The Warrant Chiefs

Ibadan History Series

Published by Northwestern University Press

Christian Missions in Nigeria 1841–1891
by J. F. A. Ajayi

The Zulu Aftermath
by J. D. Omer-Cooper

Published by Humanities Press

The Missionary Impact on Modern Nigeria 1842–1914
by E. A. Ayandele

The Sokoto Caliphate
by Murray Last

Britain and the Congo Question 1885–1913
by S. J. S. Cookey

Benin and the Europeans 1485–1897
by A. F. C. Ryder

Niger Delta Rivalry
by Obaro Ikimẹ

The International Boundaries of Nigeria
by J. D. Anene

Revolution and Power Politics in Yorubaland 1840–1893
by S. A. Akintoye

Power and Diplomacy in Northern Nigeria 1804–1906
by R. A. Adelẹyẹ

The Segu Tukulor Empire 1848–1893
by B. O. Ọloruntimẹhin

IN PREPARATION

The New Ọyọ Empire
by J. A. Atanda

The Evolution of the Nigerian State 1898–1914
by T. N. Tamuno

The Malagasy and the Europeans
by P. M. Mutibwa

For further details of the books in this series
please consult the publisher.

Ibadan History Series
General Editor J. F. A. Ajayi, PhD

The Warrant Chiefs

Indirect Rule in Southeastern Nigeria 1891–1929

A. E. Afigbo, PhD
Department of History, University of Nigeria, Nsukka

Humanities Press

First published in
the United States of America 1972
by HUMANITIES PRESS INC.
303 Park Avenue South
New York, N.Y. 10010

SBN 391 00215 5

Printed in Great Britain

Dedicated to the Old Boys of
St Augustine's Grammar School, Nkwerre, Orlu

Contents

Contents

Plates

Acknowledgements

We are indebted to the Cambridge University Press for permission to use extracts from *Southern Nigeria in Transition* by J. C. Anene.

The publishers are grateful to the following for permission to reproduce photographs:
The National Archives, Ibadan for Plate 1; Chief Adadonye Fombo for Plate 2; Faber and Faber and the Reverend W. Groves for Plate 3 taken from *Ten Africans* by Margery Perham D.B.E.; and Dr T. N. Tamuno for Plate 4.

Abbreviations

ACIR	Aba Commission of Inquiry Report
ACINE	Aba Commission of Inquiry Notes of Evidence
ADC	Assistant District Commissioner
ADO	Assistant District Officer
Calprof	Calabar Province
CC	Court Clerk
CO	Colonial Office
Conf	Confidential
CSO	Chief Secretary's Office (Lagos)
DC	District Commissioner
DO	District Officer
EP	Eastern Provinces
FO	Foreign Office
HC	High Commissioner
LGNP	Lieutenant Governor Northern Provinces
LGSP	Lieutenant Governor Southern Provinces
NC	Native Court
NCR	Native Court Rule
NCRE & CP	Native Court Rule Eastern and Central Provinces
NP	Northern Provinces
OC	Officer Commanding
OG	Ogoja Province
OP	Onitsha Province
OW	Owerri Province
SNP	Secretary Northern Provinces
S of S	Secretary of State
SP	Southern Provinces
SSP	Secretary Southern Provinces

Preface

The Warrant Chiefs; Indirect Rule in Southeastern Nigeria, 1891–1929 is a political history of the Ibo, Ibibio, Ijo and Ogoja peoples under colonial rule. It is the story of an attempt made by the British to rule these peoples through what was thought to be their indigenous political organisation. Though the origins of the policy can be traced to a period a little earlier than 1891, the first structural arrangement based on definite legislations laying down specific rules for putting it into practice was made under Sir Ralph Moor (1896–1903). Sir Walter Egerton (1904–12) followed Moor's footsteps in local government policy. But in 1912 Sir Frederick Lugard came back to Nigeria charged with the duty of amalgamating Northern and Southern Nigeria. Lugard gave his assignment a broad interpretation, and, among other things, sought to establish a uniformity of system in local government between the North and the South. He attempted between 1914 and 1919 to infuse into the local government system of the South the principles and practices on which local government in the North was based.

As soon as Lugard left Nigeria, it was found that his system could not achieve the desired results and various attempts were made to reform it. The last and most fateful of these reforms was the introduction of direct taxation in 1928, a measure which was calculated to strengthen the system and make it more acceptable to the people through the abolition of the hated forced labour and the provision of funds for local development. However, direct taxation not only failed to improve the system but brought it to ruin in the Women's Riot of 1929. The Riot marks the end of the era of the Warrant Chiefs. The Warrant Chief System failed primarily because it was based on assumptions which had no root in indigenous soil, and secondly because it brought on the people burdens which were either unnecessary or whose purpose they did not understand. The failure of the system is not primarily, as is usually thought, an adverse commentary on the political organisation of the Ibo and their neighbours, but on the ability of the British in the first four decades of their rule to understand and solve the administrative problems presented them by Ibo, Ibibio, Ijo and Ogoja society. To some extent, however, it also reflected the failure of the natives to modify their indigenous system enough to meet the needs of the changed times.

There are indeed at least two aspects to the process generally known as colonial conquest of which military subjugation is only one. In a general sense the British could be said to have subdued the Ibo and their neighbours militarily by 1914. The other aspect is the attempt by the colonial power to master and control the institutions which regulate the life of the colonised or failing that to supplant them. This book could be seen as a study of British attempts to achieve this second stage of colonial conquest over Southeastern Nigeria and of the resistance offered by Ibo, Ibibio, Ijo and Ogoja society. At the end of the period covered by the work, the British had to confess failure and more or less start trying afresh.

The book thus seeks to explain why this attempt at total conquest through institutional control failed for over three decades. The question is approached from two main perspectives. Firstly, an attempt is made to bring out clearly what the British did in the field of local government in the Eastern Provinces in the period 1891–1929. Secondly, the light in which the Ibo, Ibibio, Ijo and Ogoja peoples saw and reacted to the policy is fully discussed. No more emphasis is laid on the one or the other side of the question than is considered necessary for a balanced and effective treatment of the subject.

The main material for this work comes from the official records of the period. However, this source has been supplemented substantially with oral evidence collected from various people in the field. Material from the latter source has been used mainly to throw light on those aspects of the Warrant Chief System on which there is very scanty material in the official records. The thesis out of which this work grew carries an appendix which gives the date and place of each interview as well as the name of and other necessary details about each informant. It has not been thought necessary to include this in the book. However, two sample extracts from my field notes can be found in the Appendix.

In the period covered by this work the Ibo, Ibibio, Ijo and Ogoja peoples with whom it deals were affected by a succession of administrative arrangements originated and imposed by their British colonial masters. These changes must be outlined to avoid confusion. First, by a notification published in the *London Gazette* of 5 June 1885, they were included in the Protectorate of the 'Niger Districts', a vague and paper province of the British empire defined as including 'the territories on the line of coast between the British Protectorate of Lagos and the right or western bank of the Rio del Rey, as well as the territories on both banks of the Niger, from its confluence with the River Benue at Lokoja to the sea, as well as the territories on both banks of the Benue, from the confluence up to and including Ibi'. In 1889 this territory was named the Oil Rivers Protectorate. In 1893 it became the Niger Coast Protectorate. On its amalgamation in 1900 with the former Royal Niger Company territories which lay south of Idah, the new administrative unit came to be known as the Protectorate of Southern Nigeria. This protectorate was divided for administrative purposes into four Divisions, the Eastern, the Central, the Cross River and the Western Divisions. The Ibo, Ibibio, Ijo and Ogoja peoples of our concern were included in the first three Divisions.

In 1906 the Protectorate of Southern Nigeria was amalgamated with the Colony and Protectorate of Lagos (Yorubaland deprived of Ilorin and Kabba) and the new unit named the Colony and Protectorate of Southern Nigeria. This amalgamation was accompanied by internal administrative rearrangements as a result of which the whole unit was divided into three administrative Provinces – Western, Central and Eastern. Under this arrangement the Ibo, Ibibio, Ijo and Ogoja peoples were incorporated in the Central and Eastern Provinces. On the amalgamation of the Colony and Protectorate of Southern Nigeria with the Protectorate of Northern Nigeria in 1914, Lugard extended to the rest of the country the provincial system which already existed in the North. This involved carving up the three provinces of the South into smaller units. At the conclusion of this exercise by about 1917, Southeastern Nigeria, the home of the people dealt with in this work, was divided into four provinces – Onitsha, Owerri, Calabar and Ogoja Provinces. For the rest of the period covered by the study and in fact for many years after Onitsha, Owerri, Calabar and Ogoja were known as either the Eastern Provinces or the four provinces east of the Niger. And it is by these terms that they are referred to in this work to avoid confusion. Later still other administrative and political changes and reorganisations took place, but these lie outside the scope of the present work.

The Ibo and Ijo communities west of the Niger were in the Benin and Warri Provinces and so lie outside the area of this study. The Brass Division too was in the Warri Province. Onitsha was an entirely Ibo Province. Owerri Province was mainly Ibo, but also embraced the Central and Eastern Ijo. Calabar was the province of the Ibibio-speaking peoples though to the north it incorporated some non-Ibibio groups. The Ogoja Province contained the rest of the semi-Bantu-speaking elements in the Eastern Provinces as well as the Afikpo and Abakaliki Ibo.

In the process of producing the thesis out of which this work grew I got much help from many people. I am grateful to the late Professor J. C. Anene, who helped to draw my attention to this topic and supervised the thesis, to Dr C. C. Ifemesia, who read most of the chapters and rendered a great deal of help, to Dr P. C. Lloyd and Mr Michael Crowder, each of whom read the first three chapters, and to Professors J. E. Flint and J. A. Ballard, each of whom read the work through and suggested many useful amendments. My thanks also go to the staff of the Ibadan University Library and of Nigeria's National Archives for their willing co-operation; to Mr E. J. Usoroh, then of the Geography Department of Ibadan University, who traced all the maps but one; to my friend Mr R. U. Igwebuike of the Ministry of Economic Planning, Enugu, who rendered me invaluable assistance during my visits to the Enugu Archives; and to Mr Nicholas Ukpabi and Mr A. O. Ijere for the typing. This anthology of acknowledgements would be incomplete if I failed to mention my indebtedness to Messrs E. C. Ezekwesili and C. I. Eneli, who taught me history at St Augustine's Grammar School, Nkwerre, and gave me the initial inspiration to study history; to Mr Oji Iheukwumere, my Headmaster at Ihube Central School, Okigwi, who drew my attention to the possibilities of higher education; and to Professor J. F. Ade Ajayi, whose encouragement and support enabled me to overcome the shattering experiences of the Nigerian Civil War and who has provided me with an ideal of intellectual balance and dedication to academics which I am committed to emulate. I thank the authorities of the University of

Ibadan for awarding me the studentship which made this study possible. Finally I am deeply indebted to my wife for her kind encouragement and unsparing criticism of my style.

A. E. A.

1 Introduction: the indigenous political background

In 1891, when Britain decided to establish effective rule in the Oil Rivers Protectorate, she gave concrete proof of her intention by appointing Sir Claude Macdonald to head the new administration as commissioner and consul-general. To guide him in the execution of his duties, the Foreign Office, under which this territory was being administered, issued 'General Instructions' defining the extent of his responsibilities. With regard to local government, this document asked Macdonald not to interfere unduly with the 'tribal government' of the peoples of the protectorate, but to allow the local chiefs to continue to rule their peoples and to administer justice to them in traditional fashion. The new administration, however, was to keep a vigilant watch over the chiefs and their functionaries in order to prevent injustice and check abuse.[1] Macdonald and his successors sought to carry out these instructions through the institution of the Warrant Chief System. In so far as this system was supposed to achieve the conversion of the indigenous political system of the peoples of the protectorate into an instrument with which the new rulers would govern, 'influence' and 'civilise' the natives, it was an attempt at Indirect Rule.

This view that Indirect Rule, later known as Native Administration, was applied to Southeastern and South-central Nigeria before the imposition there in 1928 of direct taxation has often been vehemently denied by scholars and propagandists of British imperial government. The clearest and most aggressive statement of this denial was Dr Lucy Mair's in 1962. Clearly irritated by a vague allusion to this view she wrote:

[1] CSO 1/14, Despatch No. 2 of 18.4.91 containing the General Instructions from FO to Sir Claude Macdonald on the occasion of his appointment as Commissioner and Consul-General of the Oil Rivers Protectorate.

What is the source of the current myth that Britain 'tried to implant Indirect Rule' in Ibo country? . . . If one is to make any sense of it, it can only be on the assumption that some people think that any appointment of subordinate agents of government is 'Indirect Rule. . . . As a general proposition this is strangely ingenuous, as a version of Nigerian history it is unpardonably inaccurate . . . it is carrying unscholarship too far to hold it [Indirect Rule] responsible for what happened [in Eastern Nigeria] where it was *deliberately* not introduced . . .' until after the Women's Riot of 1929–30.[2]

Writing a few years later, Dr E. A. Ayandele, who believed that 'until the days of Lugard [1912–19] the moral purpose of British administration in our period was purely negative',[3] asserted that before 1914 no governor in Southern Nigeria 'established, in any formal manner, any system of administration that may be strictly described as Indirect Rule'.[4]

Many of those who subscribe to this view, including authorities like Dr C. K. Meek, Miss M. M. Green and Mr G. I. Jones, therefore speak firstly of the period before 1928 as one of Direct Rule in Southeastern and South-central Nigeria and secondly of the introduction of Native Administration into these areas with the imposition of direct taxation. On the basis of this disputable hypothesis Mr Jones went on to publish in 1966 a paper which he entitled 'From Direct to Indirect Rule in Eastern Nigeria'.[5] The error in this view of our political history has been dealt with elsewhere in detail by the present writer and by Dr Obaro

[2] Lucy Mair, 'Indirect Rule in Ibo land', *West Africa*, 2335, 1962, p. 238. The italics in the quotation are mine. Dr Mair was castigating Michael Crowder's *Story of Nigeria*, London 1962.

[3] E. A. Ayandele, *Missionary Impact on Modern Nigeria: A Social and Political Analysis*, London 1966, p. 283

[4] *Ibid.*, p. 155

[5] C. K. Meek, *Law and Authority in a Nigerian Tribe*, Oxford 1937, p. x. M. M. Green, *Igbo Village Affairs*, Cass, second ed. 1964, p. 3. G. I. Jones, 'From Direct to Indirect Rule in Eastern Nigeria', *ODU, Journal of African Studies*, University of Ife, Jan. 1966

It may be noted that Dr Obaro Ikime, in his book *Niger Delta Rivalry*, London 1969, p. 219, etc., also talks of the introduction of Native Administration into the Warri Province in 1928. This is in spite of his view, expounded in his brilliant article 'Reconsidering Indirect Rule: The Nigerian Example', *Journal of the Historical Society of Nigeria*, Dec. 1968, that the pre-Lugardian system in Southern Nigeria was Indirect Rule. The fact that these two views can be held by the same person creates the erroneous impression that Indirect Rule was one thing, and Native Administration another.

Ikimẹ. [6] What is attempted briefly here is a meaningful definition of Indirect Rule which would help us to understand the political history of Southeastern Nigerian peoples in this period as well as the development of the general concept of Indirect Rule as applied to West Africa.

The historiography of Indirect Rule has been seriously bedevilled by a failure on the part of scholars to follow the historical method. Consequently attempts to define the system, from Lugard and Margery Perham to their sophisticated later-day disciples, have been vitiated by excessive preoccupation with the version of that system which obtained in the emirates of Northern Nigeria. The procedure has been to analyse emirate Indirect Rule, usually described erroneously as the classic pattern, to isolate its basic characteristics and from these arrive at a statement called the definition of Indirect Rule as a system. This definition is then applied to the local government systems of other neighbouring groups which are described as 'direct' or 'indirect' depending on how remotely or closely they are seen to approximate to the emirate pattern. The faults of this procedure are many, but only the three main ones will be mentioned here. Firstly it does not take into account the historical evolution of the system: Northern Nigeria was not the first African territory to which the policy was applied. Secondly it does not take into account the original meaning of 'Direct Rule' in the light of which alone the original meaning of its opposite, Indirect Rule, before it became encrusted with propaganda and legend, could be understood. Thirdly it fails to take into account the obvious fact that the emirate system of government was atypical in sub-Saharan Africa and therefore that the peculiar form which colonial local government took there cannot correctly be treated as typical. On this matter Professor J. E. Flint has recently said:

> This [Northern Nigerian] feudalism, being a highly developed and strongly Islamic type known only in the savannah belt of West Africa, was quite foreign to the rest of tropical Africa, and had almost no relevance to the general principles of African administration. [7]

[6] A. E. Afigbo, 'The Warrant Chief System in Eastern Nigeria: Direct or Indirect Rule?', *Journal of the Historical Society of Nigeria* (hereinafter referred to as *JHSN*), iii, 4, June 1967. Obaro Ikimẹ, 'Reconsidering Indirect Rule! The Nigerian Example', *JHSN*, iv, 3, Dec. 1968

[7] J. E. Flint, 'Nigeria: The Colonial Experience from 1880 to 1914' in *Colonialism in Africa 1870–1960*, eds L. H. Gann and P. Duignan, i. *The History and Politics of Colonialism 1870–1914*, Cambridge 1969, p. 250

An accurate definition of Indirect Rule is thus bound up with the history of the development of British administrative practice in West Africa and with the original meaning of Direct Rule. British rule in West Africa began in those coastal enclaves generally designated as Crown Colonies in the constitutional and political history of Anglophonic West Africa. These were bits of West Africa which by the mid-nineteenth century already had a long history of direct and intimate contact with Europe and which, as a result, had evolved fairly westernised local urban communities. According to Lord Hailey these Crown Colonies comprised 'the coastal region(s) in which European influences [had] been established for a considerable time'.[8] Because of this fact the indigenous systems of government had been seriously undermined and could not be used to exercise effective rule over the educated natives and the alien elements which made up the population. Furthermore the decision to impose British rule over these enclaves was taken in the period of imperial liberalism, humanitarianism and philanthropy when it was thought necessary and possible to 'transform' the benighted peoples of Africa and Asia through the imposition of western commerce, western Christianity, western technology and British political institutions. It was for this reason that on the political plane the Crown Colony system of government was introduced into West Africa, the system giving the people on whom it was imposed the benefit of British institutions modified to suit their local conditions.[9] On this point Sir Herbert Richmond Palmer, himself a committed advocate of the emirate version of Indirect Rule, has written:

> During most of the nineteenth century the ideal of colonial adminis-
> tration was to create colorable counterfeits of the Motherland, its
> institutions, its idiosyncrasies and its peculiarities. There was a governor
> to represent the king, a Judge to represent the Rule of Law and a
> chaplain to represent the established church. Land tenure . . . was made
> to simulate the time-honoured characteristics of English Freehold. Dim
> rows of street lamps attested the high degree of civilisation reached by
> the river ports and the Beadle said 'Oyez', 'Oyez', 'Oyez' when His
> Honour the Judge bowed to his be-wigged bar and his be-wigged bar
> bowed to him.[10]

[8] Lord Hailey, *An African Survey*, Oxford 1937, p. 171
[9] A. E. Afigbo, 'The Establishment of Colonial Rule 1900–18' in *History of West Africa*, eds Ajayi and Crowder, London, ii, forthcoming
[10] H. R. Palmer, 'Some Observations on Capt. R. S. Rattray's Paper: Present Tendencies of African Colonial Government', *Journal of Royal African Society*, xxxiii, 130, p. 37

This Crown Colony system was the original concept of Direct Rule – meaning a system of rule using British institutions and implementing British ideas of government. Its opposite was a system under which British institutions and ideas were deliberately excluded; instead an attempt was made to rule through the indigenous institutions of the colonised peoples. This was the original meaning of Indirect Rule. The definite techniques by which this latter policy was implemented necessarily varied from one locality to another depending on the characteristics and the leadership articulation of the political institutions of the people. In practice, therefore, there was not, and there could not have been, a uniform system of Indirect Rule. On this matter Palmer was once again definite. In the same paper he pointed out that:

> There cannot be and [there] is not one universal sealed pattern of Indirect Rule. . . . [*All that Indirect Rule*] *was intended to mean was some variety of local administration of African antecedents which was not direct Crown Colony of the old type.*[11]

The latter-day use of the term 'Direct Rule' to mean other than the 'direct Crown Colony of the old type' has introduced infinite confusion into the study of colonial administration in Africa. Lord Hailey in 1951 sought to break the spell of this inexact, but all the same captivating, use of the term, by warning against the popular distinction between 'Direct' and 'Indirect' Rule. He said:

> I have purposely avoided discussing methods of native administration in terms of 'direct' and 'indirect' rule. There is little advantage in the use of those terms. They have no claim to precision. . . . The use of those terms conveys the impression that there are two opposing systems of rule. This is not of course the case. All African administrations are dependent to a greater or lesser extent on the use of native authorities as agencies of local rule.[12]

Lord Hailey's warning would become superfluous if scholars were to return to the catholic usage of the two terms; that is, if they employed 'Direct Rule' to describe the system which sought to impose British ideas and institutions, and 'Indirect Rule' to describe the opposite system which sought to govern through indigenous institutions and ideas instead.

In spite of the lingering effect of what has been described

[11] *Ibid.*, pp. 38–43
[12] Lord Hailey, *Native Administration and Political Development in British Tropical Africa, 1940–42*, HMSO 1951

5

elsewhere as 'the Lugardian spell',[13] scholars are gradually coming round to Palmer's view of what constitutes Indirect Rule. Thus Dr Obaro Ikimẹ, Dr J. A. Atanda and Mr I. F. Nicolson have stated quite firmly that the pre-Lugardian systems of local government in Southern Nigeria qualify for the 'sacred' and 'coveted' rubric: Indirect Rule. Says Mr Nicolson:

> Moor had decided to maintain the authority of the heads of houses, while protecting their members against acts of oppression and cruelty by their heads. In other words Moor, like MacGregor, had followed the policy of the Selborne Committee in maintaining native institutions – indirect rule in fact.[14]

More recently an international seminar on colonial government organised by the Institute of African Studies, University of Ife, broke away from the orthodox tradition of Lugard, Perham and Mair by recognising the existence of gradations within the Indirect Rule system. It isolated two of these: (i) 'Indirect Rule' (with capitals), which it equated with the system which obtained in the emirates, and (ii) 'indirect rule' (without capitals), which it equated with the system existing in Southern Nigeria before Lugard's amalgamation in 1914. 'To distinguish the Northern Nigerian system of indirect rule from indirect rule as a general pattern,' wrote the editors of the proceedings, 'we designate it "Indirect Rule".'[15] The trend of modern research on the topic would therefore seem to justify the modest conclusion that there were different gradations of Indirect Rule and that the Warrant Chief system in Southeastern Nigeria was one such gradation.[16]

In seeking to apply this policy to the Ibo and their neighbours, the British selected certain natives who they thought were traditional chiefs and gave them certificates of recognition and authority called warrants. The warrant entitled each of these men to sit in the Native Court from time to time to judge cases. It also

[13] A. E. Afigbo, 'West African Chiefs during Colonial Rule and After', *ODU, Journal of West African Studies*, University of Ife, New Series, 5, 1971

[14] I. F. Nicolson, *The Administration of Nigeria 1900 to 1960*, Oxford 1969, p. 116

[15] Eds M. Crowder and O. Ikimẹ, *West African Chiefs*, Ife 1970. See the whole Introduction; in particular, the note at the foot of p. xx

[16] A. E. Afigbo, 'The Warrant Chief System In Eastern Nigeria: Direct or Indirect Rule?', *JHSN*, iii, 4, June 1967. See in particular the two concluding sentences.

empowered him to assume within the community he represented executive and judicial powers which were novel both in degree and territorial scope. In order to see the history of this system in proper perspective, it is necessary to delineate the stage on which the Warrant Chiefs performed by describing the indigenous political system of the peoples of the Eastern Provinces.[17] This will facilitate an understanding of the reaction of these peoples to the system. It will also help to show whether the policy was dictated by objective local conditions or was based on assumptions arrived at on other grounds.

One striking characteristic of the Ibo, Ibibio, Ijo and Ogoja peoples at the time of British advent was their political decentralisation. There is no evidence that any of these peoples or sections of them ever evolved, or formed part of, even a loosely integrated empire or state of any remarkable size. Instead, each of these peoples was split into a large number of tiny, politically equivalent and autonomous units. Though none of these units was either isolated or self-sufficient, each had its own name, its own land, its own shrines and religious ceremonies, its own markets, warriors, political institutions and all those other attributes which would enable it to pursue its own way in the event of estrangement from its neighbours.[18] This lack of large-scale political integration by the Ibo and their neighbours has attracted the attention of many outsiders, administrators and professional anthropologists alike.

Writing on the Ibo, Miss Green observed: 'their most immediately striking characteristic is what has aptly been called their social fragmentation. This great people is broken up into hundreds of more or less independent, social units. . . .'[19] Dealing with the Ibibio people, M. D. W. Jeffreys, then an administrative officer in this area, said: 'There is no individual whom the tribe as a whole regard as a ruler or as a person endowed with divine powers. There is no tradition that there ever was such a person.'[20] Among the Ogoja peoples of the middle and upper Cross River the same lack of large-scale political integration was observed.

[17] J. C. Anene, *Southern Nigeria in Transition 1885–1906*, Cambridge 1966, p. 1. See also O. Ikime, *Niger Delta Rivalry*, London 1969, ch. 1
[18] S. Ottenberg, 'Ibo Oracles and Inter-group Relations', *Southwestern Journal of Anthropology*, xiv, 3, 1958, p. 298
[19] M. M. Green, *ibid.*, p. 3
[20] M. D. W. Jeffreys, *Diploma Thesis On the Ibibio*, part III, p. 6. (See the bibliography at the end of this work for a note on this thesis).

Charles Partridge, who made the first systematic study of these peoples, reported that the region they occupied was 'full of small tribes of about equal power and entirely independent of one another'. He also said that unlike some other parts of the Southern Nigeria Protectorate the region of the middle and upper Cross River lacked 'paramount chiefs through whom the natives may be influenced and instructed'.[21] Dr P. A. Talbot, administrative officer and anthropologist, was expressing a generally accepted opinion when he described the whole region between the Niger River and the Rio del Rey as 'composed of peoples living in independent unconsolidated and usually small groups subject to no central government'.[22]

Many theories or rather hypotheses have been offered in explanation for the absence of large-scale political units among the Ibo, Ibibio, Ijo and Ogoja peoples. Of these hypotheses the most favoured by scholars would seem to be that offered by the environmental determinists who see an undisputed connection between the vegetation and the lack of large states. These scholars argue that the high forest, which is believed to predominate in this region, by obscuring one village from the other severely limited the mental and political horizon of the people, thus making people from next-door villages appear to each other as strangers. Also, it is argued, that the forest kept out conquering bands, like the Fulani jihadists of the nineteenth century, who could have imposed political unity from without. Said M. M. Green:

> It is largely the forest and tsetse fly that kept out of the Ibo country the horse and cattle-owning Fulani who over-ran so much of Nigeria in their Islamic holy war in the nineteenth century. How far the protection of the forest can be correlated with the social fragmentation of the Ibo people cannot be assessed. But that there is some connexion between the two can hardly be doubted. There is also the isolating effect of the bush upon the people who live in it, which can hardly have failed to contribute to the separatist tendency that is so marked among these peoples. The mere fact that every village is as invisible from the next as though it were twenty miles away cannot but affect one's mental outlook.[23]

So pervasive has this conventional view become that even Ibo scholars are coming to succumb to it. In explanation of

[21] C. Partridge, *Cross River Natives*, London 1905, p. 138
[22] P. A. Talbot, *Peoples of Southern Nigeria*, Oxford 1926, p. 562
[23] M. M. Green, *ibid.*, pp. 10–11

the political fragmentation of our peoples, Professor Anene wrote:

> As already explained, the physical environment is one dominated to a large extent by thick forest. On the one hand, the heavy vegetation was excellent defence against large-scale invasion from outside. On the other, its inaccessibility did not aid movement and easy intercourse among people who were primarily agriculturists. The Ibo, therefore, never came under a single pyramidal system.[24]

Another school of thought maintains that the political fragmentation of this area was one of the evil legacies of the slave trade. This region, it has been argued, was the slave raider's paradise. The alleged need for safety from Jukun and Aro raiding bands, as from the coastal middlemen, is said to have forced its inhabitants to break up into little communities which could easily take shelter in the forest. Apart from creating strife, argues James Coleman, the slave trade consumed men's energies in raiding and being raided, denuded the area of its most virile men, and so hindered cultural advance of which political evolution is an aspect.[25] Allied to this is the view that the political fragmentation of peoples here was partly caused by the disintegrating influence of such oracles as *Ibini Ukpabi* at Arochukwu (Aro Long Juju) and of *Igwe-ka-ala* at Umunneoha.[26]

Yet another school has laid emphasis on the mode of livelihood of the people. It has been argued that the growth of large empires in the Sudan owed much to the fact that food could be easily obtained, a condition which it is claimed encouraged specialisation in crafts and such aspects of large-scale government as soldiering. It has also been pointed out that the Benin empire, a forest kingdom, with its elaborate cultural and political systems, 'must have been based on something more than subsistence agriculture'.[27] The Ibo, Ibibio, Ijo and Ogoja peoples were, until the imposition of colonial rule, primarily subsistence farmers. If the above hypothesis is necessarily correct, then it follows that the Ibo and their neighbours must have spent most of their creative energies earning a living. Another theory advanced in explanation of this prevailing political decentralisation is that the

[24] J. C. Anene, *Southern Nigeria*, etc., p. 12
[25] J. S. Coleman, *Nigeria. A Background to Nationalism*, California 1958, pp. 40–1. See also B. Davidson, *Black Mother*, London 1961, p. 238
[26] S. Ottenberg, 'Ibo Oracles', etc., p. 313
[27] M. Crowder, *Story of Nigeria*, London 1962, pp. 29–30, 56

people were not involved in 'mass migrations which would have induced or compelled them to form large states administered by centralised authoritative leaderships'.[28]

These are impressive hypotheses, but they fail to provide a satisfactory explanation for the line taken by the political evolution of the Ibo and their neighbours. None of the hypotheses can stand up to critical examination. The vegetation of the region was no doubt an important factor in the life of its peoples, but its major role was not that of acting as a barrier to communication and contact among local communities which the hypotheses of the environmental determinist would seem to presuppose. It has not yet been fully and generally appreciated what amount of coming and going as well as face to face contacts characterised the communities of this area. The little objective research which has been done has established that routes used by long-distance traders like the Aro and Awka ramified the whole of this region, and even extended to the area west of the Niger. In addition to this there was a great deal of coming and going by professional groups like diviners, oracle agents and their clients. The creeks of the coast also provided an excellent system of natural canals which made it possible for a canoe to travel from one end of the Bight of Biafra to the other without coming out into the open sea. According to some authorities, the Jukun in their heyday dominated ritually and economically the whole region below the Benue River down to the estuary of the Cross River in spite of the alleged high forest. There is no evidence to show that the Fulani failed to conquer these peoples because of the forest. On the contrary, it would appear that they had more than enough to occupy them in the Central Sudan. If they did not expand sufficiently far south to conquer the Tiv and the Idoma, there was no question of their conquering the Ibo and the Ibibio. The separatist outlook regarded as inherent in forest peoples did not prevent the Bini from building a large empire.

However, travel through the Onitsha, Enugu, Abakaliki and most of Ogoja areas reveals that much of the 'high forest' of the popular textbooks is a survival of the extravagant nineteenth-century romances which portrayed Africa as the jungle continent both in culture and vegetation. The vegetation of these areas is much the same as that of Northern Yorubaland, where the Oyo

[28] J. S. Coleman, *Nigeria*, etc., p. 28. See also B. Davidson, *Old Africa Rediscovered*, London 1961, pp. 193–4

empire rose and flourished depending on an army that relied to a large extent on cavalry. For most of the rest of the region the vegetation is thin secondary rather than thick high forest. Only with regard to the river basins and the coastal region extensively broken by creeks can one correctly talk of the vegetation in terms of high forest.

Contrary to the impression which the myth of high forest tends to convey, the communities in this region were far from being disparate units. There were many integrative links – common and centrally located markets, the long-range traders, the other specialists and their routes already mentioned being among these. And what was more, many of the social institutions of the Ibo and their neighbours served as agencies for cultural integration among otherwise politically disintegrated groups. Writing on the Ibo, V. C. Uchendu, himself an Ibo, said 'the *dibia* (diviner) and title-making associations aid Pan-Igbo integration. They confer on their members a Pan-Igbo citizenship',[29] and this cosmopolitan status which these institutions conferred made them powerful instruments of cultural integration throughout the region. Surely there was more to the political particularism of the Ibo and their neighbours than the vegetation.

Like objections can be made to the 'slave trade theory'. First it fails to explain why the Ibo and their neighbours did not resort to centralised organisations as an effective means of defence against marauding bands if slave raids were such a prominent factor in their lives. It has been shown that elsewhere in West Africa – for instance, where raids were the main means of recruiting slaves – the traffic in men instigated efforts towards large-scale political consolidation. The Dahomeans were a case in point. The Kingdom of Dahomey was to an extent the outcome of the need to defend the Fon against devastating raids from Oyo. If the same was not exactly true for Asante, at least that state grew in response to the need to break the stranglehold of the slave-trading coastal states over its economy. 'It may be asserted,' a student of this topic has written recently, 'that it was the desire on the part of some of the States to preserve themselves against raiders which first led to the development of strong states.'[30] Why did the slave trade not inspire a similar reaction among the Ibo, Ibibio, Ijo

[29] V. C. Uchendu, *The Igbo of Southeast Nigeria*, New York 1966, p. 83
[30] K. Y. Daaku, 'The Slave Trade and African Society' in *Emerging Themes of African History*, ed. T. O. Ranger, Nairobi 1968, p. 137

and Ogoja? Why did the Ijo communities of the coast rest satisfied with village states in spite of the advantageous position in which they stood, through direct participation in the slave trade, of expanding imperially?

Secondly it must be pointed out that no full-scale study of the organisation of the slave trade in this area has been made. Therefore it is difficult to say how far the raids went and how stirring was the need for protection. It is not certain, moreover, what proportion of the slaves sold in the ports of the Oil Rivers states was obtained through such raids and what proportion through the normal processes by which a society lacking an organised system of incarceration for prisoners rid itself of criminals and misfits.[31] The extent to which African wars of the pre-colonial era were necessarily caused by the slave trade has not been established. The theory which tends to regard raiding for slaves as the universal explanation for African wars is a relic of the myth of barbaric Africa. K. Y. Daaku writes:

> We have on record the answers of rulers of two states which are generally associated with the slave trade – Dahomey and Ashanti. When the kings had occasion to talk on the slave trade, Adandozan of Dahomey (1797–1818) and Osei Bonsu of Ashanti (1801–24), both vehemently denied that they made wars on others 'simply to catch men'. The fact that there were rich harvests of slaves after wars between states must not necessarily lead us to the conclusion that the economic motives weighed heavily in the minds of rulers during the period of the slave trade.'[32]

Even more relevant is the answer of Obi Ossai, King of Aboh, the Ibo city kingdom lying just to the west of our region of interest, to questions addressed to him on the same issue by some members of the 1841 Niger Expedition.

Commissioner:	Does Obi sell slaves for [from?] his own dominions?
Obi:	No, they come from far away.
Commissioner:	Does Obi make war [simply] to procure slaves?
Obi:	When other chiefs quarrel with me and make war, I take all I can as slaves.[33]

Assuming that the political fragmentation of the Ibo, Ibibio,

[31] P. A. Talbot and H. Mulhall, *The Physical Anthropology of Southern Nigeria,* Oxford 1962, p. 5
[32] K. Y. Daaku, 'The Slave Trade and African Society' in *Emerging Themes,* etc., p. 135
[33] T. Hodgkin, *Nigerian Perspectives,* Oxford 1960, p. 245

Ijo and Ogoja owed a great deal to estrangement engendered by constant intergroup fights, it would be wrong to attribute the absence of large-scale political units to the slave trade alone. Research into the pre-colonial history of these peoples will gain immensely from a recognition of the fact that, among densely populated agricultural peoples like the Ibo and the Ibibio, intergroup animosity was more often than not the result of conflicts over land. It is contended that the political, economic (other than slave trade) and psychological factors which cause wars in other parts of the world were by no means absent from the pre-colonial society of the Ibo and their neighbours, just as they were not absent from other African societies.

In the same way an objection could be made to the explanation which lays emphasis on a people's livelihood. Though there is a connection between a people's political system and their means of livelihood, it is not yet established what political system is always necessarily associated with a particular economy. Fortes and Evans-Pritchard have pointed out, for instance, that 'the Tallensi and the Bemba are both agriculturists but they have different political systems'.[34] The lack of mass migration theory is not more acceptable than any other. There is as yet no comprehensive study of the traditions of origin and migration of these peoples. Nor is the absence of traditions deriving them from distant lands to be taken as proof of the fact that they originated where they now live. A further objection to this theory is that not all peoples who are known to have been involved in mass migrations evolved centralised leadership. Similarly it is necessary to point out that if the oracles were instrumental in liquidating the talented and the intelligent who might have proved effective state or empire builders they also helped to eliminate misfits whose presence in a community would have caused disruption. Also, as already pointed out, visits to the oracles encouraged travel and therefore the development of a wider outlook on life.

Many of these theories which seek to explain the absence of large states among the peoples of this area derive from two assumptions and it is these which constitute their basic weakness. The first assumption would seem to derive from a belief that all human societies naturally evolve towards the same goal. Those

[34] Eds M. Fortes and E. E. Evans-Pritchard, *African Political Systems*, Oxford 1940, p. 7

who hold this view reach the conclusion that the absence of large states is an unexpected phenomenon which must be explained, that the political organisation of the Ibo and their neighbours was an earlier model of that same social organism which else-where had evolved into the western-European type of nation-state or into what in Africa is called the 'primitive' state. This assumption is probably the explanation for the fact that these theories seek not to give a clearer insight into the political organisation of these peoples, but to explain their inability to 'complete' the prescribed evolution. Yet neither social anthropology nor history teaches that in the field of socio-political engineering, as within the ancient Roman Empire, all roads lead to the same point. The second assumption would seem to be the belief that large-scale political organisation is necessarily better than the segmented and fragmented type. This view may be true for the present age, but there is nothing to show that in the particular circumstances in which these peoples lived their lives before the era of colonial rule large state systems would have served their needs better than the system of democratic village republics. Was the Roman Empire necessarily an improvement on the Greek city-states? The answer returned on this question by each scholar would necessarily depend on his point of departure.

In any case, attempts to account for the survival into the twentieth century of the absence of large state systems which ignore the ethos and genius of the people in question are bound to prove unsatisfactory. In the final analysis the culture of any people, of which its socio-political system is an aspect, is a synthesis resulting from the interaction of their genius with their geographical and historical environment and experience. But where the environment and experience can be described in more or less definite terms, their genius is a factor beyond finite comprehension or rather not amenable to scientific analysis. And it will always be a matter for controversy which of the two factors invariably determines or dominates the other.

One other characteristic of Ibo, Ibibio, Ijo and Ogoja societies is the general similarity of their indigenous political systems. Commenting on this fact, G. I. Jones, one of the better-informed authorities on the social anthropology of this region, said:

> Details vary in different localities. . . . But whether in Ogoja, Rivers, Ibo or Ibibio Provinces, the government of every local community consisted of a federation of equivalent segments whose leading men met together

in a council which was said to consist of the senior age-grade in the community and was referred to collectively as elders.[35]

More recently, in a comparative study of the political systems of the peoples of Southeastern Nigeria, Professor Anene said:

> The subtlety, complexity and stability which characterised the manner in which the Ibo communities organised their political life may be said to apply to the Ibibio.[36]

The political system of each of these autonomous communities can be said to belong to the Group B or segmentary category described by Fortes and Evans-Pritchard in their epochal study of the typology of African political systems.[37] But as Jones has pointed out, the concurrence is not absolute, the systems here differing in some ways from the classic type discussed by Fortes and Evans-Pritchard. Whereas this classic type is said to lack centralised administrative and judicial institutions and to depend mainly on the segmentary lineage system for the regulation of political relationship between one territorial group and another, the political systems of the Ibo and their neighbours 'have some centralised administrative and judicial institutions and cleavages of wealth and status corresponding to the distribution of power and authority'.[38] They also depend to a considerable extent on non-kinship associations like titles and secret societies for the regulation of political affairs between territorial segments. Being basically segmentary, central government within each autonomous unit is a federation of equivalent segments, each of which retains a large measure of power and authority and regards as binding, decisions only to which it has given assent. Even within the trading states of the Oil Rivers, which during two centuries of boom in slave and oil trade came nearest of all communities in this area to achieving centralised administration of the classic Group A type, the principle of equivalent segments remained

[35] G. I. Jones, *Report of Commission into the position, status and influence of chiefs and natural rulers in Eastern Region*, Government Printer, Enugu 1957, p. 6. See also Talbot and Mulhall, pp. 4–5, where the authors state that 'Ibo political organisation resembles that of the Semi-Bantu-speaking groups of the Eastern Provinces. There are no chiefs or heads of villages or larger groups and no kingdoms or large city-dwelling communities as are found among the Yoruba to the west of the Niger.'
[36] J. C. Anene, *Southern Nigeria*, p 14
[37] Fortes and Evans-Pritchard. See the Introduction for their typology of African political systems.
[38] G. I. Jones, *The Trading States of the Oil Rivers*, Oxford 1963, p. 4

very real and operative. With the unfavourable trade conditions which overtook these states from about the second half of the nineteenth century the operation of this principle was so reinforced that by the time colonial rule was imposed the constitutions of these communities had reverted more or less to the classic federal type of the Ibo and Ibibio interior.

For purposes of classification, however, two types of political systems will be distinguished here. These are the *Democratic Village Republic* type and the *Constitutional Village Monarchy* type. The second type is found among the riverine Ibo, the coastal Ibibio (Efik) and the Ijo. The political systems of the remaining Ibo and Ibibio and of the Ogoja fall within the first type.

It cannot be over-emphasised that this typology must not be driven too far. Each community in the second category remained in the last analysis a federation of equivalent segments. In addition the governmental systems of autonomous units within the two types shared certain basic characteristics in common. First, in both, the autonomous units were indeed small in size, the largest units being the village-groups of the Ibo. The population of a village-group usually numbered a few thousand souls at the most. Most of the 'constitutional monarchies' – Onitsha, Oguta, Opobo, Bonny, Kalabari, Brass, Duke Town and Creek Town – were village communities and each was inhabited by even fewer people than was the case in an Ibo village-group. Second, in both types political authority was widely dispersed among the lineages and kinship institutions, age-grades, secret and title societies, oracles and diviners and other professional groups. Says Miss Green: 'By dispersal we mean not only that the whole body of villagers can and do, if they so wish, take a hand in most practical affairs, but that there is often a tendency for matters to be handled in an *ad hoc* fashion by a number of different groups or sections of society rather than by one recognised centre of hierarchy.'[39] Third, there was in both types the same lack of clear separation between judicial, executive and legislative functions – the same institution(s) and persons most times performing the three functions at one and the same time and in the same place. The fourth common characteristic was the informality with which the processes of government were carried out. Miss Green has ably described this feature of

[39] M. M. Green, *ibid.*, pp. 73–4

indigenous government in her study of the Ibo village of Umueke Agbaja in what, during the period covered by this study, was the Okigwi Division.[40] Her findings here were applicable to the governmental processes of the other Ibo groups and their Ibibio, Ijo and Ogoja neighbours.

Finally there was the fact of the absence of clear distinction, or even of an attempt to distinguish, between the political and the religious in the governmental process. As a result in both types of polities law-making and its enforcement, for instance, were both political and religious in character. The autonomous unit amongst these peoples was not just a state in the secular western sense of the word but a sort of spiritual union of the living, the dead and the gods traditionally associated with the particular piece of territory in question. Emphasising this characteristic of the political process among the Ibo, Professor Anene said:

> No study of the Ibo is intelligible without a clear appreciation of the pervasive reality of the supernatural world. Among the Ibo religion, law, justice and politics were inextricably bound up. Law and custom were believed to have been handed down from the spirit world, from time immemorial, from ancestor to ancestor. The spirit world comprised a hierarchy of gods: the most important perhaps was the god of the land – the unseen president of the small localised community. No community is complete without a shrine of the god of the land.[41]

For the Ibo the largest political unit was usually the village-group, each member village being in fact largely autonomous. For the other peoples – the Ibibio, Ijo and Ogoja – the largest unit of political integration was the village. Above the village-group for the Ibo, and above the village for the Ibibio, Ijo and Ogoja peoples are loose associations of villages which the colonial administration termed 'clans', but which Jones and some other social anthropologists have termed 'tribes'. Among the Ibibio each of these clans 'had a common tutelary deity (*ndem*) and totem (*Nkpo Ibet*)' while most of the Ibo and Ijo ones did not have these institutions, though like the Ibibio clans they were in the habit of thinking 'of themselves . . . as the descendants of a common ancestor, or as derived from a single parent village'.[42] In spite of this and other similar myths of common origin, research has revealed that very

[40] *Ibid.*, see chs vii, viii, ix, x
[41] J. C. Anene, *Southern Nigeria*, pp. 12–13. Anene's terminology would be more accurate if he used 'the Earth Goddess' in place of 'the god of the land'.
[42] G. I. Jones, *The Trading States of the Oil Rivers*, p. 17

few of these larger agglomerations of villages had anything even remotely resembling centralised political institutions. The vast majority of these were only cultural groupings. One or two examples from some of the more supposedly closely knit clans will serve to illustrate the looseness which characterised intra-clan relations generally.

The Umuchieze clan in Okigwi Division, for instance, was composed of the village-groups of Lokpaukwu, Lokpanta, Lekwesi and Leru. These villages had a common *chi* (guardian spirit) to which they offered sacrifice every January. But apart from this common action every village-group in peacetime went its own way and resisted uninvited interference in its affairs by any other member of the clan. Most other common actions taken by members of this clan were usually induced by an emergency such as a threat by the Aro or their mercenaries. And even then, although in theory all the village-groups were supposed to help any member of the clan attacked by an outside enemy, there were many instances in which one or other member village-group was left to fight its own battle. 'Local jealousy or indifference,' concluded a British investigating officer, 'frequently got the better of clanship tie.'[43] In 1932 the Ediene and Itak clans of the Eastern Ibibio, before an administrative officer anxious to 'discover' centralised clan political institutions, admitted only 'grudgingly' the existence of clan councils in the days of yore.[44]

The fact is that these clans lacked centralised political organisations in the ordinary sense. In short they had no political mechanism that functioned continously or regularly to arrange and adjust intra- and extra-clan affairs and which had a readily available executive arm capable of enforcing legal or moral sanctions or both on member units. The age-grades, secret and title societies which were some of the cornerstones of political organisation among the Ibo and their neighbours were village or at best village-group institutions. Although some of these institutions of one autonomous unit might have occasional contacts with those of a neighbouring unit, they were not sufficiently integrated at the clan level to form the foundation of a regular clan administration. When two member units of a clan fell out, the dispute was

[43] CSO 26, No. 28583, Intelligence Report on the Umuchieze Clan, Okigwi Division, Owerri Province. See the enclosure No. SP 9429/43
[44] CSO 26, No. 27615, Intelligence Report on the Ediene and Itak Clans, pp. 25–6

settled by calling in another member unit to arbitrate, or in some cases by armed conflict. Commenting on the Ibo generally, Mr G. J. F. Tomlinson, Assistant Secretary for Native Affairs, wrote in 1923:

> The ... conclusion to which the opinions of officers acquainted with the Ibo country seem to point is that even where the clans are clearly defined, they were loosely organised communities which seldom or never came as a whole under a single directing power, whether that power was a clan chief or a clan council.[45]

One of the few divergences from this general pattern was provided by the Aro clan, which, it is claimed, had a general council of the component village-groups which was a going political concern. This council comprised nine *otusi*[46] men, the heads of the ten other villages which had no resident otusi, and co-opted elders of intelligence and good character. The council was presided over by the titular clan head called *onyishi otusi* of Oro village. The executive arm of this council was the *ekpe*.[47] An assistant administrative officer commented in 1935:

> The Aros were clan-conscious rather than town-conscious and today the average [Aro] man will declare with pride that he is an Aro before he gives the name of his town, recalling the spirit of St Paul triumphantly declaring 'Civis Romanus sum' followed by the information 'I come from Tarsus . . . no mean city.'[48]

This measure of political integration evolved by the Aro clan is traceable to the peculiar position which the Aro, as exploiters of the Long Juju and as monopolist middlemen, enjoyed *vis-à-vis* their neighbours. In this situation the Aro felt the need for and evolved a system which was able to adjust relations among the villages so that the secrets behind Aro ascendancy could be kept from outsiders.

The average village in the Eastern Provinces was divided into a number of subordinate units which territorially could be called wards and ward-sections. The ward-section, popularly called

[45] G. J. F. Tomlinson (Assistant Secretary for Native Affairs), *Report on a Tour in the Eastern Provinces*, Lagos 1923, p. 10
[46] The traditional title for any of the nine heads of the nine Aro patrilineages.
[47] G. I. Jones, *Report of Commission into the position, status and influence of chiefs*, etc., p. 5. See also CSO 26, No. 29017, Intelligence Report on the Aro Clan, pp. 20–3
[48] CSO 26, No. 29017, Intelligence Report on the Aro Clan, p. 18

extended-family, comprises households or single families tracing descent to a common ancestor; while the village is made up of a number of lineages or wards tracing descent to one of the sons of the original (mythical) founder, or to one of the several co-founders, of the village. [49]

The ward-section or sublineage was the smallest unit of political authority. Among the households which made up this unit there was generally one which belonged directly to the eldest son of the common father. This was the senior household of the unit. The head of this household had charge of any sacred symbols which belonged to the founding father in his lifetime and for that he was the living representative of all the dead members of that unit who were still believed to be participants in the fortunes of the unit. He therefore enjoyed a great measure of personal respect, as an insult to him was regarded as an insult to the founding father and other dead ancestors, an offence involving the impertinent member and often the whole unit in the risk of incurring the anger of these spiritual members of the unit. By reason of his special position this man was generally appealed to by a house-holder who had a problem child or wife and wanted moral pressure brought to bear on him or her. He was called upon to arbitrate in minor disputes between households. In short, he figured prominently in the composing of issues which it was thought could be dealt with through the application of moral pressure. But matters which involved the wielding of legal and political power within the unit went directly to the council of the sublineage composed of all the householders in the unit and of adult members who were of the right age. In this council the head of the senior household presided but the conduct of the meeting was generally dominated by the most intelligent or wealthiest elder who had acquired some measure of influence in consequence. The sublineage was autonomous in matters which touched only its interests and were not of such grave proportions as to endanger its corporate existence. For matters which either touched other units or threatened it with disruption it had to look up to a superior body.

This latter body was the council of the lineage. The lineage had its senior sublineage whose head stood in the same position within the unit as the head of the senior household did within the

[49] C. K. Meek, *Law and Authority in a Nigerian Tribe*, Oxford 1937, pp. 88–97

sublineage. He arbitrated in minor disputes between extended families, though at times a third extended family rather than he could be called upon to mediate. He presided over the council of the lineage, which was composed of all the heads of the component sublineages and all adult men of intelligence and repute within the unit. Here, as in the council of the sublineage, decisions were taken after a public debate at which any member could secure audience if he had something reasonable to contribute; and the decision taken could be the result of one or two influential members throwing his or their weight on this or that side. Like the sublineage this unit dealt only with those issues which touched its exclusive interests and with regard to such matters generally resisted unsolicited interference from outside. For decisions on matters which defied solution at its hands or touched outside interests the next authority was the council of the village.

Within the village the head of the senior lineage took charge of the sacred symbols of the unit and presided over the village council. The village enjoyed autonomy in its own affairs but among the Ibo was dependent on the village-group council for matters which involved outside interests or could not be compounded within it. The village-group in turn had its senior village whose head was the ritual head of the entire group and presided over the village-group council, a body which comprised all village heads, heads of all other segments as well as other elders who cared to attend. In actual fact any adult male member of the village-group could attend and insist on being heard. The core of the village-group council comprised the sublineage heads popularly known among most Ibo as *ndi ama ala* or *ndi isi ọfọ* – the ọfọ being among this people the supreme ancestral symbol, the staff of traditional authority and influence as well as the symbol of justice, truth and right living. Though it would be a gross falsification to regard the ndi isi ọfọ as the cabinet of the village-group or as the repository of sovereign authority, no legislation or other political action meant for the entire group could carry any weight or force without their support and blessing. On the other hand they could not hold the rest of the village-group assembly to ransom by withholding such assent and blessing on issues in which the *vox populi* was firm and clear and thus had come to mean *vox dei*.

The system described above could be regarded as the basic political structure of the Ibo and their neighbours. It was not in all places that each segment had a senior unit whose right it was to produce a politico-ritual leader; on the contrary, there were villages and groups of villages in which the headship went to the oldest living freeborn member of the unit concerned. Also there was no rigid rule of procedure which enjoined that difficult cases must always go from the sublineage through the lineage and the village to the village-group council. Different combinations and permutations were allowed, and the procedure adopted in each case was determined by the temper of the people concerned and by the urgency and gravity of the issue. Any analysis of the political systems of these peoples must recognise the existence of infinite patterns and procedures in spite of the underlying general similarities already isolated and discussed. But in all cases each segment in each group was in its political practice and structure a microcosm of the segment directly above it or a macrocosm of that directly below it.

In barest outline this was probably the original constitution of the communities in the Eastern Provinces for centuries.[50] Described in a different terminology, it was a constitution founded first and foremost on gerontocracy. Since generally the head of each segment was either the oldest man in the line of direct descent from the founder or at least the oldest surviving descendant of such a founder, it was generally the practice that in each segment the dominant section of the council comprised those who had reached the elders' grade in the age-set system which obtained with varying emphasis amongst most peoples of this region. The age-grade system has been graphically described as that method by which segmentary communities organised themselves for work, war and government. Under this system the age-grade which was just below manhood concerned itself with duties such as cleaning the paths, streams and public squares; those of the citizens who had reached manhood played the main part in war and in enforcing the decisions of the council of the village or its segments; while those of the elders' grade concerned themselves with deliberations and the administration of justice.[51]

The classic example in this area of how this system worked is found in Mgbom, in the Afikpo village-group of the North-

---

[50] Lokoprof No. 159/1921. Tribes of Nigeria: Inter-Relations of (Kaduna Archives). See Palmer's minute dated 11.7.21, which contains his general theory on the evolution of indigenous African political systems.
[51] *Ibid.*

eastern Ibo, which has been intensively investigated by Dr Ottenberg. In this village three age-grades were very important for purposes of government. The first was *uke ekpe*, the grade of middle-aged men who formed the executive arm of the village political system. Above this was the *oha ndi ichie*, made up of men who had graduated from uke ekpe but had not yet reached the ripe age to be numbered among the elders' grade. They played little part in government but from time to time were called upon to help the uke ekpe in enforcing the decisions of the elders, while at other times they sat with the elders, contributed their opinion in debates, but did not take part in actual decision-making. Above them was the *ndichie* grade, which constituted the supreme legislative and judicial body of the village.[52] Another illuminating example is found in the Anam group of the Anambara valley, where village government was in the hands of the *ikenyi* (elders) and *otu mpokulo* (men of over 48 years of age), while the still younger grade of *otu owanuno* formed the messengers and executive agents.[53]

Evidence from oral tradition seems to suggest that as these communities grew in wealth new elements were introduced into the system. The emphasis which came to be laid on taking titles, for example, appears to be a relic of the importance which was attached to surplus wealth at a certain time in these communities' history, a period when, for reasons which have not yet been fully investigated, the economy experienced some expansion. This increase made it possible for men, *after* maintaining their dependants, to have a surplus to spend on the taking of titles and the purchase of membership of some secret societies. The possession of wealth thus came to be regarded as a symbol of ability and good sense and the only visible proof of it was the giving of those elaborate feasts which preceded entry to these privileged societies. Membership of these closed organisations conferred a new status. In the first place it showed that the individual concerned was, at least, a man of considerable means able to build up some following and to contribute materially towards the prosecution of projects such as war on a neighbouring community agreed upon by the unit. In the second place it

[52] S. Ottenberg, 'The System of Authority of the Afikpo Ibo', Ph.D. Thesis, Northwestern University, 1957, pp. 240–3
[53] CSO 26, No. 29576, Intelligence Report on the Anam Group, paras 23–36

showed he was a free-born and a man of probity. In many areas some of these organisations enjoyed so much popularity among the people that either membership of them came to constitute a criterion for participation in government or the title societies came to be annexed to the original political organisation based on the lineage system.

Judged by the amount of political power which was attached to the possession of these titles, the *eze* and *ntinya* title systems of Onitsha province and Ibibio areas respectively were probably the most important. Without taking the ntinya title, for example, the head of a group could not hope to exercise the influence vested in that headship or enjoy the perquisites which went with it. In the Ediene and Itak clans of the Eastern Ibibio certain ntinya holders bearing special titles had exclusive rights to preside over particular types of cases. For instance, the *obong uneng*, or 'chief of fowl', dealt with all cases involving fowls; the *obong edong*, or 'chief of sheep', dealt with cases involving sheep; others were concerned with cases involving cows, nocturnal breaches of the peace, market matters, the up-rooting of people's crops and violence during the farming season.[54] In the northern sections of Nsukka (Northern Ibo) in communities like Ogboli and Enugu-Ezike, titles enjoyed great prestige, and village government lay in the hands of the assembly of lineage elders presided over by the head of the senior lineage, with title-holders called *asogwa* and *ndishi iwu* acting as executive agents. Not infrequently in this area a village segment recognised the oldest man as its head in internal affairs and the senior titled man as its representative in all dealings with other sections.[55] The title system was of some political significance even in areas where membership of a title society was not a *sine qua non* for participation in village government. In the Izzi clan of the Northeastern Ibo, though the powers of government lay in the hands of the generality of the elders called *nze*, only those who had made the *isi nze* title, which required each entrant to kill a cow for the other members of the titled group, had real political influence in the council.[56] Put

[54] CSO 26, No. 27615, Intelligence Report on the Ediene and Itak Clans, p. 32. See also G. I. Jones, *Report of Commission into the position, status and influence of chiefs*, etc., p. 17
[55] C. K. Meek, pp. 148ff
[56] G. I. Jones, *Report of Commission into the position, status and influence of chiefs*, etc., pp. 17–18

differently, the possession of a title conferred the social confidence which helped in the achievement of political leadership.

Apart from having this direct political significance, these societies, through bringing the oldest and most level-headed sections of the community together under a kind of brotherhood, helped, like the age-grade system, to minimise the strains and stresses which were inherent in a segmentary society as a result of the clashes and bickerings among the different segments. Furthermore, it was not unlikely that legislation in the interests of the public good often originated from the discussions held in the meetings of these exclusive societies. What was more, by imposing discipline on their members, these societies minimised clashes between individuals and thus reduced occasions on which there were breaches of the peace.

The secret society was another development which probably came later to modify the basic political system delineated above. This institution was characteristic of communities in this general area with the exception of such Ibo groups as the Oratta and Ikwerri. In each village, the society or club embraced all the able-bodied in the community who had paid the necessary entrance fee. These secret societies in their classic type, notably the *ekpo* of the Ibibio, the *odo* and *omabe* of Nsukka Division, the *ekang* of Aba and Bende Divisions and the *mmo* of most Ibo areas, simulated the spirits of dead ancestors reappearing in corporeal form to play a part in the government of the village or its segments. It was the elders of the community who generally constituted the oldest members that disciplined the rest of the community in the name of these societies. Each society could enforce its own decisions as well as the decisions of the council of its unit when asked to do so, and could at times initiate legislation in the name of the ancestors.[57]

A close look at these political developments reveals that in essentials the ancient constitution continued in its basic form of rule by lineage heads and elders even in those communities where the title and secret societies took a prominent part in government. Within the secret society control lay in the hands of those who had achieved the highest grades and who invariably were the elders and heads of the different lineage groups. It was the same thing

[57] *Ibid.*, pp. 21–2. D. Forde and G. I. Jones, *The Ibo and Ibibio-speaking peoples of Southeastern Nigeria*, Oxford 1950, pp. 19, 73–4. C. K. Meek, pp. 66–79

with the title society. From the predominantly subsistence character of the economy of these communities in the pre-colonial era, it is certain that those who acquired enough material surplus to enable them to join these societies were generally those who had large families and therefore a large labour force, which would usually take many years of hard work to acquire. In consequence the holders of the higher grades, in either type of society, were usually the elders and heads of village sections and sub-sections. Rule by titled men or secret societies thus came to be rule by those, or at least a majority of those, who had reached the elders' grade. In 1921 H. R. Palmer, the Lieutenant Governor of the Northern Provinces, went so far as to claim that 'what is now known as taking titles was originally nothing more than stepping from one [age] grade to another which was celebrated by some kind of feast.'[58]

Within this pattern there was still scope for individuals of genius to tower above the general herd. Some of these people could be men of wealth and large hearts, who by reason of these had been able to build up large followings who supported them in public, and in private helped to maintain them in opulence by working for them on certain days of the native week. They could also be men of sharp wit and eloquence, who by their suave manners and persuasive oratory would always sway the majority in their lineage council to their side. An example of men whose pre-eminence in their sections depended on their personal qualities was Anumudu of Onumonu in Owerri, whom Meek described in his *Law and Authority in a Nigerian Tribe*. Anumudu owed his influence in his kindred to his wealth and the judicious use he made of it. By helping his kindred in times of trouble he placed all those around him under an obligation and acquired an influence which exceeded that of his unit's *okpara* or lineage head. Men like Anumudu were not rare in the political experience of Ibo, Ibibio, Ijo and Ogoja communities.[59]

The influence which charismatic leaders enjoyed in their sections gave them more weight than they would otherwise have had in the affairs of their village. But at the village level there was little opportunity for an individual to achieve undisputed ascen-

---

[58] Lokoprof 159/1921. Tribes of Nigeria: Inter-Relations of (Kaduna Archives). See minute dated 11.7.21
[59] C. K. Meek, pp. 111–15. G. I. Jones, *Report of Commission into the position, status and influence of chiefs*, etc., p. 11

dancy over all other lineages owing to the keen jealousy which usually existed between segments and also owing to the fact that each segment would nearly always have its own political 'prodigy'. Even at the level of the lineage or sublineage the influence of these men should not be over-estimated. They could be called upon to arbitrate in disputes between individuals who held them in high esteem or they could help to form popular opinion in the group. But they could not take unilateral actions on issues of importance which were clearly the responsibility of the convocation of elders, nor could they set the executive machinery of the unit in action unless commissioned to do so by the unit's supreme authority. 'To be sure,' observes Dr Simon Ottenberg, 'elders are influenced by their most able leaders, yet decision and ultimate authority rest in the hands of the group as a whole.'[60] On this issue and referring specifically to the Ibo, Professor Anene said: 'Generally speaking, the Ibo communities were democracies in the sense that the government of the communities was the concern of all.'[61]

The above was the general pattern of political organisation in the Eastern Provinces. But as already shown there were the *Village Monarchies* with constitutions that differed from this pattern in some noteworthy respects. The more spectacular of these 'exotic' constitutions operated largely in those coastal communities which played a prominent part in the Atlantic trade, chiefly Calabar, Bonny, Kalabari, Opobo and Brass. One of the main distinctions of the coastal constitution was that in the period between 1700 and 1880 it came very near to producing real centralised chiefships. By 1880, however, reaction in the opposite direction had set in and went on throughout the greater part of the colonial era.

Each political unit here (usually the village community) was segmented into wards and ward-sections. Duke Town, for instance, by the middle of the nineteenth century comprised six wards, namely Duke Ephraim, Archibong, Ntiero Duke, Enyamba, Cobham and Henshaw. Each of these wards subdivided again into ward-sections more commonly known as houses.[62] Opobo Town divided first into fourteen wards which in turn

[60] S. Ottenberg, p. 353
[61] J. C. Anene, *Southern Nigeria*, etc., p. 14
[62] Ed. D. Forde, *Efik Traders of Old Calabar*, Oxford 1956, p. 121

subdivided into sixty-five houses.[63] The house was the fundamental unit of political authority among the Ijo and the Efik, the
coastal equivalent of the hinterland extended-family or sublineage
in a political sense. In Efik villages a person's status depended
largely on whether his genealogy could be traced directly to the
founding father of the unit; that is, on whether he was free-born.
Thus, though slaves or people of servile descent could amass
wealth and by reason of that become politically important, they
were never so completely absorbed into the Efik social system as
to come to aspire to the headship of an Efik house or ward.[64] In
the Ijo communities, whether or not a house originally began as
a community of true agnates, by the nineteenth century it had
become a 'trading and fighting corporation' in which a member's
status depended on his ability in trade and politics in the Niger
Delta. The quickest means by which a house grew was through
the purchase and absorption of slaves who were usually given
putative kinship relationship with the founder of the unit to
strengthen the corporate unity of the house. Because of the
emphasis on ability in these Ijo states a man could (and some did)
rise from slave status to the headship of the house to which he
was attached, or to the headship of a house which he could found
as soon as he was able to contribute a war-canoe to the navy of his
community. The classic example of this feature of Ijo society was
the life and career of Jaja, who, starting as a slave, rose to the
headship of the Anna Pepple group of houses and ended as King
of Opobo.[65]

The house, in its internal affairs, was an autonomous political
unit governed by a council made up of the influential members of
the unit and presided over by the house head. In Efik communities
the head had to be the ablest of the 'full-blooded descendants'
of the founder.[66] In the other coastal communities he had to be
a man democratically elected on ground of his ability to manage the

[63] Based on information collected from Chief Robert D. B. Fubra, Mr
E. M. T. Epelle, Chief S. W. K. Uranta and Chief Harvey Jim Jaja, all of
Opobo Town.
[64] G. I. Jones, *Report of Commission into the position, status and influence
of chiefs*, etc., p. 34
[65] K. O. Dike, *Trade and Politics in the Niger Delta*, Oxford 1956, pp.
182–3. See also *Eminent Nigerians of the Nineteenth Century*, ed. K. O.
Dike, Cambridge, pp. 18–19
[66] G. I. Jones, *Report of Commission into the position, status and influence
of chiefs*, etc., p. 34

affairs of the house. In the latter case he could thus be either one of the former head's sons, or if these were nonentities or near-nonentities, one of his brothers or slaves. The government of a house was far from autocratic, especially in Efik communities. But in the Ijo houses the amount of power enjoyed by a house head depended on whether or not he was the original founder of the house. If he was – in which case the members of the house were either his sons or slaves – he governed the house as more or less his private estate. But as the house grew in years and some of the members in wealth and influence, he was compelled to rule in association with the house council. In any case, for the house the era of autocracy never lasted longer than the life-span of the founder. After that the majority in the council would start to carry the vote. In spite of this a house head of ability and genius could still carry a great deal of weight. This he could do by buying many personal slaves over whom he had direct control. In the event the majority in the house assembly which carried the vote would be a majority composed largely of his personal followers. But even then no house head who was not a founding father could hope to enjoy a personal autocracy in the government of the house. 'Power in a canoe house,' says Jones, 'can be represented as distributed and balanced between the ordinary members, the leaders, and the chief.'[67]

The ward was governed by a council comprising all the house heads in the ward and presided over by a ward head, called *Etubom* by Efik. Among the Efik the *Etubom* was the ablest of the house heads, but among the other coastal communities the office was hereditary in one house, which was the 'mother' house of the ward. Thus in the Jaja ward, Opobo, which had fourteen houses, the ward head came from the Jaja house. The position, though hereditary in one house, was elective. The 'mother' house elected one of its ablest members and presented him to the ward council, which could reject a candidate considered incompetent or morally unworthy of the position. The personal authority of a ward head over the ward was less than that which a house head enjoyed over his house. The ward, containing virtually autonomous houses,

[67] G. I. Jones, *The Trading State*, etc., pp. 168–71. Supplemented with information collected from E. M. T. Epelle, Chief S. W. K. Uranta, Chief Robert D. B. Fubra and Chief Harvey Jim Jaja, all of Opobo Town; Chief Victor Allison and Chief Adadonye Fombo (Bonny); Chief B. D. Frank-Bestman, Chief E. T. Jack and Chief A. K. Bob-Manuel (Abonnema).

was a looser political unit than the house where political unity was strengthened by the fact that each house had a common fund or pool of trade goods on which each member depended at various times for sustenance. In the last resort the unity of a ward, as G. I. Jones has argued, depended on the necessity for a common front against rival wards. The ward council could not dictate to any house in its internal affairs nor could it intervene in an intra-house dispute without invitation. It existed mainly to adjust claims between houses and to assert the claims of the ward against other wards. [68]

The structural similarity in the political systems of the two groups, Efik and the Ijo, so far noticed did not continue on to the sphere of the government of the village as a unit. In the Ijo groups the final authority in inter-ward dispute, in house issues which could not be finally disposed of by the lower councils, and in legislative matters affecting the whole community was the village council, comprising all the ward and house heads and presided over by an Amanyanabo (village head). Issues which defied resolution in this body were decided by appeal either to an oracle (such as the Long Juju) or to arms. The position of Amanyanabo was hereditary in Kalabari in the Amachree house, in Bonny in the Pepple house and in Opobo in the Jaja house. [69]

In Efik villages the situation was different. In Duke Town, for instance, there was no general council of ward and ward-section heads which had the right to mediate in inter-ward disputes or to deliberate on matters of common interest. The political vacuum which might have existed as a result of this was filled by a secret organisation called ekpe by the Efik but which occurs as *egbo* in nineteenth-century records. Each village had its own ekpe lodge, though Duke Town and Creek Town had one, as Duke Town is said to have originated as a mere segment of Creek Town. It was this society, which impersonated the spirit of the dead ancestors, that actually 'ruled the village'. The elders who had brought admission to the highest grade, called *Nyamkpe*, wielded political authority through it, while those men who had reached the grade of *Okpoho*, just below *Nyamkpe*, were the executive agents. The ekpe of each village was the supreme legislative, judicial and

[68] Ed. D. Forde, *Efik Traders*, pp. 122–3. Supplemented with information collected from the informants listed in footnote 67, above
[69] P. A. Talbot, *Tribes of the Niger Delta*, London 1932, pp. 289–91

executive authority on all matters touching the village as a whole.[70]

The great expansion of wealth occasioned by the Atlantic trade, the interference of the supercargoes who wanted a more centralised system of authority capable of enforcing the order necessary for the expansion of commerce and the need of these states for a show of unity and strength *vis-à-vis* neighbouring rivals and the visiting European traders, gave the constitutions of these coastal communities a twist which made them different from the constitution of the Ibo and Ibibio of the interior from whom most of the members of these communities are said to have descended. Duke Town and Creek Town each evolved an *obong* (pl. *mbong*).[71] In the nineteenth century these were called 'kings' by Europeans. But neither of the two mbong was properly integrated into the indigenous political system. Without a general council of the village through which they could act, or their own independent bureaucracy, army or police, the mbong were, in the internal affairs of their villages, the most fascinating of constitutional nonentities. Their true position was that of the mouthpiece of the community in its external affairs.

The operation of the same forces had also given the village heads of the coastal Ijo communities an opportunity to improve on their positions within the same period. G. I. Jones has pointed out that in the eighteenth and early nineteenth centuries the heads of Bonny, New Calabar and Nembe came near to becoming 'potentates of centralised pyramidal government'.[72] However, neither they nor the two Efik mbong actually achieved that status. As Jones has also pointed out, even the most pre-eminent in the Calabar line of mbong, men like Duke Ephraim and Eyo II, did not possess any appreciable political power outside their wards, and even there they depended greatly on the support of other men of wealth, position and intelligence.[73] In Calabar, for instance, the title 'king' applied to these two most successful of Efik merchant princes of free birth was freely assumed by lineage heads and even by heads of secret societies. When the super-

---

[70] Ed. D. Forde, *Efik Traders*, etc., pp. 135–42. G. I. Jones, *Report of Commission into the position, status and influence of chiefs, etc.,* p. 22
[71] Ed. D. Forde, *Efik Traders*, etc., pp. 124–30
[72] G. I. Jones, *Report of Commission into the position, status and influence of chiefs,* etc., p. 38
[73] Ed. D. Forde, *Efik Traders*, etc., pp. 131–2

cargoes applied this or a similar term to the head of any of the communities between the Rio del Rey and the Niger Delta, they were largely giving vent to a hope that such an institution might evolve in these communities for effectively maintaining the public peace. When these communities applied these terms to their nobility, they were also at times largely ostentatiously displaying that they had imbibed enough of western culture to apply to themselves foreign terms which they half-understood or completely misunderstood. Duke Ephraim preferred the title 'duke' to the title 'king' because he thought it more expressive of power and magnificence.[74]

Certain historians, perhaps out of mistaken belief that a chiefly constitution is inherently superior to a 'chiefless' one, have been inclined to romanticise on the status achieved by these men. In this connection it is necessary to bring out two important points. Firstly, if it is true that these men adequately served the needs and met the challenges of their own day, they did not need to be despotic monarchs in order to do this. Secondly, however able they were, neither the Pepples of Bonny, nor the Amachrees of Okrika, nor the Enyambas of Calabar were able to modify considerably the basic segmentary structure of the constitutions they inherited. In consequence, after the first half of the nineteenth century, when the Europeans who had helped to shore up these men lost interest in doing so, and the trade which built up the material pedestal on which these kings and chiefs of the coast had attempted to stand left their hands, they sank back to what they had in essence always been but had vainly struggled to outgrow – village heads. In any case the fact still remains that however tantalisingly near these men came to being autocratic chiefs in the conventional sense, by the beginning of the period covered by this study they had atrophied into the most pathetic relic of the trick which the Atlantic trade had played with the political systems of these coastal communities.

Other examples of the *Constitutional Village Monarchy* type were to be found in Onitsha and Oguta towns. The constitutions of these village-groups differed from the constitution of the hinterland groups in the Eastern Provinces in the following ways. In the first place they were based on dominance by a narrow plutocracy and thus differed from the broad-based democracy of the other. Secondly, though the Onitsha and Oguta constitutions

[74] *Ibid.*, p. 126

were based on title systems as were the other constitutions described as distinctly autochthonous, the Onitsha and Oguta titles were not generally the ordinary 'open' type; that is, they could not be obtained by any free-born who had reached the appropriate age and acquired the necessary material means. Instead the very important titles were either conferred by a man who was the titular head of the political system or they were hereditary in certain lineages. In Oguta, for example, the *eze igwe* and *iyasere* titles were hereditary in well-defined segments. Finally there is evidence from oral tradition that this particular political constitution was borrowed from outside – most likely from Benin.[75]

At the apex of the political system in Onitsha was the *obi*, who held the title of *eze*, the most elevated title in the community. Under him were three colleges of titled men called ndichie. The most senior college, *ndichie ume*, contained six titled men who acting in concert with the obi were said to constitute the traditional government of Onitsha. It seems more probable, however, that sovereignty in the village lay in the hands of the general assembly which comprised the obi as chairman, the ndichie ume and the two other title colleges of *ndichie okwa* and *ndichie okwaraza*. The decisions of this assembly were enforced either by the mmo society (a secret organisation) or by one of the age-grades into which the men were organised. The ndichie title was usually conferred by the obi though the fees paid by the candidates were shared by the obi and those who had already bought the title in question.[76] In Oguta the chief executive council was formed by the ndichie titled men. This council had twelve members, of which the head was eze igwe followed by the deputy head of the town known as iyasere. Other members of the ndichie title college worthy of mention included the *ogene*, who was the oldest man in all Oguta; the *ogana*, who for his eloquence in debate was the spokesman of the council; and the *Eze Ani*, who as the okpara of Oboagwa, the ward occupied by those alleged to be the descendants of the first inhabitants of

[75] D. Forde and G. I. Jones, *The Ibo and Ibibio-speaking Peoples*, pp. 20, 36–7. G. I. Jones, *Report of Commission into the position, status and influence of chiefs*, pp. 19–20, 27–8, 36–7
[76] D. Forde and G. I. Jones, *The Ibo and Ibibio-speaking Peoples*, etc., p. 37. G. I. Jones, *Report of Commission into the position, status and influence of chiefs*, etc., p. 28

Oguta, was the priest of *ani*. The full assembly which was the supreme governmental body of Oguta comprised, in addition to the ndichie, two other colleges of title-holders – the *oririnze* and *ndi okpara*. The oririnze was a lesser ndichie title, while okpara was the title given to the head of any of the twenty-four wards of Oguta.[77]

Neither the Onitsha nor the Oguta constitution was a well-integrated monarchy or even a thoroughgoing oligarchy in view of the large powers which the segments and the age-grades have been shown to possess.[78] After investigating the Onitsha constitution in the 1930s, Dr C. K. Meek came to the conclusion that 'indeed in many respects' the obi 'was not so much a king as president of a bureaucratic society'.[79]

The conclusion which emerges from the whole analysis is that at the time British rule was imposed on the Ibo and their neighbours no community east of the Niger had a leader who could be made, without doing violence to the traditional constitution, to fulfil the role of a chief under Indirect Rule as the system was then interpreted. Under this system, as then operated, a chief was believed to represent the executive authority of his unit, or to be one from whom such an authority was believed to derive. There was nobody in any community in the Eastern Provinces whose traditional status within the indigenous constitution fitted him for such a role. In each autonomous community decisions were taken in matters of public interest by a collectivity of those who had attained the ripe status and this was done in the name of the community. In traditional social philosophy 'the community' meant the living members, the dead ancestors and the convocation of local deities and spirits. These deities and spirits were conceived as closely associated with and interested in the weal and woe of the unit. If the lineage head stood as the living representative of the ancestors, nobody ever made pretensions to, or was ever regarded as, compounding in his own person all the elements which made up a 'community'.

For the purpose of his report to the Eastern Nigeria Government in 1956 on the status and influence of chiefs in the then Eastern Region, the social anthropologist Jones said a chief could

[77] G. I. Jones, *Report of Commission into the position, status and influence of chiefs*, etc., pp. 19–20
[78] *Ibid.*, p. 28
[79] C. K. Meek, *Law and Authority In a Nigerian Tribe*, etc., pp. 189–95

be defined as anybody referred to by a 'term signifying head'.[80] By this definition the okpara, isi ozo and isi nze of Ibo areas, the obong isong and the ekpe leader of Ibibio groups would all be chiefs. For the purpose of this study, as for Indirect Rule as understood in the Eastern Provinces before 1930, this definition is unsatisfactory. The Warrant Chiefs were expected to *be* and *act* as chiefs not just as people referred to by a 'term signifying head'. The position of a village head among the Ibo and their neighbours was not wholly or even mainly a political office, but signified the ritual status which its occupant enjoyed through his standing in the genealogical history of the group. This helps to explain why many of the lineage heads were often decrepit and senile and confined by innumerable taboos to their compounds. Had their position mainly signified political headship it would have been politically shortsighted to appoint such men to it. To be a lineage head one needed not political ability, but free descent, reputation for moral rectitude and generally the right age. In trying to understand the proper position of these lineage heads who keep the ancestral symbols of the group, Miss Green observed that:

[80] G. I. Jones, *Report of Commission into the position, status and influence of chiefs*, etc., para. 28. This definition of the term 'chief' by Mr Jones is startling but probably understandable in the light of the trend of Nigerian party politics at the time. During that time the National Council of Nigeria and Cameroons (NCNC), which was the ruling party in the Eastern Region and a powerful opposition party in the Western Region, was under double pressure. In the West the Action Group Party spread the propaganda that if the NCNC should come to power there, the position of the Obas would be in serious jeopardy, since the NCNC 'was' the party of the republican Ibo, who, having no traditional chiefs of their own, could not be expected to understand, respect and uphold chieftaincy and royalty in other lands. At the same time certain groups of NCNC supporters in the East clamoured for the creation of a House of Chiefs in the Eastern Region which the party would manipulate for political purposes and to which loyal party members who failed to secure election into the House of Assembly could be sent as reward for loyalty. It was in this circumstance that the NCNC, determined to prove the Action Group propagandists wrong and to satisfy its own supporters in the East, called on Mr Jones to conduct the inquiry into the position, status and influence of chiefs in the Eastern Region. Mr Jones, it would appear, knew he was expected to find arguments on which the NCNC could create an Eastern House of Chiefs. This would seem to explain why, in spite of all the arguments to the contrary which the Report contains, Mr Jones came to the rather amusing conclusion that a chief was anybody referred to by 'a term signifying head' and by this meaningless definition 'proved' that the Eastern Region had 'chiefs' and ought to have a House of Chiefs!

Dr Nadel has recently pointed out that in a Nupe village membership of the council is an official political appointment even though it goes to heads of the kinship group. In this Ibo village, however, one could hardly say that the dozen or so *nde ama ala* were differentiated as a body from the kinship structure. *They might exercise certain political functions but basically they were there in virtue of their position in the kinship system.*[81]

It was peoples who had evolved the political system and constitutions analysed in this chapter that the British colonial administration in Nigeria expected to operate a local government system that at the time was assumed to presuppose, for its smooth running, the existence of chiefs of more than nominal political standing.

[81] M. M. Green, *Igbo Village Affairs*, etc., p. 73. Italics in the last sentence of the quotation are mine.

2 The origins of the Warrant Chief System

The Warrant Chief System was synonymous with the Native Court System in the Eastern Provinces in the period 1891–1929. Whatever position of influence, responsibility and power which Warrant Chiefs enjoyed in this era derived from their possession of the warrant which made them members of the Native Court. Even when they functioned as executive authorities in their different villages, they did so as members of the Native Court, which really was the local government body. When they made by-laws to regulate local affairs they derived their legislative authority from their membership of the same institution. Therefore in investigating the origin of the Warrant Chief System one is involved in finding answers to such questions as when and how the first Native Court in this area came into existence, what general principles and considerations underpinned it and how the first members or Warrant Chiefs were appointed.

On the question of how the system came into existence there is reason to agree with Mr S. M. Grier, the Secretary for Native Affairs, who in 1922 said that the Warrant Chief System was fathered by the Court of Equity.[1] What was the Court of Equity and how did it come into being? It is necessary to discuss these questions in full in view of the powerful spell which this institution seems to have cast over the imaginations of later British administrators who grappled with the problem of providing an effective local government system for the area which in 1900 became the Protectorate of Southern Nigeria.

In the palmy days of the city-states of the Oil Rivers their indigenous political system had been able to cope with the problem of maintaining law and order both among their own

---

[1] S. M. Grier, *Report on a tour in the Eastern Provinces*, Lagos 1922, p. 4. See also *Report of the Native Courts (Eastern Region) Commission of Inquiry*, 1953, p. 2

people and between the latter and the trading community of
Europeans. G. I. Jones, in his masterly survey of the history of
these coastal communities, wrote:

> In the time of King Opobo [of Bonny] integration and co-ordination
> between the two communities (the African and the European) had been
> provided by the king who took care to establish a personal relationship
> with the captain and supercargo of every trading vessel. The British
> traders were prepared to accept his authority because they regarded
> him as the supreme authority in the area. It was the same in Old Cala-
> bar at this time where an appeal to the King of Duke Town as head of
> Egbo could also mobilise the agents of this secret society for the collec-
> tion of a trader's debt.[2]

But towards the end of the first half of the nineteenth century the
indigenous political system of these states entered a period of
progressive decline owing, partly, to the fact that the men who
succeeded to the headship of these communities lacked the political
astuteness of their predecessors and partly owing to the economic
decline which overtook these states with the suppression of the
slave trade and the determined effort of European merchants to
undercut the position of the coastal middlemen.[3] The need was
therefore felt by the commercial community along the coast for a
political institution that would be able to perform in the new era
this function which the indigenous system had hitherto carried
out so effectively. This need was the background to the rise in
Bonny either just before or in 1854 of the first Court of Equity.[4]

The Court of Equity thus came into being entirely on the
initiative of the European and African merchants, the latter being
mainly the 'kings and chiefs' of the community concerned. It was
presided over by the commercial agent who had stayed longest on
the river, but later in a place like Degema the presidency was
held by each agent in turn irrespective of his length of stay on
the river. The decisions of the court were arrived at by a simple
majority vote. The court punished the convicted by means of
fines and could impose an economic embargo on any trader who
refused to abide by its decision. Appeals lay from it to the British

[2] G. I. Jones, *The Trading States of the Oil Rivers*, Oxford 1963, pp. 79–80
[3] For European attempts to penetrate the interior in the first half of the
nineteenth century which helped to set the coastal states on the road to
decline, see C. C. Ifemesia, *British Enterprise on the Niger 1830–1869*, unpublished Ph.D. Thesis, University of London 1959, ii–vi.
[4] G. I. Jones, *The Trading States*, etc., Oxford 1963, p. 80. Alan Burns,
History of Nigeria, 7th impression 1958, p. 135

consul, a procedure which, it was hoped, would help check the miscarriage of justice. But in view of the consul's many duties, of his lack of an independent means of transport and of the general poverty of communication in the thickly forested region of the coast, it can be understood if this safety mechanism did not function faultlessly, and if the Courts of Equity were to a great extent left to themselves. But whatever must have been the shortcomings of the institution, it is indisputable that it succeeded in maintaining a certain amount of law and order among the wild 'gentlemen' of the commercial community of the coast. That the Court of Equity satisfactorily met a deeply felt need is evidenced by the fact that by 1870 it had spread from Bonny to the Benin River, Brass, Okrika, Opobo and Calabar, as by the fact that in 1872 an Order-in-Council gave it a legal basis and brought it fully under consular control.[5]

In many ways the Court of Equity was the forerunner of the Native Court as it came to be constituted under the Warrant Chief System. Firstly, it contained the essential germ of the principle of associating native rulers with the work of the 'new' administration in the Oil Rivers and their hinterland. The African merchants who sat with the European supercargoes in the court were generally the members of the old aristocracy – the heads of houses and of the city-states – for it was these men who held the main strings of the middlemen trade of the coast. Secondly, it was a manifestation of the feeling which was then current that indigenous African systems of government needed to be re-inforced through the infusion of European ideas and practices before they could meet the increased demands being made on them as a result of the incursion of European economic and other interests. Thirdly, it was a pointer in the direction of the possibilities of a cheap administration. The legalisation of this system in 1872, which vested the administration of the coast of the Oil Rivers on a group of unpaid merchants, under-lined for the intelligent observer the fact that London would give its blessing to a cheap solution of the problem of local administration. Fourthly, the Court of Equity, like the Warrant Chief System, was based on the principle that one or two

---

[5] G. I. Jones, *The Trading States*, etc., pp. 77–8. A. Burns, pp. 135–6, 140. S. M. Tamuno, *The Development of British Administrative Control in Southern Nigeria, 1900–1912*, unpublished Ph.D. Thesis, University of London, pp. 21–2

members of the local community, acting in concert with some Europeans or under the guidance of a representative of the British Government, could, contrary to traditional constitutional practice, lay down the law for the rest of the community.[6] And lastly, it established for the British the principle of charging such a single institution with judicial, executive and legislative functions.[7] In spite of these important resemblances, however, the Court of Equity differed from the Native Court of later days in four ways. Firstly, its members were traders, African and European; secondly, it administered no particular body of law but merely adjusted claims among merchants; thirdly, it had jurisdiction over three sets of people, British subjects, the indigenous elements and other foreigners not subjects of Britain;[8] and lastly, it never pretended to supersede the indigenous system of government as far as the internal affairs of any community were concerned.

These differences notwithstanding later experiments aimed at providing a local government system for the Oil Rivers area and its hinterland owed much to the example of the Court of Equity; in fact some of these experiments could be described as having aimed at reconstituting the Court of Equity and extending its jurisdiction to cover the whole of indigenous political and social life. In 1885 the British formally declared a protectorate over the Oil Rivers partly as a result of international developments which do not concern us here, and partly because Britain had come to realise that her trade there was on the increase and 'that the absence of civilised rule makes it essential that the lives and property of the traders should be protected by British officials'. Under the protectorate it was hoped that the local 'chiefs will, as hitherto, manage their own affairs, but will have always at hand counsellors and arbitrators in matters of difficulty and dispute'.[9]

---

[6] By this I mean that when the Court of Equity laid the law for *trade*, one of the principal bases of coastal society, the rest of the community was forced to conform although the law in question was not made by its own sovereign body. There is no intention to say here that the court dictated the law in other aspects of the coastal states' existence, though of course its trade regulations affected other aspects of society indirectly.

[7] G. I. Jones, *The Trading States*, etc., p. 78. 'The Court [of Equity] had administrative and legislative functions as well as judicial. . . .'

[8] A. Burns, Appendix 'E', articles 5, 6, 7

[9] S. M. Tamuno, pp. 25–6: quoted from C/4279: Lister to Bramston, 5.10.1883

But in practice British performance fell far short of this promise. 'Counsellors and arbitrators', by which were meant consuls and vice-consuls, were few and far between. To make the situation more unsatisfactory the Court of Equity had been abolished in 1885. The practical impossibility of the consul, who at times worked without a European assistant, effectively maintaining the peace between the various local communities and the European merchants resident in them forced the more imaginative and adventurous of the consuls to try their hands at providing a reliable system of local government for the area. The first attempt was made in Bonny by Consul Hewett in 1886. That year the Bonny community was brought to the brink of civil war as a result of animosity between the two leading house heads – Oko Jumbo and Waribo Manilla Pepple. In a bid to restore peace and quiet to the town Hewett stepped in, side-tracked these two over-mighty 'barons' and set up a council of five 'chiefs' in which he vested legislative and executive powers and the right to rule Bonny. He also gave it the right to determine all disputes which might arise between Bonny citizens and people from neighbouring groups. Hewett retained for himself the veto power. This experiment is remarkable for its exclusion of European merchants, but has a limited significance since no attempt was made to extend it to other Oil Rivers states.[10]

But the most ambitious experiment along these lines was projected by H. H. Johnston when he was acting consul in 1887. Johnston's deportation of Jaja had nearly led to complete social disruption in Opobo. He was therefore faced with an urgent need for a system of local government which would help to restore quiet in the city-state and pave the way for a stable administration. This need was the origin of his scheme for 'Governing Councils' or what Dr S. M. (now T. N.) Tamuno has called his 'reformed

[10] J. C. O. Anene, *Establishment and Consolidation of Imperial Government in Southern Nigeria (1891–1904)*, M.A. Thesis, London 1952, p. 63. This thesis has since been drastically revised and published as *Southern Nigeria in Transition, 1885–1906*, Cambridge 1966. In one respect I find the thesis more useful than the published revision. In the thesis the raw facts are more easily distinguishable from what might be called the disputable interpretations. By the time *Southern Nigeria* was written the author had acquired more confidence as a historian than he had when he wrote the thesis. As a result the opinions and the hard core of facts are now more difficult to distinguish one from the other. For this reason I shall refer to the thesis and the book as the occasion demands.

type of Court of Equity'.[11] A Governing Council as projected by Johnston was to comprise a president who was to be the consul, a vice-president and a secretary who were to be Europeans, three African chiefs, four European traders and an *ex officio* member who was to be the senior naval officer in the area. It was to meet weekly and appeals from it were to lie with the consular authority. It was charged with keeping the peace, maintaining the highways and other means of communication, regulating commerce and hearing minor disputes. It could impose a fine of five pounds or a term of imprisonment not exceeding one week but could not inflict corporal punishment without the written permission of the supreme consular authority. It could also impose direct taxation not exceeding three shillings per head per year on people who had resided in Opobo for longer than one month. After establishing this system at Opobo, Johnston proceeded to extend it to Brass, Bonny, Degema and Calabar.[12] Alarmed at what it considered the illegality of these proceedings the Foreign Office disallowed the measures setting up these Governing Councils and reminded the acting consul that his duties were limited to 'the administration of justice and the maintenance of order among British subjects'.[13] In short, that he had no right to interfere with the internal government of the city-states. The importance of this stillborn project lies in the fact that it continued the traditions which the Court of Equity had established and that it exercised an undoubted influence over the men who later tackled the same problem it had tried to solve.

As already pointed out it was not until 1891 that Britain came finally to grapple with the problem of actually governing the Oil Rivers (later Niger Coast) Protectorate and to this end appointed Sir Claude Macdonald as the Commissioner and Consul-General of the Protectorate. 'Macdonald's appointment,' noted Dr S. M. Tamuno, 'was a significant development in the history of British administrative control of this protectorate. Great Britain, in many respects, established a new administration after 1891.'[14] In these circumstances, therefore, the problem of providing the Protectorate with a reliable system of local government, which the metropolitan government had hitherto fought shy of, had to be

[11] S. M. Tamuno, p. 29
[12] J. C. O. Anene, *Establishment and Consolidation of*, etc., pp. 64–5
[13] Quoted *ibid.*, p. 67 from FO 84/1881, FO draft of 10.2.1888 to Johnston
[14] S. M. Tamuno, p. 54

faced in earnest and solved in so far as a solution was possible. It was in this period that the Warrant Chief System with its specific court and chiefs endowed with warrants came into being as a definite instrument of local administration. 'To avoid, where possible, an open rupture with the [local] chiefs,' wrote J. C. Anene in 1952, 'was a corner-stone of the policy of Sir Claude Macdonald. That disputes internal and external were bound to occur, he was fully aware. He therefore created a machinery for local administration which he intended to serve a variety of purposes. This machinery for local native administration was a kind of revival of the Governing Councils set up by H. H. Johnston and rejected by the Foreign Office.'[15] It must however be emphasised that Macdonald and his successors did not revive Acting Consul Johnston's scheme lock, stock and barrel. What they did was to adopt the principle of using what was thought to be the indigenous political system for purposes of local government, subject it to the central government and reject the inclusion of European traders in the new local machinery. Before dealing with the implementation of this policy, it will be necessary, in order to bring the whole story into focus, to examine in some detail those factors and assumptions which in the first instance forced the Protectorate Government to attempt to solve its local government problems by seeking to rule indirectly through what it thought was the traditional system of government of the communities in its area of authority. The intention here is not to analyse and expound the considerations which generally led to the adoption of the policy of Indirect Rule. This is already a beaten track and in the context of the present work would be neither illuminating nor interesting. Instead the objective is to examine those factors which were specifically applicable to Southern Nigeria and which clearly determined the course which its local government history ran under British rule.

In the first place the system was implicit in the British conception at the time of the political relationship known as 'protectorate' which was applied to this area. According to the official British view in the 1880s, a 'protectorate' was a political relationship between a 'protecting' power and a 'protected' state under which the former took charge of the foreign relations of the latter, which continued to manage its internal affairs.[16] When, for

[15] J. C. O. Anene, *Establishment and Consolidation of*, etc., p. 188
[16] S. M. Tamuno, pp. 43–4

instance, King Jaja of Opobo asked for the definition of the word 'protection' before he could append his mark on the treaty proposed by Consul Hewett in 1884 he received the following answer:

> I write as you request with reference to the word 'protection' as used on the proposed treaty that the Queen does not want to take your country or your markets, but at the same time is anxious that no other nation should take them. She undertakes to extend her gracious favour and protection, *which will leave your country still under your government*.[17]

British policy-makers evolved this system of political relationship with native rulers and states as a reaction against Direct Rule or the Crown Colony system which in their minds and experience was associated with too many problems. They argued, writes Professor Flint,

> that they could not carry any more administrative costs, that the mortality rates for colonial officials were too high to contemplate, and that the implementation of the abolition of slavery (which would be obligatory if the territories fell under British Colonial jurisdiction) would raise social problems which a colonial office regime could not solve.[18]

But as time went on, however, the 'narrow legalistic concept of protectorate',[19] as Professor Flint has aptly called it, had to be abandoned in favour of a looser concept which enabled the British to intervene more actively in the domestic government of 'protected' states and peoples with a view to securing needed reforms while still working through the indigenous institutions of the state or people. It was in this way that Indirect Rule, in its original meaning already discussed, evolved. Some of the factors which brought about this change in our area of interest have been fully analysed by Professor Flint. They included 'the influence of the man on the spot', the expansion of British business in the Oil Rivers and the increasing 'failure of indigenous institutions to provide stability' unaided.[20] All these factors as well as the

---

[17] J. E. Flint, 'Nigeria: The Colonial Experience from 1880 to 1914' in *Colonialism In Africa, 1870–1960*, i, *The History and Politics of Colonialism*, Cambridge 1969, eds L. H. Gann and P. Duignan, quoted on p. 226. Italics added. J. C. O. Anene, *Southern Nigeria in Transition, 1885–1906*, Cambridge 1966, quoted on p. 66

[18] J. E. Flint, 'Nigeria: The Colonial Experience from 1880 to 1914', etc., p. 225

[19] *Ibid.*, pp. 230–4

[20] *Ibid.*

international obligations which Britain incurred through signing the Berlin (1885) and the Brussels (1890) Acts dictated that the narrow legalistic view of 'protection' should be sufficiently modified to make it possible for the imperial power to assume within the territories of the 'protected' state powers which in time came to be almost equal to those exercised in a crown colony. By 1886 the British Foreign Office was already lecturing Consul Hewett in the Oil Rivers that a protectorate must be seen to imply

> the promotion of the welfare of the natives of all these territories taken as a whole by ensuring the peaceful development of trade and facilitating their intercourse with Europeans. It is not to be permitted that any chief, who may happen to occupy a territory on the coast, should obstruct this policy in order to benefit himself.[21]

Yet whatever was the consequence of this change, it never entailed a total departure from the earlier recognition that under the protectorate system the indigenous institutions of the 'protected' would still find an essential part to play in administration. Rather what emerged was a closer definition of the position which these institutions were to occupy in the new scheme of things. Even three years after the Foreign Office instruction to Hewett, C. P. Ilbert, a law officer of the crown, pointed out, in language reminiscent of the Old Testament, that by a 'protectorate' Britain meant 'not to upset the native chief, or to replace native customs or institutions in their application to his subjects, but to assert authority over all foreigners within his gates'.[22] Later still in 1891 Claude Macdonald was advised, as already shown, not to attempt a radical reform of the indigenous system but to supervise its working in order to ensure the administration of justice.[23] Since the British idea of 'protection' in this period did not envisage the absolute supersession of indigenous institutions in their application to the 'protected', it was practical common sense for an administrator faced with the question of providing a local government system acceptable to the people under his charge to seek to do so by merely forging a link between the central government and these institutions. It was further

---

[21] *Ibid.* Quoted on pp. 233–4. See also F. D. Lugard, *The Dual Mandate*, Edinburgh 1922, pp. 34–5, for the part which British concern to fulfil international obligations on the Niger played in undermining the narrow legalistic concept of protection.
[22] Quoted in S. M. Tamuno, pp. 45–6
[23] CSO 1/14, Despatches from FO and CO, No. 2 of 18.4.91

imperative to prevent the indigenous political system cluttering the ground and causing obstruction and also to avoid the more arduous and unrewarding task of abolishing it altogether in the teeth of spirited opposition by the people.

Another consideration which dictated the use of the indigenous system for purposes of local government was the quest for a cheap administration. The British treasury in the nineteenth century was notorious for its parsimony with regard to grants to dependent provinces of the empire. This fact lay behind the many expedients which Britain tried as a means of achieving her objectives in much of what later became Nigeria. The measure of 1872 which brought the Courts of Equity under the legal control of the consul and vested in them the administration of the Oil Rivers area derived largely from the fact that it was financially convenient: the members of the Court of Equity received no pay.[24] Hewett's recommendation in 1882 for the formation of a 'loose protectorate' between Benin and the Cameroons was rejected because such a step would entail 'heavy demands upon the British taxpayer'.[25] It was largely for reasons of economy that Britain granted a charter to Goldie's Company as 'the cheapest and most effective way' of meeting the obligations imposed on her by the Navigation Act of the Berlin Conference (1885). For the same reason she later wanted to transfer the administration of the Oil Rivers to the same or some other company.[26] When in 1891 Britain decided on administering the Oil Rivers in practice and not just on paper, the decision was taken on the understanding that the protectorate would be able to pay its way.

This tight-fistedness of the metropolitan government in matters of colonial expenditure meant that the Protectorate could never afford to pay the large number of European staff that would make direct administration possible. In this situation it was wise and convenient to seek to use local rulers who could be, and were, maintained cheaply. 'If the tribal system of government is allowed to fall into decay,' it was argued by the advocates of this system, 'it will be necessary to increase to an extent beyond the resources of the Protectorate the staff necessary for doing work

[24] S. M. Tamuno, pp. 21–2
[25] Quoted in R. Robinson and J. Gallagher with Alice Denny, *Africa and the Victorians*, London 1961, p. 165
[26] *Ibid.*, pp. 180–1, 184–7, 188. See also J. E. Flint, *Sir George Goldie and the Making of Nigeria*, Oxford 1960

which is now done under the tribal system.'[27] There was another side to the economic argument for the system. It was thought that through the indigenous system it would be easy to levy direct taxation, for the tax could then be portrayed as customary service levied by the people's traditional rulers. Also if the tax bred discontent the 'chiefs' would act as a buffer between their angry people and the European officers. On this Sir William N. M. Geary has written:

> *A Native ruler of the same colour and religion as the ruled is a convenient buffer for the Central Government* and makes the easier the enforcement of Law and Order by the Central Government.[28]

An equally important fact which helped to persuade the Protectorate Government to seek to use the indigenous system in local government was official determination to achieve continuity in administration in a region which, according to contemporary popular European opinion, was remarkable for its inhospitable climate. Even by the late nineteenth century the climate of West Africa had not outlived this notoriety. It was still acceptable to make such statements about it as that 'men's blood rapidly

[27] CSO 1/15, No. 9 of 15.9.01. There are no statistics for the earlier period, but the economic argument for indirect rule is clearly illustrated in a comparison of the following figures for the Eastern Provinces in 1924:

Division of District	Total cost of Warrant Chief fees		
	£	s.	d.
Calabar	603	17	6
Eket	840	0	0
Opobo	743	5	0
Abakaliki	431	5	0

It should be pointed out that some of the districts had upwards of 108 Warrant Chiefs who shared among them some such sum as those indicated above. About the same time the salary of a district officer was £720–£960 p.a. plus seniority allowance of £72 p.a., the salary of an ADO was £500–£690 p.a., that of a cadet was £500 p.a. All this was exclusive of free quarters and transportation costs from Britain to Nigeria and back – expenditure which was never incurred on Warrant Chiefs. See Sessional Paper No. 31 of 1924, pp. 3–7; Nigeria Blue Book 1924, Lagos 1925, pp. 153–8

[28] It must be pointed out that although direct taxation was introduced into the Eastern Provinces only in 1928, the question of its introduction occupied official minds from the very early days of the Protectorate. W. N. M. Geary, *Nigeria Under British Rule*, Cass Reprint 1965, p. 272. The italics are added.

putrefies under the tropical zone', 'tropical conditions favour the growth of pathogenic bacteria'. At this time too the death rate of Europeans working in West Africa was placed at thirty-five per cent.[29] Because of what was regarded as the debilitating effect of this particular environment on Europeans, long periods of leave were considered necessary for those serving there to recuperate their health. This meant, first of all, that those on the political establishment were never all on the spot at the same time, as some members of the staff had to be on leave to recoup their health. Also the fact that this establishment was constantly being reshuffled, new and inexperienced men taking the place of older officers, raised the question of continuity in administration.[30] These issues cropped up over and over again and influenced the making of official policy.[31] In 1894 Sir Claude Macdonald had noted that the 'good work' done by the Native Pastorate Church derived largely from the fact that since the officials were Africans they were 'capable of withstanding' the climate better than Europeans and of bringing about 'a continuity of work'. At the same time he expressed the opinion that the inability of the missions run by Europeans to achieve a continuity of service hampered their progress.[32] When faced by the need to secure this continuity of service which was considered invaluable for an efficient administration, the Colonial Government solved the problem in the field of local government by seeking to work through the indigenous ruler. The local chief, it was believed, would never need leave, and once instructed on what to do would be able to go on even under the supervision of an inexperienced cadet.

The fact that the British penetration of the Eastern Provinces was accomplished from the coast also contributed to the decision to use indigenous rulers in local government. Although effective administration was inaugurated in 1891, it was not until 1901–2 that the British acquired anything like fairly reliable knowledge of the character of the hinterland of the Oil Rivers. By that time the main lines which local government would take had been worked out along the coast. As the interior was conquered this system

[29] M. H. Kingsley, *West African Studies*, London 1901, pp. 250, 283
[30] CSO 1/13, Despatches to the FO, No. 139 of 8.8.98
[31] See for instance CSO 1/14, Despatches from the FO, No. 118a of 12.8.98
[32] *Report on the Niger Coast Protectorate August 1891–August 1894. Africa*, No. 1, 1895 (C 7596), p. 10

elaborated for the coastal region was introduced. Thus in the crucial years opinions on the layout of the whole region were based on what were seen and heard on the coast. This was very important.

In spite of the network of creeks and rivulets connecting one community with the other, touring in the region of the coast was not a very pleasant exercise. Without a sure knowledge of the interior the administration had no reason to suppose that touring inland would be easier and more pleasurable than it was along the coast. What officers felt about touring along the coast can easily be gathered from one who knew them and their area of work fairly well, E. D. Morel:

> Indeed, people at home [in Britain] have no conception of the natural difficulties under which the administrator, the merchants etc. labour in carrying out their respective tasks . . . in the deltaic and forest regions of Nigeria. For six months in the year a very large portion of the Central and Eastern Provinces is perpetually submerged. The Niger overflows its banks, every forest rivulet becomes a river, the creeks and channels spread their waters upon the land, the forest is flooded over an enormous area and the pathways inter-secting it are impassable.

From this he went on to paint a piteous picture of commissioners passing nights in dugouts, 'marching in the rear of weary carriers, through reeking, soaking and steaming forest; negotiating streams swollen into torrents, camping when and where they can'.[33] This was not a situation in which direct European administration could be attempted. Under indirect administration, on the other hand, the commissioner could be content with seeing the chiefs once in a while and the business of government would be carried out all the same. Moor was fully aware of this fact and he wrote to one of his commissioners:

> I cannot concur in your view that Oguta is difficult of access for nine months of the year. From December until May . . . it is accessible by land without any difficulty and in August, September and October it is accessible by water, so that for over seven months of the year it is fairly accessible. In any case, *if Native Councils are established there the District Commissioner Agberi will have to make it his business to visit the place at least once a quarter . . . to see that work is properly carried on.*[34]

[33] E. D. Morel, *Nigeria: Its Peoples and Problems*, London 1912, pp. 65–6
[34] Calprof 9/2. Letter No. 3 of 19.6.02 from Moor to the Divisional Commissioner, Central Province. The italics are mine. The communication problem also partly explains the employment of the so-called 'Native

Under direct administration quarterly visits would reduce the drive for effective administration to a farce.

Furthermore, the Warrant Chief System was set up to serve as an instrument of political 'pacification' and consolidation. 'The new local bodies,' wrote J. C. Anene, 'were set up as a sequel to military subjugation and were expected to give stability and permanence to what was considered pacification.'[35] The point was that the Protectorate lacked troops sufficient to subdue all the people quickly and absolutely. For instance, to deal with the Aro, a single clan whose population was estimated at about five thousand in 1901, the government had to borrow troops from Northern Nigeria and Lagos and thought of getting troops from Sierra Leone and British Central Africa.[36] In this situation, therefore, after the initial overawing of any people by the use of, or the threat of using, the available forces the administration had recourse to winning their supposed leaders to its side. This ruse was supposed to deprive the die-hard adherents of the old order of tried leadership. Moreover busying the supposed chiefs with the work of local administration, especially where this brought some material reward to act as a bribe, was an effective way of limiting the time and inclination they might have to plan mischief. In the neighbouring Lagos Administration Governor McCallum talked of the need to 'engage the chiefs in Administration and make them happy'.[37] This general point was clearly illustrated by Sir Ralph Moor's action after the first serious military expedition in the interior in 1901–2. 'Immediate action,' he reported to the colonial secretary, 'is being taken to establish Native Councils at suitable centres throughout the whole of these

Political Agents' by the protectorate government. They were men who combined in their persons the functions of what later came to be known as a Native Authority and those of a quasi-vice-consul. They were sometimes the heads of their communities and included people like Chief Coco Otu Bassey at Itu, Daniel Henshaw at Idua, Ani Eniang at Ikpa, Young Ekpe Bassey at Uwet, Henry Black Davis in Western Ekoi, Chief Cookey Gam at Opobo and Magnus Duke at Calabar. Stationed in some of the more remote areas, they, among other things, presided over Minor Courts and dealt with certain grades of cases privately. These men were also cheaply maintained.

[35] J. C. O. Anene, *Establishment and Consolidation of*, etc., p. 273
[36] CSO 1/13, No. 218 of 3.8.1900 and No. 181 of 25.6.01
[37] I. F. Nicolson, *The Administration of Nigeria 1900–1960*, Oxford 1969, quoted on p. 32

territories in order that there may be an immediate means provided for the natives to settle their disputes and difficulties.'[38] In such a case the Native Court was supposed not only to act as the watchdog of the administration but also to endear the government to the people through providing them, for the first time it was believed, with a means for settling their disagreements peacefully. If this policy was considered important in 1902, it was even more so in 1891.

Some of the leading scholars of the evolution of British administration in the Protectorate of the Oil Rivers have increasingly come to recognise the important part which the personal inclinations of Sir Claude Macdonald and Sir Ralph Moor, in particular the former, played in determining the character of local government in this region during the period covered by this study. It has been argued that Macdonald was rare among his contemporaries in his belief that it was necessary and beneficial to consult and respect African opinion as well as collaborate with African leaders in the process of determining policies which would impinge vitally on African interests. Macdonald, argues Professor Flint,

> came to the Niger with certain fixed ideas which were to prove important when seen in the perspective of developing British attitudes to the West African peoples. He assumed without question that the wishes, ideas and opinions of the African, whether he was a chief or a slave, were of great, if not paramount, importance in making administrative decisions and he also took it for granted that the purpose of British control in West Africa was to achieve social reform by means of dynamic economic development. . . . For him 'Imperial interests' were the interests of the Africans.[39]

Macdonald demonstrated this consideration for African opinion and interest in the manner he conducted his inquiries of 1889 as a special commissioner sent out to determine the political future of the peoples of the Niger Coast Protectorate – that is, whether they would be handed over to the Royal Niger, or some other company or should be brought under the direct administration of the crown. He also showed it in the recommendations which he made.[40] It has even been suggested that these recommendations helped to determine the nature of the job which he was assigned

[38] CSO 1/13, Despatches to FO, No. 203 of 17.5.02
[39] J. E. Flint, *Sir George Goldie*, London 1960, pp. 129–30
[40] *Ibid.*, pp. 130–1

later in 1891, as contained in the General Instructions mentioned and discussed earlier in this work. According to Professor Anene, Macdonald's handling of the 1889 assignment endeared him to the coastal peoples and chiefs, who therefore came to look upon him 'as a man they could trust'. Therefore, argues Professor Anene, the choice of Macdonald in 1891 to inaugurate the new era of effective British rule in the Oil Rivers 'was in many ways a wise one', as 'what the new task . . . required was not a rabid imperialist but a diplomat',[41] and Macdonald was the latter.

Professor Flint and Professor Anene believe that Macdonald adopted this policy which led to the upholding of native institutions because though an imperialist, 'he was also a man of great humanity, averse to bloodshed', but two other scholars of the subject disagree. 'It is the view of the present writer,' warns Dr Obaro Ikimẹ, that 'existing studies of the career of Macdonald pay too little regard to the circumstances of his rule. Consequently his actions tend to be explained largely in terms of his ideals and beliefs.' On his side, I. F. Nicolson thinks Macdonald's attitude to the natives and their institutions had much to do with his being a Scot. 'Like McCallum and MacGregor in Lagos,' he writes:

> Macdonald was a steadfast believer in consulting native opinion and basing policy firmly on the wishes and aspirations revealed in the process of consultation. It may not have been Scottish egalitarianism which inspired the respect for African self-determination; but these may well have been influenced by unhappy ancestral memories of theMacGregors and Macdonalds – memories of terrible mistakes made by alien governments, in the treatment of Scottish highland clans.

This controversy cannot be resolved here.[42] What is important for our purpose is that the origin of the policy to associate the native institutions of the Protectorate of the Oil Rivers with the work of the new administration owed something to the personal attitude of Macdonald whether that attitude was rooted in his humanity or practical common sense or his innate Scottish suspicion of alien rule divorced from the interests and wishes of the ruled.

[41] J. C. Anene, *Southern Nigeria*, etc., p. 41
[42] J. E. Flint, 'Nigeria: The Colonial Experience from 1880 to 1914', etc., p. 237. J. C. Anene, *Southern Nigeria*, etc., pp. 141, 142, 172, 173. Obaro Ikimẹ, 'Sir Claude Macdonald in the Niger Coast Protectorate – A Reassessment', in *Odu*, New Series No. 3, April 1970. I. F. Nicolson, *The Administration of Nigeria*, etc., p. 84

The distribution of Native Courts in the portion of Southern Nigeria
Protectorate east of the Niger in January 1903

With regard to Moor, opinion is divided. Professors Flint and Anene are reluctant to attribute to him any respect for African opinion. In their works he appears as the impatient and un-diplomatic man of 'blood' and 'punitive' expeditions who broke Ebrohimi and Benin, shelled and burnt Ediba on the Cross River and smashed up the Long Juju (Ibiniukpabi) of the Aro. Professor Flint describes him as having 'theoretically believed in indirect rule'. Under Moor, he maintains, following Professor Anene, 'penetration was largely military in character. Negotiation played little part; and the effect, if not the intent, of policy was destructive of traditional institutions.'[43] This is not the place to contend against this view which makes the contrast between Moor and his predecessor too sharp to be convincing. A detailed and objective study of the administrative history of this period, however, is bound to lead to the conclusion that there was a great continuity of policy until the advent of Lugard in 1912, yet this should not have been the case if Moor had been such a marked contrast to Macdonald.[44] This much is clear from Mr Nicolson's book, which in many respects contains a more balanced assessment of Macdonald and Moor than Anene's. 'The chart by which Moor navigated,' Mr Nicolson has written,

> had been drawn in outline by his predecessor and former chief in the days of Foreign Office Protectorate, Sir Claude Macdonald; but it was left to Moor, who succeeded him in 1896, to fill in the details and to do the actual navigation.[45]

If therefore the initial decision to associate indigenous rulers and institutions with the work of the colonial government owed much, as has been cogently argued, to Macdonald, its continuation after the latter's withdrawal from the scene also owes much to Moor's commitment to that policy, and to his ability, as will be shown below (see chapter 3), to elaborate the machinery for that indigenous and alien co-operation in local government.

These were the general ideas, mental attitudes and administrative needs and other circumstances which led to the institution of the Warrant Chief System. A year or so after Macdonald's appointment, the earliest of the Native Councils had already come into existence. By 13 February 1892 what was called the

[43] J. E. Flint, 'Nigeria: The Colonial Experience from 1880 to 1914', etc., p. 240. J. C. Anene, *Southern Nigeria*, etc., pp. 178–80
[44] I. F. Nicolson, *The Administration of Nigeria*, etc., pp. 82–3
[45] *Ibid.*, p. 82

'High Court of the Native Council of Old Calabar', of which the consul-general himself was the president and which acted as a court of appeal for a number of Minor Courts established on the Cross River, was already in existence. Also by 2 July the same year Native Courts had been established at Bonny, Buguma and Degema, but could not function effectively owing to lack of clerks to record their proceedings.[46] It is not known how many of these courts were actually established by Sir Claude Macdonald but it is known that before he left the country these local arms of the central government were already functioning at Calabar, Bonny, Degema, Buguma, Akpayafe, Tom Shott, Adiabo and Itu. Each met for business twice a month.[47]

Under Sir Ralph Moor, who succeeded Sir Claude Macdonald as Commissioner and Consul-General and who in the period before 1914 did more than any other single man to give the local government system of the Eastern, Benin and Warri Provinces its distinctive character, the number of these courts grew rapidly as new territory was brought under British control. In the period 1898–9 there were already about twenty-three of these courts in the Niger Coast Protectorate.[48] In the years 1899–1900 the District of Calabar alone had one Native Council and fifteen Minor Courts, while for the same period the total for the portion of the protectorate lying between the River Niger and the boundary with the Cameroons was about six Native Councils and twenty-four Minor Courts distributed as shown:[49]

District	Native Council	Minor Court
Old Calabar	1	15
Opobo	1	3
Bonny (including Okrika)	2	1
New Calabar (Degema)	1	3
Brass	1	—
Akwete (sub-district)	—	2

At all events by 1900 the coastal regions and the areas adjoining them were already punctuated with these outposts of government. The courts in the hinterland came after 1900 as a result of the increased control which the Protectorate Government gained

[46] Calprof 8/5, Enclosure of 13.2.92; *Correspondence respecting the affairs of W. Africa. Africa*, No. 11, of 1893, p. 6. See ch. 3 for the distinction between Native Council and Minor Court.

[47] J. C. Anene, *Establishment and Consolidation of*, etc., p. 271

[48] *Ibid.*, p. 273

[49] CSO 1/13, Despatches to FO, No. 260 of 25.9.1900

over the interior. By 1903 the Native Courts of the Southern Nigeria Protectorate numbered about sixty. Some idea of the extent of territory which they spanned can be gained from the fact that when Mr Justice M. R. Menendez set out to inspect them in 1903 he covered one thousand six hundred miles and the tour took him one hundred and nine days.[50]

The government believed that 'chaos' 'reigned' throughout the Eastern Provinces and that this derived from the lack of a means of adjusting disputes arising between village and village, tribe and tribe. Not surprisingly, therefore, it saw the institution of a Native Court as the introduction of sanity into a deranged society. For the same reason too the establishment of a Native Court was seen as the next logical step after an area had been subdued militarily or agreed to sign a treaty of friendship with the Protectorate Government. Unfortunately we do not have full information on the establishment of most of these courts. In most places in Southeastern Nigeria military confrontation was the most dramatic incident marking the advent of British rule, while the establishment of the Native Court generally passed off without much incident. Thus elders are wont, when asked about the coming of the white man, to dwell at great length on the fighting and the military preparations preceding it, and to pass over the establishment of the Native Court casually, yet in the long run this institution was to bring more revolutionary changes in their lives than the fighting did. For example, Chief Udo Akpabio, a former Warrant Chief of the Anang, in an account of his life given to the Rev. W. Groves, spent many words on the fighting and then casually remarked:

> The court was then established at Ikot Ekpene. Summonses and Warrants were issued free of charge. Okodi Iya of Ikot Ekpene, Akpan Etok Akpan of Ikot Esetan, and Inyang Ata Udo of Ikot Obong were the first Warrant Chiefs.[51]

Compared with the British political officers who would just send in the names of those proposed for membership without comment, Chief Udo Akpabio was prolix.

In a few places, however, the position was the reverse, the establishment of the Native Court coming as the climax of British advent, and on these we have a great deal of information.

[50] CSO 1/13, Despatches to FO, No. 16 of 7.1.03, with enclosure
[51] 'The story of Udo Akpabio of Anang Tribe, Southern Nigeria', recorded by the Rev. W. Groves, in *Ten Africans*, ed. M. Perham, London 1936.

It would therefore pay to describe in some detail the institution of one or two such Native Courts of which there is detailed information in order to show how the people concerned saw the whole question.

In 1902 the village of Obosi in Onitsha Division was on the verge of civil war in consequence of a conflict which had arisen between a group of young men who no doubt had come under missionary influence from Onitsha on the one hand, and the elders on the other. The former, to the horror of the latter, demanded the abolition of time-honoured customs like the killing of twins, facial scarification and the taking of certain traditional titles. The Divisional Commissioner of the Central Division of the Protectorate, Mr W. Fosbery, saw the solution to this trouble in the establishment of a Native Court. He therefore went to Obosi and established a court to serve the village and its neighbours. Through this court, Fosbery secured the passage of laws banning those customs which had 'revolted' the 'progressives'. One of these laws vested on the court the sole right to 'confer rank (titles) on natives of Abutchi (Obosi)'.[52] Obosi elders of today insist that the Native Court came as an instrument of unwelcome revolutionary change and as a perpetuator of a rift which missionary influence had introduced into the village group.

The second example reveals even in a more startling fashion that the local people did not always see the establishment of a Native Court among them in the same light as the government did. In December 1906 the government had decided to open a court at Okomoko to serve the Etche people, and in March 1907 sent Mr Isaiah Yellow to superintend the erection of the court buildings, after which he would become its first clerk. While the work on the court compound was on, Mr Yellow and the people who had been appointed Warrant Chiefs for Etche grew impatient of the delay and proceeded to try cases illegally. In the process they charged exorbitant fees, imposed heavy fines and forced people to refer cases to them. The widespread extortion and blackmail in which Yellow and the chiefs indulged served to reinforce the case of 'a strong party of irreconcilables in the Etche country ... who ... offered passive resistance to all

<hr>

[52] Calprof 10/3, Report No. 14 of 5.8.02 from Fosbery to Moor. This example and the one following *help* to show how some of the Native Courts actually came into being.

government proposals'. On the completion, but before the formal opening, of the court Mr Yellow sought and obtained permission to start road-making. His attempt to recruit labour for this purpose was the last straw that broke the camel's back. On 17 July 1907 the Etche rose against Mr Yellow, the Warrant Chiefs and the court, razed the court buildings to the ground and chased the court clerk and all those who collaborated with him out of Etche. This, however, was not the end of the story. A strong military force under Captain W. Haywood over-ran Etche, forced the people to surrender their guns, to rebuild the court houses and to pay compensation for all property damaged or looted in the uprising.[53] The Etche still deny that the coming of the Native Court meant the dawn of an era of peace and contentment; it was, they insist, the occasion for bloodshed and devastation carried out in a manner that was unparalleled in their history.

Questions arising from the siting of these courts came to loom large in the 1920s. The haphazard way the courts originated made it inevitable that their areas of jurisdiction should often cut across ethnic boundaries. In siting the courts the colonial government was guided in the main by considerations of administrative expediency. Many courts, like many district headquarters, were situated among people who were considered troublesome and therefore in the greatest need for constant government observation. For many other courts the over-riding consideration was to get them located at the geographical centre of the villages and clans they served. Some others situated at certain district headquarters did not fall into the one or the other category since district headquarters were chosen with an eye on the healthiness of the environs, the availability of good water supply and the like. It is not surprising therefore that guided by these purely practical considerations those who drew the boundaries of the provinces, districts and Native Courts failed to take into account ethnic and cultural boundaries and groupings.[54]

The decision to rule the Eastern Provinces indirectly should not necessarily have led to the Warrant Chief System. But that it

---

[53] CSO 1/15, Despatch Conf GD 86/07 of 5.8.07 from J. J. Thorburn, Acting Governor to S of S. See Enclosure No. EP Conf T 43/1907 of 22.7.07 in Despatch GD 123/1907 of 5.12.07 from Egerton to S of S.
[54] S. M. Grier, *Report on a Tour in the Eastern Provinces*, etc., p. 2. See C 176/19. Remarks by F. P. Lynch, the comments of the LGSP on the Grier Report on the Eastern Provinces.

did lead to this attempt to rule a chiefless society through chiefs is to be explained by a number of factors which helped to determine official policy. In spite of three centuries or more of European presence in the Bight of Biafra, the British had very little reliable knowledge of the social and political system of its interior peoples by 1900. The early years of colonial rule which were taken up with the hurly-burly of military subjugation gave neither the administration the time to collect and collate, nor the people the confidence and inclination to offer, information on the indigenous political system. In this matter the British formed their opinion of the whole region from what they saw on the coast. Without proper investigation they assumed first that the heads of houses and sections whom they saw along the coast were autocratic chiefs, and second that the house system was common to the whole region.[55] 'The administration,' wrote J. C. Anene on this issue, 'applied to the hinterland what it knew of the coastal towns and thus talked of "boys" and "chiefs" (with reference to the hinterland).'[56] And finally, as already pointed out, Indirect Rule in this period was believed to presuppose rule by chiefs. On this Professor Crowder says:

> It is necessary to emphasise that indirect rule, at least in theory, did not mean government of African peoples through their chiefs. In practice (however) indirect rule laid heavy emphasis on the role of the chief in the government of African peoples, even for those peoples who traditionally did not have political as distinct from religious leaders.[57]

It was this misplaced emphasis on the role of the chief that predisposed British officers to find 'kings and chiefs' wherever they went in the provinces to the east of the Niger.[58]

[55] The House Rule Proclamation, for instance, was made applicable to the whole of the area which in 1900 became Southern Nigeria.

[56] J. C. O. Anene, *Establishment and Consolidation of*, etc., p. 274

[57] M. Crowder, *West Africa Under Colonial Rule*, London 1970, p. 169

[58] Examples of this abound in the political reports of this period. After a futile attempt in 1894 to traverse the interior of Calabar, Roger Casement, a political officer, reported of a certain 'king of the Anang' who denied him passage through his land. In 1895 Mr W. V. Tanner, the Acting Vice-Consul at Akwete, made a tour of certain parts of the large Ngwa clan. In the report which he sent to headquarters he talked of a 'king of Ngwa' who promised to do what he could to send him 'as far as his authority extended'. He also talked of meeting at Ohia (another inland village) 'a chief' who was happy to see him and promised to do what he could to keep things quiet. Also the following year Mr A. B. Harcourt, a political officer who accompanied a government expedition into the hinterland of Akwete, reported that 'Aquetta [Akwete] gives its name to a tract of country in

Though it was thus the official policy that local government in the Eastern Provinces should be conducted through 'traditional kings and chiefs' the story of the appointment of the first Warrant Chiefs does not reveal that there was any plan or system designed to ensure that those chosen for the job were in fact the right men; that is, the traditional leaders of the people. In this matter it would appear that many political officers were at times concerned to recruit energetic and promising leaders who could secure compliance with the government's demands.

Along the coast there was not much difficulty in fishing out chiefs. The leaders of city-states like Brass, Bonny, Degema, Opobo and Calabar had had long commercial and social dealings with European merchants and, latterly, they had also come into contact with European missionaries. Their cultural sophistication not only made them less prone than their hinterland neighbours to fear and suspect the white man, it also made the latter very chary of committing among them acts like the beating of village heads which he indulged in with abandon in the interior with resultant panic and distrust among the people. In short the coastal communities were spared many of those situations which in the interior made people unwilling to be appointed Warrant Chiefs.[59] The general pattern of Warrant Chief selection along

which there are several towns under the influence of Wabara King of Aquetta.' He also talked of being introduced to 'King Annanaba of Obegu' and of having interviewed many other 'kings and chiefs'. A little later the same year, Mr Arthur G. Griffith, the Acting Commissioner in charge of Calabar, paid a visit into the Ibibio interior and talked of having held a successful meeting with the 73 most important 'chiefs' of the area he visited. It was reports such as these which confirmed the government in the false opinion that the Communities of the Eastern Provinces had chiefs. Calprof 8/2: Reports dated 3.11.95 by Tanner; 1896 by A. B. Harcourt and 5.7.96 by A. G. Griffith. D. Forde and G. I. Jones, *The Ibo and Ibibio-speaking peoples of Southeastern Nigeria*, Oxford 1950, p. 83

[59] Cf. the following opinions on the matter: (a) Anene, in *Southern Nigeria*, says: 'The political organisation of the coast communities was easily appreciated, though with considerable misgivings, by the aliens who intruded into coast affairs during the nineteenth century', p. 11. (b) Flint says: 'Here [along the coast] the history of contact with Europe, the existence of kingship and the house system, the use of pidgin English as a *lingua franca*, the presence of an educated element at Calabar, and the labours of African clergy of the delta pastorate throughout the coast towns, had permitted steady accommodation of African institutions to British demands.' In 'Nigeria: The Colonial Experience from 1880 to 1914', in *Colonialism in Africa*, eds. L. H. Gann and P. Duignan, p. 248

the coast was for the political officer to call upon the assembly of house and section heads to 'elect' those of its members it considered fit for warrants. But there were occasions when the section head or amanyanabo or obong of the unit was called upon to make the selection. How far this was done in consultation with the rest of the assembly is not known. In 1902 Obong Eyo Honesty VIII of Creek Town sent in the names of four people whom he said he had appointed to replace some deceased members of the Native Council. The same year the 'sub-chiefs' of Henshaw Town, Calabar, protested to the District Commissioner against the selection by their leader, Chief Ekang Henshaw, of some people they did not 'approve of their representing' their town 'in any public place or gathering' though they 'quite recognised them' as their 'town gentlemen'.[60]

Judged by their mode of selection the Warrant Chiefs of the interior fall into two broad groups: those arbitrarily chosen by the government without reference to anybody, and those chosen after some sort of 'consultation' with their people. Examples taken from the two groups will now be considered in order to illustrate the procedure in each case.

The first Warrant Chief from the Ikwo clan in the Abakaliki Division was one Anyigo Agwu, of whom it has been said that 'neither he nor his father was a village head before the coming of the whiteman'. After the subjugation of the clan, a meeting of the representatives of its component villages was held and there, it is reported, 'the whiteman just looked at Anyigo Agwu and called him out to be a chief'. This, it was admitted, was because Anyigo Agwu looked a strong and courageous man who could give effective leadership.[61] In Oraukwu in the Onitsha Division there was a similar case. On this village having been disarmed, the British political officer who came with the troops held a meeting of those of its men who were immediately available. After surveying the assembly he is said to have called out Ubaejesi Mbanefo, Ugochukwu Mbanefo, Okoye Ezinwa, all of Amaeze ward, and Nmetu Ububa of Amuda. The first two were brothers and were chosen because, oral tradition claims, they were huge and personable men who had also managed to bring chairs on

[60] Calprof 9/3, ii, letter to DC from Henshaw Town, Old Calabar, dated 25.4.02. See another from Creek Town dated 2.5.02
[61] Based on information collected from Chief Nwancho Atuma of Ikwo in Abakaliki

which they sat while others were either sitting on the ground or standing about. The obvious conclusion would seem to have been that they were 'kings' sitting on thrones. Surely the white men were not that naïve. But just as the white man often thought the black man had the mental equipment of a child and was naïve, so the black man at times had an equally low opinion of the white man. This should be a chastening revelation. The other two who were also called out from the assembly had helped to induce the villagers to surrender their guns during the first visit of the soldiers. When the purpose for their selection was announced the unbelieving crowd protested against the 'taking away' of two brothers and eventually secured the 'release' of Ubaejesi.[62]

One of the first Warrant Chiefs of Ihitte in Okigwi was Onuoha Nwosueke, the village crier of Dimneze in Onicha Uboma. Being a very old man, Onuoha had not been as quick as his fellow villagers in taking to the bush on the first entry of Southern Nigerian troops into Uboma and consequently had been caught by the soldiers. When forced to rally his people, he beat his drum as he would do to announce either a general meeting or communal work. On this occasion some of the brave young men responded to his call. To the European officer who came with the soldiers this was positive proof of Onuoha's authority over this people. When the time came to appoint chiefs Onuoha was called to take a warrant. But since he was very old and felt incapable of carrying out satisfactorily the functions of a Warrant Chief, he pushed forward one of his slaves to take his place. No other person in the village was consulted when all this was taking place. Another Ihitte man, Ogoke Nwoke, was caught on the road by the military and forced to lead the way. And because he did so to the satisfaction of the administration he was subsequently made a Warrant Chief.[63] In like manner an Aro man, Okereke Udensi, became a Warrant Chief of Ihiala, a non-Aro community, simply because he helped the government to enforce the disarming of the village-group.[64] A point about these guides was that after their first forced meeting with the soldiers and the white officers

[62] Collected from Abraham Ejidike of Oraukwu, who worked as a court messenger before the 1920s

[63] Information collected from Chief S. A. Ogueri of Lowa in Uboma Okigwi, and corroborated by another old man in Uboma who requested that his name be kept secret

[64] Information collected from J. N. Udensi, the son of this Warrant Chief. He is an ex-court clerk and now lives at Abakaliki

they generally came to be considered as experts on relations with the new régime. They encouraged this attitude among their people through the ostentatious display of such articles as the metal chairs, axes and cloths with which they were generally rewarded for their services. If the expedition returned to their villages they were generally the first to come out to meet it and to help it get its demands met. Not surprisingly, therefore, they were easily mistaken for chiefs by European officers.

In the category of those selected after some sort of consultation with their people there were equally fascinating cases. When the Akwurakwu village-group in Agba clan, Abakaliki Division, was asked to produce its chief, the demand led to the spread of the gruesome rumour that at death such a chief would be divided lengthwise into two equal halves, one part going to the white man and the other to the chief's people. This rumour was perhaps merely a vivid symbolical representation of the people's conception of the appointee's novel position as a servant torn between two irreconcilable loyalties, but it was sufficient to make people not want to become chiefs. However, one Ukpai Ereshi managed to ask the district commissioner's interpreter what truth there was in the story only to be assured that it was a mere fabrication. He then volunteered to be made a chief and as there was no rival candidate he was later given a warrant.[65] His courage in approaching the white man's interpreter when all others feared to come forward was proof of his fitness to lead his people in a time of crisis.

Another interesting case was the selection of the Warrant Chief of Umuariam in Obowo, Okigwi. The choice here was a man who was considered a social misfit and had some time earlier been sold as a slave to Azumiri merchants who traded to the coast. There he had made contact first with coastal traders, then with white men and learnt to dress in the latest fashions introduced by the invaders. Later he managed to find his way back to Umuariam. When the government asked the village of Umuariam for its chief, the elders thought they were required to pay tribute in men and regarded this as an opportunity to do away finally with this man, as it was then believed that the person surrendered would be either killed or sold into slavery. This problem son of Umuariam was therefore pushed forward as the chief of his village-group.

[65] Collected from Ukpai Ereshi in the presence of eight other elders of Agba who nodded their heads in approval as Ukpai Ereshi talked

When soldiers led him away the elders congratulated themselves on their cleverness. But when he came back with a piece of paper which made him the chief of this and many other neighbouring villages they were so astounded that, as my informants put it, 'we could not talk'.[66]

Sometimes the consultation was not with the general assembly of the village, but with any of its prominent members who were known to the government. This, for instance, was the case in the choice of the Warrant Chiefs of Isu and Oratta clans in Owerri Division. Njemanze of Owerri was a very powerful and influential slave-dealer in pre-British days and for this was well known to Aro men. The Royal Niger Company was said to have heard of him in 1895 and to have made contact with him that year from their Oguta station through an Aro agent. During the Aro Expedition of 1901–2, when two of the military columns heading for Arochukwu passed through Owerri, Njemanze helped to provide them with local guides to Bende. After the expedition he was made use of in gathering the chiefs of neighbouring village-groups like Akabo, Nekede, Naze, Emekuku, Ogi, Egbu, Nguru, Irete and so on.[67]

It was not always that the selections in this category were made by political officers; sometimes the initiative was taken by a court clerk or some other government agent. The selection of the Warrant Chiefs of Odot, a community between Ikoneto and Okoyon in the Cross River basin, was a case in point. For want of their own Native Court, it was said, the Odot took all cases which arose among them to Ansa Ansa Ani, the clerk of the Ikoneto Minor Court who had no legal right to try these cases. To end this anomalous situation Ani went to Odot on 6 July 1898 and in consultation with the village head selected six men whom he thought competent to hold warrants.[68]

It is important to emphasise here the fact that none of these approaches to the problem of selection was fool-proof. The same 'method' often produced opposite results in different and often adjacent village groups and clans. It has already been shown how

[66] Collected from Chief James Onwunali (former Warrant Chief) and Chief R. J. Onyeneho, both of Obowo, Okigwi
[67] Collected from Chief J. O. Njemanze (Owerri Town), Chief G. O. Iheanacho of Ugwa in Owerri and Chief J. N. Nwansi of Ikeduru in Owerri
[68] Calprof 6/1, iv. Letter dated 12.7.98 from Ansa Ansa Ani at Ikoneto

the appointment of the man who first came to hand led to the absurd situation in which an Aro was made the chief of a non-Aro group. But in Nteje the same method led to a directly opposite result. The Warrant Chief here was one Okuefuna, who incidentally was the head *Ndichie* (the senior title-holder) of his village. He was given a warrant not on the strength of this, however, but because he had helped the British to disarm Nteje and neighbouring villages.[69] Selection after some consultation with the people produced 'good' results along the coast as well as in some places in the hinterland, for instance in the Oratta clan. But even in the latter place the results varied from village to village. In Emekuku and a few other villages of this clan the headmen were notorious slave-dealers. Fearing deportation on a charge of slave-dealing they hid themselves and sent younger men to take their places.[70] This particular method of working through a local dignitary produced an interesting result in Ubakala. The Ibeji family of Olokoro had supplied guides to two columns of the Aro Field Force when they passed through Olokoro on their way to Bende. Later this family was rewarded through three of its members – Nwakpuda, Nwosu and Madumere – being appointed Warrant Chiefs. Use was made of this family's local knowledge in the choice of Warrant Chiefs for many other villages which came under the Olokoro Native Court. At the time there was in the Ibeji family one refugee from justice who some years before the British advent had fled his village of Ubakala on a charge of murder. This man was one of those whom the Ibeji family sent to show some columns of the Aro Field Force the way to Bende. Later on he got a warrant and was sent back to Ubakala to be their Warrant Chief.[71]

Also selection through the village assembly did not produce the same result in all places. In the Umuariam village-group of the Obowo clan, as already seen, it led to the appointment as Warrant Chief of a man who, but for the British advent, should have been 'eaten' by the Long Juju. In Eziama of the Nneato clan,

[69] Collected from Chief Igwe Ezeabasili of Nteje, son and successor of Okuefuna, and from A. E. Chiegbu, a former court clerk who was a rate clerk at Nteje at the time of the interview.
[70] Information supplied by Chief J. O. Njemanze of Owerri Town, Chief G. O. Iheanacho of Ugwa in Owerri Division and Chief J. N. Nwansi of Ikeduru, Owerri
[71] Information supplied by Chief E. I. Madumere, Nwamaghoha Nwabuisi and Samson Nwakpuda, all of Olokoro in Umuahia

Okigwi, it led to the choice of a man who has been described as a nonentity. When Eziama elders were faced with the usual demand for their chief they reasoned among themselves that to surrender Ihionu Ogbuewu, their village head, would bring eternal shame on them. They decided therefore to surrender someone whose disappearance would mean little loss to the village.[72] In Akawa, a village of the same clan, the same procedure led to the choice of the village head as Warrant Chief since he did not hide from the government and as his people feared that if they hid him the white man to whom they attributed oracular insight would find out and punish them.[73]

Why, one is compelled to ask, did the search for chiefs not generally lead to the choice of the traditional head of the community concerned? The answer to this question is to be found in the circumstances of the time and in some particular methods adopted by the colonial government in the process of subjugating this area.

The general atmosphere of the early years of the colonial régime was thickly charged with mutual suspicion, mutual ignorance and fear on the side of the people and of the government. As already briefly mentioned above, one of the things which puzzles a newcomer to the study of the history of these peoples is the abysmal ignorance which pervaded the hinterland with regard to Europeans up to 1900 and after. This state of affairs owed something to the middlemen traders of the coast who,

[72] Based on information collected from Mr Edo Eze and Chief Ogbuewu (son and successor of the Warrant Chief in question), both of Eziama Nneato in Okigwi. The belief that only the most stupid would and should follow the white man was widespread and even helped to determine the people's attitude to the earliest Christian missionaries. Compare the following: 'None of the converts [of the new religion] was a man whose word was heeded in the assembly of the people. None of them was a man of title. They were mostly the kind of people that were called *efulefu*, worthless, empty men. . . . Chielo, the priestess of Agbala, called the converts the excrement of the clan, and the new religion was a mad dog that had come to eat it up.' Chinua Achebe, *Things Fall Apart*, London 1958, p. 128. Note: It is necessary to point out that, comparing my notes on the attitude of most people to the British advent with the section of Chinua Achebe's *Things Fall Apart*, which tells of the first contacts of the 'village of Umuofia' with the white man, one is likely to form the opinion that that section of the novel can, with appropriate caution, be treated as containing reliable historical information.

[73] Information collected from Chief Maduka Ezurike of Akawa, Edo Eze and Chief Ogujiofor Ogbuewu of Eziama. Both villages are in Nneato clan.

for selfish reasons, had deliberately kept the Europeans on the coast apart from the people in the interior. The result was that when European penetration of the hinterland was effected many communities were found to have known practically nothing about the newcomers. Chief Obiukwu Nze of Umulolo village of the Otanzu clan in Okigwi, when asked why Umulolo people deserted their village when the British first got there answered *O mere onye ma ihe ha wu?*[74]

In many places there were people who had no doubt that the first white men they saw were either ghosts or beasts. Many people thought that the early Europeans were spirits since they 'had no toes', at times 'had four eyes' and also 'riveted' pieces of iron to their chests.[75] The people of Ahiara still claim they killed Dr Stewart, a medical officer attached to a patrol that went into the hinterland about 1905, because they did not know that he was a human being.[76] It is small wonder then that many villages were not just reluctant, but uncompromisingly determined not to accede to the demand to hand over their traditional leaders. Such leaders were not only generally wise (and therefore an asset) but religiously and ritually indispensable. And it was believed that to 'sacrifice' them to the unknown 'white creatures' was likely to provoke the anger of the gods and of the ancestors whose interests they were believed to represent among the living.

Another important factor which helps to account for the way the choice of the early Warrant Chiefs was made is to be found in

[74] 'Who knew *what* they were?' The use of *ihe*, meaning what (neuter), in place of *ndi*, meaning *who*, is significant. It conveys vividly the doubt which was rife at the time as to whether the British were human beings or ghosts or beasts. Cf. Chinua Achebe, p. 125. Obierika, one of the characters in the book, said, some time after the British advent, 'But I am greatly afraid. We have heard stories about white men who made the powerful guns and strong drinks and took slaves away across the sea, but no one thought the stories were true.'

[75] They had no toes because they wore shoes, had four eyes because they wore goggles and the buttons on their clothes were generally regarded as pieces of iron riveted to their chests. Cf. Chinua Achebe, p. 65, 'It is like the story of white men who, they say, are white like this piece of chalk. . . . And these white men, they say, have no toes.'

[76] Information collected from Chief James Onwunali and Chief R. J. Onyeneco of Obowo as well as from Chief S. A. Ogueri of Uboma, all in Okigwi. It is said that before they killed Dr Stewart the Ahiara people took him to their neighbours, among whom were the Obowo, to show *what* they had caught.

indigenous reaction to the high-handed procedure of the colonial government in the days of military conquest and subjugation. The traditions of various villages as well as the official reports of the military patrols are full of stories of burnings of towns and seizures of traditional village headmen as a means of overawing the people. But these were actions which could not but create a state of general panic and breed distrust among the people. A few examples will help to illustrate the methods of the early administration and the unforeseen results they produced.

It was the policy of the Protectorate Government to disarm any community its forces over-ran as a means of ensuring its future good behaviour. During the Aro Expedition the policy was to demand guns from a village at the rate of one gun for every four houses. If the villagers failed to surrender guns to the satisfaction of the political officer accompanying the column, the soldiers either burnt the town or lived off it until the demands of the government were fully met.[77] The effect of this policy on the people was often heightened recalcitrance and increased distrust of the government. The case of the Ubium of Eket District is typical. Some of these men had been forced to surrender their guns and for this would have nothing to do with the British until their guns were returned to them. Between May and October 1900 political officers made strenuous but futile efforts to bring them to a peace parley. The Ubium later told Assistant District Commissioner A. C. Douglas that their guns must be returned to them first and that they would not even accept compensation for the guns as 'they have a law that only those who have guns can cut palm nuts'.[78]

It was also official policy to seize local leaders and keep them as hostages to be released only if government demands were met by their people. Lt-Col. A. F. Montanaro, the Officer Commanding the Aro Field Force, ordered his officers to treat as 'hostile' any village in which the leaders did not surrender as soon as the military patrol entered it, and to keep any leaders who surrendered until guns had been handed in, food provided for the troops and roads made. On taking Arochukwu, Montanaro himself, in accordance with his own instructions, seized Ezeala, Kamalu,

[77] CSO 1/13, Despatches to FO of 1902. See copy of a letter from OC Aro Field Force dated 3.1.02.
[78] Calprof 9/1, i. Letter from Gallway dated 19.10.1900. See also letter from A. C. Douglas dated 5.5.1900.

Ugbaja, Ifunwueze and Ijeomanta – heads of different sections of Arochukwu.[79] Again during the Ezza military patrol of 1905 'important Assaga chiefs' were called to negotiate with the commanding officer, Captain Margesson. But on the day after their surrender 'the five principal chiefs' were seized and handed over to the political officer, Mr Phillips, as hostages.[80] On the general effect of this policy an experienced officer, Major Gallway, has left the following revealing comment: 'The practice of calling chiefs to meetings and then seizing them and of calling in guns to mark and then destroying them has resulted in a general distrust of the government and its policy.'[81] Since the villages in this region were closely situated, rumours and news travelled very fast. The often highly coloured story of the manhandling and maltreatment of the head of one village was likely to precede the patrolling troops in the surrounding villages. It is not surprising therefore that in many places those sent to meet the troops, and who were generally seized under the mistaken impression that they were chiefs, were either courageous young men or rascals sent to take the place of the elders. Those sent in for warrants by Obosi, said the Rev. Mr Ekpunobi of Obosi, were chosen by the village not because they had title or wealth, but because they were brave and fearless men who were considered able to face the challenge offered by the new situation. They were people, he said, who if the occasion demanded the exchange of blows could rise to it. This was so because some time previously some Obosi old men, for reasons which are now obscure, had got into trouble with some white men (identified as Royal Niger Company agents) and had been sent to prison at Asaba, where some of them died. From this the conclusion was drawn that the challenge of the times needed able young men.[82]

Early official attitude also conveyed the impression that the duties of the 'new style chief' were incompatible with roles expected of village elders in the traditional system. According to custom, for instance, the elders were the custodians of the land of

---

[79] CSO 1/13 of 1902. Copy of a letter from OC Aro Field Force dated 3.1.02. See also CSO 1/13 of 1901. Report No. 8 from OC attached to No. 440

[80] Conf 21/05. Ezza Country – unsettled state of. See report No. 1 from the Ezza patrol dated 20.3.05.

[81] Calprof 9/1, i. Letter dated 19.10.1900 from Gallway to Moor

[82] Information collected from the Rev. Mr Ekpunobi, Mr E. A. Arinze and Chief Okoma (ex-court clerk), all of Obosi, Onitsha.

the community and could not alienate any portion of it. But a village head like Njemanze of Owerri was bullied and bamboozled by Gallway into alienating a portion of the land of his village. After the Aro Expedition, one military column to which Major Gallway was political officer had camped for a night at Owerri. The Major, it is claimed, took the opportunity to 'ask' Njemanze to show him a piece of land on which the government would build a station. Njemanze took him to various sites until they came to the present location of the district office which Njemanze refused to give away because he considered it very fertile. But Gallway on his part refused to accept any other piece of ground and blandly argued that after all the government was going to build only one or two houses on any acquired plot. In the presence of the forces (in fact they had just looted his yam barn) and the news of what they had done to the Aro still in the air, Njemanze had to swallow his objections. Consternation followed at Owerri when later a large area was surveyed and marked out as crown land. The story of the acquisition of Owerri government station was said to have spread like wildfire, and no village elder who heard it could be expected willingly to place himself in a position where he could be forced to bring upon himself the grave responsibility of alienating that of which by tradition he was the custodian.[83]

Apart from being incompatible with traditional functions the duties of a Warrant Chief were in themselves difficult. The office called for frequent visits to district headquarters to ascertain the needs of the district commissioner. In the early days, when the districts were few in number and very large in extent and when generally there were only one or two courts in a district, to be a chief was a difficult assignment. Take the case of Okigwi Division, for example. At first the headquarters were at Umuduru. This meant that a Warrant Chief from Ihube would travel at least 16 miles and one from Nneato 23 miles in order to answer a duty call from the political officer at headquarters. If the Warrant Chief were lucky and did not have to cover long distances, he might be required to recruit young men to carry government luggage from one destination to another. Since in those days more often than not his people would dive into the bush at the sight of a court messenger or on hearing that it was their turn to supply carriers, executing this order sometimes meant, for the

[83] Information collected from Chief J. O. Njemanze of Owerri Town.

Warrant Chief, taking an active part in chasing young men from one corner of the village to the other. If he failed to produce the specified number of young men or to do any other job assigned to him he was promptly punished by the administrative officer who was not likely to be interested in why an assignment was not satisfactorily done. In September 1906, for instance, the district commissioner at Umuduru, Captain A. E. Heathecote, went into Aro Ndizuogu to find that the people had failed to do some work assigned to them at the government station. He arrested all but one of the leaders and kept them in custody until the work was finished after a fortnight.[84]

The traditional village head, who generally owed his position to age, was almost invariably physically incapable of carrying out this kind of onerous assignment. In many places traditional village heads who were selected for warrants promptly declined the offer and instead put forward younger men to take their places. In the Izzi clan of Abakaliki the first man chosen as Warrant Chief was one Ukwa Egbe, the *Ishiala* of Igboagu, but he felt too old to carry the burdens of the office, and so passed the offer on to Igboji Ola, a relation of his, who was a younger man. *Ishiala* Akwashi, one of the first Warrant Chiefs of Ngbo, soon found that trekking to Abakaliki regularly was too much for him and pushed forward his son Ale Adagba to take his place.[85] In Ubahu Nneato (Okigwi) the village head, Okpara Nwukam, would not accept a warrant because being deformed he could not easily make the 46 miles round trip to headquarters, while Ako Agidi and Nwanaku, one of whom should have taken his place, were too scared of white men to accept a warrant. At this point one Okereke Osuchukwu, a bold and courageous man, presented himself and since nobody challenged his right was made a Warrant Chief. He is said to have proved himself a 'dreadful' chief.[86]

The spread of rumours which were often false was in some places responsible for the refusal of the elders to be made Warrant

[84] CSE 1/11/42. Report on OW Dist. by Capt. Heathecote, p. 5. The title is misleading for the report is actually on Umuduru (later Okigwi) District.
[85] Information collected from Chief Idika Igboji (Izzi), Chief Elei Adagba and Oduma Uduonwo (Ngbo) in Abakaliki Division.
[86] Information collected from Chief Onwubiko Ako (son and successor of Ako Agidi, the village head in question) and from Chief Ogujiofo Ogbuewu of Eziama Nneato, Okigwi.

Chiefs. The Aro Expedition conveyed the impression that the government was out to liquidate all slave-dealers. Since every man of importance in those days was implicated in the traffic either as an active participant or as an accomplice, the demand for chiefs was in some villages interpreted as a demand for the surrender of all prominent slave-dealers.

The spreading of false information was at times an aspect of the war of the middlemen on the British for undermining their position through penetrating into the interior. In 1902 the Divisional Commissioner of the Cross River Division found that there was certainly a connection between the activities of these middlemen traders and the fact that in many places the local people and their headmen refused to have anything to do with the white man. On Abragba for instance he reported:

> There are a number of Akunakuna traders living here. I find [that in] the towns in which there are many of these and Calabar traders, it is much more difficult to approach the chiefs and people and much more difficult to get any orders carried out or arrive at the truth about local matters etc. than in places where there are none. I sat in the king's compound for half an hour while Enyamba my interpreter hunted about for chiefs and induced them to come and see me.[87]

The Aro in particular put their knowledge of these areas to profitable use. In places they would inspire fear in the elders and induce them to run away. They would then take pay from the British officer to ferret out the chiefs; and when these chiefs got warrants these same Aro agents took money from them for helping to make them big chiefs. But no simple formula can summarise satisfactorily the part played by these middlemen in the momentous events of these early years of the colonial era. It was Aro and Awka guides, for instance, who informed the government that Nze Osuoji of Umulolo was the head of Otanzu clan and Ogujiofo Umeojiaku of Ihube the head of the Otanchara clan. The Aro were also instrumental in pointing out Njemanze of Owerri. In these places therefore these middlemen traders were responsible for the fact that it was the traditional heads who got warrants.[88]

[87] Calprof 10/3, ii. Report on the Cross River Division No. 3, dated 18.3.02
[88] Information collected from Chief J. O. Njemanze (Owerri Town), Chief Obiukwu Nze of Umulolo Okigwi, Chief Mbabuike Ogujiofo of Ihube, Okigwi.

However, it would be insufficient to explain the difficulty in getting traditional village heads to volunteer for warrants at this time only in terms of the factors analysed above. The events of 1891–1914, the period which saw the military conquest of this area by the British, constituted for the communities in this region one of the gravest crises in the history of their civilisation. Men and women saw themselves forced to accept an order of things which was openly paraded as a total contradiction of all they knew, valued and respected. Conservatism aside, they believed it was their duty to maintain intact what they had inherited from their fathers. They sought to do this not only by refusing to conform to the new ways but also by seeing that the chief custodians of the old way of life did not betray it. The wholesale and total association of the traditional aristocracy with the new régime would have dealt a severe blow at the root of their inherited culture. It would have meant that these ritual personages would have to be in the vanguard of the campaign against practices like the killing of twins, trial by ordeal and human sacrifices; practices which the British administration denounced as barbarous but which formed part of the social and religious life of the community and still enjoyed the support of responsible opinion which was as yet unreconciled to the new. These elders were meant to see that the life of the community was in harmony with the wishes of the ancestors and the gods who were believed to enjoin these practices. Furthermore the association of the elders with the new régime and its reformism would have meant their breaking at least some of the many taboos which they had to observe in order to maintain the semi-sacred character of their positions. For instance, like their counterparts in Igala and other parts of black Africa, some of the heads of Ibibio communities were not allowed to cross certain streams or to see dead bodies or to sleep outside their *efe* (compound). Yet they could not carry out the functions required of Warrant Chiefs without breaking these rules. Such outrages of the wishes of the supernatural members of society would, it was ardently believed, bring about grave consequences. When these villages refused to surrender members of their ancient aristocracy they were, among other things, trying to prevent a total collapse of the old order.[89]

[89] C 176/19: Memo. by R. B. Brooks, Resident of Owerri, dated 20.1.20 and based on his experience in the Calabar Province. Supplemented with information from Chief Udo Udo Ibanga of Ikot Ekpene Town.

Most of the Warrant Chief appointments discussed above were made in the difficult early days which saw the imposition of British rule; that is, in the period before and around 1906. One may then ask to what extent the absence of pattern or definite method highlighted above continued or changed as things 'settled down' and the British gained more information about the people and the latter came to understand the purpose of the whole exercise. As for the period before 1906 or so, there is no record on this matter surviving from the years 1906 to 1914. Political officers continued to report the constitution of courts and to submit the names of those proposed for Native Court Warrants without any comment on the processes by which they arrived at the choice of the men they were recommending.

Thus no record earlier than about the middle of the 1920s has been found which gives worthwhile information on the appointment of Warrant Chiefs. In fact only from about 1919 did it come to be widely confessed in official circles that no particular care had been exercised in the selection of the members of the Native Courts. It was not until 1923, and as part of the reorganisation following S. M. Grier's report on the Eastern Provinces (discussed in chapter 5), that the government ordered inquiries into the traditional status and mode of selection of then living Warrant Chiefs. The surviving records would seem to show that this inquiry was carried out only in one or two areas in the Calabar Province and there not even in sufficient detail.[90]

Of the available documents on the matter the only informative and useful report was that by Major Sealy-King on the three Native Court areas of Ndealichi, Aro and Enyong. Here Sealy-King investigated the cases of thirty-five Warrant Chiefs.[91] Of

[90] Calprof 14, C 582/22. Pedigrees of chiefs in Calabar Province 1922–4. See Report by Major Sealy-King dated 2.5.24. See also list attached to No. 506/A.118/1923 of 22.8.24 from ADO Abak to the DO Ikot Ekpene. This latter document is virtually uninformative. Of the eighty Warrant Chiefs in the Abak District the ADO was unable to collect information showing the status of any of them in traditional society. Of the eighty, fifty-one names had against them 'No information, probably elected by Government'; then seventeen were described as 'Nominated on Merit' without showing by whom; two were described as elected by people; of the others nothing was said. Even the dates of their appointment were not given.

[91] Calprof 14, C 582/22, Pedigrees of Chiefs, etc. See Report by Major Sealy-King dated 2.5.24. Except where otherwise indicated, what follows is based on this document.

these, eleven got their warrants between 1902 and 1911 when British rule in Calabar Province was at the stage of being firmly consolidated. Of the remaining twenty-four, ten were appointed between 1918 and 1922, while no date was ascertainable for the selection of the remaining fourteen. Most of these later twenty-four were second-generation Warrant Chiefs, that is chiefs who got their appointments because the first Warrant Chiefs from their villages had either died or been disgraced for misdemeanour. Of the eleven 'sub-tribes' or clans in the three court areas only in one, Enyong, was the 'sub-tribal' head appointed a Warrant Chief, the other clan heads were not. Nine of the thirty-five chiefs were traditional village heads, five were from the same families as their village heads but were not qualified by tradition to be village heads, while of the remainder nothing was known.

Even more revealing is the analysis of the methods and reasons for the appointment of some of these chiefs. From the document there were two main methods of appointment. The first was, as in the earlier period already analysed, an arbitrary choice by the colonial government without reference to the people whom the chief was supposed to rule. The other was a choice made in consultation with the people, in particular with the village assemblies in which the chiefs were elected by popular vote. As in the earlier period also neither the first nor the second method invariably led to the choice of the traditional village head as Warrant Chief. Of the nine chiefs who represented the Aro clan in the Aro Native Court, for instance, two were chosen by the government before 1910 and seven by the people. Of the two who were chosen before 1910, one had helped the Protectorate forces in the Degema area some time before his choice, while the other had helped in making roads in the Aro district when it was first brought under British control. The British therefore rewarded them with appointment to Native Court membership. Neither of them happened to hold a traditional political office. In the same way neither of the seven chosen by the people had traditional leadership status; only three of these came from the same family as the traditional heads of their villages. Thus, even though before each choice was made the political officer harangued the people on the need to elect traditional village heads, the assembly was more concerned with choosing those who would give effective representation at the court. About one particular case in the

Idere 'sub-tribe' of the Enyong Native Court area, Major Sealy-King recorded: 'He was chosen by the people in 1918 on account of his good sense and undoubted ability to represent them.' It is certainly likely that there were other cases in which other considerations weighed with the people.

From the point of view of this study, the above analysis is very important for two reasons. The pattern or lack of pattern in the choice of later-day Warrant Chiefs which emerges from it agrees largely with the conclusions reached earlier in this chapter on the basis of the analysis of oral traditions collected by the author about forty years after Major Sealy-King's own investigations. This goes to confirm the general reliability of the oral traditions used in this study as well as the value of the methods used in checking them. This issue has been examined in some detail elsewhere.[92] Secondly the analysis clearly shows that the problem of choosing a Warrant Chief had not been simplified by the reign of more stable conditions – if anything it had become more confounded. Many of the careerists and rascals who got warrants in the early years of British rule had lived to become 'powerful' and wealthy chiefs, and therefore 'successful' men. They thus had shown that careerism could pay in the new era. Furthermore Warrant Chiefship soon came to be seen as a profession requiring acute mental qualities and sturdy limbs. It became impossible, for all these reasons, to convince everybody that only traditional heads should become Warrant Chiefs. The tradition also soon came to be established that a man needed either to have a smattering of book knowledge or to have served his apprenticeship as a headman (messenger-boy) to a Warrant Chief to qualify for election as a Warrant Chief. For only then would he be in a position to master the baffling intrigues of the Native Court, to stand up to the court clerk, and therefore to ensure effective representation for his people.[93] We shall hear more of this issue later (see chapter 5). What is important now, however, is that the lack of pattern which characterised the appointments made in the

[92] See also A. E. Afigbo, 'Oral Tradition and History in Eastern Nigeria', parts I and II, in *African Notes*, Bulletin of the Institute of African Studies, University of Ibadan, iii, 3, and iv, 1, 1966

[93] Based on information collected from various informants in the field, *e.g.*, from Chief Mbabuike Ogujiofo of Ihube, Chief Obiukwu Nze of Umulolo, Chief James Onwunali of Ikenanzizi (all in Okigwi); Chief Nwancho Atuma of Ikwo (Abakaliki), Chief Ngadi Onuma of Oloko (Bende), Chief Luke Obiasogu of Nnewi (Onitsha), etc.

period before 1906 set a dangerous precedent which not even the exertions of the administration could do much to alter.

Within the territorial confines of what in 1914 emerged as Nigeria, the Warrant Chief System was one of the two earliest serious and systematic attempts at indirect administration. The other was within the Lagos Protectorate (Yorubaland). Goldie had also been forced by circumstances to proclaim indirect rule as one of the administrative instruments of his company. But for his company indirect rule was a cloak for inaction, a policy of non-interference in the affairs of the indigenous peoples designed to spare the Royal Niger Company the expenditure implicit in setting up a definite machinery for local government. It was in fact a policy of division of labour. Under it the indigenous rulers were to be encouraged to maintain law and order among their people, while the company concerned itself with excluding 'foreigners' or trade rivals from its territory. Consequently the Royal Niger Company made no effort worth the name to organise a definite system which would embody Goldie's ideas of local government.[94]

But for the men of the Niger Coast Protectorate Indirect Rule was a policy of active participation in the local administration of the indigenous peoples and they set up the machinery for this purpose. The next chapter deals with the nature and structure of this machinery.

[94] J. E. Flint, *Sir George Goldie*, etc., pp. 94–5. See also M. Perham, *Lugard: The Years of Authority*, London 1960, pp. 38 9, 207–10

3 The structure of the Warrant Chief System, 1891–1912

For a considerable part of the period 1891–1900 the structure of the Warrant Chief System was in the process of formation, and it is not known for certain whether during these years there was a definite legal enactment setting out clearly the directives to guide procedure in the Native Courts. Instructions on the institution of these local government bodies were issued *ad hoc* and necessarily changed rapidly as new situations were met with in the penetration of the interior and as past experiences were re-evaluated.[1] It is probably understandable that throughout this period of more or less 'blind' experimentation no attempt was made to legislate on the constitution and procedure of Native Courts, for experience was just being gained and legislation has a way of turning flexible convention into rigid tradition.

From a patient and critical study of the documents it would appear that in the first years of the Niger Coast Protectorate the administration tended to regard the Native Court as the Court of Equity reorganised specifically for settling disputes arising among the indigenous elements. The extent to which the traditions of this earlier institution and Johnston's stillborn programme for Governing Councils dominated official thinking can be illustrated from an analysis of the membership of a 'Governing Council' which the vice-consul at Forcados proposed for Warri in 1891. This court, which comprised seven members, excluding the vice-consul, who perhaps presided, contained four European traders – D. P. Bleasby of the African Association, R. Kerr of Miller Brothers, J. W. Brownridge of Pinnock and Company and H. Fischer of Bey and Gunmer. Actually, one unaware of the fact that the Courts of Equity were abolished in 1885 would think the 'Governing Council' was one of such courts.[2]

[1] J. C. Anene, *Southern Nigeria in Transition 1885–1906*, Cambridge 1966, see footnote on p. 252
[2] Calprof 6/1, In-letters to the Commissioner and Consul-General 1891–

The absence of system and consistency which characterised local government in the Protectorate in this period is writ large in many other features of the Native Courts. There was no uniform terminology for them. In Warri in 1891, as already seen, a Native Court was called 'Governing Council', a name which recalls Acting Consul Johnston's stillborn programme of the 1880s; in Bonny in 1892 it was called the 'Native Council'; in Calabar in the same year it was called the 'Court of the Native Council for the District of Old Calabar', but by 1895 the name of the latter had been changed to the 'High Court of the Native Council of Old Calabar'. Courts presided over by native chiefs were called 'Minor Courts' on the Benin River in 1896 and 'Local Councils' at Degema in 1897. Furthermore, it would appear there was no fixed number of members who could sit as shown by the records of the High Court of the Native Council of Old Calabar in 1897. On 25 April 1895 Chief J. J. Henshaw was both sitting member and court clerk.[3]

The confused experimentation which characterised local government policy in these early years has baffled many a scholar of this period. Dame Margery Perham, the first of many to give full attention to the study of native administration in Nigeria, failed to track down even the outlines of the structure and growth of the Warrant Chief System. In her book devoted to the study of that subject, *Native Administration in Nigeria*, she was able to describe in some detail the structure and evolution of native policy in Northern Nigeria and, to some extent, in Yorubaland. But for the area covered by the present study she contented herself with describing how deeply the natives revolted early European visitors and administrators because they were 'particularly barbarous and intractable' and had to be forcibly brought to share in modern civilisation in the form of British colonial rule. The history of Southern Nigeria between 1900 and 1906 she summarised as 'the gradual opening up of the interior, with a parallel increase of trade and revenue'. By her silence on the issue of the structure of local government she gave the impression that in the matter of native administration there was hardly anything

1899, see letter No. 11 of 15.9.91 from the Vice-Consul at Forcados. It is not known whether the formation of this court was approved. The other three members of the proposed court were to be African chiefs.
[3] Calprof 8/5, Court Records 1891–9. See Native Court records dated 30.6.93, 25.4.95 and 11.11.95.

in Southern Nigeria before 1914 worthy of note and that whatever there was was uninspiring. 'The Government of Southern Nigeria,' she wrote, 'to judge by the paucity of information given upon this point in their reports, do not seem to have been proud of their native administration in their two eastern provinces.'[4] There is in fact enough information on the matter to sketch at least the bare outlines which a diligent search would have revealed and which is evidenced by what follows in this chapter.

In the same manner the fluid character of local government policy and structure in these early years led Professor Anene into a welter of confusion, the extent of which would appear not to have been fully recognised by the reviewers and readers of his book, *Southern Nigeria In Transition 1885–1906.* On the structure of the Native Courts, for instance, he wrote:

> A remarkable appendage (to Macdonald's local government institutions) was the establishment at Old Calabar of a High Court of the 'Native' Councils as a kind of Court of Appeal. The first few years of British rule saw two parallel régimes – one 'Native' and the other alien. The 'Native' was at every point subordinated to the 'alien'.[5]

One needs to observe only briefly here that the High Court of the Native Council at Old Calabar presided over by the Commissioner and Consul-General himself could not have been a mere appendage to the local government which Macdonald was seeking to establish. If it was anything, as a court with an original and appellate jurisdiction it was an organic part of the system, the key institution by which Macdonald maintained control on the functioning of the local government machinery. Again one needs to point out that if the Native and Consular Court systems ran parallel as Professor Anene asserted, then the native system could not have been subordinated at every point to the alien one as he correctly pointed out. Professor Anene in the same chapter also surprisingly conceded, thus contradicting himself, that the native and alien systems coalesced to form one system of administration in the early years:

> Up to 1898 the protectorate records speak of four categories of Court. . . . The divorce between the Native Court and the unmistakably British Court Systems had not yet emerged.[6]

---

[4] M. Perham, *Native Administration in Nigeria*, Oxford 1937, pp. 21–32
[5] J. C. Anene, *Southern Nigeria*, etc., p. 253
[6] *Ibid.*, p. 260

WARRANT APPOINTING MEMBER OF NATIVE COURT.

I *Hy. gilbecky. acting Vice-Consul for* H.B.M's Commissioner and Consul-General for the Niger Coast Protectorate, do hereby appoint *Chief Brajini* to be and to act as a Member of the *Benin Minor Native* Court subject to the Rules and Regulations drawn up for the guidance of Members of the said Court.

Given under my hand and the seal of the Niger Coast Protectorate this *14th* day of *January* 1896.

Hugh Bedford a.v.c

H.B.M's Commissioner and Consul-General.

H.B.M's Consulate-General,
Old Calabar.

1 A specimen Warrant appointing member of native court

2 Chief Udo Akpabio, a Warrant Chief of Ikot Ekpene, with his school-
master son

The fact is that, even though Macdonald and Moor, unlike Lugard, did not expressly say:

> The essential feature of the system is that the Native chiefs are constituted as an integral part of the machinery of administration. There are not two sets of rulers – British and native – working either separately or in co-operation, but a single Government in which the native chiefs have well defined duties and an acknowledged status equally with British officials,[7]

they did not see themselves as setting up parallel administrations. On the contrary, they saw the Native Court system in its judicial capacity as the local arm of the Consular Courts and in its legislative and executive capacities as the arm of the protectorate government generally. It was for this reason that the district commissioners were so closely associated with the Native Courts, and the chief law officer of the Protectorate supervised both the Native and Consular Courts. The outlook which saw the two systems as parts of the same chain of authority became more pronounced as time went on. In time it led, as will be shown later in this chapter, to the complete subordination of the Native Court system (in its judicial aspect) to the Supreme Court and its commissioners.

In spite of the lack of a definite system in the structure of local government in the early years, the period saw the steady crystallisation of certain principles and practices in native administration which were later carried over from the Niger Coast Protectorate to the Protectorate of Southern Nigeria and its successor. By 1900 it was already established, for instance, that all members of Native Courts must hold warrants from the government,[8] and that there was to be a distinction in name, jurisdiction and status between a court sitting at headquarters, where a European political officer could regularly act as its *ex officio* president or at least keep a vigilant eye on its working, and a court sitting away from headquarters which could at best receive periodic and hurried supervision from a political officer. In fact in this, as in some other aspects which will be pointed out below, the Native Courts Proclamations of 1900 and 1901 were an attempt to build into a system the practices and experiences of the years of the

[7] Lord Lugard, *The Dual Mandate In British Tropical Africa*, Edinburgh 1922, p. 203
[8] Calprof 8/5, Court Records 1891–9. See copies of Warrants issued by Hugh Lecky, Acting Vice-Consul on the Benin River.

Niger Coast Protectorate. The proclamations tried to bring to an end the era of structural and procedural confusion in Native Court organisation.

From a study of these proclamations the history of the structural evolution of the Warrant Chief System emerges as the story of the process by which the British colonial administration sought to modify what they thought was the indigenous political system in order to fit it for carrying out the programmes of a reforming central government. In his study of colonial rule in West Africa Professor Michael Crowder has correctly pointed out that 'the use of indigenous political institutions for the purpose of local government was contingent on certain modifications to these institutions', and he distinguishes two kinds of modifications. In the first category were modifications designed to rid the supposed indigenous institutions of those 'aspects of traditional government that were repugnant to European ideas of what constituted good government'. Among these were the abolition of human sacrifices and of certain forms of punishment like maiming, which were considered barbarous. In the second category of modifications were those 'designed to ensure the achievement of the main purpose of colonial rule, the exploitation of the colonised country'. An example of the latter was the introduction of taxation 'designed to stimulate the production of cash crops for export'.[9] There was a third aspect which Crowder failed to mention even though it loomed very large in the policies of all indirect rulers. The very facts of colonial conquest, European presence, missionary propaganda as well as of the intrusion of new economic forces were apt to act as solvents of indigenous institutions and authority. Of this fact the administrators were immensely aware. And it was this that created the need for the third category of modifications which were designed to shore up the indigenous institutions in the face of the disintegrative forces just enumerated.

In the end the result of the three-sided modifications of the supposedly indigenous system was a far-reaching transformation of it amounting to a revolution. But, says Professor Anene, the administrators 'firmly believed that they were doing nothing revolutionary'.[10] This belief in preservation through transformation is characteristic of all indirect rulers. The modifications of

[9] M. Crowder, *West Africa Under Colonial Rule*, London 1970, p. 169
[10] J. C. Anene, *Southern Nigeria*, p. 252

the indigenous system which the Government of the Protectorate of Southern Nigeria considered necessary in this period were enshrined in the various Native Court Proclamations (from 1906 Ordinances) which were issued to guide the constitution and running of these local government bodies. The first of these proclamations was issued in 1900 and came into operation on the first of May that year.

This proclamation, like the ones which came after it, clearly reflected in its provisions the assumption which was at the time widespread in European circles that the natives of the Protectorate were incapable of ensuring good government for their peoples unless they received adequate guidance from European political officers. Acting-Consul Johnston had earlier justified his creation of Governing Councils dominated by Europeans on the ground of his conviction that the chiefs of the Oil Rivers unaided were incompetent to administer the affairs of their country 'in a wise and just manner'.[11] This belief was also rife in the Colony and Protectorate of Lagos (Yorubaland) as in the Protectorate of Northern Nigeria. This is the explanation for the fact that the three administrations laid emphasis on European supervision and control. But the question which each administration had to decide in the light of the indigenous political situation that faced it was whether to exercise the necessary control from within the local government body, or to stand outside it and issue instructions which in Northern Nigeria were known as *advice*. In the latter place, where the emirate system of administration was highly centralised and autocratic, the administration decided to exercise the necessary control from outside the local government body. In Yorubaland, where the powers of the oba were not as centralised and autocratic as those of the Fulani emir, the administration decided to exercise that control from within the local government body and thus made the political officer a member, but *not* the president, of the native authority council. In the Eastern Provinces, where political authority was widely diffused, the administration decided that the ideal thing was to make the political officer not just a member of the Native Council, but also its president. But from considerations of practical politics it was discovered that the political officers could not preside over all the Native Courts which political necessity forced the government to create. Therefore it was decided that

[11] *Ibid.*

political officers should be presidents of only a few Native Courts which would then serve as an example to the many others which were left largely on their own.

The Native Courts Proclamation of 1900 therefore created two categories of Native Courts. In the lower category were all courts, presided over by a 'native authority' or a local chief, and which were known as Minor Courts. Above these were courts called Native Council which were presided over by political officers, and all of which were located at district headquarters. The benches of both grades of courts consisted of people holding judicial warrants from the high commissioner or his representative and who could not be deprived of their membership without his express sanction. For any session, a Native Court bench was to comprise the president, the vice-president, three other members and one member specially summoned to represent the village or district in which the dispute arose. For the Minor Court the president was to be elected quarterly by the members. The two classes of courts were to be guided, as far as possible, by 'native law and custom not opposed to natural morality and humanity'. At first sight this latter provision sounds superfluous, since from the composition of the bench and in the absence of special training in English law for the African members the court could hardly be guided by other than customary law. But the emphasis was on the last seven words of the quotation and the provision was meant to ensure that the courts did not uphold and apply such aspects of traditional jurisprudence which the administration looked upon with horror. When required the courts were also to administer some other laws of the Protectorate.[12]

Minor Courts and Native Councils exercised different jurisdictions in spite of the fact that their Warrant Chief members were generally people of equal standing or at least people locally accepted to be so. The explanation lay in the official conviction, already analysed, that without close European supervision the chiefs could not function satisfactorily and efficiently. Therefore those of them who operated right under the nose of the European officer were to enjoy wider powers than their colleagues who were left more to themselves as a result of having to function in

[12] *Laws of Southern Nigeria for 1900 and 1901* (1903), p. 430; Calprof 10/2, Proclamations 1900–2. See Native Courts Proclamation No. 9 of 1900

villages far away from headquarters. In civil matters, Minor Court jurisdiction was limited to twenty-five pounds in matters of debt or damage and to fifty pounds in matters of inheritance. In the same class of matters Native Council jurisdiction was limited to cases in which the claim or damage or inheritance in dispute was not more than two hundred pounds. In land cases both categories of courts enjoyed unrestricted jurisdiction. In their criminal jurisdiction they dealt with petty assault, and disobedience to the lawful orders of a house head or insult to him. The Native Council had the power and duty to supervise Minor Courts, inspect their records and enforce on them orders prescribed by the government. Legal practitioners were excluded from both classes of Native Courts.[13]

Further, to achieve that close European control considered indispensable for the efficient working of the system, the courts were placed squarely under the European political staff. A district commissioner could at any stage in the trial of a case transfer it from a Minor Court to a Native Council or from the latter to the District Court. A defendant in a case could apply to the district commissioner for a transfer while a litigant dissatisfied with the findings of a Native Court could appeal to the district commissioner who could order a retrial of the case, annul or vary the decision of the court. Also in order to achieve efficiency and enforce justice the high commissioner retained a large measure of power in his own hands. He enjoyed the power to withdraw for a definite period the right of any Native Court, which abused its powers, to function as such. He could likewise suspend or dismiss individual Native Court members who abused their powers. He could issue orders regulating the fees of the members, the execution of their judgments and the keeping of court records.[14]

In time the judicial duties of these courts came to overshadow their executive and legislative duties. This derived partly from the belief of the administration that the greatest need of the peoples of this region was some institution which would enable them to settle the numerous inter-village 'palavers' which were believed to arise among them and which they were supposed to have no means of settling except by recourse to war and blood-

[13] Calprof 10/2, Proclamations 1900–2. See Native Courts Proclamation No. 9 of 1900
[14] *Ibid.*

shed. In late September 1902, for instance, inter-village fighting was reported around the Taylor Creek in the Delta. Early in October Moor wrote to the divisional commissioner under whose jurisdiction the disturbed region came:

> Pending Government action would it not be possible to get some native emissaries to send to the locality to talk and consult with the natives there with regard to the formation of some form of Native Court for settling their difficulties? It seems to me that the majority of these outrages occurs through the natives of the locality having no means of settling inter-tribal or inter-town differences.[15]

This belief that what the region needed most was peace was also related to the government's economic policy. Sir Ralph Moor in particular believed that the region being rich in a natural produce, a major aspect of economic policy should be to impose and maintain that measure of *Pax Britannica* which would enable the natives to collect and market the sylvan produce of their land unharassed. Early in 1902 he reported to the Colonial Office that he had instructed the district commissioners for Bende and Arochukwu

> to take immediate action to form Native Courts for the settlement of individual and inter-tribal disputes, which is really the surest method of inducing the natives to take up the produce trade, for by it a means is provided of settling all disputes and the lives of individuals are rendered safe and property secure: so that there is no seizing of either person or property on the roads, and the man who works to obtain produce is ensured of a return for his labour in that he can take his goods to the market and return in safety.[16]

Thus in peaceably settling 'palavers' that would otherwise lead to war and disruption of economic life, these courts were seen to be contributing to the realisation of the main purposes of colonial rule – the exploitation of the colonised country. Also Moor's emphasis on peace and the settlement of quarrels without resorting to fights and war owed something to his psychology as a former police officer.[17]

Another reason was the consideration that if European control was to be a reality, then the procedure of the courts should be such that the political officer would understand it when he found

[15] Calprof 9/2, Out-letters from this High Commissioner 1900–6. See letter No. 12 of 3.10.02
[16] CSO 1/13, Despatches to FO and CO 1891–1906. See Despatch No. 157 of 12.4.02 from Moor to CO
[17] I. F. Nicolson, *The Administration of Nigeria 1900–60*, Oxford 1969, p. 87

time to sit in, or when he failed to be present, be able to determine whether justice had been done by merely reading the recorded proceedings. It was largely for these reasons that the administration spent so much time and energy drawing up detailed regulations which were to guide the Native Courts in their judicial duties. Some idea of how detailed and ponderous these legal regulations were could be gathered from a brief discussion of the procedure laid down for the courts as well as of the duties of the court clerk whose responsibility it was to ensure adherence to the prescribed rules.

Each Native Court had at least one clerk whose duty it was to prepare the lists of all cases which came up for hearing in such a way that all cases arising from any one area would be dealt with by the court at one sitting or at a number of continuous sittings. The clerk summoned the members who were to attend each day's meeting. Every proceeding in the court started with his filing the summons and for each summons issued he had to keep a duplicate on the back of which he entered the date of its issue, the date when each witness was summoned, the date of hearing the case, and the page of the book on which the judgment of the court was entered. On it too he stated the date of the satisfaction of the court's judgment.[18]

Every court had a paged judgment book in which the clerk recorded its sittings, the date of each sitting, the names of the president, vice-president and the ordinary members by whom each case was tried, as well as the names of the witnesses called and interrogated. The judgment in each case was to be signed by the president or, in his absence, by the vice-president. There was also a cash book on the credit side of which moneys paid into the court were entered as well as the reference number of the case for which each payment was made. On the debit side were entered all expenditure such as fees paid to members out of the court's funds.[19] The clerk's duties were highly specialised and tedious. It can therefore be understood if the largely illiterate members held him in awe, and if these clerical formalities caused delay, irritation and frustration.

The summons cost two shillings where there were only one plaintiff and one defendant, three shillings and sixpence where there were more than one on either side or where there was one

---

[18] *Laws of Southern Nigeria 1900 and 1901*, p. 431
[19] *Ibid.*, pp. 431–2

on each side but in a representative capacity, and double the sums given above where the case arose before 1 January 1900. Hearing, where the claims were confessed, cost two shillings in a Native Council or one shilling in a Minor Court. Where the claim was neither defended nor confessed and therefore needed proof, hearing cost two shillings, plus threepence for every pound claimed in a Native Council; or one shilling, plus three pence for every pound claimed in a Minor Court. Whether the claim was contested or not, but arose before 1900, hearing cost was one pound plus one additional shilling paid for each pound claimed in excess of ten pounds in a Native Council, or ten shillings plus an additional sixpence paid for every pound claimed in excess of ten pounds in a Minor Court.[20]

It cost a shilling to summon a witness, sixpence for each hour 'necessarily taken' to serve the summons. But the extra charge for serving summons could not exceed three shillings and six pence without the special sanction of the court. Before the issue of summonses, the hearing of any case or the summoning of witnesses the correct fee for each stage of the proceedings had to be paid into the court. A waiver for these charges could be granted by the district commissioner to indigent men who had genuine grievances, but were unable to pay for the court's services. In criminal cases no fees were charged but if the prosecution was found frivolous or malicious the complainant paid costs. In districts where payment of fees and fines in cash could not be enforced, payment in trade goods, brass rods or manillas but not in gin or other spirits was authorised. In all such cases, successful litigants had to accept indigenous moneys or trade goods as payment for any costs awarded them.[21]

The administration also recognised that the members of the Native Courts needed inducement to shoulder their onerous, and at times despised, duties. Thus during the sitting of the court the vice-president of a Native Council and the president of a Minor Court got ten shillings a day while the other members, including the special member summoned from the district where the case arose, got five shillings. In criminal cases, this special member got no fee. Where a Warrant Chief had to come from a distance which necessarily involved his walking more than one hour, he got a special fee at the rate of sixpence for each additional

---

[20] *Ibid.*, pp. 433–4
[21] *Ibid.*, pp. 430–2

thirty minutes taken, but this special fee was not to exceed five shillings for any one session of the court irrespective of the number of days the court sat for the session.[22]

But with all the emphasis which the administration placed on the judicial side of the Native Courts' duties, it did not forget that the maintenance of peace involved much more than the settlement of 'palavers', nor that Native Courts had a role to play in helping to realise the administration's self-imposed mission of 'civilising' and educating the people. Mr I. F. Nicolson writes:

> The very greatest importance was attached by Moor and his officers to the Native Courts and Native Councils. They were intended to be the chief instruments of progress employed directly by Government, supplementing the civilising influences of commerce and education.[23]

For these reasons, therefore, the Native Courts were endowed with specified executive and legislative powers. Thus every Native Court enjoyed the power, with the approval of the high commissioner, to make by-laws for 'the peace, good order and welfare' of their areas of authority and to revoke or amend these as required. By-laws were to deal with matters like the construction and maintenance of roads, the establishment and preservation of landmarks, the prevention and abatement of nuisance and the provision of grounds for burying the dead.[24] This grant of power to make by-laws to Minor Courts was an innovation. In the period before the Proclamation only Native Councils enjoyed that power.[25] The Native Court was also granted specified executive powers. Each had the authority of a justice of the peace: the power to bind people over to keep the peace; to prevent or suppress public disturbances such as riots and affrays; to execute Supreme Court orders or the orders of a district commissioner; to seize and send to the Supreme Court people accused of serious crimes like robbery, murder and slave-dealing.[26]

The Native Courts Proclamation of 1900 was enacted in a

[22] *Ibid.*, p. 433
[23] Nicolson, p. 88
[24] Calprof 10/2, Proclamations 1900–2. See Native Courts Proclamation No. 9 of 1900
[25] CSO 1/13, Despatches to FO and CO 1891–1906. See Despatch No. 167 of 3.10.99
[26] Calprof 10/2, Proclamations 1900–6. See Native Courts Proclamation No. 9 of 1900

hurry. On the amalgamation of the Niger Coast Protectorate with the southern portion of the Royal Niger Company's territories in 1900 the existing Native Courts were abolished at only three days' notice and the Proclamation hastily introduced. Not surprisingly before the end of the year experience revealed several defects in the act and therefore the necessity for sundry amendments and additions. These reforms were embodied in the Native Courts Proclamation of 1901, which came into operation on the first day of January that year. This later act did not embody any revolutionary principle – the innovations which it brought were confined to structural details and legal technicalities, especially to the more precise definition of the powers of the courts and to provisions for supervising and controlling them more closely. Some of these additions or amendments will now be treated.

Under this proclamation, the district commissioner acquired the right to appoint a Warrant Chief to act as the president of a Native Council during sittings which he could not attend.[27] It had now become obvious that it was practically impossible for a political officer to discharge effectively his many duties in that capacity as well as his duties as Commissioner of the Supreme Court and president of Native Councils. But this concession created a convenient loophole for officers who were too lazy to exercise effective supervision over the courts under their charge. By conceding that the Warrant Chiefs, while functioning in the absence of the district commissioner, could exercise the powers of a Native Council, this amendment subsequently constituted one of the strongest arguments for the total exclusion of political officers from membership of Native Courts.[28]

In order to ensure that the Native Courts were patronised by the people, it was made illegal for any other person or body to exercise jurisdiction 'on any pretext whatsoever' in any area under the jurisdiction of a court founded under this law.[29] This was the origin of the policy and process by which the councils of village elders as well as the secret and title societies – some of the real indigenous political institutions of the people – were driven underground. Under cover of this very provision Sir Ralph Moor in May 1902 felt it necessary to emphasise for his officers that

[27] *Laws of Southern Nigeria 1900 and 1901*, p. 421
[28] See the next chapter.
[29] *Laws of Southern Nigeria 1900 and 1901*, p. 421

the only legal means of administering justice in these territories are through a Commissioner's Court or by Native Council, and though in unsettled territories the District Officers are allowed to assist and advise chiefs in . . . cases brought before them as chiefs, it must be understood that this is an unauthorised method. . . . It is not one to be encouraged but . . . should be done away with as soon as practicable.[30]

The background to this amendment is that in many places people newly subjugated continued to order their affairs through their indigenous institutions, thus treating the Native Courts with studied neglect.

The control of the central government over these courts was also strengthened. The high commissioner could thenceforth at pleasure restrict or extend the jurisdiction of a Native Court, specify offences which it could deal with, declare any building a 'Native Prison' for the detention or imprisonment of persons arrested or sentenced by Native Courts.

The appointment, duties and pay of inspectors of Native Courts and the administration of Native Prisons were all included in the list of matters on which he could make and unmake rules. In their judicial capacity and functions the courts were brought, to some extent, under the Supreme Court. In matters where the prescribed punishment exceeded five pounds or a term of three months' imprisonment appeals lay from the Native Courts to the Supreme Court. The hearing and determination of such appeals lay with a judge of the Supreme Court sitting with between two and five Warrant Chiefs as assessors. The decision of the Supreme Court on these matters was final. Native Court clerks were given orders to send their monthly returns to the judicial department through the district commissioner. This detour through the political officer was instituted to offer him a chance of explaining occasions in which he had absented himself from Native Court sittings. By this means, it was hoped, the Chief Justice would obtain full information on the degree of supervision which the courts received and report cases of laxity to the high commissioner. These detailed regulations, which were part of the drive for efficiency, unfortunately only served to encumber the Native Courts with bureaucratic novelty and routine.[31]

Placing the Native Courts under British Courts was not in

[30] Calprof 9/2, Out-letters from the High Commissioner 1900–6. See letter No. 9 of 22.5.02 from Moor

[31] *Laws of Southern Nigeria 1900 and 1901*, pp. 426–8. CSO 1/13, Despatches to FO and CO 1891–1906, see Despatch No. 16 of 1903

fact a totally new departure. During the early years of the Niger Delta Protectorate the Native Courts were under the Consular Courts, and their organisation, reorganisation and overall supervision were directly under the control of the law officers of the central administration.[32] The tenuous link which Proclamation No. 9 of 1900 provided between the Native and the British Courts must have derived from the hurry with which that law was rushed into being. Other noteworthy provisions made by the Native Court Proclamation of 1901 included limiting the jurisdiction of Native Courts in land matters to cases in which the land in question was worth not more than £200 for Native Councils and not more than £25 for Minor Courts.

The following year (1902) an attempt was made to define precisely the duties of messengers attached to these courts. Even in the period before 1900 each Native Court had its posse of court messengers, but what their duties were remained vague in the extreme. In fact it was the practice for a plaintiff to serve the summons on the defendant while the court messengers worked in the prison department as warders, served consular court processes and acted as orderlies. This way of serving Native Court summonses which entailed the parties to a quarrel confronting each other before it was settled, especially in those early days when summonses were novel and dreaded, often led to collisions between litigants and to actual or further breaches of the peace. Because it was unsatisfactory it was decided to use court messengers in serving Native Court processes. At first the messengers went directly to the defendant but this method proved equally unsatisfactory for two reasons. In the first place it frequently led to violent clashes between the messenger and the defendant supported by his people, and did not ensure that the defendant would unfailingly respond to the summons. In the second place it tended to undermine the authority of the local Warrant Chief who felt he was not fully made use of as 'native authority'. Consequently Moor ruled in 1902 that messengers serving processes or carrying ordinary executive messages from the court should go first to the Warrant Chief of the 'district' whose duty it would then be to arrange for the carrying out of the necessary instructions in each case.[33]

[32] CSO 1/13, Despatches to FO and CO, see Despatch No. 167 of 3.10.99
[33] Calprof 10/3, Reports, see Report dated 4.1.01. Calprof 9/2, Out-letters from High Commissioner. See letters Nos. 2 and 8 of 22.5.02

Moor was meticulous about the technical organisation of the courts. He insisted on each of them being formed and founded strictly according to law – having its warrants and those of its members properly endorsed. He was no less particular about the efficiency of the court scribes in clerical and accounting matters. Before 1899 he audited the accounts of the Native Courts himself, but in 1899 he appointed a local auditor who, after inspecting the court books, reported to the auditor-general of the protectorate and to Moor. In 1902 the office of local auditor was abolished and a travelling supervisor of Native Courts appointed. By 1907 there were two of these latter officers in the Eastern Province alone, one being stationed at Calabar and the other at Opobo. These officers spent their time going round the courts checking clerical and accounting matters. This was also the period of travelling commissioners who helped to supervise the courts and to instruct the clerks and other court officials in their duties. The most famous of these travelling commissioners in this area, F. S. James, for instance, toured the villages in Bende District telling the people that when a man received a summons it should be understood to mean that the case between him and his adversary would come before the Native Court for settlement.[34]

It is interesting to note that while Moor lavished tender care on the bureaucratic side of the system, such questions as the right of the Warrant Chiefs to hold the positions given them and how far the territorial extent of the courts' jurisdiction harmonised with ethnic or sub-cultural boundaries (issues which were later to loom very large) did not bother him at all. Nor did they bother Egerton and Lugard after him. But while highlighting this fact it is only fair to add that even if Moor and his immediate successor, Egerton, had shown interest in such questions they might not have arrived at a satisfactory solution of them. As already shown in chapter 1, so unsettled were their times and so suspicious the people that inquiries into these matters might have proved nugatory as well as caused dangerous delay in the implementation of government policies. But with Lugard the situation was substantially different, as by his time the Protectorate had more

[34] CSO 1/13, Despatches to FO and CO. See Report dated 4.1.03 attached to Despatch No. 16 of 7.1.03. Calprof 9/2, Out-letters from High Commissioner. See letters No. 2 of 22.5.02 and No. 14 of 2.9.02. *Southern Nigeria Annual Report 1907*, p. 36

or less settled down and alien rule become an established, though from the point of view of the people a sad, fact.

To Moor the problem of setting up a Native Administration in the territories under his charge did not end with the mere institution of Native Courts. He came to the Bights of Benin and Biafra at a time when, owing to the rapid decline of the middleman trade monopoly and the spread of Christianity, coastal society, which had been built on the trade boom of the eighteenth and early nineteenth centuries, was facing the threat of total collapse and disintegration. There was the danger that the slave population might seize this opportunity to desert the houses in their thousands. In the circumstance the success of Moor's policy of ruling through the 'tribal system'[35] was endangered. Moor was therefore not prepared to leave to the Native Courts alone the vital job of upholding the authority and position of the house heads; rather he proceeded to enact specific measures directed to this end. Since he regarded these measures as 'purely for native administration', any detailed examination of the system which he set up and which Lugard later said he reformed must include an analysis of these acts in order to illustrate their proper place in Moor's scheme. A study of their provisions helps to show how far Moor was prepared to go in order to rule indirectly.

The first of these measures (which, however, is little known) was the proclamation for 'the better maintenance and guidance of the trade system of the New Calabar people', which was issued in 1899. According to the preamble the purpose was 'to maintain intact the Native System of House Government, and to establish cordial relations between the chiefs . . . and their boys, so as not to interfere with the rights of the chiefs or the responsibility of the boys'. It regulated the services of house members to their house head in such a way as to uphold the economic position of the latter, and with it his political authority. The proclamation was first to apply to New Calabar (Degema) and if successful was to be extended to the other portions of the Niger Coast Protectorate.[36]

[35] CSO 1/13, Despatches to FO and CO. See Despatch No. 134 of 25.8.99
[36] The proclamation abolished the old system of 'topping' or 'trade tax', since it had failed to satisfy all parties. The life of the trading boy was divided into three periods. The first or the 'probationary' period lasted three to five years, depending on the conduct of the boy. During this period

The enactment of the Native House Rule Proclamation in 1902, which was designed to supersede this earlier law, was perhaps a confession of its failure. The later act has proved the more widely known of the two measures. It applied to the whole of the Protectorate of Southern Nigeria, since the house system was thought to obtain throughout the entire area. By its provisions every member of a house who refused to submit 'to the control, authority and rule of the head of his house in accordance with native law and custom' was to be liable to prosecution and, on conviction, to a fine not exceeding fifty pounds, or imprisonment for not longer than one year, or both. Any house member wandering abroad without visible means of subsistence could be arrested without a warrant by a court official and sent to the district commissioner for forcible return to the house head. No employer could engage a house member without the consent of his house head. A breach of this provision brought on the delinquent prosecution in a court of law. The only section which concerned a head of house provided that if he neglected his customary duties to his house members he was to face prosecution.[37]

These two measures were the result of clear-headed political realism and common sense. Moor was no less opposed to the slave trade and slavery than any other administrator before or after him. Largely out of a desire to eradicate these evils he had enacted the Slavery Proclamation of 1901 and partly for the same reason he fought the Aro in 1901–2. But he would not therefore watch with unconcern the dissolution of what he thought was responsible for the maintenance of law and order in

the boy traded for, and all profits accrued to, the head of his house. The second or 'taxed' period, which started on the termination of the first and lasted five years, was that during which the boy traded for himself but paid tax to the chief at the rate of ten shillings for each puncheon of oil, four shillings for each cask of kernel and 50 per cent on other articles sold. The third or 'free' period was that during which a boy became a 'free trader', trading for himself and enjoying 'all the rights, privileges and prerogatives' of the head of a house. To graduate from one stage to the other the boy needed a certificate of good conduct from the district commissioner and Native Council, and 'good conduct' meant that a boy had in no way done anything to defraud his master. Any boy convicted three times under the provisions of this act was considered ineligible for graduation to the next stage. See CSO 1/13, Despatches to FO and CO. See Despatch No. 34 of 25.8.99 and the Enclosure
[37] *Laws of Southern Nigeria 1900 and 1901*, pp. 435–9

the Protectorate of Southern Nigeria, the rock on which he intended to anchor his ship of indirect administration.

Another step taken by Moor to build up the structure of the Warrant Chief System was the issue in 1903 of the Roads and Creeks (Rivers) Proclamation. The basis of this enactment was the belief that in pre-British days the peoples of the region undertook communal labour 'for the good of their country' and should continue to do so under the colonial régime. It was argued that throughout Southern Nigeria the inhabitants of each town were subject to the control of a chief and by tradition were liable to be called out by him for the purpose of maintaining roads linking them with neighbouring villages as well as for the construction and maintenance of their defence walls and trenches. The establishment of British rule, it was argued, had removed the necessity for building and maintaining defence works, and the labour or part of the labour thereby saved was to be used in providing the needs of the new era, for instance, in better roads.[38]

In exercise of the powers granted him by this Proclamation the high commissioner could at any time declare that a waterway or road was to be maintained by the chiefs of the villages through which the river or creek or road ran. It was for the district commissioner to inform a chief when a road, creek or river needed clearing. Once thus instructed a Warrant Chief had the right to call out any man between the ages of fifteen and fifty or any woman between fifteen and forty years old residing within his area of authority to work on the road or waterway or part of it for a length of time not exceeding six days in a quarter. A chief who failed to carry out orders given him under this act was liable, on conviction, to a fine not exceeding fifty pounds or to imprisonment for not longer than six months. Anybody who disobeyed a chief engaged in executing an order received under this proclamation was liable on conviction to a fine of not more than one pound or to imprisonment for not longer than one month.[39] The execution of their duties under this proclamation and the ruthless exploitation of the opportunities which it offered for personal enrichment later became one of the reasons

[38] Calprof 9/2, Out-letters from the High Commissioner. See letters Nos. 14 and 23 of 14.10.02. See also Memo. on Road Construction in file No. C 224/1913, Native Chiefs Recognised by Government, Trial of, etc. The enactment also derived from the fact that no direct tax was imposed.
[39] *Laws of the Colony of Southern Nigeria*, ii, 1908, pp. 1226–8

which corroded away much of the respect which the Warrant Chiefs could otherwise have received from those under them.[40]

As already shown, the Native Courts were from the onset projected and constituted as fully rounded local government bodies. They were not only judicial institutions but had legislative and executive functions. To ensure that they effectively and satisfactorily served their executive functions each was provided with its own treasury. The unsettlement which accompanied the imposition of British control gave Moor no scope to institute direct taxation. Consequently the local treasuries were, under him and Egerton, at an embryonic stage of development and derived their revenue entirely from court fines and fees. Each Native Council and each Minor Court had its own treasury into which all its income went.[41]

By means of these local treasuries Native Court houses were built, good roads were made linking village to village, rest houses were put up and maintained and chiefs and their headmen were rewarded 'for good work' done. In general court clerks and messengers depended on these local treasuries for their pay, each official being a charge on the court he served. The chiefs too got their sitting fees from the same source.[42] For much of this period the control of the expenditure of the courts was vested in the divisional commissioner, subject in certain cases to the authorisation of the high commissioner and in other cases to his confirmation. Each court was empowered to spend, with the approval of the divisional commissioner, not more than five pounds on an improvement work in its area of authority. Before giving his approval the political officer was to satisfy himself that the expenditure could be incurred without embarrassment to the financial position of the court. In this way it was hoped an effective check would be kept on injudicious expenditure. If a court desired to spend more than five pounds on a project, it had to obtain the approval of the divisional commissioner, who in turn had to seek the sanction of the high commissioner. From 1906 this sanction had to come from the provincial commissioner.[43]

---

[40] See ch. 7
[41] CSO 1/13, Despatches to FO and CO. See Despatch No. 167 of 3.10.99
[42] CSO 1/13, Despatches to FO and CO. See Despatch No. 167 of 3.10.99 and No. 16 of 7.1.03
[43] CSO 1/13, Despatches to FO and CO. See Despatch No. 409 of 26.8.03. C.176/19 Remarks by F. P. Lynch, etc. See Conf OG 35/20 of 30.3.20 from Resident, Ogoja Province

To Moor the chief merit of the institution of local treasury was its educative value to the Warrant Chiefs. He believed that the participation of the chiefs in the expenditure of these local funds provided them with 'an object lesson in civilised administration' and he hoped that by means of it they would be made to realise that the position which they occupied was one of power and trust. It was for this reason that he ordered that no expenditure, except on the clerical staff, should be made without the consent of the court members.[44] Here was an institution which with patience and understanding could have been developed to the great benefit of the people.

The Native Treasury is generally regarded as having been invented in Northern Nigeria. According to the accepted chronology of events Lugard laid the foundation of the institution between 1900 and 1906 by streamlining direct taxation in the emirates and by establishing the practice by which the emir retained a stated fraction of the proceeds of direct taxation in his emirate for meeting the traditional obligations of his office. Then between 1906 and 1911 Herbert Richmond Palmer completed the edifice by institutionalising the Native Treasury through converting the fraction of the yields of taxation hitherto retained by the emir into the fund of the Native Administration, out of which the personal salary of the emir and the public needs of the emirate were met and which was then subjected to a regular check. It has been contended, rather unconvincingly, by the admirers of Emirate Indirect Rule that the basic principle of the Native Treasury is that its main revenue is derived from direct taxation. By this questionable criterion the experiment described above which Moor initiated in the nineteenth century would not qualify for the name 'Native Treasury'.

It is, however, contended here and elsewhere[45] by the present writer that the essence of the Native Treasury, as of all local finance under any local government system, is that a local authority should not be entirely dependent on the central government for the money it requires for meeting local needs. Seen in this light therefore, and from the foregoing, it

[44] CSO 1/13, Despatches to FO and CO. See Despatch No. 409 of 26.8.03
[45] A. E. Afigbo, 'The Native Treasury Question Under The Warrant Chief System In Eastern Nigeria 1899–1929', in *ODU*, University of Ife, iv, 1 July 1967

is clear that Sir Ralph Moor anticipated Lugard and Palmer in this matter. By 1899 the system under which each Native Council and Minor Court was made to have its own treasury and disburse its funds under the guidance of the district commissioner was already firmly established and widespread in the Niger Coast Protectorate. In that year Moor routinely reported to the Foreign Secretary that

> by this means (i.e. the funds of the Native Treasuries) Court Houses are erected for the administration of justice and good roads made from village to village, and other works of public utility carried out.[46]

Moor's policy in this regard, as in other matters, was faithfully continued by his successor, Sir Walter Egerton.

The formalisation of the structure, and to a large extent of the philosophy, of the local government system of the Protectorate of Southern Nigeria was thus largely the achievement of Sir Ralph Moor. By the system he set up the Government of the Protectorate was able to maintain some measure of contact, albeit perfunctory and unsatisfactory, with the people.[47] It does not appear that this achievement of no mean importance would have been possible if Sir Ralph Moor were as black as Professor Anene sought to paint him in the pages of his *Southern Nigeria in Transition 1885–1906*. It may be true that the history of the Protectorate under Moor was more punctuated with 'punitive' expeditions than was the case under Macdonald. But then, it must be borne in mind that while Macdonald dealt mainly with coastal communities which had already lost their political independence by 1891, Moor had to impose British rule on hinterland communities which still cherished untrammelled independence and entertained deep-rooted suspicion of the white man. Anene's prejudice against Moor is undoubted. He even attributed to Moor expeditions which took place long after he had

[46] CSO 1/13, Despatches to FO and CO. See Despatch No. 167 of 3.10.99
[47] CSO 1/13, Despatches to FO and CO. See Despatch No. 139 of 18.8.98. Moor was a strong believer in the need for constant contact between the administration and the people. On this he wrote in the despatch quoted above: 'I am of course taking it for granted that the Administrator should spend a considerable portion of his time in moving about the territories for in my opinion it is not possible for a man to be an able Administrator in Africa without almost continuous contact with the Natives.'

left the service of the Protectorate.[48] This is not the place to rehabilitate the much neglected and maligned Sir Ralph Moor. But it is in place to state that an objective study of his administrative, economic and educational policies clearly shows him as a realistic and painstaking administrator, one of the real founders of effective British authority in Southern Nigeria.[49] This conclusion has been confirmed independently by Mr Nicolson in his full-scale and critical study of the administration of colonial Nigeria.[50]

Moor left Southern Nigeria in 1903 and was succeeded by Sir Walter Egerton in 1904. In 1906 the Southern Nigeria Protectorate was amalgamated with the Lagos Colony and Protectorate and brought under one governor. The same year the new political unit was divided for administrative purposes into Lagos or Western, Niger or Central, and Calabar or Eastern, Provinces. These were large territorial and administrative units. For instance, the Eastern Province comprised what in 1914 became the Provinces of Calabar, Owerri and Ogoja. The Central Province comprised what later became Benin, Warri and Onitsha Provinces. What was more, the men who were appointed commissioners and placed in charge of these three provinces in 1906 – Widenham Fosbery (Western), Fredrick Seton James (Central) and Horace Bedwell (Eastern) – were officers who had seen service in Southern Nigeria from the earliest days of British administration on the coast.[51] A man like F. S. James was said in 1900 to know more of the area lying between the Niger and Cross Rivers, a territory then believed to be under the rule of the Aro, than any other officer in the service of the Protectorate.[52] It was therefore to be expected that these officers should be given extensive responsibilities in administrative matters and that these powers should be reflected in their increased control over the Native Courts and their members.

[48] J. C. Anene, *Southern Nigeria*, p. 181. There he wrote: 'Military expeditions dominated the history of the period 1896–1906 because Ralph Moor believed in the efficacy of punitive expedition. . . .' Here it is only fair to note that Moor left Southern Nigeria in 1903.
[49] A. E. Afigbo, 'The Background to the Southern Nigeria Education Code of 1903', in *JHSN*, iv, 2, 1968. A. E. Afigbo, 'Sir Ralph Moor and the Economic Development of Southern Nigeria 1896–1903', in *JHSN*, Dec. 1970
[50] I. F. Nicolson
[51] *Government Gazette*, 2 May 1906 (Lagos), notifications 2 and 3
[52] CSO 1/13, Despatches to FO and CO. See Despatch No. 287 of 7.9.01

This need, together with the decision to bring the Warrant Chief System in its judicial aspect more directly under the judicial department, and the general need for reorganisation as a result of the 1906 amalgamation, led to the enactment of the Native Courts Ordinance of 1906, which then superseded the Native Courts Proclamation of 1901. The new ordinance did not inaugurate any spectacular departure from the general pattern spelled out by Moor but introduced a few modifications in detail. Only the important additions need be discussed here.

The provincial commissioner and the assistant district commissioner were included as *ex officio* members of the Native Court and whenever they or the district commissioner presided over a Minor Court it acquired the powers and dignity of a Native Council. This was further proof of the contention that it was generally believed by the administration that only the presence of a European officer in, or his close identification with, these courts could qualify the chiefs to exercise large judicial powers. The provincial commissioner could at any time sit as the president of any court in his province, and the presidents, vice-presidents, members and officers of the Native Courts in his province were made subject to his direction.[53]

The Native Court became subject to the orders of the chief justice or of any other judge of the Supreme Court as far as its judicial duties were concerned. The chief justice or a puisne judge could at any stage in the trial of a case transfer it from one Native Court to another or to the Supreme or the Commissioner's Court, and a Native Court could of its motion apply for the transfer of a case. Every month each Native Court had to forward to the chief justice or a judge appointed by him a full list of the criminal cases decided by it in which penalties of more than twenty pounds' fine or three months' imprisonment had been imposed. This list operated as an automatic appeal on behalf of every convicted person whose name appeared on it, and the chief justice or puisne judge could, 'without hearing any argument', annul or amend the judgment.[54] Thus the subordination to the Supreme Court of the Native Court system in its judicial aspect, a process which began with Moor, became complete under Egerton. The Native Court became in fact the local judicial arm of the British Court. Presumably this arrangement was made in

[53] *Laws of the Colony of Southern Nigeria*, ii, 1908, pp. 1267–8
[54] *Ibid.*, p. 1272

order to ensure that Native Courts dispensed justice in accordance with British conceptions of it.

This total subordination of the Native Court system to the Supreme Court marked the triumph of the legal system and ideas of the Lagos Colony and Protectorate over those of Southern Nigeria. It may be true, as Nicolson has persuasively argued, that Sir Walter Egerton's plan for the amalgamation of the two Southern administrations 'was not a scheme for complete fusion', since he (Egerton) held the 'idea . . . that a partial fusion would permit the retention of the different methods of administration until the time came to amalgamate the whole of Nigeria'.[55] But the provisions of the Native Courts Ordinance of 1906 clearly show that Egerton was unable to resist successfully the clamour of the Lagos lawyers for larger doses of English judicial procedure and, perhaps, his own innate convictions as a trained lawyer that the Supreme Court system of law administration, since it was the closest local approximation to the English system, represented for 'primitive' peoples the far-off divine legal system towards which all tribal judicial institutions and practices should move. Thus Professor Flint talks of 'the Southern Nigeria Protectorate [falling] under the sway of Lagos'.[56] But while pressing home this point and deprecating the subversive effects of the arrangement on indigenous legal systems and institutions, one should also emphasise that Egerton, like all paternalistic colonial governors, believed that it was good for the people. Professor Anene commented:

> It is fair to add that the subordination of the Native Courts to the Supreme Court Judges was a measure of the awareness of the administration that a great deal of injustice and terrorism might otherwise be inflicted on innocent but impecunious natives alleged to have committed an offence against the many but hardly comprehensible proclamations and regulations issued by the 'big white man . . .'[57]

Meanwhile, the 'opening' up of the country had been proceeding rapidly. The previous year Colonel Moorhouse had subjugated the Onitsha hinterland; Abakaliki Division had been 'opened' with the defeat of Ezza, and Ikot Ekpene Division was speedily being brought under control. In the year 1906 Okigwi Division

[55] Nicolson, p. 100
[56] J. E. Flint, 'Nigeria: The Colonial Experience from 1880 to 1914', in *Colonialism in Africa 1870–1960*, eds L. H. Gann and P. Duignan, p. 250
[57] Anene, *Southern Nigeria*, p. 266

was started with headquarters first at Umuduru and then at its present location.[58] This rapid expansion underlined for the authorities the importance of the Native Court as the outpost of the new order of things which the British represented. In this situation the chances of the institution making a lasting impression on a recently subdued area depended on its ability to suppress violence with promptitude. As a recognition of this fact the new ordinance provided that every member and officer of a Native Court as well as every Warrant Chief and headman could, within his own area of authority, arrest without warrant a person who committed, or was charged on oath with having committed, a breach of traditional or protectorate laws.[59]

By 1908 some of the coastal areas and the hinterland regions immediately adjoining them had been under Native Court rule for over fifteen years. In such areas these institutions were coming to win a measure of acceptance, albeit unenthusiastic. This meant that many more people were taking their complaints to the courts. The administration, however, saw this as evidence of 'litigiousness' on the part of the people. It was partly to check this so-called litigiousness and partly to make the courts more self-supporting in view of their enlarged personnel that the cost for taking out a summons from the Native Courts was raised in 1908. Where the claim did not exceed ten pounds or the suit was not for the recovery of goods but for other type of relief the summons cost five shillings. If the claim arose more than five years before the application for relief was made or was more than ten pounds the fee was doubled. A criminal summons, which was formerly free, now cost five shillings unless it was issued at the instance of the president or the vice-president of the court. From all indications it would appear that people had abused the earlier concession in criminal matters.[60]

The structural organisation of the executive side of the Warrant Chief System in these early years is of great interest. All messages from the government to a Warrant Chief passed from the district officer to the court clerk. Then the latter either sent for the chief

[58] Conf 21/05: Ezza Country, Unsettled state of; 236/06, Ikot Ekpene: Handing Over Notes; E3828/08, Report on Okigwi District for Nov. 1908. See also Report on Okigwi District for 1906 by Capt. Heathecote – Unnumbered, located at Enugu Archives.
[59] *Laws of the Colony of Southern Nigeria*, ii, 1908, p. 1277
[60] *Government Gazette*, 9 Sept. 1908, p. 1299

or sent a court messenger to convey the message or instructions to him. Theoretically the Warrant Chief then carried out the order. In practice, however, each Warrant Chief parcelled out the area under his control into wards over each of which he appointed a headman or a messenger known among the Ibo as *Udumani*. It was these headmen who in fact formed the ultimate agents for carrying out the orders of the government. This development started early in the history of the Warrant Chief System. In many places the demand for chiefs had led to each ward of the village pushing forward its representative, whether he was the traditional ward head or not. Generally only one of these got a warrant and the others automatically became the representatives of the Warrant Chief in the wards. In other places where the Warrant Chiefs were ambitious and scheming men eager for power, they chose their own representatives without any reference to the wards concerned. In all cases, however, care was taken to choose strong and audacious young men, for the duties of a headman called for a man endowed with these qualities.[61]

The headman, in cooperation with the court messenger, arrested criminals against whom warrants had been issued, served summonses, recruited forced labour under the Roads and Creeks Ordinance, gathered in carriers, saw to the maintenance of rest houses and ensured that a touring government officer was provided with water, firewood and the like. These were unpopular jobs and their execution entailed, especially early in the history of the administration, forceful conscription of young men. It was also the duty of headmen to follow their chief to the court whenever it was his turn to sit, and it was through them that litigants wanting to influence their master approached him.[62]

The central government soon accorded recognition to this spontaneous development. Headmen who did their work satisfactorily and were well spoken of before the political officer got

[61] *Udumani* was an early Ibo rendering of the English word *Headman*: now it would be *Edimani*. Information collected from Chief Nwancho Atuma (Ikwo, Abakaliki), Ukpai Ereshi (Agba, Abakaliki), Samson Onyeama (Ohuhu, Bende), Chief Mbabuike Ogujiofo (Ihube, Okigwi) and many others.

[62] Information collected from the men mentioned in footnote 61 above and from Chief Jonah Ikpe (Ibekwe, Opobo), Chief Udo Udo Ibanga (Ikot Ekpene Town), Jacob Aweze (Ezzagu, Abakaliki), B. N. Aniekwe (Abakaliki Town).

official recognition in the form of caps. One of them could also hope to step into his master's shoes in the event of his death or dismissal. The practice of giving caps was started at Ikot Ekpene by the district commissioner, Mr Reginald Hargrove. He gave fez caps bearing metal engravings of the crown to all Warrant Chiefs and satisfactory headmen, and special staffs with decorated heads to chiefs who were considered more influential than others. This created a new hierarchy of status in society. An ambitious and successful young man could become a 'capped' headman, then a Warrant Chief and perhaps earn a staff. The 'cap and staff' system proved very popular and spread from Ikot Ekpene to other divisions. It gave political officers a firmer control over the headmen and the chiefs. To be deprived of one's cap or staff was an obvious disgrace, a proof that the victim had been found wanting in certain respects. But to lose one's warrant was a more serious affair; in fact it was regarded as a political and economic calamity, for with the warrant went the right to sit in court, the prestige and authority one enjoyed in his village and the spoils of office attaching to these. The 'cap and staff' system made the chiefs and their headmen more painstaking and more zealous in the discharge of their duties. In course of time, however, it was to prove politically and socially disruptive.[63]

Throughout the years before 1914, and even after, most officers who were brought up under the system described above

---

[63] OW 413/16 Caps and Staff System at Orlu and Okigwi. See Enclosure No. 27/13/20 of 24.1.20 from DO, Okigwi Division to the President, Owerri Province, E 1108/12 Caps and Sticks Owerri Province. See Enclosure No. 279/Indent 24/14 of 28.4.14 from J. C. Maxwell, Commissioner, Owerri. Also the file OW 715/15 Uniforms for Warrant Chiefs. See Enclosure 1, letter No. 636/15 of 21.12.15. In the letter just cited the District Officer, Aba, advocated a distinctive uniform for Warrant Chiefs. 'I am much in favour,' he wrote, 'of allowing Warrant Chiefs to wear some distinguishing mark. The following suggestion is submitted for consideration (a) Warrant Chiefs should be allowed to wear a long flannel cloth shirt of cerise (Nigerian) colour, with a band of dark green round the neck forming a "V" on the chest in front. That the arms of Nigeria be worked on the pocket in green silk. The colours are picturesque and will be appreciated. (b) A double terai hat of dark green with a cerise plume or feather with a small silver badge of the arms of Nigeria to pin on the front of the hat. This is a type of hat commonly worn by chiefs and is much preferred by them to the fez, which is not sufficient protection against the sun.' If this suggestion had been implemented it would have, in the minds of the people, completed the transformation of the Warrant Chiefs into outright government employees like the court messengers or even the Nigeria police.

looked upon it as good. In 1903 Mr Justice M. R. Menendes described it as without parallel in West Africa.[64] In 1907 the Commissioner, Eastern Province, wrote: 'This system has worked well and the increasing demand for the establishment of new Native Courts shows the trust and confidence which the courts enjoy among the Native population.'[65] An objective assessment reveals, however, that even in the years before 1914 the system had many shortcomings. The many precautions which had been taken to ensure that it functioned smoothly proved largely unavailing.

The control which the Supreme Court was allowed to exercise over the Native Court had proved both ineffective and harmful. The Supreme Court itself was understaffed and had only about three or four judges, who, apart from their normal judicial duties, had to review all cases tried by the Supreme, District, Police Magistrate and Native Courts in the Central and Eastern Provinces. In 1912, 44,800 cases needed review. Apart from the practical impossibility of three or four men giving this large number of cases adequate attention, there was the extra handicap that the cases which came to them from the Native Courts were poorly reported by the half-literate court clerks.[66] In fact some of these cases were so complicated that they could be understood only by the man on the spot. It was highly doubtful whether Supreme Court supervision, apart from discovering laxities among a few district commissioners, directly conduced to the dispensation of justice in any way. There is evidence from the days of Sir Ralph Moor's high commissionership that the work of supervising and organising the judicial side of the Native Courts was more than the chronically short-staffed Judicial Department could cope with. Chief Justice H. G. Kelly of Southern Nigeria wrote in 1903,

> When the Native Courts were recently constituted, Sir Ralph Moor informed me that they were to be placed under the Judicial Department, and I thereupon pointed out to him that having regard to the great volume of judicial work here, it was practically impossible for one man to supervise them satisfactorily, which he readily admitted at the time and it was agreed that these courts which numbered about 69 and are continually increasing as time goes on, should until other arrangements were made remain temporarily only under the Judicial Department.

[64] CSO 1/13, Despatches to FO and CO. See the attachment to Despatch No. 16 of 7.1.03.   [65] *Southern Nigeria Annual Report 1907*, p. 36
[66] B 486/1914, New Court System – Reasons for Introduction

Chief Justice Kelly also objected to the arrangement on the ground that this work of supervision, which was administrative rather than judicial, was not a proper assignment for the Judicial Department. He therefore suggested that 'a separate Department such as exists in other colonies should be constructed for this purpose'.[67] But as already has been shown, nothing was done in this regard. Instead the Native Courts were brought more and more under the Supreme Court, with the results already sketched.

Instead of proving helpful the subordination of the Native Court to the Supreme Court was pernicious. It tended to incapacitate the divisional commissioner, who feared that his intervention in a case might be set aside by the puisne judge on grounds of some obscure legal technicality. The belief of certain political officers that the Supreme Court would scrutinise all cases tended to make them neglect their duties. The knowledge that the record of a case could be called for by the Supreme Court made the political officer, whenever he was present, encumber the Native Court with rigid adherence to procedural minutiae.[68]

The right of appeal to the Supreme Court created a loophole for the intervention of legal practitioners whom the government had wanted to exclude from the Native Courts. A litigant who lost his case in one of these courts was usually besieged by a horde of cut-throats eager to lend him money with which to appeal. While investigating abuses in one court in 1909, W. Buchanan-Smith discovered that these money-lenders included the court clerk, the messengers and often the Warrant Chiefs also, who generally followed a disappointed litigant out of court to persuade him to borrow from them at exorbitant rates of interest the money with which to pay for a counsel and an appeal. Hovering around the courts too were lawyers' touts who solicited clients for their masters and made defeated litigants pay them considerations before they took them to their master. The result for the litigant was generally more debt incurred from bootless litigation and further prosecution for debt. In any case the provision for appeal from a Native to the Supreme Court fostered protracted litigation.[69]

[67] CSO 1/15, Southern Nigeria Confidential Despatches to CO, 1900–7. See Despatch No. 7 of 11.9.03 and the Enclosure from Mr Kelly, Chief Justice, dated 10.9.03.
[68] OW 122/16, Native Courts – Memorandum On, the whole file. See especially paras 5 and 6
[69] CSO 26/3, File No. 24412, Comments on the Aba Commission of Inquiry Report – see minute by the Lieutenant Governor Southern

Also the constant supervision by the European political officer in which both Moor and Egerton trusted for attaining efficiency in the courts could not be secured. As the courts grew in number and the duties of the political officer grew in volume and complexity it became impossible for the administrative officer to be present at every meeting of each court in his district. It was not even possible for him to attend all the meetings of the court sitting at his headquarters. R. C. Sayer, District Commissioner for Aba, complained in 1911:

> Here, in common with other Districts the really necessary work is much impeded by a mass of monthly and weekly returns, which have to be sent in. As every Provincial Head of Department can call for any fresh return which comes into his head, the list is constantly increasing. . . . Many of these returns are redundant and obviously unnecessary.[70]

Routine office work was already interfering with political work, especially with the effective supervision of the courts. An examination of available statistics on the attendance of district commissioners at ten Native Courts will help to illustrate this point.

Native Court	Year	No. of sittings	No. presided over by district commissioner
Calabar		78	24
Creek Town		31	1
Eastern Ekoi	Jan. and Sept. 1905	11	1
Uwet		18	—
Adiabo		15	—
Owerri		89	12
Aba		56	8
Degema	June–Sept. 1914	69	37
Ahoada		34	9
Okigwi		76	31

The Chief Justice, commenting on the statistics from the Calabar District, said: 'If the Native Council of Calabar and other courts in the District give wrong decisions it is probably due to want of supervision by the District Commissioner or the Assistant District Commissioner.'[71] There was thus a pressing

Provinces (hereinafter LGSP), para. 71. C 176/19, Remarks by F. P. Lynch, etc. See Enclosure Conf No. 30/20 of 20.1.20 from Mr Sasse, para. 19
[70] E 2227/11, Half-Yearly Report on Aba District dated 1.7.11 para. 17
[71] Conf 152/5, Native Courts Calabar – the entire file. OW 122/16, Native Courts – Memorandum on. In this memo. the resident for Owerri wrote:

need for a revision of the whole basis of Native Court organisation east of the Niger.

The failure of the political officer to attend the meetings of the courts regularly had also given the constitution of the Warrant Chief system an unforeseen twist. It had led to a situation in which the court and its proceedings were dominated by the court clerk – an evil which was to grow from strength to strength and, in spite of all checks, was to attain alarming heights after 1914.[72] With his western education, which enabled him to understand better than the illiterate chiefs the 'mysteries' of the Native Court regulations, which were patterned on those of the Supreme Court, the clerk was able to assume status and powers which were not assigned to him by law. Indeed, there were court areas where it was widely accepted by the people and their chiefs that he had the power to choose sitting members, to discipline by long periods of suspension or by open disgrace chiefs who disagreed with him, and to interfere with the trial of cases as well as influence their outcome. Some clerks were reported to have assumed the airs and powers of administrative officers and by so doing to have made the chief very submissive to their whims and caprices.[73]

What was worse, the pretensions of the clerks were matched neither by efficiency nor honesty on their part in the discharge of their official duties. Between 1900 and 1906 in the Akwete District the clerks, with the probable exception of Mr Allen, who was at Obohia, were frequently accused of corruptly making considerable sums of money by charging ignorant litigants excessive court fees and pocketing the difference.[74] Nothing was more damaging to the reputation of the court clerks in this period than the reports

'The statistics for Court sittings in this Province for June and September Quarters of 1914 – the last six months during which the old system functioned – are as follows: At Owerri the Native Court sat 89 days the District Commissioner (DC) was present only 12; at Aba the Court sat 56 days, the DC was present 8; New Calabar Court at Degema sat 69 days the DC was present 37; the Ahoada Court sat on 34 days, the DC was present on 9; the Okigwi Court sat on 76 days, the DC was present on 31. In some of the outlying Courts, nothing was even seen of the DC during this period.'

[72] See ch. 5

[73] B 486/1914, New Court System, Reason for Introduction, Memorandum by H. O. S. Wright

[74] Calprof 10/1, Minutes 1900–6. See letter from Ag. Divisional Commissioner, Eastern Division to Secretary, Calabar

of the travelling supervisors of Native Courts. In 1912 Mr Archibong III, Assistant Travelling Supervisor of Native Courts, toured the courts of Owerri District only to find that 'the work of the clerks generally had not been satisfactory'. The clerks 'charged' insufficient fees, and where they had received correct fees and fines had entered in the cash book either a smaller amount than was received or nothing at all. The accounting situation in the two Minor Courts of Ngor and Nguru will suffice to illustrate this point. In the Ngor Court there were seven instances in which the fees should have been ten shillings each but in each case only five shillings were 'charged', while in two other cases the fee should have been one pound each but only ten shillings were 'charged' in either case. In two cases dealt with by the Nguru Court the clerk 'charged' five shillings instead of ten shillings for each, in four others ten shillings instead of one pound for each; and then four fines were paid but no traces were found of them in the cash book.[75]

A similar report submitted by Mr Bob-Manuel on the courts of Aba District was equally damaging to the reputation of the court clerks. To his surprise Bob-Manuel discovered that the clerks, with one exception, did not know the fees to be paid by litigants before obtaining copies of court proceedings. Yet these were laid down in specific instruction.[76] Throughout the district no receipt books were kept for money which was either received or paid out. The value of property claimed by litigants and what time each claim arose were not stated, with the result that the right summons fees could not be 'charged'. At Azumini the dates on the cash book, the cause book and the counterfoils of writs did not agree.[77] These discrepancies in accounting were partly the result of deliberate dishonesty and partly due to poor education. In this

[75] E 1280/12, Native Courts Owerri District, Reports and Queries by Assistant Travelling Supervisor of Native Courts. See Queries No. 4/11 and 6/11. It must be pointed out that the entries did not necessarily show how much the clerks actually charged in each case. Being very corrupt the clerks must have pocketed parts of what they actually collected for the courts and then confused issues by incorrect entries and claims of ignorance.

[76] These were 2s. for the first 150 words and 1s. for each additional 100 words or part thereof. This was to be paid in stamps to be placed on the counterfoil. Search Book in the custody of the Administrative Officer. *Nigerian Gazette*, 1908, p. 1298

[77] E 660/13, Native Courts, Aba District, Report on the accounts of by Ag. Travelling Supervisor of Native Courts, Mr Bob-Manuel

period court clerks were generally men of 'little dangerous knowledge' owing to the fact that the poor rate of pay drove away better educated men, while the searing scrutiny and emphasis on the technicalities of the job which followed the visits of travelling supervisors scared off others. In 1903 Mr Justice Menendez while on an inspection tour of the Native Courts experienced some difficulty in persuading the recently employed clerk of the Okrika Native Council to remain in his position. The clerk's reluctance derived from his feeling unequal to the rigorous system of book-keeping then existing at Degema. It was the same thing with the clerk of the then recently established Umukurushi Minor Court.[78]

The travelling supervisors did good work in enforcing discipline and making the Native Courts adhere to legal rules. As a result of their vigilance in 1907 245 queries involving a total of £290 were issued in the Eastern Province alone. Before the end of the year 166 of these queries were answered and £175 recovered.[79] In spite of these, however, the supervisors themselves were not immune from laxity and corruption. For a period of two and a half years they did not visit the Native Courts of Owerri District and for that length of time the accounts were unaudited. When Mr Archibong III visited the district in 1912 he could audit the accounts only from June 1909 to December 1911.[80] The story of one Mr R. M. Jumbo, Assistant Supervisor of Native Courts for the Eastern Province, will serve to show that these officials too were at times men of little faith.

On taking over Opobo District in July 1912, Mr Reginald Hargrove discovered that, contrary to authorised practice, there was no general expenditure book for the Native Courts of the District. When he recalled the abstracts for the quarters ending March and June from Calabar, he discovered that the entries were altogether incorrect. Later, all the court clerks confessed to him that they had been accustomed to alter the entries in respect of expenditure and receipts so as to force the abstracts to balance. These abstracts had always gone to Jumbo, who, after checking, presented them to the district commissioner for signature.

[78] CSO 1/13, Despatches to FO and CO. See Justice Menendez's Report attatched to Despatch No. 16 of 7.1.03
[79] *Southern Nigeria Annual Report*, 1907, p. 36
[80] E 1280/12, Native Courts Owerri District Reports and Queries by Assistant Travelling Supervisor of Native Courts, para. 2

Neither he nor the political officer who preceded Mr Hargrove in Opobo 'discovered' these gaping flaws in the accounting: a proof that no firm checking was applied. Nor was that all. According to the system then obtaining at Opobo the clerks submitted to Jumbo at the end of each month their books together with cash representing the difference between receipts and expenditure. They added the latter in pencil. They also sent to him manillas which they received as court fees and fines. Jumbo was then expected to audit the books, check and ink the pencil addition, sell the manillas and credit the sales on the receipt side. After these he was expected to present the books to the district commissioner for signature. It was now discovered, however, that in some cases Mr Jumbo had added the sales from the manillas on both the receipt and expenditure sides, thus making it possible for the sum to disappear 'safely' into his pocket. In some cases the proceeds from the sales were not shown at all while in one entry there appeared 'payment of £1 to Mr Jumbo for manillas sold to him'.[81]

It was further discovered that Mr Jumbo had at one time taken seven pounds ten shillings, and at another two pounds ten shillings for the purchase of handcuffs and chairs respectively for the courts in Opobo District, but had misused the money. Inquiries revealed that Mr Jumbo was actually in embarrassed financial circumstances and that his creditors were already applying for summonses against him.[82] Mr R. M. Jumbo's career and the fact that he could indulge in such impudent dishonesty for months without discovery were convincing proofs that the safety mechanism of the structure set up by Moor and Egerton had hopelessly broken down. By the end of the first decade of this century, therefore, the system was due for review, but not necessarily the type of review to which it was subjected under Lugard between 1914 and 1919.

The House Rule Proclamation of 1901, the act by which Moor had hoped to halt the decline in the authority of the coastal chiefs, was also being undermined by the progress of events. Many things in this period demonstrated its growing anachronism. While it prevented the house members from running off at will

[81] Conf 410/1912, Jumbo (Mr) R. M. Assistant Supervisor of Native Courts, Eastern Province, Arrest of etc. See letter from Mr Hargrove dated 16.10.12.
[82] *Ibid.*

3 Chief Young Briggs, a Warrant Chief of Abonema, with his son, 1905

4 Sir Ralph Moor, Consul-General of Niger Coast Protectorate 1896-1900, High Commissioner of the Protectorate of Southern Nigeria 1900-1903

and thus offended 'progressive' elements like the missionaries, it failed in visibly increasing the authority of the house heads. The latter had become very lazy and rarely, if ever, visited the distant inland markets where their boys traded. The result was that the boys lacked control and on occasions precipitated disturbances in the interior which often led to military patrol. The chiefs gave the right granted them to settle petty disputes between their house members privately such a liberal interpretation that they began to handle cases which should have gone to the Native Courts; and for these cases they charged fees contrary to law.[83]

It was further discovered that the proclamation had over-emphasised the duties which house members owed to their chiefs, while leaving very vague the duties which the house heads owed to their house members. This situation encouraged indolence among the house heads. Also it encouraged them to develop that narrowness of outlook which made them see the house as made for them and not they for the house. In consequence there were widespread complaints against the Bonny, Opobo and Degema heads of houses. As early as 1905 F. W. Sampson, acting commissioner for the then Eastern Division, had called for an amendment to this proclamation and the redefinition of the duties of house heads towards their members individually and collectively. But while Mr W. Fosbery, the provincial commissioner, agreed with Sampson's strictures on the law, he refused 'to hasten its end by trying to amend it'.[84] The subsequent amendment of 1912, which made it possible for house members to purchase their freedom, was a tardy acknowledgement of the fact that the House Rule Proclamation had become outdated and useless. After this its final repeal was a matter of time.

In spite of the shortcomings analysed above, the period covered in this chapter was one of comparative quiet for the Warrant Chiefs and their makers. This was partly because the years 1900 to 1915 coincided roughly with the period when the Ibo, Ibibio, Ijo and Ogoja peoples were being conquered. The turmoil and the widespread fear of the white man that characterised this

[83] Conf 133/5, Native House Law No. 26 of 1901. See letter from Mr Sampson dated 5.8.05.
[84] *Ibid*. See Minute by Honourable Provincial Commissioner. He wrote: 'There is a good deal in what Mr Divisional Commissioner says. . . . I certainly will not touch the law myself. It is a useful tho[ugh] archaic piece of legislation which is doomed as it is, but I don't want to hasten its end by trying to amend it.'

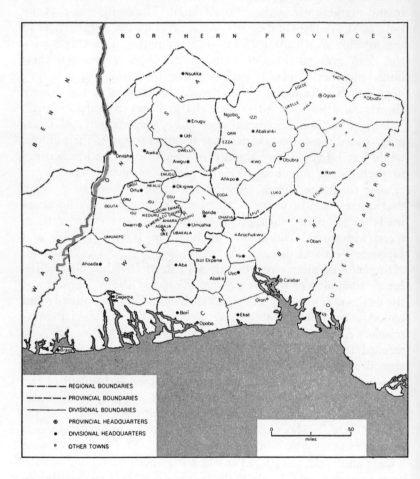

The Eastern Provinces in 1922

period favoured the Warrant Chiefs, court clerks and messengers, and enabled them to build up the power which they wielded with great effect for many years after. 'The men put forward as Warrant Chiefs in the early days,' observed Mr Ferguson, Divisional Officer at Owerri, 'quickly consolidated their position through the Native Courts . . . and attained their maximum power about 1915. Since then their power has decreased partly because times do not permit of the same means being employed.'[85]

For much, if not the whole, of the years before 1915 the minds of the indigenous people were dominated by the first shock of the encounter with the newcomers and the universal demonstration of British military invincibility. Furthermore, there was too much for the Warrant Chiefs to do. Roads, court houses and quarters for the court staff had to be built, carriers were constantly being requisitioned and all the orders for these were executed through the 'new men' attached to the novel institution of the Native Court. Any disobedience of these orders or molestation of the 'new men' who transmitted them to the people brought swift punishments. In this way it came to be accepted by the peoples of the area that these 'new men' were the authentic voice of the Colonial Government.

There were also other factors which operated in favour of these men. The status of a Warrant Chief or a court messenger was not as yet an enviable one. For a long time it continued to be the fashion to regard the 'new men' as people given in tribute to white men. For as long as this view lasted people declined to be closely identified with the Native Court. In the interior recruitment into the court messenger service continued for many years to be by means of conscription.[86] Because of the general attitude of hostility to the idea of being a Warrant Chief or a court messenger those who became either court members or messengers or clerks enjoyed what might be called a security of tenure in this period. There was very little scheming to unseat any of them in order to succeed him, unlike in the period after about 1915.

[85] 61/1924, Annual Report Owerri Division 1924, p. 2
[86] Chief Mbabuike of Ihube, Okigwi, who became a court messenger around 1909, said he was conscripted into the service. He deserted a number of times but on each occasion was caught, thrashed and confined to the lock-up in order to persuade him to accept the post. He submitted to recruitment only after his family had begged him to do so if, as he put it, 'I did not want the white man to kill them'.

Another factor which in this period guaranteed security of tenure to these men was the fact that owing to the general lack of sophistication on the part of the local people it needed an extraordinarily courageous and desperate man to proceed to headquarters to report a chief or court staff for oppression, bribery or extortion. Even if a man did report, it was at this time the official policy to support the chiefs as much as possible. Added to this was the fact that it was generally known that the Warrant Chiefs often sat with the district officer to try cases. This gave them further prestige and protection. 'The political officer being associated with the Native Administration [in the pre-1914 years],' said S. W. Sproston, the Resident of Ogoja, in 1920, 'was a visible support to the chiefs whereas at present [in post-1914] it is somewhat veiled.'[87] The extent to which the court and its personnel benefited from the reflected glory of the political officers is illustrated by the fact that to this day an investigator meets people who proudly refer to the fact that their fathers, as Warrant Chiefs, sat in the same court with district commissioners. Along the coast, where a long tradition of general sophistication should have made it easy for the oppressed to complain vociferously, the operation of the House Rule Proclamation was an effective instrument for checking revolt against 'established' authority. In delta traditions the final collapse of the political authority of the so-called chiefs is widely dated from the repeal of the House Rule Proclamation in 1915.[88]

Also aiding the Warrant Chiefs and court staff to consolidate their position in this period was the fact that for long these 'new men' were only feeling their way to power. They were still subject to the general initial fear of white men, and the popular belief that the government had a mysterious way of finding out things which were supposedly hidden. For long too the Warrant Chiefs were in the habit of telling the village elders the purposes and results of their visit to headquarters. They were still to a large extent what the people expected them to be – those who went between the local community and the government. But towards the end of the period the chiefs and their headmen became more confident, realised their independence of village elders and, by acting in accordance with this new awakening, stirred up oppo-

[87] C 176/19, Remarks by F. P. Lynch, etc. See Memo. Conf OG 25/1920 dated 30.3.20 from Resident, Ogoja.
[88] See next chapter

sition. In this earlier period the court staff too were more restrained than they became later.[89] Thus the period of Lugard's governor-generalship marked the end of an epoch in more ways than one. Firstly, it saw the inauguration of Lugard's scheme for introducing into the South the pattern of Indirect Rule which he had instituted in the North. Secondly, it marked the beginning of the era during which the full impact of those forces which eventually helped to discredit the Warrant Chief system was felt. The next chapter deals with the events of this momentous period in the history of the Warrant Chief System.

[89] It must be said that in the case of the court clerk he felt from the beginning that though lower than the political officer he was higher than any chief. It was the more or less closer supervision of those days that came near to keeping him in his place. Based on information collected from Chief Ukpai Ereshi (Agba, Abakaliki), an ex-Warrant Chief; Chief Obiukuru Nze (Umulolo, Okigwi), ex-Warrant Chief.

4 Lugard and Lugardism in Southeastern Nigeria, 1912–19

In 1912 Sir Frederick John Dealtry Lugard returned to Nigeria charged with the duty of amalgamating the Colony and Protectorate of Southern Nigeria with the Protectorate of Northern Nigeria. It was while carrying out this assignment that he attempted to dismantle the local government system which his predecessors in Southern Nigeria had set up. He then struggled, but failed, to erect one that would be in line with his own ideas of how the affairs of native peoples should be administered by a colonial power.

If, as already shown, the amalgamation of the Colony and Protectorate of Lagos with the Protectorate of Southern Nigeria in 1906 had meant in some measure the extension to the latter Protectorate the administrative ideas and policies of the Crown Colony system,[1] even more so did the amalgamation of 1914 lead to the imposition on the South of the peculiar pattern of Indirect Rule which had been evolved in the emirates. Lugard himself was positive on this point, and he returned to it again and again in his *Report on the Amalgamation*, which he published on retiring from Nigeria. 'The system [of Indirect Rule]', he argued, 'may thus be said to have worked with good results in the North, and I desired to introduce its principles in the South.'[2] At another point in the *Report* he also said that he imported into the South the Northern system 'with the objective . . . both of reforming the judicial system of the south, and of establishing uniformity throughout Nigeria'.[3] Mr Edwin Speed, the Chief Justice, who drafted the ordinances embodying Lugard's reforms, said that

[1] An example was the complete subordination of the Native Courts to the Supreme Court. See ch. 3
[2] F. D. Lugard, *Report on the Amalgamation of Northern and Southern Nigeria* (hereinafter *Report on the Amalgamation*), London 1920, p. 27
[3] *Ibid.*, p. 47

he was guided in this work by the desire 'to evolve a system applicable to the whole country'.[4] Leading scholars of Nigeria's political and administrative history such as Dame Margery Perham, Mr A. H. M. Kirk-Greene, Professor J. E. Flint and Mr I. F. Nicolson, who have investigated this problem in detail, are agreed that, in the words of Perham:

> The Amalgamation of Nigeria meant the extension to the south of principles of Native Administration which had been worked out in the north.[5]

But whereas the general outlines and even many of the details of Lugard's policy in Yorubaland are generally known, the basic facts of, and stages in, the application of his policy to South-central and Southeastern Nigeria have until recently not been fully investigated. In spite of this, many scholars have blamed Lugard's attempt to impose emirate Indirect Rule on the present Mid-west and former Eastern Nigeria for the many administrative errors and even tragedies which took place there. This has induced a defensive attitude in Lugard's admirers, who have therefore sought to shelter Lugard by putting forward the view that whereas he sought to introduce emirate Indirect Rule into Yorubaland he never extended the same policy to South-central Nigeria (except probably Benin) and to the Southeast. Dr Lucy Mair's view on this matter has already been dealt with in this work and elsewhere by the present writer.[6] But she is not alone in holding it. Perham has written:

> Even the critics of Lugard's dealings with the Yoruba would admit that he had a policy for them and that he applied it with deep and lasting effect. This cannot be said of the southeast which presented him with an entirely different administrative situation which he was unable to master.[7]

[4] *Ibid.*
[5] M. Perham, *Native Administration in Nigeria*, Oxford 1937, p. 201. A. H. M. Kirk-Greene, *Lugard and the Amalgamation of Nigeria*, Cass 1968. A. H. M. Kirk-Greene, *The Principles of Native Administration in Nigeria*, Oxford 1965. J. E. Flint, 'Nigeria: The Colonial Experience from 1880 to 1914' in *Colonialism in Africa 1870–1960*, eds L. H. Gann and P. Duignan. Nicolson, *The Administration of Nigeria, 1900–1960*
[6] See ch. 1. See also A. E. Afigbo, 'The Warrant Chief System in Eastern Nigeria: Direct or Indirect Rule?', *JHSN*, iii, 4, 1967
[7] M. Perham, *Lugard: The Years of Authority 1898–1945*, London 1960, p. 457. Here Perham is unusually vague. She means either that Lugard had no policy for the southeast or that if he had he did not apply it with

For Perham the Southeast includes the former Warri Province. In his book *Niger Delta Rivalry*, Dr Obaro Ikimẹ has convincingly shown that Lugard also applied the Northern version of Indirect Rule to the Warri Province. Here an attempt will be made to establish the same thesis for Southeastern Nigeria and to give the main stages and details in the application of this policy as well as its impact on the administration and peoples.

But while concentrating on the Eastern Provinces it is necessary to emphasise that Lugard's policy was part of a wider policy for Nigeria which derived from the peculiar circumstances of early British political and administrative arrangements for the country. Objective research has established that Lugard had nothing but contempt for the administrative system of the Colony and Protectorate of Southern Nigeria – for its judicial system, its provincial arrangement and its native policy. According to Perham, his official biographer, Lugard 'looked at the government of the south with something close to disgust'.[8] Mr Kirk-Greene rightly says that this attitude was 'perhaps not unnatural for an administrator bred in the Northern emirates'.[9] A full-length study of the reasons for the vehement dislike for the south which was widespread amongst Northern officers has not yet been made, but some can be suggested here. The Northern and Southern administrations had been estranged from each other early in the establishment of British rule in the two territories. They quarrelled over boundary questions and railway policy as well as over the division of customs revenue collected by the Southern administration on goods which later found their way into Northern Nigeria. The Northern administration also inherited the Muslim dislike and contempt for 'pagans', especially the residual antagonism between the Sokoto caliphate and Yorubaland. Added to this was the fact that the Northern administration, handicapped by poverty and unable to ensure for its staff the conditions of living considered necessary for European workers

'deep and lasting effect', neither of which is correct. Lugard had a policy for the Southeast and, as the rest of the work will show, he applied it with 'deep and lasting effect'. The effect remained with the Eastern Provinces until about 1950, when it was decided to jettison the idea of traditional native authorities.

[8] Quoted in J. E. Flint, 'Nigeria: The Colonial Experience from 1880 to 1914', etc., pp. 255–6

[9] A. H. M. Kirk-Greene, *Lugard and the Amalgamation*, p. 14

in West Africa, was jealous of its Southern neighbour, which was better placed financially. The truth is, as Professor Flint has said, that

> in comparison with the southern administrations, the northern was a failure, whether judged in terms of administrative efficiency or of economic development (the normal criteria for assessing the progress of a colony).[10]

Probably it was consciousness of this failure that induced in the Northern administration an attitude of 'vehement defensiveness' and a tendency to assert 'that it alone had discovered the true principles of African administration'.[11]

Lugard and his wife (née Flora Shaw) spearheaded this propaganda[12] and it is here that it becomes clear how fateful it was that he was chosen to carry out the work of amalgamation which had been in the air since 1898. In addition Lugard had another complaint which also helped to determine his attitude to the Southern administration. He would appear to have had a feudal conception of society and authority which, reinforced by his military training, produced in him a peculiar predilection for a highly regimented system. Says Nicolson:

> He had the soldier's love of discipline and ranks, each rank obedient through the official hierarchy to its head; for him law and authority proceeded downwards; they were not working arrangements evolved through discussions and democratic process.[13]

The emirate system of Northern Nigeria to which many scholars have applied the epithet 'feudal' offered Lugard an opportunity of realising his ideal of a closely regimented society. It is not surprising, therefore, that when on his return to Nigeria in 1912 Lugard, in the words of Perham, 'subjected the south to a searching examination by the standards of northern administration'[14] he found it wanting in many respects to the extent that he not only 'doubted its existence' but also 'decided that what was needed was the creation of an administration'.[15]

He found the Southern administration untidy and inefficient,

[10] J. E. Flint, 'Nigeria: The Colonial Experience from 1880 to 1914', p. 250
[11] *Ibid.,*
[12] I. F. Nicolson, *The Administration of Nigeria*, ch. vi
[13] *Ibid.*, p. 45
[14] M. Perham, *Native Administration in Nigeria*, p. 61
[15] A. H. M. Kirk-Greene, *Lugard and the Amalgamation*, p. 14

the Southern Nigerians of low racial type, lawless and immoral. On one occasion he wrote to his wife,

> Extraordinary, N[orthern] Nigeria runs itself. . . . In S[outhern] Nigeria, on the other hand, papers pour in and they have large questions of policy which might have been decided 12 years ago.[16]

Clearly, to Lugard and his close associates there were many features of the pre-1914 systems of administration in Yorubaland and the rest of Southern Nigeria which stank in their nostrils and Perham, continuing the onslaught on the South, says 'the defects of Southern Nigeria could have been demonstrated by any standards of good government'.[17] Lugard's criticisms of the administration of Southern Nigeria generally and of native policy in Yorubaland in particular have been ably analysed by many scholars. What remains is to investigate fully his complaints against native policy east of the Niger, and the many schemes which he sought to implement there in a bid to effect a change for the better.

The criticisms of Sir Frederick Lugard and his disciples against native policy in Southeastern Nigeria centred on the Native Courts, which were the sole instrument of local government there. A dispassionate analysis of these criticisms shows that Lugard and his men were not just saying, as was said in the last chapter, that the system they inherited was not working extremely well, but that it was no system of native administration at all. This means that even if the system had been functioning as expected by its formulators, they still would have tried to supplant it with another they approved of. Sir Edwin Speed, the Chief Justice first of Northern Nigeria and then of the amalgamated country, thus said of these courts, 'the main and to my mind insuperable objection to the Southern Nigeria native courts is that they are not native courts at all'.[18] Herbert Richmond Palmer, another of Lugard's enthusiastic lieutenants, even argued that the courts had never been intended to operate as Native Courts. They were set up, he said, to meet the needs of district commissioners who, anxious to avoid 'the wholesale introduction of British law and European methods', wanted an arrangement that would enable them 'to use common sense and summary

[16] *Ibid.*
[17] M. Perham, *Native Administration in Nigeria*, p. 61
[18] F. D. Lugard, *Report on the Amalgamation*, p. 77

jurisdiction in dealing with primitive peoples'. But because these officers were unable to sit constantly owing to the distractions of their many duties, the courts 'were made to do duty as a spurious kind of native tribunal', thus developing 'in a manner quite contrary to the spirit in which they were designed'.[19] To Lugard and those of his disciples who preached the superiority of emirate Indirect Rule to all other forms of native policy the Native Courts of the Eastern Provinces, owing to the operation of a number of factors, were not real Native Courts.

The first of these was the subordination of the Native Courts to the Supreme Court. With regard to this, what bothered the Lugardians was not that Supreme Court control had not been effective as already shown, but that whatever little supervision which the Judicial Department exercised had led to the penetration of indigenous society by English legal ideas, thus causing disruption and confusion.[20] For one thing, they argued, it was in order to satisfy Supreme Court requirements that the Native Courts had come to be encumbered with forms and procedural regulations alien and meaningless to the people.

The second factor was the arrangement by which the political officer sat as president of the Native Court. Here again, what affronted Lugard and his men was not that the political officer was no longer able to fulfil his duties in this regard, though they produced statistics to show it,[21] but that no matter how infrequently he attended the sittings of the Native Courts he dominated the proceedings to such an extent that the Warrant Chiefs could not develop a sense of independence and responsibility. In short, they said, he dwarfed the chiefs, thus making it unlikely that the system would lead to the emergence of powerful or real chiefs. The political officer, argued Dr J. Crawford Maxwell, one of these men, 'was the court and the native members were merely figureheads: he took the evidence when he was present, he gave the judgment without even consulting the native members, and the more experienced he was the less important were the native members'.[22] On one occasion, they

[19] Palmer's Report in C 210/1915: System of Native Administration hitherto obtaining in the Southern Provinces
[20] B 486/1914, New Court System, Reasons for Introduction of – the whole file. See also Lugard, *Report on the Amalgamation*
[21] OW 122/16, Native Courts – Memorandum on. See Memo. by Maxwell No. 97/OW 122/16 of 19.2.16.
[22] *Ibid.*

said, a political officer in reporting the proceedings of a court he attended had admitted that

> I informed the court that I would adjourn the case until such a time as they might find themselves in agreement with me and would not come back in the meantime. Eventually they acquiesced.[23]

On such occasions as that just outlined, the Lugardians maintained, the Native Court became 'the court of the District Commissioner for the trial of Native cases'.[24] And yet, it was argued, the European officer who gave the decisions was not necessarily responsible for them, since in law the court was a Native Tribunal. Furthermore, they maintained, a Native Court should normally deal 'with cases brought before it in accordance with Native Law and Custom ... such as Matrimonial disputes, Debts, Petty assaults and the like', and all these belong to a class of cases which the political officer was ill-equipped to handle.[25]

The third factor which, in the opinion of these men, was responsible for the fact that the Native Courts were not in fact *native* was the false position which the Native Court clerk had come to occupy in it. Because political officers no longer found it possible to sit frequently the clerks had become the leading spirit of these institutions of local government. The influence of the Supreme Court, the Lugardians maintained, was also partly responsible for the ascendancy of the clerk in the Native Court. Ventilating the faults of the system before the Legislative Council, Lugard said the need to conduct the Native Courts according to Supreme Court procedure and the use of very many forms gave the clerk who had a smattering of knowledge of the English language an immeasurable advantage over the chiefs.[26] The clerk had become so powerful, argued Palmer, that he had in effect become the village headman as understood by that

---

[23] B 486/1914, New Court System, Reasons for Introduction of. See draft memorandum prepared by H. O. S. Wright for use by Lugard in the Legislative Council.

[24] OW 122/16, Native Courts – Memorandum on. See Memo. by Maxwell – No. 97/OW 122/16 of 19.2.16.

[25] F. D. Lugard, Memo. on Native Courts in Southern Nigeria in the file OW 225/14

[26] B 486/1914, New Court System, Reasons for Introduction of. See speech delivered by Lugard in the Legislative Council on 12 March 1914, Lugard: Native Courts in Southern Nigeria in the file OW 225/14.

phrase in Northern Nigeria.[27] Not surprisingly therefore, pointed out Mr H. O. S. Wright, people had come to treat the Native Court clerk as

> a big man saying, as their excuse, that he had the power of imprisonment and release, that he would not allow the members to disagree or argue with decisions given by himself and (if they dared to do so) would suspend them for a lengthy period, that he would permit only those members who had not much sense and whom he could easily sway to his will to sit in judgment. . . .[28]

'In such a case,' argued Lugard, 'gross injustice may result' and, what was worse from his point of view, 'the whole endeavour to teach the chiefs to administer justice to their own people is nullified and brought into disrepute.' This he described as a 'catastrophe'.[29]

The fourth factor which deprived these courts any claim to the epithet *native* was the fact that the Warrant Chiefs were not in fact traditional chiefs. Argued Palmer:

> In a system of this character there is really no room for Native Chiefs, hence the present Warrant Chiefs are as a class merely the more adaptable natives of the successful trader type who act as advisers to the court on the one hand, and as subordinates or allies of the Native Court Clerk on the other.[30]

In the light of these views it is understandable that some of Lugard's more radical disciples called for a clean sweep of the existing system. 'Real Native Courts therefore,' warned Palmer, 'cannot be created by amending the present Courts. Entirely new Courts are necessary.'[31]

In addition to the above criticisms centred on the Native Courts as courts, Lugard and his disciples were also very critical of other aspects of the existing local government arrangement. They thought there were too many Warrant Chiefs in the Eastern Provinces. Because the chiefs added up to an unwieldy crowd, they argued, it was impossible to single out and encourage promising chiefs who could be built up into paramount authorities. Also because they were too many, many of the chiefs had grown

[27] Palmer's Report, in C 210/1915, System of Native Administration hitherto obtaining in the Southern Provinces
[28] B 486/1914, Native Court System, Reasons for Introduction of. See draft Memo. by H. O. S. Wright for use by Lugard in the Legislative Council.
[29] F. D. Lugard, Native Courts in Southern Nigeria in the file OW 225/14
[30] Palmer's Report, in C 210/1915, System of Native Administration hitherto obtaining in the Southern Provinces [31] *Ibid.*

apathetic to their responsibilities. 'Many chiefs who have held warrants for years,' it was claimed, 'have rarely put in appearance at court either from apathy, old age or sickness.'[32]

Lugard also castigated the House Rule Ordinance which Moor had used to shore up the declining authority of the coastal chiefs. Lugard had a simplistic idea of the House system. He saw it as a species of slavery. According to him the members of a House consisted largely of slaves and were recruited by the addition of new slaves. He saw the House Rule Ordinance as a legalisation of the institution of slavery in the Delta, an arrangement by which the British administration, and in particular the judicature, were made to lend their weight to the preservation of an institution whose continued existence was inimical to the Slavery Ordinance. The political and administrative place of the House system in Delta society he never understood and never investigated.[33]

Also using the standards of Northern Nigeria, Lugard found Moor's Native Treasury arrangements objectionable on two grounds. The first was that these treasuries were not subject to central auditing. It may be pointed out here that this lack of central control was not the case at first: up to 1899 the commissioner and consul-general himself had audited the accounts of the courts. But after that date, as the courts grew in number, a local auditor was appointed to do the work and to report directly to the auditor-general of the protectorate and to the high commissioner. By 1903, however, it had been found that the searching inquiries which this practice entailed scared away many of the court clerks who were hard to find, and who when found felt themselves unequal to the rigorous accounting thus required. Moor therefore decided that it was 'inadvisable and unnecessary' to continue with this practice. Instead he trusted to the supervision of divisional commissioners and the travelling supervisors of Native Courts to check dishonesty and peculation. Furthermore, the revenues of these courts were often in the form of trade goods, a form of wealth which could not be easily subjected to scientific auditing and accounting since their values fluctuated unpredictably.[34]

[32] Conf C 242/1914, Lists of Warrant Chiefs in Calabar. See Confidential Memo. No. E Conf 133/13 dated 3.1.14.
[33] F. D. Lugard, *Report on the Amalgamation*, para. 23
[34] A. E. Afigbo, 'The Native Treasury Question under the Warrant Chief System in Eastern Nigeria 1899–1929', *ODU*, iv, 1 July 1967

But Lugard was not interested in such history. Had his main objection been absence of central check he should have been able to create one. But he had a more serious objection to these treasuries as they existed and this was that they were associated with the Native Courts, both in the sense that they were controlled by the Native Court members and in the sense that all their revenue came from court fees and fines. 'The distinction between a Native Court and a Native Treasury,' he warned, 'must also be clearly observed . . . a Native Court is not a Native Treasury,' and should have nothing to do with the disbursement of funds. 'I am entirely in favour of organising Native Treasuries,' he said, as long as that institution is understood to mean 'a fund formed primarily from taxation, and from fees for market-stalls and such like sources. To this fund the fines and fees of Native Courts may be added. The fund is administered by the Commissioner in consultation with the paramount chief (or perhaps with more than one chief where there is no single paramount chief). It is devoted to paying salaries to chiefs and others who are responsible for the control of their communities, and (if Native Court receipts are added to it) also the salaries or sitting fees and other expenses of Native Courts.'[35]

Judged by this criterion Moor's experiments along this line were no Native Treasuries. Lugard regarded the arrangements by which the main funds of those treasuries were derived from court fees and fines as open to gross abuse. It constituted a standing temptation to the chiefs to impose fines out of all proportion to the offence and to fine criminals whom they should imprison – all in an attempt to have enough money in the court funds with which to pay themselves. He said:

> The system which has hitherto, I believe, been in vogue in some districts, by which the sums received by a court were in the whole or part received by the Members of the Court or in part by the Native Chiefs . . . is subversive of the elementary ideas of justice, and tends to induce the Court to award fines in preference to other more deterrent sentences, and if a Court be corrupt it may even happen that the party best able to pay is fined.[36]

These were the main criticisms which Lugard and his disciples levelled against the pre-1914 local government system of the Eastern Provinces. There were a number of minor complaints

[35] F. D. Lugard, Native Courts in Southern Nigeria in the file OW 225/14
[36] *Ibid.*

against the same system but these will be dealt with along with the reforms and attempted reforms. Most of the Lugardian critics of Moor's system were not prepared to concede any virtues to it. But there were a few who while equally insisting on far-reaching changes believed that in the existing political condition of South-eastern Nigeria at the time British rule was imposed Moor's system was the only arrangement that possibly could have worked at all. But having succeeded, they continued, in establishing a measure of law and order which would make the introduction of the Northern system possible, it had outlived its usefulness. To such people the reforms which they advocated were not a sudden break with the past but logical and healthy development from it.

Under the pre-1914 system, for instance, inexperienced political officers exercised, as presidents of the Native Courts, wider powers than they had as commissioners of the Supreme Court. The grant of limited powers was one of the features of the system advocated by Lugard and his men. This was now said to lie in the logic of the fact that the country had settled down, thus undermining the circumstances that originally justified the grant of extended judicial powers. Dr J. C. Maxwell argued:

> It has been the experience, not merely of this but of other tropical dependencies, that while it is necessary at the outset to grant extended judicial powers even to junior and inexperienced officers if the development of the country must proceed, it is equally necessary after a time to withdraw these powers from junior officers and confine them to officers of greater experience. Even had the former system of Native Courts been maintained it would have been advisable to amend the section whereby an Assistant District Officer acquired these great judicial powers by sitting as president of a Native Court. Still more was it desirable to reduce the powers where Native Courts sat without any European Officer.[37]

It was also argued that at the time British rule was imposed the political situation east of the Niger was such that the Native Courts would have proved ineffective unless they were presided over by members of the European political staff. Again Dr Maxwell argued:

> The communities lacked cohesion and were mutually jealous of, and frequently antagonistic to, each other. In the face of this an attempt to found Native Courts on any other basis would probably have failed. The District Commissioner was the authority whom the rival and contending

[37] OW 122/16, Native Courts, Memorandum on. See Memo. by Maxwell No. 92/OW 122/16, dated 19.2.16

communities had to admit was superior and therefore formed the bond of union that enabled the Courts to be conducted successfully.

By 1914 the 'beneficent' presence of the political officer had achieved the desired end, it was contended, since the courts had engendered 'the habit of court going'. Therefore, the argument ran, the continued retention of the political officer as president had become manifestly superfluous.[38] What was more, Lugard added, Moor's system was structured as it was owing to the fact that chiefs had become powerless through the 'disintegrating influence of (coastal) middlemen traders and the Aro'. But since by 1914 the system had helped to 're-establish tribal authority' and to create 'unity' among the various communities, it had paved the way for a 'further advance' which was seen to lie logically in the introduction of the Northern system.[39]

Having spotlighted the main areas in which the pre-1914 local government system in the Eastern Provinces fell short of the system in the emirates, Lugard proceeded to impose his own system without consulting with the senior political officers of the Old Southern Nigeria Protectorate who had helped to introduce and had operated for about two decades the system inveighed against by the newcomers. The first official intimation which these officers had of the coming far-reaching changes came late in 1913. 'On (coming) January 1st,' ran an official circular of December that year addressed to the three provincial commissioners of the South, 'the administration generally will undergo considerable change. . . . Important changes will shortly be introduced in the administration of native affairs. . . .'[40] When the changes came they entailed the far-reaching decision to

[38] *Ibid.*
[39] F. D. Lugard, *Report on the Amalgamation*, p. 45. On this Palmer had a different opinion. He believed that the pre-1914 system had merely led to the disintegration of indigenous society. He argued that 'The attempt therefore to preserve Native Custom has so far resulted in steadily destroying it and among these relatively primitive peoples full Europeanised individualistic government is being introduced. The Government machinery is steadily grinding to powder all that is Native and transforming the peoples into black English men.' See Palmer's Report in C 210/1915, System of Native Administration Hitherto obtaining in the Southern Provinces
[40] See Memo. from James Watt, Colonial Secretary. Sent under cover of Conf No. C 388/1913 of 18.12.13 in OW 2/13. Political Staff and New Organisation which comes into force on 1 Jan. 1914, Memo. on duties of, etc.

extend to the south the Supreme, Provincial, Native Court, Native Authority and Native Revenue Ordinances of Northern Nigeria after these laws had been amended in minor details only. Here, as already said, attention is focused only on how these innovations affected the Warrant Chief system of local government east of the Niger.

First and foremost the subordination of the Native Courts to the Supreme Court was brought to an end. The jurisdiction of the Supreme Court was limited to the urban areas and their immediate environs in order to shelter unsophisticated villagers from its 'pernicious' influence. In the Calabar Province, for instance, the territorial extent of Supreme Court jurisdiction was restricted to a radius of five miles from the Court House at Calabar, and three miles from the Court Houses at Opobo and Eket respectively. In spite of this attempt to protect the Native Courts from the influence of the British courts, Native Courts were still to serve Supreme and Provincial Court processes.[41] In addition, said Lugard, the Native Courts were to co-operate with the British courts in arresting criminals wanted by the latter and in holding preliminary investigations in cases whose nature is such that 'judges of Native Courts [are] better able to get at the real facts than a British court, both because of their more intimate knowledge of native habits of thoughts and motives, and because witnesses are more likely to tell the truth'.[42] This cooperation between the Native and British courts, Lugard said, should be promoted in every way, as it would encourage the Native Courts to feel that they form 'part of the Government of the country'.[43]

The Provincial Court Ordinance which came into effect on 1 October 1914, through the operation of its section 3, introduced to the South the provincial system of Northern Nigeria. As a result the areas which until then comprised the Eastern and Central Provinces of Southern Nigeria were broken up into six smaller provinces. Four of these lay east of the Niger, forming the Eastern Provinces of those days or the Eastern Nigeria of later days. These four provinces were Calabar, Ogoja, Onitsha and Owerri. The Calabar Province, for instance, formed less than

---

[41] EP 1138, vol. 1. Calabar Province, Annual Report 1915, p. 2. *Nigerian Gazette*, 15 Jan. 1914. See Native Courts Ordinance, Section 17
[42] F. D. Lugard, Native Courts in Southern Nigeria in the file OW 225/14
[43] *Ibid.*

a third of the Eastern Provinces of which it had been a part. It was divided into three divisions each of which was subdivided into districts. The European officers in charge of these administrative divisions were constituted into Commissioners of the Provincial Court and given powers graded according to experience and seniority, with the Commissioner (later Resident) in charge of the province enjoying full powers.[44]

The Provincial Court was set up partly as a barrier against too frequent contact between British law and unsophisticated natives and partly as a guarantee of justice to people who should not normally go to the Supreme Courts but who were involved in cases in which the Native Courts were considered unlikely to do justice for a number of reasons. Lugard defined the classes of cases which should usually be dealt with in the Provincial Court as including those which:

(a) Deal with offences which under native law are not offences, and are only made such by British law, such as those under the Slavery, Customs, Firearms, Wild Animals Preservation, and other such Ordinances. . . .

(b) Deal with offences in which superstition is likely to pervert the course of justice (especially in pagan districts), such as the Poison Ordeal, the murder of twins or their mother, cases of alleged witchcraft, etc.

(c) Demand exceptional measures for suppression owing to the prevalence of the particular crime, when the Native Court does not appear willing to take adequate measures.

(d) Afford grounds for doubt whether the Native Court is likely to do substantial justice, owing to the position of influence of the accused.[45]

As a general rule, said Lugard, offences against the person would be left to a competent Native Court, while offences against public order should normally go to the Provincial Court; but whenever an offence was sufficiently serious it should go to the Provincial Court. This had to be so because he could not yet trust Native Courts to do impartial justice and because, since native punishments like mutilation had been abolished, Native Courts which had no prisons would be incapable of imposing condign punishments.[46]

[44] EP 1138, vol. 1. Calabar Province, Annual Report 1915, pp. 1–2
[45] F. D. Lugard, Native Courts in Southern Nigeria in the file OW 225/14
[46] *Ibid.*

The virtue of the system, claimed Lugard, was that it brought British justice to the door of everyone without exposing native society to the wholesale penetration of alien judicial ideas. To this end the procedure was summary and there was no question of automatic appeal from the Provincial Court to the Supreme Court. Also legal practitioners were barred from the Provincial Court as from appeals going from that Court to the Supreme Court.[47]

Having severely limited the influence of the Supreme Court as well as conceived the Provincial Court as a buffer between the Supreme Court and the generality of the people, Lugard went on to create Native Courts after his own heart. The Native Courts Ordinance which he introduced in 1914 considerably altered the existing system in the Eastern Provinces. One of the more revolutionary changes dealt with the relationship of the political officer with the Native Court. The district officer ceased to be a member, let alone the president, of the Native Court in order, claimed Lugard, to enable that institution to evolve into an 'independent tribunal' and the members 'to acquire a sense of responsibility'. These ends would not be attained, he said, if the Native Court continued to be 'dominated by the presence of a European'.[48] This change was, for the Eastern Provinces, probably the most radical departure from the pre-1914 arrangement and argument over its wisdom or unwisdom was to rage between the Lugardians and their opponents until the Warrant Chief System collapsed in a scene of riots.

But if Lugard believed that European membership of the Native Courts thwarted the realisation of the ends for which they were instituted, he did not doubt that these institutions would equally go splendidly astray if denied constant and intensive European supervision. The exclusion of the district officer from the Native Court did not mean for that officer relief from Native Court work. It in fact meant increased responsibility for the healthy development of that institution. 'But the fact that the District Officer does not sit as President', wrote Lugard in his instruction to political officers,

> should enhance rather than decrease his duties of supervision. It lies with him to develop the Courts in his Province, and to constantly

[47] F. D. Lugard, *Report on the Amalgamation*, paras 49 and 50
[48] F. D. Lugard, Native Courts in Southern Nigeria in the file OW 225/14. See also *Report on the Amalgamation*

endeavour to make them fit to exercise larger and larger powers. He can only achieve this by being in constant touch with them so as to see that they exercise strict impartiality, and to inculcate in them the idea of a patient and full examination of all available evidence so that justice may be done.[49]

After sounding this hortative note, Lugard went on to prescribe in detail the means by which the district officer was to realise this lofty ideal. He, as well as the resident, was to attend the meetings of the Native Court frequently. But at the same time he was to abstain from a too frequent intervention in the business of the court, except where manifest injustice was about to be done, or he would undermine the reputation and prestige of the court as well as the self-confidence of the members. All the same, in order to keep the court straight the district officer had the powers to 'transfer cases from it to the Provincial Court before, during or after trial'. Also litigants dissatisfied with the judgments of the Native Court could 'appeal to the Commissioner in his administrative capacity' and if the political officer should see good cause in the case of the appellant he could rehear the case in the Provincial Court. Furthermore the political officer had the powers to 'attend the Native Courts from time to time and check Court returns' as a way of detecting injustice and corruption. And finally, that is on the issue of the relationship of the political officer to the Native Court, Lugard enjoined that the policy of the government, which was 'to increase the influence and prestige of the Native Courts and to make them in every way effective instruments of justice', could only be achieved firstly by constant European supervision, which would infuse in the Warrant Chiefs 'the principles of British justice', and secondly by establishing as many courts as possible, 'so that complainants may be able to obtain redress without travelling prohibitive distance'.[50]

Supervision and guidance from the European officer constituted the linchpin of the Native Courts proposed by Lugard. Thus while he took care to remove the political officer from the bench of the Native Court, he also took care to ensure that he was able to guide the development of that institution. Moor's reliance on the

[49] F. D. Lugard, Native Courts in Southern Nigeria in the file OW 225/14
[50] *Ibid.* As a remedy against litigants having to travel prohibitive distances, Lugard even recommended courts formed for the occasion to deal with a specific case. He said: 'If a crime is brought to the notice of a Political Officer in a district where no Native Court has been set up . . . he may appoint a temporary court for the trial of the particular crime.'

district commissioner to guide the growth of the Native Councils from *within* that body failed because that officer could not find the time to sit as often as necessary. As this study develops it will also be seen that Lugard's district officer was not able either to do the rigorous supervision from *outside* on which the reformer pinned hopes for the success of his system.

The other important change introduced by the new ordinance concerned the hierarchy of courts created. The pre-1914 two-tier arrangement setting up Native Councils and Minor Courts was abandoned in favour of one distinguishing between Judicial Councils and Native Courts. The Judicial Council was conceived as 'a deliberative body consisting of the chief functionaries of an organised Native State' and its duties were more than judicial. In this sense the Judicial Council resembled Moor's Native Councils which carried administrative and legislative functions in addition to the judicial. No Judicial Council was ever set up in the Eastern Provinces, as the prerequisite indigenous political set-up did not exist there. Lugard himself said the chances for that body being set up in the South existed only in the three Western Provinces and Benin District. The Native Courts proper were divided into two sub-groups. The first was the single judge court, which could have assessors and advisers or no. The classic example of this was the *alkali* Court in Northern Nigeria. This class again did not exist in the Eastern Provinces. The other type was the Native Court, which comprised 'petty chiefs' and exercised only limited civil and criminal jurisdiction. With the application of this ordinance the former Native Councils were reduced to 'C' grade and the Minor Courts to 'D' grade. The powers of these 'petty chief Courts' were very limited indeed, but then it was hoped that as they acquired experience in handling cases they would be granted extended powers.[51] In fact in the Eastern Provinces it was soon discovered that the jurisdiction of these courts was too limited to cope with the rising wave of litigation. As a result many of the courts originally granted 'C' grade jurisdiction moved up to 'B' grade while others granted 'D' grade moved up to 'C' and even 'B' grade.

Lugard was anxious to avoid having to encumber the Native Courts with alien associations. But at the same time he shared the then prevailing pet European prejudices on the minimal conditions which an African tribunal must meet to satisfy European

[51] *Ibid.*

ideas of a court of justice. The result was that in spite of his protestations to the contrary, Lugard imposed on the Native Courts alien forms and modes of procedure. 'I consider it of importance,' he insisted, 'that a certain formality should be observed in order to add to the dignity of the Court.' Thus each court had to sit on a day and at an hour previously promulgated, and maintain strict order and decorum in and around the court house. Each court had to be established by warrant which alone gave legality to its status, proceedings and sentences. This was necessary to check the rise of self-constituted tribunals. Court members were to be appointed by warrant. The other processes and forms of the courts were still to be used – including civil and criminal summonses. Each Native Court was to keep a book in which were to be entered laws or rules made by it with due approval.[52]

The insistence on a certain measure of formality, the decision to allow the use of printed forms and the recording of the proceedings and transactions of the Native Court, as well as the fact that the court members were in most cases illiterate chiefs, compelled Lugard to attach to each court a clerk to keep the records. But in order to prevent this official from gaining ascendancy over the chiefs, Lugard laid down detailed regulations for keeping him in check, but as will be shown in the next chapter these turned out to be ordinary paper controls. He stipulated that the political officer was to visit the courts in his division as frequently as possible to examine the records, question the clerks, the chiefs and all persons who had something to do with the hearing of a case in order to check the correctness of the entries made by the clerk. The clerk was to keep a counterfoil receipt book from which to issue receipts for all moneys paid to him. The record of court proceedings was to be as brief and simple as possible. In certain classes of cases – matrimonial, debt, theft, petty assault cases or the like – the record of proceedings was to consist only of the names of the litigants and their witnesses, the fees paid and the decisions given. But in land cases the record was to be as full as possible.[53] This regulation with regard to Native Courts records broke down almost as it was being made since it was mainly on the records that political officers relied for their understanding of cases which came to them for review. In making the regulations about the records, Lugard seemed to forget that what made it

[52] *Ibid.*   [53] *Ibid.*

possible for the clerk to dominate the court in the past was not the length of the records he took but the fact that he was literate while the chiefs and the litigants were not.

In addition to the rules on records, the clerk's wages were to be paid to him by the president of the court for which he worked. The Warrant Chiefs constituting a court were to be encouraged to engage their own clerk and to regard him as their servant. In no case was a clerk to be allowed to remain in one station for longer than two years. The president of the court, said Lugard,

> should, if possible, keep a separate tally of fines and fees by means of a notched stick or other simple device. With a uniform hearing fee such a record of number of cases heard will form a useful check on the counterfoil book.[54]

Since Lugard also abolished the office of the Travelling Supervisor of Native Courts it meant the business of keeping an effective check on the clerks now devolved on the district officer alone. As will be shown in the next chapter, Lugard's plan for keeping a check on the Native Court clerk remained a dead letter from the start. Curiously enough Lugard inconsistently proceeded to undermine some of these controls. Formerly the clerks had been dependent on the revenue of the courts they served for their salaries, this revenue being administered locally by the chiefs and the political officer. But Lugard not only abolished these local treasuries, hoping to set up his own (which he never succeeded in doing), but also converted the court clerks into 'government' clerks by paying their salaries out of the general revenue of the Colony and Protectorate. When in 1912 Mr A. Willoughby Osborne, the Chief Justice of Southern Nigeria, commented on the draft bill, he said:

> The worst evil attendant on the native court system is not touched by the bill and will flourish under it just as badly as it does now. I refer to the Native Court Clerks who are responsible for keeping the court Records.[55]

The future was with him and against Lugard and Edwin Speed.

The policy of curtailing or seeking to curtail all influences considered inimical to the growth of chiefly authority also left its mark on the court messenger service. In spite of Sir Ralph Moor's

---

[54] *Ibid.*
[55] F. D. Lugard, *Report on the Amalgamation*, p. 77

orders to the contrary in 1902,[56] these officials of the court had
continued in many places to side-track the Warrant Chiefs when
serving court processes, had on occasions undertaken the duty of
arresting criminals, and were being used for purposes other than
those strictly pertaining to the Native Court. These practices
Lugard, like Moor, considered unorthodox. He held that the
maintenance of order, the detection of crime and the arrest and
prosecution of criminals were some of the responsibilities of
chiefs and that the excessive use of court messengers in such
cases was apt to diminish chiefly authority and control. 'Court
Messengers,' he said, 'are not designed to undertake police
functions' and 'must not be confounded with the police.'[57] He
continued:

> When a Native Court had need to arrest or summons any persons or to
> call witnesses, it will despatch the Court Messenger to the village with
> the requisite instructions to the chief, who will be responsible for
> arresting or summoning the persons required and for sending them to
> the Native Court.[58]

In short the name 'Court Messenger' was to be a literal definition
of the bearer's duties, namely carrying messages or summonses or
warrants for execution to Warrant Chiefs who then had to see
that the people concerned were brought to court or arrested
according to what the writ demanded. Because of this simple
definition of their duties Lugard decided on a drastic cut in the
number of court messengers employed by the courts. He believed
that two or three court messengers should suffice for any court.[59]
The reduction was effected in spite of the protests of the officers
in the field. As will be shown later, this very change was to have
untoward consequences, for the duties of the court messengers
grew by leaps and bounds in the Eastern Provinces, where chiefs
of influence who could carry the responsibility mapped out by
Lugard did not exist. However, one other point about the cut
was that apart from wanting to protect the authority of the chiefs
Lugard wanted to effect economy in administration. Fewer

---

[56] See ch. 3
[57] Enclosure No. A 17/1914 of 10.3.14 from the Secretary Southern
Provinces in OP 29/1914 Native Courts Onitsha Province: Messengers
allowed for. F. D. Lugard, Native Courts in Southern Nigeria in the file
OW 225/14
[58] F. D. Lugard, Native Courts in Southern Nigeria in the file OW 225/14
[59] *Ibid.*

court messengers meant less money spent in paying the court staff.

Apart from these more or less negative measures designed to clear the way for the growth of chiefly authority, Lugard had more positive schemes designed to achieve the same end. The situation which existed east of the Niger, in which a Native Court bench often consisted of upwards of one hundred Warrant Chiefs who sat in rotation, and all of whom had equal powers or rather lacked real powers, was very unsatisfactory to Lugard, who considered it unsuitable for the introduction of his own brand of Indirect Rule. It was the proclaimed policy of Lugard to force the pace of evolution of centralised leadership in decentralised communities. In the section of his *Political Memoranda* dealing with the duties of a political officer under the new dispensation he wrote:

> If there is no Chief who exercises authority beyond his own village he [the DO] will encourage any Chief of influence and character to control a group of villages, with a view to making him Chief of a district later if he shows ability for the charge.[60]

Putting this idea more graphically later in his *The Dual Mandate in British Tropical Africa*, Lugard argued that the first step towards the introduction of Indirect Rule in 'primitive (i.e. chiefless) societies'

> is to hasten the transition from the patriarchal to the tribal stage, and induce those who accept no other authority than the head of the family to recognise a common chief. Where this stage has already been reached, the object is to group together small tribes, or sections of a tribe, so as to form a single administrative unit whose chiefs severally or in council . . . may be constituted a Native Authority . . . through whom the District Officer can work.[61]

It was such instructions as this which transformed the order 'find the chief' into the highly disruptive injunction 'make the Chief'.

The attempt to implement this policy in the Eastern Provinces started badly. In November 1913 an order went out to the provincial commissioners to the effect that from 1 January 1914 all the existing Native Courts would be abolished and one Native Court established for each district. This court would hold sittings at all the centres where Native Courts existed under the pre-1914

[60] F. D. Lugard, *Political Memorandum* No. 1, 1918, p. 11
[61] F. D. Lugard, *The Dual Mandate in British Tropical Africa*, Edinburgh 1922, pp. 217–18

system. Also, members would be chosen for this court out of the existing Warrant Chiefs, but the jurisdiction of each chief would be limited to the area which he represented. 'Existing lists' of court members, it was ordered, 'should be carefully revised for this purpose. . . . It is thought possible that existing lists are in some cases too long and this should receive your careful consideration.' In any case, it was insisted, 'twenty men would be an out-number for any court and . . . in many cases twelve would be sufficient'.[62]

In obedience to this order political officers went on to curtail drastically the number of Warrant Chiefs in their districts. The district officer at Okigwi, for instance, proposed reducing the membership of the Okigwi and Umuduru Native Courts from fifty to ten and from forty to ten respectively. Soon, however, a frantic telegram went out from headquarters withdrawing the order because 'temporary advantage of reduced numbers fails outweigh disadvantages'.[63] The fact is that 'it had become the custom for each town to have one or more representatives on the court' and to abandon this practice would have escalated the already existing evil of chiefs holding private courts. This, it was feared, would undermine the confidence which the people were assumed to have in the official courts.[64]

Lugard then thought of other methods of achieving the same end. He contemplated the creation of very many Native Courts so that the membership of each bench could be kept small. To attain this end he was prepared to countenance what he called 'clan' or 'tribal' courts, an arrangement by which each court would serve only one clan, and every town or village would have either a Warrant Chief who was a member of the court or a 'recognised' chief who was not. By a 'recognised' chief Lugard meant a chief who was excluded from membership of the court, but who had a certificate of recognition, not a Warrant, which would give him the status of a Native Authority within his unit. He was to exercise certain limited executive, but not judicial,

[62] Conf C 242/1914, Lists of Warrant Chiefs, Calabar Province. See the enclosed circulars
[63] Conf C 242/1914, Lists of Warrant Chiefs, Calabar Province. See Telegram A 678 dated 31 3 14 and sent from A 510/14
[64] Conf C 242/1914, Lists of Warrant Chiefs, Calabar Province. See Enclosures: No. C 366/13 of 28.11.13; No. E Conf 133/13 of 17.1.14 and Telegram A 678 of 31.3.14. F. D. Lugard, *Political Memorandum*, No. 8, 1916, p. 272

powers over his people. Through this programme of courts with reduced personnel Lugard hoped it would be possible to appoint permanent presidents who, with encouragement, could grow into sufficiently influential chiefs. The practice by which Native Court presidents were chosen on a quarterly basis was to be treated only 'as a transitional expedient'.[65] Lugard was able to enforce the appointment of permanent presidents in a number of places, but his scheme of 'recognised chiefs' and 'clan' courts remained a paper one. The number of chiefs on the bench of each court continued to be larger than Lugard considered healthy for the system and the legal adviser, T. D. Maxwell, was left to complain of 'the large number of 1067 chiefs' authorised as 'Warrant Holders' within 'the small geographical area of Calabar Province'. The Ikot Ekpene Court alone had as many as 108 Warrant Chiefs.[66]

But Lugard's main programme for remodelling the indigenous political system of the Eastern Provinces to a point where it would be capable of operating emirate Indirect Rule, and the one which he applied systematically in spite of all odds, was the Native Authorities Ordinance of 1916. Under his system a Native Authority should ideally be a single chief rather than a council or court. Only where this ideal condition could not be met would he reluctantly go on to constitute councils of chiefs, or worse still Native Courts, into Native Authorities. Thus early in 1917 he called on the residents east of the Niger to submit lists of chiefs to be constituted Native Authorities under the Ordinance.[67]

The Resident of Owerri Province, Dr J. C. Maxwell, in his reply warned that the implementation of the scheme in his province would lead to the creation of 'a very large number of Native Authorities each exercising a limited and ineffective control over a small area and the objects aimed at in the ordinance would not be attained'. He advised the appointment of Native Courts as Native Authorities and recommended the gazetting of nine of these courts each as Native Authority in its area of jurisdiction. In 1918 all the Native Courts in the province were

---

[65] F. D. Lugard, *Political Memorandum* (1918), pp. 272, 274
[66] Conf C 242/1914, Lists of Warrant Chiefs, Calabar Province. See Minute by T. D. Maxwell dated 20.10.14.
[67] Telegram dated 9.3.17 in EP 3759, Native Authorities Southern Provinces

appointed Native Authorities.[68] The Resident of Ogoja Province piped a similar note to Dr Maxwell's. As a result, not a single individual in the province was recommended for appointment as Native Authority. Instead each Native Court was made a Native Authority over its own area of jurisdiction.[69] The Residents of Onitsha and Calabar Provinces, however, showed more enthusiasm and optimism than their colleagues at Owerri and Ogoja and recommended 'Sole Native Authorities' for certain court areas. Their recommendations were as shown below:[70]

Province	District	Chief	Area of authority
Calabar	Calabar	Obong of Duke Town	Duke Town Area
	„	Obong of Creek Town	Creek Town Area
	„	Fourteen other chiefs	for various sections of Calabar
	„	Daniel Henshaw	Oron NC Area
	Ikot Ekpene	Anoyom Iya of Nja	Enyong Area
	„ „	Mba Nkoli	Ibe 'Tribal Area'
	Opobo	Mark Pepple Jaja	Opobo NC Area
	„	Udom Okom	Essene NC Area
Onitsha	Onitsha	Chief Mba	Onitsha Waterside
	„	Obi Okosi	Onitsha Inland Town
	„	Ezeokoli	Nnobi NC Area
Onitsha	Onitsha	Orizu	Nnewi NC Area
	„	Walter Amobi	Ogidi NC Area
	Awka	Igwegbe of One	Ajalli NC Area
	Udi	Onyeama of Eke	Oye and Achi NC Area
	—	Chukwuani of Nkanu	Owelli, Agbani, Ogui NC Area
	—	—	

In most other places in these two provinces the Native Courts were made Native Authorities for their respective areas of jurisdiction. Later, however, the Resident of Calabar Province recommended the staggering number of 116 chiefs for gazetting as Native Authorities for the Calabar district alone. The earlier arrangement under which a few hand-picked chiefs were so recommended had caused much bickering as it created disparity among the *etuboms* (ward heads), who were traditionally equals.

[68] See Letters Nos 165/OW 214/17 of 17.5.17 and No. 21/OW 214/17 of 19.1.18 in EP 3759, Native Authorities Southern Provinces
[69] *Nigerian Gazette*, 1917, p. 353
[70] *Ibid.*, pp. 352–4. See also Letter No. OP 117/1917 of 25.6.17 in EP 3759, Native Authorities Southern Provinces

It was in a bid to end this situation that all the various heads of houses, wards and villages were accorded the envied position. But this only made a travesty of the policy.[71]

On the surface the response of the residents of Onitsha and Calabar Provinces to the policy may appear justified in the light of the fact that the two provinces contained most of those communities whose indigenous political systems were classified in this work as constitutional monarchies. But even in such communities the singling out of the kinglet for elevation to a Sole Native Authority and the failure to limit his new powers to his village or ward did violence to the traditional constitution and made his position more artificial than would otherwise have been the case. What was worse, some of the communities in which Sole Native Authorities were created did not have traditional constitutions of the village monarchy type. More will be heard of these Native Authorities later in this work, but here it suffices to point out that some of these chiefs were strangers to the communities on which they were imposed as Native Authorities. For instance Daniel Henshaw was an Efik and a former political agent of the government. But he was made the Native Authority for the Oron Native Court area, which was a non-Efik territory.

But the appointment of 'Sole Native Authorities' who were to exercise executive powers independently of the Native Courts was, as already shown, only part of a larger policy designed to bring the local government system of the Eastern Provinces in line with that existing in the North. As part of this policy Lugard went forward to make some of the 'Sole Native Authorities' Paramount Chiefs over their respective Native Court areas. Among the more celebrated of these men were Chief Igwegbe Odum of One, Chief Onyeama of Eke and Chief Chukwuani of Nkanu, of whom more will be heard later. Other aspects of the same policy dealt with the implementation of three schemes which were dear to Lugard's heart.

The first of these was the establishment of Native Prisons. Lugard argued that if Native Authorities and Native Courts were to be worth their salt and grow in power they had to be given the opportunity to execute their own sentences; in other words they had to have their own prisons. Persons sentenced to imprisonment by a Native Court were to serve the sentence in a Native

[71] EP 3759, Native Authorities Southern Provinces. See Memo. OC 651/1922

142

Prison, not in a central government prison, since no European officer took responsibility for the sentence.[72]

It was in obedience to this maxim that in March 1914 Lugard asked the residents of the Eastern Provinces to report to him on the feasibility of the project in their areas of authority.[73] The replies which he received were disappointing. On this issue the attitude of political officers in the Owerri Province was typical. They pointed out that there were no chiefs of sufficient stature to manage the prisons and that to introduce the scheme into their province would only add another feather to the cap of the court clerk, for he would quickly seize effective control of prisons located far from headquarters. In the absence of direct taxation, which would yield the money for maintaining the prisons, the scheme, they said, was premature. If the prisons were to be real Native Prisons there was also the danger that they would become engines of tyranny in the hands of ambitious Warrant Chiefs anxious to augment their shadowy authority. In the light of this, they pointed out, a Native Prison would undermine the harmony and repose of a Native Court area as each chief would angle to see it sited in his village. If these institutions were actually left to native control sanitation might be so elementary that the prisons would become death-camps. If the prisons were not to be a curse, it was argued, strict European supervision would be a must. In that case the prisons would be 'native' in name only and there would be no real difference between them and district prisons. In view of all this, the general opinion ran, the scheme was 'desirable in theory but unworkable in practice'.[74] The very attempt to impose the idea on the provinces east of the Niger where the conditions did not warrant it is illustrative of Lugard's pre-occupation with 'ideal forms' and his neglect of objective local situations.

The second scheme was about the education of chiefs. This idea sprang from Lugard's desire to improve the class of chiefs then existing in many parts of the Protectorate and his belief that this end could be realised through educating each chief for his job

[72] F. D. Lugard, Native Courts in Southern Nigeria in OW 225/14
[73] Memo. No. A 536/1914 dated 6.3.1914 in OW 195/14 Native Prisons – Establishment of in connection with Native Courts. F. D. Lugard, Native Courts in Southern Nigeria in the file OW 225/14
[74] See Enclosures 2, 3, 5, 6, 7, 12, 13, 15 and 17 in OW 195/14, Native Prisons – Establishment of in connection with Native Courts

while he was still young. These 'young chiefs' were to reside in boarding houses, returning home only during holidays. While in school the prospective chiefs were to be taught not only literary subjects 'but also and primarily the meaning of discipline, good behaviour and a high moral tone' so that when they finally returned home they would easily 'make themselves leaders of their compatriots and become of inestimable value in the better administration of the country'.[75]

Again Lugard called upon the Residents to report to him on which schools they considered best suited for carrying out this plan, the source from which the money for it could be derived, whether the fathers of the prospective chiefs would raise any objection and whether at the conclusion of their instructions the young chiefs would be regarded as aliens by their communities. Since the residents were not called upon to say whether the scheme was workable – perhaps owing to lessons learned from the fate which the prison scheme of the previous year met in their hands – a man like E. D. Simpson, the Resident of Ogoja Province, did not consider the scheme critically. He merely gave the details which Lugard asked for and concluded: 'The object and scope of the scheme is entirely admirable and . . . I am hopeful in regard to a successful issue finally. . . .'[76] The residents of Onitsha, Owerri and Calabar went beyond their terms of reference and subjected the scheme to searing criticism in the tradition of that of the previous year. From Onitsha Hargrove said the parents would refuse to pay the necessary fees, some because they had not the money, some because of prejudice, others because of both. But, he concluded, the scheme had no chance of success because chieftaincy did not necessarily descend from father to son, a situation which made it impossible to forecast who would in time become a chief so that he could be educated from childhood.[77]

Dr Maxwell replied that the scheme was admirable where there were chiefs, but that there were no chiefs in his Province, Owerri. What was needed, he said:

[75] Circular Letter B 895/1915 in B 893/15, Education of future chiefs. Question of

[76] *Ibid.* See Enclosure No. 869/OG 286/1915 dated 11.9.15 from the Resident, Ogoja

[77] Enclosure OP 386/15 of 13.10.15 in B 893/15, Education of future chiefs, Question of

was education on a broad basis, not the institution of a system by which education is restricted to a small and artificially created class which would be a curse, because this artificial class will resort to all measures to maintain a position to which they know they have no natural rights.[78]

Here we see the wide gulf between the realism of the man on the spot and the romanticism of the man at headquarters.

Lugard was offended by what appeared to him the unadventurous spirit stalking the provinces east of the Niger, and by the treatment meted out by the political officers there to a scheme which he believed was 'of great value to Government and to the country'. Consequently he ignored the advice of the residents and ordered that if the Lieutenant-Governor of the Southern Provinces (Mr A. G. Boyle), the Secretary of the Southern Provinces (Colonel Moorhouse) and the Director of Education were agreed on the scheme they should implement it without further argument and instruct the residents to 'treat it as a government policy and to apply it loyally' instead of regarding it as a topic for 'an academic thesis'.[79] Eventually the scheme died a natural and unceremonial death, not because Lugard had been warned that it was unrealistic and would fail but because the Europeans who were expected to head the proposed schools were not available.[80]

The third scheme was designed to lead to the introduction into the Eastern Provinces of Native Treasuries in the form they then existed in Northern Nigeria. When Lugard came back to Nigeria, he already had definite ideas about what a Native Treasury should be, just as he also had definite ideas about other aspects of local government. He abolished Moor's experimental treasuries because they did not meet the conditions which in his mind Native Treasuries should satisfy. As already shown, the origin of the Native Treasury is traditionally associated with Palmer in Katsina in 1906 after Lugard had left Northern Nigeria. But Lugard, regarding it as an organic and logical development of the system he had established between 1900 and 1906, fully accepted it as one of the pillars of a rightly guided Native policy. This much is clear from his writings. He soon came to argue that without a

---

[78] Enclosure No. 468/OW 530/15 dated 27.9.15 in B 893/15, Education of future chiefs, Question of
[79] Minute No. 46 of 23.2.16 by Lugard in D 893/15, Education of future chiefs, etc.
[80] Minute No. 45 of 16.2.16 by A. G. Boyle in B 893/15, Education of future chiefs, etc.

Native Treasury no system of local government could successfully prepare Africans for eventual self-rule.[81]

The abolition of the pre-1914 treasuries left the way clear for the introduction of a full-fledged Native Treasury system on the pattern existing in the emirates. 'It has been my hope,' he said, 'that I should be able to gradually introduce a system of indirect taxation into the Southern Provinces such as exists in the Northern Provinces and in practically every British (and foreign) possession in Africa.' His arguments for this policy fell into two groups – administrative and financial, but of the two the former was to him more important.[82]

To Lugard the weightiest argument for extending direct taxation to the south was that it would enable him 'to set up a system of administration through the Native chiefs somewhat on the model of the Northern Provinces',[83] as it was the surest way of selecting the most capable and most influential men and investing them with authority and responsibility. By participating in the assessment, collection and disposal of revenue, he pontificated, the chiefs would become an integral part of the government of the country. This close association with the government would speedily help to expose incompetence and dishonesty, and by progressive elimination competent and responsible rulers would emerge to the inestimable benefit of the country. What was more, in order to keep the chiefs from the temptation to indulge in bribery, extortion and the imposition of unjust fines, it was necessary to provide them with a regular income on which they could live and with which they could maintain the dignity of their position. Direct taxation was the best means to this end, for with its logical concomitant, the Native Treasury, it would provide the means of giving each person who held a public office an adequate and assured salary.[84]

The other argument which Lugard advanced in support of direct taxation was the need to augment the revenue of the Protectorate. This reason, though initially secondary, acquired added importance by 1914 as a result of the economic exigencies of the First World War. 'Recent events in Europe,' he argued,

[81] F. D. Lugard, *The Dual Mandate*, p. 219
[82] Despatch of 10.8.14 from Lugard to CO in CSO 9/1/8. Secret file No. 35, Taxation in the Southern Provinces
[83] *Ibid.*
[84] *Ibid.*, Despatch dated 13.3.15 from Lugard to CO

'have completely altered the outlook and it may be that the institution of direct taxation will be necessary not only for its indirect benefits but in order to enforce revenue.' The bulk of the revenue of the Protectorate at the time came from customs duties (chiefly on spirits) and from railway freights. Trade spirits were entirely in the hands of traders from continental Europe. The staple export of Southern Nigeria – palm kernel – was also sent largely to continental Europe. It was therefore certain that the dislocation of trade between the British empire and continental Europe which was sure to result from the war would drastically affect the revenue of Nigeria. 'I anticipate,' warned Lugard, 'a very serious shortage of imports and exports for some time to come which will decrease the revenue both from customs and railways freights. In the circumstances it may be imperative to augment the revenue by direct taxes.'[85]

On 10 August 1914 Lugard asked the British Colonial Secretary, Lord Harcourt, to grant him 'the same discretion and initiative' with regard to the introduction of direct taxation into the South as had formerly been granted him in the North.[86] But since Lord Harcourt considered it important that as long as the war lasted no rash step should be taken to precipitate a colonial revolt, he advised Lugard that 'the general question of direct taxation in the Southern Provinces . . . should stand over for the present'. The Colonial Secretary added, however, that if in any specific area it was felt taxation could be introduced with safety definite proposals could be forwarded to him.[87]

The following year (1915) Lugard sought to exploit the opportunity offered by this loophole by pushing through a modified programme of taxation. If he could not introduce taxation throughout the South at the same time, he could at least do so piecemeal. To support his case he produced a disquisition on the typologies of political systems of Southern Nigeria to justify the initial introduction of the measure into certain areas. At the top of the pyramidal scheme which he produced Lugard placed the Yoruba and the Bini, who, he said, were 'some centuries in advance of the Eastern Provinces' through having developed a 'highly organised social system'. Below these he

[85] Despatch dated 10.8.14 from Lugard to CO in CSO 9/1/8. Secret file No. 35, Taxation in the Southern Provinces
[86] *Ibid.*
[87] *Ibid.*, Harcourt to Lugard dated 30.4.15

placed the coastal communities of the Oil Rivers, who, 'though belonging to the most primitive communities – Ibos, Ijaws, Efiks – have acquired a more advanced organisation by means of houses organised for trading purposes'. At the base of the pyramid he placed the other communities east of the Niger, who, he said, were at 'varying stages' of social organisation and whose polities ranged 'from the agglomeration of families who recognise no common head to the tribal organisation reached by Aros'.[88]

Lugard now proposed to impose direct taxation on the first two groups for a number of reasons. Firstly, according to him, being 'more highly' organised, they possessed the necessary machinery for collecting the tax. Also, since their peoples were already 'used to' the payment of tribute in one form or the other, direct taxation would not be an innovation or stir up revolt. Rather it would lighten the burden of the people by consolidating and systematising their duties to their rulers and replacing the haphazard demands of the old régime with all their numerous openings for extortion. Secondly the immediate introduction of taxation was necessary in order to arrest the disintegration of traditional society which was being encouraged by the influence of the missions and other 'aliens', the lingering influence of the Supreme Court, the Aro and the decline of the middleman's trade monopoly.[89] Lugard had also, as already mentioned, sent Mr H. R. Palmer, one of his lieutenants with Northern experience, on a roving tour of the Southern Provinces. At the end of the trip Palmer had reported to his chief what he knew the latter was only too ready to hear: that there was no opposition to the idea of direct taxation in the South, except, perhaps, in Lagos; and that its implementation would be as easy and as smooth as it had been in the North.[90]

This closely argued case did not sweep the British Colonial Secretary off his feet. On the contrary, Lord Harcourt remained as determined as ever not to incur any risk, however remote, of disaffection among the people of Nigeria at a time when practically the whole military force of the colony was either engaged in the Cameroons or stationed near the frontier with that German colony and when there had already been sporadic risings in the interior districts of the Protectorate. He was rather highly impressed by Lugard's concession of the possibility of some

[88] *Ibid.*, Despatch dated 13.3.15 from Lugard to CO
[89] *Ibid.*   [90] *Ibid.*

agitation from Lagos and by the influx of 'aliens' into the principal towns of the interior. The history of a land agitation which had taken place earlier in the Eastern and Central Provinces had taught him that the capacity of these 'aliens' for 'mischief' was not a factor to be underrated. For these reasons he was unable to sanction the proposal.[91] If the first hindrance to a full realisation by Lugard of his taxation scheme for the Southern Provinces was the Colonial Office, the second was the determination of the British officers east of the Niger not to be stampeded into an incautious line of action.

After repeated pressure Lugard had been allowed to introduce direct taxation into Oyo in 1916. By 1918 all the provinces west of the Niger, except Warri, had been brought into line on this matter. Lugard had been allowed the free hand which he fought for only on the conditions that the impost on the people did not exceed what they already paid in the form of tribute; that it had the consent of their chiefs; and was not likely to precipitate any disturbance.[92]

These conditions were not easy to satisfy east of the Niger. If it was possible to equate 'topping', which on the coast House members paid to their head of House, to a form of tribute, there was nothing among the rest of the people of the Eastern Provinces which even remotely resembled tribute. If in the West and North there were chiefs who by tradition had the power to negotiate on behalf of their people and who were able to impose on them a programme which enjoyed their support there were no such dignitaries east of the Niger. The Warrant Chiefs had no real political influence. Nor was there any British officer in the Eastern Provinces who was prepared to assure the Colonial Secretary that the imposition of a novel tribute on the people would not lead to disturbance.

Nonetheless in March 1918 Lugard and the Lieutenant-Governor of the Southern Provinces, A. G. Boyle, felt themselves 'encouraged' by 'the success which was meeting the introduction of direct taxation into Oyo, Abeokuta and Benin Provinces' to request that the foregoing conditions imposed by the Colonial

---

[91] Despatch dated 30.4.15 from CO to Lugard in CSO 9/1/8. Secret file No. 35, Taxation in the Southern Provinces
[92] See Memo. C 49/1918 of March 1918 from LGSP to the Residents east of the Niger in the file Conf C 49/1918, Introduction of Universal Taxation in the Southern Provinces

Secretary be withdrawn so that the other provinces of Southern Nigeria which were still immune from taxation would be brought under the same dispensation. In order to see that the South fell into line with the North, Boyle and his chief were prepared to fly in the face of stubborn facts. Although it was a cardinal belief of the administration that the ideal condition for the introduction of direct taxation was the existence of influential chiefs, Boyle told his officers that where these did not exist village heads should be used as tax agents. It was also held that taxation could be introduced successfully only with the closest European supervision. Yet, while 'fully' realising that the political service was badly depleted, Boyle pressed his proposal, for, he argued, 'to make a beginning would be a great advance'.

When, however, Boyle called upon his residents east of the Niger to express their views on this great matter, particularly on whether it was a viable proposal, [93] the replies which came in were a sad disappointment of the high hopes which obtained at headquarters; there was no spontaneous enthusiasm for the scheme among the officers serving in the Eastern Provinces. But, as in the scheme for Paramount Chiefs and permanent presidents, [94] the resident of Calabar was less positively pessimistic than his counterpart at Ogoja or at Owerri, and it is doubtful whether his view reflected the opinions of his officers, who appeared uncertain about the prospects of the scheme. For the purpose of introducing direct taxation, he said the peoples in his province fell into two political types. There were first the communities of the coastal region – for instance Calabar Town and Opobo, in which he said it would be relatively easy to 'build up' Paramount Chiefs through whom taxation could be imposed. Then there were the 'interior tribes' among whom 'the whole position becomes much more difficult and will require great patience, perseverance and tact before any effective result can be hoped for'. In this group there was no hope of obtaining Paramount or even District Chiefs and the whole scheme would have to rest on the narrow shoulders of the village heads. Here he anticipated incessant disturbances and punitive expeditions, but he did not believe that these could develop into a general threat to peace. [95] In contrast to the resi-

[93] *Ibid.*   [94] See above pp. 143–4
[95] See Memo. No. C Conf 6/1918 dated 19.6.18 from Resident Calabar Province to LGSP in Conf C 49/1918, Introduction of Universal Taxation in the Southern Provinces

dent, neither R. B. Brooks, District Officer at Ikot Ekpene in 1918, nor M. D. W. Jeffreys, who was at Eket in 1919, shared this last opinion. Their view could be summarised with Jeffreys's cynical remark that 'given sufficient force anything is possible'.[96]

The Ogoja resident, W. E. B. Copland-Crawford, regretted his inability to recommend the scheme in view of the absence of chiefs 'who by character, influence or ability . . . stand out conspicuously for special distinction' and also in view of lack of enough European staff. Since no tributes were ever imposed in the province, he argued, any rate recommended as direct taxation 'would exceed what at present docs not exist' and would be in conflict with one of the Colonial Secretary's provisos. In his reply he seized the opportunity to castigate the tendency to dress the Eastern Provinces in jackets fashioned for other provinces, as well as Mr Palmer's optimistic opinion that except perhaps in Lagos there was no objection to taxation in the South. 'Mr Palmer's inquiries in the Ogoja Province,' he concluded, 'were of such a nature that his impression, so far as this province is concerned, should be largely discounted.'[97] With this scheme, as with the Native Prisons project, Lugard's second period of office in Nigeria was, as far as the Eastern Provinces were concerned, one of unrealised ambitions. It was not until 1926, eight years after his departure, that the question of direct taxation in this area became once again a live issue.

By means of these reforms, implemented and projected, Lugard attempted to confer on the Eastern Provinces what he thought were the benefits and glories of the local government system which he had set up in Northern Nigeria between 1900 and 1906, but he failed. Why?

Firstly, even before the system was fully put into operation its foundation had given way. The rest was near-chaos. The Native Authorities Ordinance, one of the main columns supporting the structure, was passed in 1916 and was not applied to the Eastern Provinces until 1917, but the First World War had started in 1914. The latter event led to a rapid fall in the number of

[96] Memo. Conf 24/1918 dated 1.6.18 from Mr Brooks, DO, Ikot Ekpene, in the file Conf C 49/1918, Introduction of Universal Taxation in the Southern Provinces. See also Memo. by Jeffreys dated Awa 26.6.19 in Calprof 16. Conf 1/26, Introduction of Taxation 1917–27

[97] Memo. No. Conf OG 12/1918 from Resident Ogoja Province to LGSP in Conf C 49/1918, Introduction of Universal Taxation in the Southern Provinces

European staff available for political duties in Nigeria, as officers who had military experience – and these were many – re-entered the army. Nigeria supplied officers for the defence of the Nigeria–Cameroon border and in 1917 had to surrender further staff either for military duties within the country or to take drafts to oversea fronts. The reduction in the civil establishments was such that Lugard himself told his officers that he would not expect 'the same results as under normal circumstances' and that all that was to be aimed at was 'to maintain the country in comparative peace and order and collect revenue essential for its administration'.[98]

One or two examples will serve to show the paralysing effects which this severe staff shortage had on the administration. In 1916 Mr E. Dayrell, who was stationed at Ikot Ekpene, wrote frantically for an additional political officer. He was the only senior officer in the very large Ikot Ekpene Division made up of the five districts of Ikot Ekpene, Abak, Uyo, Itu and Aro-Chukwu. With him at headquarters was an Assistant District Officer, Mr Price, who had only limited judicial powers, and in any case could not leave the station on account of treasury, prison and other routine work. At the time of writing Mr Dayrell had dealt with all Provincial Court cases which were outstanding at Abak, Uyo and Etinan, but still had at Itu and Aro-Chukwu cases which, he estimated, would take him two months to dispose of. Some of these cases had been outstanding for more than twelve months. Parts of Ikot Ekpene District itself had not been visited by a political officer for nearly one year. Bende Ofufa, a section of the district, was said to have seized the opportunity offered by this neglect to renounce all alien control. Its people refused to attend any court, to obey any summons or to allow arrest to be made there. It became a place of refuge for 'criminals' and run-away prisoners. In 1914 a policeman, a court messenger, a road-maker and a carpenter had been sent there to make a rest house and roads but had been chased out by the people, and yet by 1916 nothing had been done to punish 'this outrage'.[99] In the

[98] Telegram No. 489 dated 6.2.17 in Calprof 14: C 118/17, Native Labour for the Front, Recruiting of. See also Conf Memo. from F. D. Lugard, dated 31.1.17 in same file
[99] Letter No. 9/L4/16 dated 4.1.16 from Mr E. Dayrell, DO, Ikot Ekpene in Calprof 14: C 397/14, Reorganisation of Ikot Ekpene Division. A number of those who had enthusiastically supported the changes introduced by Lugard in 1914 must have watched this worsening staff situation,

face of this severe staff deficiency the vigorous supervision by the political service on which Lugard largely relied for the efficient working of the Native Courts and Native Authorities could not be secured.

The second important force working against Lugard was the fact that the times were changing fast. The initial fear and suspicion by the people of the white man and his régime had died down. Those who were appointed Warrant Chiefs, court messengers and headmen had had time to show that the whole business was lucrative in terms of the material gain and perceptible prestige and authority which flowed from it. As the country settled down and the period of widespread building of rest houses and the like was gradually coming to an end, the duties of a Warrant Chief or headman became less onerous. There had also been time for it to be demonstrated that those villages and clans on whose territories the Native Courts were built had much to gain and little to lose therefrom; it made them, as one officer put it, the Mecca of their surrounding neighbours.[100] The relevance of all this was that this greatly changed situation helped to generate a severe conflict, which will be dealt with in full below, between the demands of what was considered sound administration on the one hand, and the dictates of the indigenous political situation on the other. The political traditions of the people and the changes noted above demanded almost unlimited proliferation of Native Courts as well as the appointment of a large army of Warrant Chiefs to represent almost every social segment. But administrative convenience demanded fewer courts and fewer chiefs, as well as the emergence of paramount chiefs. Ultimately the British failure in the Eastern Province was the failure to resolve this conflict.

In this period also the Native Court personnel became more and more alienated from the people. Chiefs and their headmen began to take scant notice of their village elders. The decline of effective supervision consequent on the depletion of European

which meant a drastic drop in the frequency of supervision of the Courts, with increasing dismay. 'The Native Courts,' Dr Maxwell had warned in 1915, 'cannot be left entirely to themselves . . . [or] they would become in some cases utterly useless, in others actively mischievous.' Events proved this gloomy prognosis correct. See EP 1308/3. Annual Report, Owerri Province 1915, p. 27

[100] Ikom Division (Ogoja Province) Annual Report for 1917, p. 2, found as Onitsha Province file No. 427/1922

staff caused by the First World War enabled corruption and oppression to multiply. The clerks became masters of themselves, of the courts and of the people. In fact it was in the period which started about 1915 that the chiefs, court clerks, court messengers and headmen made their influence most felt by the people and earned for the Warrant Chief system that notoriety which it never succeeded in living down.[101]

Along the coast the full implications of Lugard's repeal of the House Rule Proclamation in 1915 were only realised gradually. A year after the repeal, an officer serving in Calabar jubilantly reported that the measure had not had the disintegrating effect on chiefly authority which the pessimists had foretold.[102] But from about 1917 the story, as told even in the official records, became different. In the annual report of that year the district officer of Opobo, writing to the resident of Calabar Province, said: 'Opobo had become a mere name, the heads of houses are heads in name only, they have no money and very little power left, they depended to a great extent on house rule and also on subscriptions from their heads of markets for the upkeep of the house. The trading firms do not now keep the house percentage of trade but pay direct to the boy who brings the produce, thus the chiefs in many cases get nothing.'[103] Later F. S. Purchas, also reporting on Opobo, wrote: 'It is not for me to discuss the wisdom of the repeal of the House Rule Ordinance. I did not know Opobo before that event. I have no hesitation in saying, however, that there is neither more happiness nor less persecution generally than existed in former years. . . . Now the people are scattered like sheep without a shepherd.'[104] Also the resident of Calabar Province wrote of the so-called chiefs of Calabar in the following words: 'The Calabar chiefs have undoubtedly lost all power since the repeal of the House Rule Proclamation. There is no unity of purpose among the people of a House.'[105]

Even before the repeal, the coastal towns were declining fast because their people could no longer maintain their traditional position as middlemen. As the European firms penetrated the interior the indigenous producers learnt to bring down their

[101] See the next chapter.
[102] EP 1138, vol. i, Calabar Province, Annual Report, 1915, pp. 4–5
[103] Calprof 14: C 278/1918, Opobo Division Annual Report, p. 1
[104] EP 1138, vol. vii, Calabar Province Annual Report, p. 10
[105] *Ibid.*, p. 6

produce themselves to the European factories. But before the repeal, coastal traditions assert, the position was not as hopeless as it became after, because the House still functioned as a corporate unit, and competition in trade was more or less between the middlemen and the interior producers. But the repeal introduced into the House the disturbing principle of everybody for himself and thus engendered bitter competition among even the members of the same House. The House heads had to cater for themselves. The impact of this new situation on the Warrant Chief System is shown by the following description given by Chief B. D. Frank-Bestman of Abonnema of the change in moral tone which these changes brought to the Native Court. He said:

> In those early days, that is, up to 1914, there was very little corruption in the Native Court because the first members who were still able to exploit slave labour through the House Rule Proclamation were rich and did not frequently condescend to take bribes. But from 1915 the first [Warrant] chiefs started to pass away and the younger men who took their places and who could no longer exploit slave labour as in the days of yore had to look for other sources of wealth. Those of them who got into the courts consequently became brazenly corrupt.[106]

This marked change in moral tone later helped to discredit the courts and their personnel, while the realisation that the legal and illegal perquisites attaching to warrants could to an extent make up for what was lost through trade decline and loss of slave labour also heightened the eagerness and ruthlessness with which warrants came to be sought for.[107] All this was disturbing for the Native Court.

Another factor which militated against the successful implementation of Lugard's schemes was his failure to carry the officers of the old Southern Nigeria administration with him. Since he looked with so much contempt on the administrative achievements of these men and their predecessors, it would not be surprising if he also considered them not very competent. One result of the amalgamation was that a number of senior officers from the North moved down to Lagos to work at headquarters and elsewhere.[108] Lugard relied largely on these men, and it

[106] Information collected from Chief B. D. Frank-Bestman, a House Head in Abonema, Degema Division
[107] See the next chapter.
[108] It has not so far been realised that the amalgamation brought about a wide dispersal of Northern Officers all over Southern Nigeria. Apart from those who served in the Central Secretariat, from where they were able to

would appear he took many decisive actions affecting Southern Nigeria without so much as consulting the officers who served there before 1914. A notorious example of this was Palmer's tour of and report on the Southern Provinces which took place without the knowledge of the senior Southern officers.[109]

The wholesale condemnation of the pre-1914 system which Lugard and the Northern officers indulged in offended the Southern group deeply and demoralised them, as will become clear from the chapters that follow. Mr Osborne, who saw the ordinances in their draft form, protested against the proposed reforms. He wrote:

> So far as my experience goes, I am of opinion that the Natives of the Central and Eastern Provinces have not got to that stage where they should be entrusted with powers of life and death. I am inclined that the present system of Native Courts goes far enough, and that in the more important cases native tribunals require the guiding influence and impartial judgment of a European officer.[110]

The political officers who were in the field had not the opportunity which Osborne had of commenting on the proposed reforms before they were introduced. But the controversy over the Palmer

influence policies powerfully, or were attached to the headquarters of the Southern Provinces, or served in the Yoruba Provinces, there were also some who served in the Eastern Provinces. This latter fact has not so far been recognised. One such officer was Mr Cator, who in 1920 was divisional officer at Calabar. In the Half-Yearly Report for Calabar Province (1920) there is the following entry about him: 'Mr Cator whose experience has been in the Northern Provinces writes: "There are no District Heads as such. . . . There are no finances as there are no Native Administration Estimates and I should very much like to see them here." ' Mr Reginald Hargrove, Resident, and an officer of old Southern Nigeria, commented: 'I have no desire to see District Heads established in Calabar Province or a Native Administration which the Province is at present quite unsuited for.' The conflict between the two groups would appear to have taken place at all levels in the administrative hierarchy and in all parts of Southern Nigeria, including the Eastern Provinces. The Rev. Groves at Ikot Ekpene later confessed to knowing a few Northern officers who were posted down to the Eastern Provinces after the amalgamation. Calprof 14: C 395/20 Half-Yearly Report, Calabar Province, 1920, pp. 2–3. See also *Aba Commission of Inquiry Notes of Evidence*, Lagos 1930, para. 18742.

[109] A. E. Afigbo, 'Sir Herbert Richmond Palmer and Indirect Rule in Eastern Nigeria 1915–28', *JHSN*, iii, 2, 1965. C 210/1915, System of Native Administration hitherto obtaining in the Southern Provinces

[110] A. Willoughby Osborne, Memorandum as to Proposal to Establish Provincial and Native Courts dated 12.12.12 in F. D. Lugard, *Report on the Amalgamation*, Appendix III, p. 77

report of 1914 offered them the opportunity of ventilating their own grievances against the reformers. They condemned the tendency to judge the South by the standards of the North, protested against the removal of the political officer from the bench of the Native Courts, against the failure to consult them before the imposition of the new-fangled ways and deplored the insinuation that they were incompetent. One of them wrote:

> I would suggest, there appears to be a suggestion running through the report . . . that political officers in old Southern Nigeria have not been doing their duty which is to be deprecated more especially as coming from an officer who only paid this part of Nigeria a very fleeting visit.[111]

These men believed, like Osborne did, that their system was basically sound though it needed minor structural changes. But the Lugardians saw it as unviable and as deserving to be swept into a limbo. There is no evidence to suggest sabotage but the polarisation of the service into Lugardians and anti-Lugardians surely hampered the implementation of Lugard's schemes. At least the enthusiasm and optimism with which policy was formulated could not be ensured for its execution. This was more so as the Lugardians were mostly senior men who were at headquarters while most of their 'opponents' were in the field. The argument between the two 'parties', which was kept at the level of a murmur[112] under Lugard, developed into a roar as soon as he left Nigeria and raged until the demise of the Warrant Chief system. The energy and time expended on this ultimately futile controversy, if directed to an objective study of the problems posed by the Ibo and their neighbours, would probably have staved off the final tragedy.

And finally there was the fact that the Lugardian reforms were not guided by the objective realities of the Eastern Nigerian political scene. No evidence has yet come to light that before (or even after) his reforms Lugard made any effort worth the name to understand the political situation east of the Niger; and it is not out of place to suspect that he never gave the problem serious thought. His was a time when it was coming to be firmly believed that anthropologists had a vital part to play in guiding the

---

[111] Memo. by A. B. Harcourt dated 1 3 15 in C 210/1915, System of Native Administration hitherto obtaining in the Southern Provinces
[112] EP 1138, vol. i, Annual Report, Calabar Province, pp. 1–4. Calprof 14: C/277/18 Annual Report on Aro-Chukwu for 1917, p. 18. These contain subdued criticisms of Lugard's system.

administration of 'primitive' peoples. The Government of Southern Nigeria recognised this fact and had engaged an anthropologist, Northcote Thomas, in 1909, to study the people and their society. But it is revealing that just before he introduced the new measures Lugard had dismissed Northcote Thomas on the theoretical ground that political officers who *should* be in daily contact with the natives ought to make better practical anthropologists. But Lugard did not ensure that these already overworked officers would have the time and interest to engage in amateur anthropological research. Discovering the structural and theoretical defects in Moor's system was one thing, while reconciling that or any other system with the political realities of the Eastern Provinces was another. Only the latter would have led to administrative success. But Lugard was concerned with the former.

Thus Lugard did not concern himself with the question of the traditional qualifications of the Warrant Chiefs to enjoy the large powers which the ordinance conferred on them. On the contrary he thought of a system by which the new Native Courts would include two types of chiefs: those he called 'traditional chiefs' and others who were to be 'persons who exercised great local influence and commanded confidence by their superior intelligence', and who could, if necessary, be 'elected' by the whole community. Apparently if chiefs of influence were going to emerge 'through the use of the ballot box', Lugard was ready to make the necessary concession. He even argued that a chief's son should not necessarily succeed to his warrant merely because he was his son or heir.[113] On the issue of how to discover 'traditional Chiefs' and encourage them to accept political office under the colonial government Lugard was silent. Yet for the Eastern Provinces this was already the crucial issue and remained so for decades after Lugard's departure. It is probably true to say that like his predecessors in Southern Nigeria Lugard did not suspect the existence of this problem.

Even before Lugard left the country indications had been received that his local government policy for the Eastern Provinces would be a failure. The first of these signs was the deposition of Chief Idigo of Aguleri as subordinate Native Authority because, said the Resident of Onitsha Province, Chief Idigo had shown that he had little influence, let alone authority, in the

[113] F. D. Lugard, *Political Memorandum*, 1918, pp. 272, 274

Aguleri Court District. Two murders were committed that year at Umuleri but Chief Idigo was unable to do anything to aid the government to apprehend the murderers. When urged to do something on the side of law and order Idigo confessed that he had no more influence than any other Ndichie of Aguleri.[114]

The career of Chief Igwegbe Odum, an Aro refugee who lived at One and who, as already shown, was made a Native Authority and Paramount Chief for the Ajalli Court district in 1917, is another case in point. His Paramount Chieftaincy was to be on probation for one year, after which, if he justified the confidence of the government, he would be confirmed in the position.[115] Less than four months after Igwegbe's elevation, however, Mr J. G. Lawton, the district officer at Awka, wrote to the Resident of Onitsha: 'The appointment of a Paramount Chief for the Ajalli district is not working satisfactorily. The Ajalli court is utterly divided at present between those who support Chief Igwegbe and those who demand his removal.'[116] In another report a few months later W. H. Lloyd, who had taken Lawton's place at Awka, again wrote: 'The political and court situation here is most unsatisfactory. The outburst against Igwegbe is universal. He has no friend outside one village now and one quarter which he used to control is seceding. The time of the Court and other chiefs is entirely taken up with raking up charges against Igwegbe, his brothers and ex-servants.'[117] Less than eight months after his appointment as Paramount Chief Igwegbe was destooled because, argued Resident R. A. Roberts (Onitsha), 'it is evident the Paramount system will not work at present at Ajalli and . . . it will serve no purpose to continue with the same'.[118] Less than three months after this Igwegbe lost even his membership of the court.

[114] Letter No. OPT 27/1917 dated 15.7.17 from the Resident of Onitsha Province to Secretary, Southern Provinces, in OP 298/17 Chief Idigo of Aguleri: Cancellation of subsidy
[115] Memo. No. OP 307/1917 dated 31.7.17 from Resident, Onitsha Province, to Secretary, Southern Provinces, in OP 307/1917 Chief Igwegbe, Creation of as Paramount Chief
[116] Memo. No. OP 307/1917 dated 21.3.18 from Resident, Onitsha Province, to Secretary, Southern Provinces (SSP), in OP 307/1917 Chief Igwegbe, Creation of as Paramount Chief
[117] Letter No. 461/1915 of 10.6.18 from DO Awka to Resident, Onitsha Province in OP 307/1917 Chief Igwegbe, Creation of as Paramount Chief
[118] Memo. No. OP 307/1917 dated 21.3.18 from Resident OP to SSP in OP 307/1917 Chief Igwegbe, etc.

Subsequent investigations revealed that no sooner did Igwegbe 'achieve' 'paramountcy' over the other chiefs than he proceeded to bleed the Ajalli Court district white. He engaged in the most brazen extortion, sought to reduce the other chiefs and their villages to subjection and posted his personal servants to his fellow chiefs' 'areas of authority' whence they would inform him about everything the chiefs said or did or both. He even sponsored revolts against the chiefs so that he would frequently be called upon to intervene as Paramount Chief and by so doing give greater substance to that position. Igwegbe's crimes were such that after a full inquiry the Resident of Onitsha gave him the option to leave the district and return to his home town, Aro Ndizuogu, or face prosecution and deportation. Around mid-November 1918 Lloyd reported from Awka that Chief Igwegbe Odum had left the Province.[119] Chief Igwegbe's rise and fall was perhaps the most dramatic and romantic in the story of the fortunes of individual Warrant Chiefs, but it was by no means singular as will be fully shown in the next chapter.

Lugard, claimed Margery Perham, 'was well aware that he was very far from having found the complete answer to the question of administration in the southeast'.[120] Is this correct, the critical scholar would ask. To this question one can only answer that Lugard did not confide this in the Colonial Office, nor did he tell the public. The *Report on the Amalgamation*, which contains an official account of his stewardship in Nigeria, could be regarded as one of the greatest tricks Lugard played on his contemporaries and even on later historians.

In compiling that report he made a guided selection of the opinions about his work which he gave publicity. Take the quotation from Dr J. C. Maxwell, the resident of Owerri. Maxwell was one of the new men whom Lugard superimposed on officers east of the Niger. And what was worse in Maxwell's own case, according to these officers, he had no experience at the district level before he was made resident of one of the most difficult provinces then in Nigeria. Before he was acquainted with his area he showed much enthusiasm for Lugard's reforms. At the

---

[119] Minutes of a meeting held by the DO Awka with the Chiefs of Ajalli NC at Ajalli on 24.10.18 in OP 307/1917 Chief Igwegbe, etc. A. E. Afigbo, 'Chief Igwegbe Odum: The Omenuko of History', *Nigeria Magazine*, No. 90, 1966

[120] M. Perham, *Lugard: The Years of Authority*, p. 461

end of the first year he reported: 'On the whole the Courts have worked efficiently. . . . The majority of the District Officers report a general improvement.'[121] However, there were a few officers who had reported adversely on the new system, but these officers were equally unfavourably described by Maxwell as those 'who [had] exercised the least supervision [over the Native Courts] and toured least.[122] It has to be remembered', continued his acid comment on these dissenting officers,

> that there are certain minds to whom a new idea is positively painful, something to be looked upon with grave suspicion; to them a change in the settled order of things can only be for the worse – [to them] the past is as a rose whose faded petals are for ever sweet.[123]

These words were written about the end of the first year of the new dispensation when this Lugardian looked upon his master's work and saw that it was good. But by 1917, when the other instalments of the projected reform came, Maxwell had begun to understand the Eastern Provinces a little better. And a comparison of his reluctance to support the proposals for Native Authorities, Native Prisons and the education of sons of chiefs with his earlier enthusiasm is revealing. But none of his adverse opinions on these issues found a place in Lugard's report.

Thus what Lugard presented to the Colonial Office and the general public was, in places, not the mature opinion of those quoted as praising the system. Mr Nicolson has also shown how in the same report Lugard doctored Mr Osborne's Memorandum on the proposed ordinances.[124] In any case, judging from his report, Lugard left Nigeria confident that he had laid the foundations for inevitable progress, or as he put it, established a system 'adequate for the needs of the community . . . capable of expansion and development, sufficient for any situation which can reasonably be anticipated for a considerable time to come'.[125] The next chapter will show how far Lugard was justified in his belief.

[121] F. D. Lugard, *Report on the Amalgamation*, p. 82
[122] *Ibid.*, p. 82
[123] OW 122/16, Native Courts, Memorandum on. See Memo. by Dr Maxwell dated 19.2.16.
[124] I. F. Nicolson, *The Administration of Nigeria*, etc., pp. 201–3
[125] F. D. Lugard, *Report on the Amalgamation*, para. 52

5 Lugardism on trial or the years of uneasiness, 1919–27

In sum, what did Lugard's reforms amount to in the Eastern Provinces? On the negative side Lugard had insulated the Native Courts from Supreme Court control, abolished the pre-1914 Native Treasuries, the House Rule Ordinance and the arrangement by which the political officer sat as president of the Native Court. He also curtailed the number of court messengers attached to each court. On the positive side he had extended the Provincial Court system manned by the political officer to the Eastern Provinces, interposing the Provincial Court between the Supreme and the Native Courts. He had also introduced the idea of Sole Native Authorities and Paramount Chiefs. There were, however, some of the projected reforms which were later to prove more fateful for the Warrant Chief System than the others which Lugard had actually implemented. Among these was the idea that the number of Warrant Chiefs for each court should be kept as low as possible, which created the tradition of leaving unfilled all but very necessary vacancies on the court bench created by the demise or disgrace of chiefs. The other was the credo that a real native authority must have a native treasury deriving its main revenue from direct taxation.

As shown in the last chapter, the Lugardian system ran into difficulty as soon as it was introduced. Here and there a few subdued voices hinted at the fact that the system was unsatisfactory but none in a sustained manner drew attention to the fact that it was totally out of tune with the political realities of the Eastern Provinces. In 1915 Mr Horace Bedwell, the Commissioner for Calabar Province and a veteran of the Old Southern Nigerian system, pointed out that the most important and immediate result of the Lugardian reform was that, through the Provincial Courts, it threw the burden of judicial work on political officers. The removal of Supreme Court control and the severe curtailment of the jurisdiction of the Native Courts meant that most of the cases affecting natives went to the Provincial Court run by political officers. The result, he said,

> is that judicial work now takes up a very large part of a political officer's time and, with a reduced staff, this has meant that travelling has suffered. To those who know the Southern Provinces visiting his district is one of the most, if not the most, important of the duties entrusted to a District Officer and his assistants.[1]

In 1917 a district officer in the Calabar Province mildly protested against Lugard's abolition of Moor's Native Treasuries because, said he, there was a great need for that institution among the Ibibio 'to provide revenue for chiefs and local administration generally'. Such a treasury would derive its revenue from Native Court fees and fines and from licences since it would be unwise to impose a direct taxation on the people, as 'it would be difficult to collect'. A Native Treasury had become all the more necessary, he pointed out, since the abolition of House Rule had deprived the chiefs of the income they formerly made from the trading ventures of their slaves. And unless a fund was formed out of which to pay the chiefs a reasonable salary they were bound to grow increasingly venial.[2] This was a reassertion of the essential validity of the pre-1914 system and a criticism of Lugard, who had abolished institutions even in areas where he was unable to find substitutes.

These hints were not taken and apparently nobody went further than these two officers had gone to focus official attention on some of the unsuspected implications and results of the extension of Lugardism to the Eastern Provinces. The result was that throughout the period of the governor-generalship of Lugard political officers grappled as patiently as they could with innumerable difficulties which they encountered in the actual application of the system. Though opposition to the Lugardian system was widespread and deep-seated among Southern officers, these men were reluctant to vocalise their views because Lugard, convinced of his own administrative ability,[3] was intolerant of criticism. It might be recalled that when political officers east of the Niger subjected his scheme for the education

---

[1] EP 1138, vol. i, Annual Report Calabar Province 1915, pp. 1–4
[2] Calprof 14, C 277/18 Annual Report on Aro-Chukwu, Itu and Uyo Districts for 1917, p. 18
[3] One is tempted to use the word 'infallibility' in place of 'ability'.

of 'future chiefs' to sober analysis he got angry with them, accusing them of treating the proposal as an academic thesis.[4] When in 1915 Dr J. Crawford Maxwell, the Commissioner for Owerri Province, pointed out that the parsimony of the 'new' régime had led to the severe shortage of even basic necessities like writing materials in the Native Courts Lugard rebuked him, ostensibly for including a criticism of the government in an annual report, but in fact for exposing the shortcomings of his policy.[5]

There is reason to believe that Lugard was of the stuff of which autocrats are made. This has increasingly impressed students of his career. Margery Perham, putting the matter euphemistically, said 'he had such an aptitude for administration that he hardly seemed to need the process of reasoning either with himself or with others'.[6] But there is something odious in a human being so able as to outlaw the normal processes of debate and dialogue so basic to democracy. Thus Dr P. C. Lloyd, in reviewing Perham's book, described Lugard as 'an autocrat, a terrible autocrat, determined to run Nigeria as a one-man show'.[7] This view has been upheld by Professor Flint and Mr Nicolson.[8] And like all autocrats Lugard preferred praise-singing to informed and objective criticism. In 1914, when he was full of his schemes for

[4] See ch. 4

[5] EP 1308/3, Annual Report Owerri Province for 1915, p. 28. See also Minute by F. D. Lugard dated 2.8.16. Dr Maxwell had written: 'Considerable inconvenience has been caused during the year by the failure to supply courts with the necessary books of records etc. On inspection of the courts it was found that clerks had been obliged to use blank pages of old cash books, flimsy manuscript books got locally or even loose sheets of paper to keep the records on, while counterfoil books for warrants of imprisonment had been converted into civil and criminal summons books. This should not have occurred as the requisition for the necessary books was submitted in ample time to ensure supply.'

[6] M. Perham, *Lugard: The Years of Authority 1898–1945*, London 1960, p. 140

[7] P. C. Lloyd, 'Lugard and Indirect Rule', *Ibadan*, 10 (a journal published at the University College Ibadan), p. 19

[8] J. E. Flint, 'Nigeria: The Colonial Experience from 1880 to 1914' in *Colonialism in Africa 1870–1960*, eds. L. H. Gann and P. Duignan. Flint shows that in his first period of office (in Northern Nigeria) Lugard wanted to 'centralise power in his own hands'; and that in the process of the amalgamation Lugard created for himself 'a strongly authoritarian position', pp. 252, 256. I. F. Nicolson, *The Administration of Nigeria, 1900–1960*, Oxford 1969, pp. 44–5. See also ch. 4, above

reform, for instance, he preferred the flattering views of people like Palmer and Dr Maxwell, who had little knowledge of the Southern system, to the sober advice of men like Horace Bedwell, R. B. Brooks and James Watt, who knew the land and its people.[9]

Under Lugard a practice had developed in the Nigerian colonial service by which officers who criticised government policies or projects too vociferously were accused of disloyalty. Mr F. P. Lynch, while raising an alarm on the deplorable state of the Warrant Chief System barely four months after Lugard's retirement, wrote: 'It may . . . be objected that representations of the nature made in this report [on the Warrant Chief System] have never been made by any other officer, to which I would reply that officers (including myself) have been afraid of incurring the charge of criticising the policy of the Government and of want of loyalty.' Also, said he, officers were generally loath to alter anything which those before them had apparently sanctioned and eulogised. In any case, he argued, should an officer report disquiet where a predecessor had given the impression that all was well he was suspected of incompetence.[10] By these remarks Lynch showed that he had a sound knowledge of the system which he was criticising. After reading his indictment of the Warrant Chief System, Colonel Moorhouse, the Lieutenant-Governor of the Southern Provinces, a man who had worked with Lugard at headquarters, made the absurd comment: 'I cannot bring myself to believe that had these practices been as widespread as Mr Lynch suggests they would not have been brought to the notice of Government by such officers as Mr Roberts, Dr Maxwell, Mr Copland-Crawford and Mr Simpson and Mr Watt.'[11] In other words, since Mr Lynch had not the experience and seniority of these officers, and though as a junior officer he was closer to the people than these residents were, he was not expected to know whether the system worked well or not, or he was not expected to report what he observed.

[9] See Memo. dated 20.1.20 by Mr R. B. Brooks, Resident, Owerri Province, in C 176/19, Remarks by F. P. Lynch on the Native Courts. See also Minute dated 6.11.19 by Col, H. C. Moorhouse
[10] Memo. dated 14.10.19 by F. P. Lynch in C 176/19, Remarks by F. P. Lynch, etc.
[11] Minute dated 6.11.19 by H. C. Moorhouse in C 176/19, Remarks by F. P. Lynch, etc.

In any case it is instructive that only about four months after Lugard ceased to head the government of the Colony and Protectorate of Nigeria Lynch felt himself sufficiently safe to send to headquarters a trenchant memorandum which called attention to the fact that the Warrant Chief System had been given an unforeseen twist by Lugard's reforms. According to Lynch all the chiefs and court staff were corrupt, the people were being badly oppressed under the system and the court clerk had become the lord of all he could survey. It is also instructive that while Colonel Moorhouse was inclined to brush the memorandum aside Sir Hugh Clifford, the new Governor, who as yet had not fallen in line with the practices in the Protectorate, took the hint and called for outspoken reports from his officers in the field. He called on them to report on three aspects of the existing system: (*i*) the quality of justice which the people received at the hands of the Warrant Chiefs; (*ii*) the fitness of the chiefs to exercise the powers entrusted to them; and (*iii*) whether any improvement in the authority and influence of the chiefs as in the general attitude and spirit of the people under them had been noticed since the Lugardian reforms were introduced.[12]

In their replies the political officers fell more or less into two groups. The first group consisted of almost all the officers in Owerri, Calabar, Onitsha and Warri Provinces and of C. Howard, who was stationed at Obubra, and was led by veterans of the pre-1914 system, for instance by R. B. Brooks, at the time Resident of Owerri. These men held that Lugard had distorted rather than reformed the system set up by Moor. In their opinion the courts did not dispense anything that could be called justice and the chiefs were not fit to exercise the powers given to them unless subjected to rigorous supervision by European officers. They also maintained that the authority of the chiefs had not increased since 1914, as the large powers which they exercised were not rooted in the confidence of their peoples. The attitude of the people, this group insisted, was that of a race under a terrible oppression against which they were helpless as the chiefs could boast ultimately of the support of the Nigerian police and army.[13] In the second group were about four or five officers, the

---

[12] Circular dated 26.11.19 from SSP to all residents of the Warri and Eastern Provinces in C 176/19, Remarks by F. P. Lynch, etc.

[13] See the Memos. sent in from Calabar, Owerri and Onitsha Provinces in C 176/19, Remarks by F. P. Lynch, etc. See in particular Memo. dated

majority of whom came from Ogoja Province, and one, E. R.
Palmer, the administrative officer at Obollo (Nsukka) in Onitsha
Province. The distinguishing mark of the reports sent in by this
group was studied moderation. They contended that the decisions
of the chiefs were fair, that the quality of the chiefs varied
according to the personality of each and that the attitude of the
people was that of general indifference. At times, however, the
people tended to look up to the Warrant Chief, who had perceptible authority, as the real power in the village rather than to the
'obscurantist' and powerless elders. With all their moderation
the officers in this group conceded that the chiefs could achieve
little without close supervision.[14]

By and large, however, there was a general concurrence in the
view that the court clerks and court messengers had come to
occupy positions which were not meant for them and that the
blame for most of the administrative evils of the time could with
fairness be laid at the door of Lugard. Resident Brooks attributed
the faults already mentioned to inadequate European supervision,

20.1.20 from R. B. Brooks; Memo. Conf OP 35/1919 dated 3.2.20 by
P. A. Talbot, Acting Resident, Onitsha; Conf L 4/1919 dated 11.1.20
from Mr Lyon, DO Udi; Conf 15/15/19 dated 18.12.19 from Bewley,
DO Okigwi. See also two Memos. from Frank Hives, Acting Resident
Warri, Conf No. 79/1919 dated 2.2.20 and another dated 12.11.19, etc.
[14] Memo. Conf No. 36/20 dated 20.1.20 from Mr Sasse, Acting Divisional
Officer; Memo. Conf OG 35/1920 dated 30.3.20 from S. W. Sproston,
Resident, Ogoja Province; Memo. Conf No. 23/1919 dated 28.12.19 from
G. G. Shute, Acting Divisional Officer, Abakaliki. From the tone of most
of the reports from Ogoja it is tempting to think that since the province
was opened up much later than the others that the choice of Warrant
Chiefs there was more in harmony with traditional principles, the government having learned from its mistakes elsewhere. But a study of other
records on the matter shows that this was not the case and that the
problems which afflicted the system at Owerri or Onitsha Province also
afflicted it in the Ogoja Province. Corruption was also rife. The main
difference between Ogoja and the other provinces was that western
education had made little progress there and this meant that the people,
to use a local but picturesque parlance, had not 'opened eye too much'. As
a result few complaints against the Warrant Chiefs, the court clerks and
the messengers would reach the ears of the over-worked political officers
because the oppressed were too frightened to be vociferous. There is
hardly any doubt that if these officers had carried out more patient
investigations than they did and put their ears close to the ground they
would have picked up the same signals as Lynch and the other officers did.
The report of Mr Howard stationed at Obubra, also in Ogoja, belies the
complacency of the other reports.

the attempt to limit the number of warrant holders, the appointment of permanent presidents for some courts, the reduction in
the number of court messengers and the fact that the political
officer, as a result of his exclusion from membership of the Native
Court, had lost touch with the people – developments all of
which were traceable to the period of Lugard's governor-
generalship. With this analysis Colonel Moorhouse was in full
agreement. He and Mr Brooks and many other officers who were
brought up under the earlier régime exhibited some bitterness at
the fact that during his reforms Lugard had given more weight
to the opinions of 'new men' like H. R. Palmer and Dr J. C.
Maxwell, who were ignorant of Southern Nigeria, than to their
own considered opinions based on definite knowledge of the
ground.[15]

The most startling revelation made by the memoranda sent
in by the political officers in Warri and the provinces east of the
Niger was the fact that Lugard had no ardent follower among
them and that there was a general lack of faith in his system.
Those who did not attack it vigorously did not defend it passionately. In spite of minor variations in the emphasis which each
officer placed on the facts the general opinion was in favour of
the emphatic assertion by Mr Lyon, who was district officer at
Udi. 'I wish to state as strongly as possible,' he said, 'that in my
considered opinion the present system is an unnatural one . . .
based on a system that is borrowed from a country [Northern
Nigeria] of dissimilar customs.'[16] In any event even the moderates
subscribed to P. A. Talbot's mild conclusion that 'the present
Native Court System is, to some extent, a failure'.[17] It is tempting
to think that the withering criticism which these officers made of
Lugard and his system could be explained in terms of their
having been infected by Clifford's attitude to Lugard. But it must
be borne in mind that the officers had their own independent
grievances against Lugard and that Clifford had hardly had time

[15] Memo. dated 20.1.20 from R. B. Brooks, Resident, Owerri Province,
and Minute No. 4 dated 6.11.19 by H. C. Moorhouse in C 176/19,
Remarks by F. P. Lynch, etc. S. M. Grier, *Report on a Tour in the
Eastern Provinces*, Lagos 1922. See Minute on p. 26 by H. C. Moorhouse
[16] Memo. Conf L 4/19 dated 11.1.20 from Mr Lyon at Udi in C 176/19,
Remarks by F. P. Lynch, etc.
[17] See Conf OP 35/1919 dated 3.2.20 from P. A. Talbot, Acting Resident,
Onitsha Province, and Memo. dated 27.12.19 from E. R. Palmer, District
Officer, Obollo (Nsukka) in C 176/19, Remarks by F. P. Lynch, etc.

to advertise his views of Lugard. And in any case, turning against Lugard Perham's blast against Moor, the defects of Lugard's system could have been 'demonstrated by any standards of good government'.[18]

The fact is that a survey of the history of the Warrant Chief System during the years covered by this chapter reveals that the pessimists were in the main justified. In the first place Lugard's attempt to achieve centralisation in local government through the creation of Paramount Chiefs, sole Native Authorities and permanent presidents of Native Courts had met with utter failure. The cases of Idigo and Igwegbe Odum, which were discussed in the last chapter, were, as already noted, no exceptions, for with embarrassing consistency the other Warrant Chiefs who were raised to one or other of these artificial positions demonstrated that they had neither the traditional right nor the personal merits to justify their appointments. A number of examples will help to illustrate the futility of the policy under discussion.

At Nnewi the appointment of Chief Orizu as Native Authority transformed the Native Court into a bear garden with two irreconcilable groups clutching murderously at each other's throats. At the head of the anti-Orizu party was Chief Nwosu, one of the oldest chiefs in the court and the man who had mediated between Colonel Moorhouse's Onitsha Hinterland Patrol of 1905 and the Nnewi people. He was closely related to Orizu: it is in fact said that they were second cousins. Nwosu had brought up Orizu, who was the younger man. He had also dominated the Nnewi Court until 1917, when Orizu was made a Native Authority. This event started what Nwosu regarded as the unnatural ascendancy of a young man over his elders. In 1920 Orizu was given the special privilege of sitting as a permanent member of the court. To Chief Nwosu and his supporters the 'exaggeration of Orizu's position' meant the violation of 'our constitution' and the creation of 'a super-chieftainship . . . over and above other chiefs who were hitherto in some cases head chiefs in their domain'.[19]

Unsettlement was also a persistent feature of the Ogidi Native Court district, thanks to Chief Walter Amobi's 'paramountcy'. It was alleged that Chief Amobi did not hesitate to use his privileged

[18] M. Perham, *Native Administration In Nigeria*, Oxford 1937, p. 61
[19] Memo. No. 139/1922 dated 9.10.22 from the DO, Onitsha in OP 414/1922, Nnewi Native Court, Unsatisfactory state of. See also the enclosed petition from Chief Nwosu and others dated 7.9.22

position as Native Authority to filch lands from his neighbours. One of the serious cases which caught the attention of the government in the early 1920s concerned Nkpo village. Amobi laid claims to a piece of land inhabited by a ward of this village and had proceeded to institute legal proceedings against Udeze, the senior Warrant Chief of Nkpo. Feeling unequal to a tussle with Amobi, Udeze was said to have accepted the claims of the powerful Nzekwu family of Onitsha town to the piece of land and to have undertaken to act as chief witness in the case against Amobi. Amobi replied by intensifying his suit against Udeze to the extent that the latter was forced to appeal to the government for the transfer of his people to the Onitsha Native Court district. 'I hold no brief for Walter Amobi,' said J. G. Lawton, district officer (Onitsha) in 1924, 'and I certainly think that the Ogidi court would be better if he were not so paramount.'[20]

The creation of permanent presidents was equally futile, equally productive of intra-court disquiet and very unpopular with all but the few chiefs who benefited from the policy. The appointment of a permanent president in any court deprived the other chiefs of the opportunity to sit as president and enjoy the coveted prestige and material rewards attaching to that position, while the political subordination which the new arrangement implied for the excluded majority was vehemently detested and resisted by them as contrary to the deeply laid political instincts and established practices of the people. As early as 1918 the political officer at Ikot Ekpene had announced that the whole experiment was both unworkable and hampering progress.[21] The permanent presidents, like the Paramount Chiefs, were not slow to seek to make it known that the government had vested them with great and unusual authority. One of these presidents, in under three months of his elevation, had actions in the court of which he was permanent president claiming all the land of 'his' clan. His pretensions were all the more unbearable to those he represented as he was an Ibo slave purchased before the British occupation and

[20] Memo. dated 3.1.24 from DO, Onitsha to the Resident, OP in OP 7/24. Representation made by Mkpo Town for separation from Ogidi Native Court. See also MP No. 4/1924 dated 11.1.24 from DO, Onitsha, to the Resident, Onitsha. Walter Amobi was not actually a Paramount Chief, but as a recognised Native Authority he played at being one.
[21] Memo. Conf 24/1918 dated 1.6.1918 from the DO, Ikot Ekpene, to the Resident, Calabar Province, in Conf C 49/1918, Introduction of Universal Taxation in the Southern Provinces

later pushed forward to represent an Ibibio clan in the court. Another permanent president within four months of his appointment instituted court actions against almost every neighbouring village and conducted the suits with forced contributions from the people he represented.[22]

The fact was that the influence of even the most powerful of the Warrant Chiefs was so circumscribed that the least attempt to extend his authority bred intense jealousy and led to all kinds of abuses. In Owerri Province no attempt was made to carry out this experiment because, warned the resident, 'any attempt to enforce paramount chieftaincy will bring trouble'.[23] Though Njoku Nwansi was called, but not recognised, as Paramount Chief of the extensive and populous Isu sub-tribe, he was able to claim only a shadowy authority over a fraction of the Isu which was included in Owerri Division. In the Isu section under Okigwi Division he was a mere name. The little precedence he enjoyed in the Owerri half he owed to his wealth and personal qualities. A great slave-dealer in the pre-British era, he became very opulent by local standards under the new régime and was famed for being the first son of Owerri Division to ride a bicycle, a motor-cycle and a car. He was also the first to build a two-storeyed house.[24]

By 1922 senior political officers in the Eastern Provinces had come to see the futility of this scheme and called for its abandonment. The reaction against this policy is best seen in happenings in Calabar and Onitsha Provinces, where the policy of Paramount Chieftaincy, Sole Native Authorities and permanent presidents had been applied with some vigour and optimism. In 1922 R. B. Brooks, then the Resident of the Calabar Province, ruled that as the permanent presidents died out no further attempt should be made to replace them, for they were 'of no use or assistance in any way'.[25] In Calabar Division most of the permanent presidents, including the *Mbong* of Duke Town and Creek Town, were pulled down and rotatory presidency adopted. The same

[22] Memo. dated 20.1.20 by R. B. Brooks, resident, Owerri Province in C 176/19, Remarks by F. P. Lynch, etc. Brooks was reporting from his experience in the Calabar Province.
[23] EP 1308/6, Annual Report Owerri Province for 1919, p. 2
[24] Based on information collected from Chief J. N. Nwansi of Ikeduru in Owerri. The informant succeeded his father as Warrant Chief.
[25] EP 3759, Native Authorities in the Southern Provinces. See Memo. MP No. C 651/22 dated 29.5.26 from Acting Resident, Calabar Province.

year the district officer reduced the policy of appointing Sole Native Authorities to absurdity by recommending the staggering number of 116 chiefs as Sole Native Authorities, some of these exercising authority only over ward-sections.[26] With the death in 1924 of Chief Anoyom of Nja, permanent president of the Enyong Native Court, the permanent presidents in the province were reduced to only three – Chief J. Z. Baillie of Oku Native Court, Chief Ebong of Ibesit in Abak Native Court area and Chief Nkomang of Utu Etim Ekpo. In 1926 F. P. Lynch, Acting Resident of Calabar, recommended that the Native Courts of Calabar and Creek Town be appointed Native Authorities in place of the individuals who had hitherto occupied the position. Though it is not clear whether this was immediately sanctioned, the recommendation by itself was a confession of the failure in the Calabar Province of Lugard's scheme for artificially building up influential chiefs.[27]

The same period witnessed similar happenings in the Onitsha Province. In 1922 Frank Hives, resident, recommended the removal of Chief Chukwuani of Ozalla as Native Authority, as he appeared 'to have no paramount authority over the Nkanu tribe'. In his place the Native Courts of Ogui and Agbani were made Native Authorities. In 1923 Chief Walter Amobi of Ogidi got the Warrant Chiefs of Ogidi Court to petition the government that he be made a Paramount Chief. The Lieutenant Governor, Colonel H. C. Moorhouse, replied that though he was not unaware of the fact that Amobi had been 'of immense use to the Government', he was unable to appoint him a paramount chief because, as he put it, 'it is contrary to the present policy of the Government to place any one chief as paramount chief over towns and villages he has no hereditary right of control, and I personally believe it to be contrary to the custom of the Ibo people'.[28] Although the idea of Paramount Chieftaincy was to linger on in a few minds until a later period, here was a renunciation of one of the foundations of Lugard's policy in the Eastern Provinces.

[26] Memo. MP No. 651/22 dated 29.5.26 from acting resident, Calabar Province in EP 3759, Native Authorities in the Southern Provinces
[27] EP 1138, vol. x, Annual Report on Calabar Province for 1924, p. 12. See also Memo. MP No. 651/22 dated 29.5.26 in EP 3759, Native Authorities in the Southern Provinces
[28] Memo. MP No. 4/1923 dated 31.1.23 by DO, Onitsha in OP 56/1923, Petition for the recognition of Walter Amobi as Paramount Chief. See also letter dated 6.2.23 from SSP to Resident Onitsha

Subsequently Chief Onyeama of Eke was pulled down from his artificial position as Native Authority because, said the resident, 'as a paramount chief', he was 'a mushroom growth'. Chief Walter Amobi went down in 1924. In 1926 Mr R. A. Roberts, Senior Resident Onitsha, 'strongly' recommended that the Native Court of Onitsha be made Native Authority for the Onitsha Native Court district and that the appointments of Chiefs Obi Okosi and Mba be cancelled. They too had failed to prove that they had authority beyond 'the range of their vision and the sound of their voice'. A Native Authority like Orizu of Nnewi had conveniently died before his turn came. 'The matter of appointing individuals as Native Authority,' said the resident, washing his hands like Pontius Pilate, 'was in accordance with the wishes of Sir Frederick Lugard . . . but in the south it has proved a failure.'[29]

As already shown, one important aspect of the Lugardian scheme was the proposal to reduce drastically the number of Warrant Chiefs in each court so that eventually powerful chiefs would emerge from each Native Court area. Though the plan of an immediate and outright dismissal of the majority of the chiefs had been abandoned at the last minute as likely to cause discontent, the official policy continued to be not to appoint new chiefs just because a Warrant Chief had died or lost his warrant for scoundrelly behaviour but to make appointments only in cases where large groups of villages had come to lack a representative chief. In Okigwi Division this policy led to a situation in which by 1920 the Orlu Native Court had only fifty-seven chiefs instead of the officially sanctioned sixty-two, the Umuduru Native Court twenty-five instead of thirty-nine and the Okigwi Court thirty-one instead of thirty-three.[30] In Aba Division in 1921 the position was as follows:[31]

29 See Memos. No. OP 117/1917 dated 30.9.22 from Frank Hives, Resident, Onitsha; A 563/17 dated 11.10.23 by Cooke, Resident, Onitsha; A 563/17 dated 14.2.23 from R. A. Roberts, Resident, Onitsha; OP 117/1917 dated 21.1.24 from Palmer, Resident, Onitsha; and Extract from Annual Report on Onitsha Province for 1926 all in EP 3759 Native Authorities in the Southern Provinces.
30 OW 416/20 Native Court Membership Instructions, etc. See Enclosure No. 6, Memo. No. 1936/3/1920 dated 19.11.20 from the DO Okigwi
31 Memo. No. 18/6/1921 dated 4.1.21 from DO Aba in OW 95/21 Aba Native Court, Reorganisation of

Native Court	No. of towns recognised	No. of chiefs approved	Actual no. of chiefs	Unrepresented towns
Owerrinta	35	35	30	10
Asa	27	27	24	10
Obohia	16	25	24	1
Aba	71	60	51	25
Omuma	25	25	21	5
Azumini	37	35	27	4

This policy was being applied in the teeth of much opposition. Experience had shown that the possession of a warrant meant political and economic power, and the Native Court Warrant was superseding the ancient titles as a symbol of status and achievement. Consequently this period saw very bitter rivalry and scheming for warrants. Retired or sacked government servants angled for warrants. At Nguru in Owerri, for instance, one Ukegbu, a former police constable, did what he could to bring his chief, Onyekwere, into disrepute in order to take his place as Warrant Chief.[32] In these contests the indigenous political constitution of the village based on lineage segments of about equal power and size provided a most admirable weapon. Heads or pretended heads of wards, ward sections and ward sub-sections, or even of fictitious sections which sprang up mushroom-like, joined the splendid quest for warrants. Any man who could rally round himself a few scores of obstreperous hot-heads put in a claim for a warrant. Usually the section real or fictitious of which the would-be warrant holder claimed to be head was presented as an autonomous village which had never been subordinate to any other group.[33]

A few examples will illustrate how fierce the scramble for warrants had become. Between 5 September and 10 October 1923 Mr F. L. Tabor, District Officer at Owerri received over eighty applications for warrants. On investigation, he said, he generally found that most of the applicants were 'mere heads of families and their dependants numbering as a rule less than 100 males who live in one hamlet or compound'.[34] The experience of

[32] Extracts from Intelligence Book dated 10.5.18 and 15.5.19 as well as Memo. No. 302/19/19 by DO, Owerri in OW 202/19, Nguru Native Court – Conduct of Ukebu (ex-constable)
[33] Memo. No. 855/2/1920 dated 12.10.20 by DO, Aba in OW 416/20 Native Court Membership – Instructions, etc. OW 279/20, Half-Yearly Report for Owerri Division, 1920, para. 2
[34] Memo. No 855/2/1920 dated 12.10.20 by DO, Aba in OW 416/20, Native Court Membership – Instructions, etc.

Mr J. G. Lawton, District Officer of Onitsha in 1923 at Uke is another revealing example. This village, situated between Abatete and Umoji, is divided into two main sections, each subdivided into three wards. Mr Lawton was the first district officer to visit it for ten years. As he entered the village, he said, he was met by 'innumerable candidates of all ages for the position of the two deceased chiefs'. The meeting which he held with the villagers was so stormy that no decision could be arrived at on any of the issues discussed. One of the wards, called Umuazu, 'had six candidates at least, each with a mob of supporters and opponents howling yes and no'. One of the contestants was an ex-court messenger, by name Okonkwo.[35] The policy of centralisation was therefore a total failure even at the level of the village. If anything the lure of the warrant helped to emphasise the tendency towards the decentralisation of authority and the segmentation of social units which were inherent in the indigenous structure.

The ruthless reduction of the Native Court messenger service carried out by Lugard in 1914 not only failed to achieve the purpose for which it was effected but led to very undesirable developments in the working of the Warrant Chief System.[36] In less than one year after the reduction was made there were unmistakable signs that the measure was unwise, impracticable and foredoomed to failure. The district officer at Idah (then a district in Onitsha Province) had been forced to reduce the court messengers in his area of authority to three on 5 May 1914.[37] By 5 March the following year he was calling frantically for the addition of two more men to the contingent. His police establishment had also been reduced to ten men, a number which was barely sufficient to guard the treasury and the post office, to provide a daily and nightly beat at the waterside where urban conditions of life were fast developing and to furnish the district officer with an escort when on tour. Yet shortage of court messengers forced him on occasions to use policemen in serving Native Court processes, a practice which Lugard had roundly

[35] Intelligence Book 'B' for Onitsha Province. See entry on Uke dated 13.12.23
[36] On the origin and the official duties of the court messenger service, see ch. 3
[37] Telegram No. 345 from the Resident, Onitsha Province, to the DO, Idah, in OP 29/14, Native Courts, Onitsha Province, Court Messengers allowed for

condemned.[38] In Ikot Ekpene Division, which had seven Native Courts, the court messenger establishment had been reduced from sixty-four to twenty-four. In Ikot Ekpene Court area the establishment had been cut from twenty to five. It was this small gang which was expected to serve the two hundred and thirty summonses and thirty warrants which on the average the court issued weekly.[39] At Bende in 1920 the processes amounted to three thousand but only twenty court messengers were available for serving them. To serve a Native Court process a court messenger at times had to cover between sixteen and twenty miles each way.[40]

If court messengers were required only to serve court processes, Lugard's plan might not have collapsed as quickly and as completely as it did. But in addition they guarded the properties of the courts, maintained order during court sittings, guarded criminals under arrest, carried messages between the district officer and court clerks, between the former and the resident and between the court clerk and individual Warrant Chiefs, or 'recognised' village or quarters headmen.

The desire for economy during the 1914 reforms had also led to the abolition of the post of road inspectors. These men were responsible for supervising the construction and maintenance of roads which did not come under the Public Works Department and had to be maintained by compulsory labour from the local people. These were the so-called provincial roads of those days. After 1914 the district officer became, in theory, directly responsible for supervising work on this class of roads, but in practice it was the court messengers who now became inspectors of provincial roads. In Aba in 1921 the roads which fell into this category exceeded one hundred miles in length and the sum granted for their maintenance was so paltry that it was barely sufficient for the upkeep of the temporary bridges on the roads. The court messengers also looked after rest houses. In Aba Division there were twelve of these rest houses in 1921 and no grants were made for their upkeep. If a chief was asked to carry out repairs on either the rest house or road his first request

[38] Memo. No. L 176/15 dated 22.3.15 from DO, Idah, in OP 29/14, Native Courts, Onitsha Province, etc.
[39] EP 1138, vol. viii, Annual Report for Calabar Province 1922, pp. 16–17
[40] Memo. No. 123/5/21 dated 15.2.21 by DO, Bende, in OW 98/21, Native Courts Owerri Province, Organisation of

generally was for a court messenger whose presence would convince the local people that the work was being done by the order of the Native Court.[41]

To the people court messengers had come to be an incarnation of the central government and of the Native Court. As a result they had to be everywhere the government or the Native Court wanted a job done. If the Nigerian Railway asked for building supplies or for labour, court messengers had to accompany the chiefs to get the order executed, and when officers went on tour they also had need of court messengers if their wishes were to be carried out. Government surveyors discovered to their chagrin that whenever they were not accompanied by court messengers they experienced great difficulties in getting their job done. The Warrant Chiefs would take no notice of such surveyors, would even positively obstruct them and provide them with neither water nor firewood. Furthermore, in view of shortage of policemen, court messengers had to do the work of rural constables in the court areas in which they served and had on occasions to arrest or serve summonses on offenders whose cases fell under the jurisdiction of the Provincial or even the Supreme Court.[42] Lugard, in 1914, had not shown a full appreciation of the extent to which these court messengers could be used in a place like the Eastern Provinces or of the possible untoward consequences of a drastic curtailment of the strength of the service at the same time as the strength of the regular police was being reduced.

Political officers who were in the field protested against the reduction before it was effected, but their objections were brushed aside by Lugard. After it had been carried out they vainly applied for increases in the court messenger establishment.[43] Eventually they were compelled by circumstances to make their own improvisations. In 1914 the government had spoken vaguely of the need to form small contingents of 'native police' which would be under the control of Paramount Chiefs in order to relieve the court messengers of minor police and other duties outside the premises of the Native Courts.[44] But this plan

[41] Memo. No. 123/50/1921, dated 6.2.21 by DO, Aba, and No. 123/5/21 dated 15.2.21 by DO, Bende, in OW 98/21, Native Courts, Owerri Province, Organisation of

[42] *Ibid.*

[43] EP 1138, viii, Annual Report, Calabar Province, 1922, pp. 16–17

[44] Circular Letter No. A 17/1914 dated 10.3.14 from SSP to all Residents, in OP 29/1914 Native Courts, Onitsha Province, etc.

could not be implemented owing to the exigencies of the political situation east of the Niger. Not only were Paramount Chiefs non-existent and, as experience bitterly revealed, impossible to create, but no Warrant Chief had the revenue from which to maintain a personal police contingent. Nonetheless, as the officers found themselves in stringent need they made use of this vague proposal. They connived at a practice by which a Native Court employed 'special court messengers' called 'recruits'. These men had no official status, no regular or stated salary. They inherited the discarded uniforms of official court messengers, subsisted on private payments which plaintiffs made for the service of sum-monses and on the free food which they got from those who asked for their service. In reality, however, the special court messengers did not stop at any objectionable practice to make their undefined status pay. Though it cannot be said with certainty that they were any worse than the official court messengers, Mr H. S. Burrough, District Officer at Degema, complained in 1921 that the system was 'most unsatisfactory and dangerous' and had caused 'much trouble'. In his division the situation became so bad that he was forced to dismiss the recruits *en masse* and to adopt the practice by which the presiding Warrant Chief provided two or three men to run special messages for the court.[45]

In 1921 the position in Owerri Province was as follows:[46]

Division	No. of NCs	Official messengers	'Recruits'
Aba	6	37	37
Owerri	6	47	24
Bende	?	23	40
Ahoada	6	29	—
Opobo	1	?	None
Degema	8	34	Dismissed *en masse* in 1920
Okigwi (District)	2	24	12

In Okigwi Division in January 1921 it had been found that some courts had as many as twenty-five 'recruits'. The number was, however, drastically cut down to six for each court.[47]

By 1922 it had become so clear that the use of these 'hangers-on at Court' was unsatisfactory that the government was forced to grant each court an increase in the official messenger establish-

[45] See Enclosures Nos 1 to 8 in OW 98/21, Native Courts, Owerri Province, Organisation of   [46] *Ibid.*
[47] Memo. No. 272/20/21 dated 15.2.21 by DO, Okigwi, in OW 98/21, Native Courts, Owerri Province, Organisation of

ment. The Ikot Ekpene Division, for example, got sixty extra men added to its establishment.[48] Here again Lugard's scheme had proved ill-conceived, impracticable and had to be abandoned. The handicap of the shortage of European staff which had always afflicted the administration but which the war had worsened, outlasted the war. 'The whole of the Province,' wrote Mr Reginald Hargrove, the resident of Owerri in 1919, 'is of course suffering from being understaffed and Assistant District Officers are urgently required at Okigwi, Owerri, Aba and Degema. Okigwi is the most urgent.' Mr O. W. Firth at Okigwi had not only the districts of Okigwi and Orlu to administer, but was also the local treasurer in the two areas and supervised the Bende District, where an inexperienced political officer was in charge. He was also in charge of the 'troublesome' Lengwe area, which was virtually still unconquered. It was considered necessary to form a sub-district in the southern portion of Okigwi Division and to establish new Native Courts at Amakohia and Añara. Orlu district needed a new Native Court to serve Uruala and its neighbours. But all these proposals were shelved owing to lack of European staff.[49] In 1920 the resident of Calabar lamented that supervision had suffered as a result of the shortage of administrative officers, and looked back longingly to the period before 1914 when it was possible for the Calabar Province to station a political officer at Abak, another at Aro-Chukwu and two at Eket.[50]

It was not only shortage of staff that was responsible for the lack of supervision which the Native Courts and their personnel enjoyed. Equally serious in its consequences for political work was the fact that political officers continued to represent all the various departments of government and to spend too much of useful time on routine work. The evil which Syer complained of in 1911 still afflicted the administration.[51] Every district officer had to prepare returns for the police, prisons and treasury departments, to mention only a few, while Native and Provincial Court returns were, of course, some of the foremost responsibilities of the political service. In some districts, observed

[48] FP 1138, vol. viii, Annual Report, Calabar Province, 1922, p. 17
[49] OW 454/19 Owerri Province Handing Over Notes; Hargrove to Brooks, paras 3, 16, 17
[50] Calprof 14, C 395/20, Half-Yearly Report, Calabar Province 1920, pp. 14–16   [51] See above p. 108.

S. M. Grier in 1922, there were Native Courts with as many as eighty Warrant Chiefs, and lists of these chiefs, the number of times they sat on the bench and other such intelligence were being meticulously prepared. As few offices had typewriters at that time, this work had to be done by hand. As there was persistent complaint of inefficiency against the clerical service, the political officer had to do the writing himself, especially as it was widely believed by officers that the value of their work was judged 'almost entirely by the accuracy and neatness of their returns'.[52] Under these conditions political officers travelled chiefly along the main roads, and Native Court supervision came to mean a hurried visit to each court once a month. Thus the Warrant Chief System, as modified by Lugard, had to function under conditions which Lugard had, surprisingly, not taken into consideration. The result was disastrous.

If in the pre-Lugardian era the influence of court clerks was not unfelt in the courts, in the period after 1914 it became one of ascendancy. In this later period there were complaints against them everywhere and no annual report of the Eastern Provinces was complete without a reference to the nuisance which court clerks constituted. In fact, the years from about 1914 to about 1930 could be properly called the 'golden age' of court clerks in the Eastern Provinces, the era during which the clerk sitting at his table commanded and was obeyed. Instances of their baneful dominance of the courts were many.

In 1918 a group of people who called themselves 'the community of Bonny' described the local court clerk as 'the chief cause of disintegration and disquiet at Bonny'. In a petition to the resident the same year the members of the Bonny Native Court complained of 'a practice which has become not uncommon . . . of the Native Court Clerk of Bonny assuming a policy of debating with both the sitting members and ordinary persons on matters affecting his interest in the court'. They charged him with intimidating members 'by pretending to have better knowledge of court procedure and Government laws' and with perpetually manœuvring to refer to the district officer Native Court cases in which he was interested and which had gone

[52] S. M. Grier, *Report on a Tour in the Eastern Provinces*, etc., pp. 18–19. G. J. F. Tomlinson, *Report on a Tour in the Eastern Provinces*, Lagos 1923, pp. 24–5. Memo. No. 757/37/22 dated 5.10.22 by Capt. Hanitch in Calprof 14, C 582/22D, Pedigrees of Chiefs, etc.

against his wish.[53] About this time too Mr F. P. Lynch, district officer, wrote: 'There is no doubt whatever and it is indeed natural that the courts are to a large extent run by the court clerk. Frequently does the petitioner say that the chiefs gave one decision and the clerk another and then the chiefs agreed with his decision.'[54] After his tour of the Eastern Provinces in 1922, S. M. Grier reported that it was the custom for the Warrant Chiefs to address the clerk as 'master'. 'We are administering these Provinces,' Grier concluded, 'through a junior political service composed of semi-educated Africans, who in many cases are alien to the people they control.'[55]

Practical manifestations of this ascendancy were legion but one of the most revealing which have come down to us was the rise and fall of Chief Igwegbe Odum of One as the Paramount Chief and Native Authority for the Ajalli Court district in the Awka Division. Igwegbe Odum, as a very wealthy trader and farmer, was a good friend of court clerks and interpreters. Though the details of how he obtained a warrant are obscure there is reason to believe that it was through the influence of these powerful men at headquarters. The fact that he became a Paramount Chief and Native Authority through the intervention of the same men is fully documented. At the time of his elevation to these prominent positions the clerk of the Ajalli Native Court was Mr Nzekwu, an Onitsha man. Igwegbe formed a formidable coalition with Nzekwu and the district interpreter that was able to bully the chiefs of the Ajalli Native Court into petitioning that Igwegbe be made a Paramount Chief. 'We do hereby,' read the petition which they were made to sign, 'of our own free will on behalf of ourselves and our people elect Chief Igwegbe of One to be our Paramount Chief.' The force of this pressure could easily be estimated from the fact that it was sufficient to prevent the reluctant and grumbling chiefs from revealing their objections to the appointment from 1916, when first they 'asked' for it, to 1917, when it was made and for many months after the triumph of the plot.[56]

Chief Igwegbe's woes started with the departure of Mr Nzekwu

[53] Petition by Bonny Chiefs dated 15.6.18 in OW 383/18, Bonny Native Court – Complaints by Chiefs against clerk of
[54] Memo. dated 14.10.19 by F. P. Lynch in C 176/19, Remarks by F. P. Lynch, etc. [55] S. M. Grier, *Report on a Tour in the Eastern Provinces*, p. 5
[56] Petition dated 11.5.17 from Warrant Chiefs, Ajalli, to DO, Awka, and Memo. No. T 2/1917 dated 25.6.17 from DO, Awka, to resident, Onitsha, in OP 307/1917 Chief Igwegbe Creation of as Parliament Chief

from Ajalli. The man who took Nzekwu's position, one Mr Kerry, for undisclosed reasons, refused to fit into Igwegbe's scheme of things. It was only then that Chief Mbonu of Ndikelionwu was able to tell the government that they 'were forced to sign the petition asking for Igwegbe's appointment as Paramount Chief', and that 'Igwegbe made friends with clerks and interpreters putting honest people in prison'.[57] Igwegbe's fall was a triumph for Mr Kerry just as his rise was for Mr Nzekwu. His career was a clear evidence of the power of court clerks in this era, of their ability to make and unmake Warrant Chiefs.

The practical consequences of the ascendancy of court clerks in this period are also richly illustrated in the oral traditions of the people. Mr Jacob Aweze of Ezzagu in Abakaliki, a confident-looking small man, who was a court messenger during this period, recently asserted that no other group of Africans employed by the government in those days or after enjoyed as much prestige and authority or aroused as much envy and fear as did the court clerks. They were, he said, so important and so arrogant that most people believed the court was theirs. In the view of some people they tended to bulk larger than the district officer.[58] Chief Nwancho of Inyimagu Ikwo (Abakaliki) said that if a clerk fell out with a chief he would start openly disregarding whatever that chief said and that litigants were generally quick to notice that such a chief was losing influence. One Mr Jumbo from Bonny, who was once stationed at Abakaliki, was even reputed to have flogged chiefs who fell foul of him and to have asked court messengers to disgrace them in court.[59] Chief James Onwunali of Ikenanzizi Obowo, Okigwi, who himself was a Warrant Chief, told stories of how a clerk of the Obowo Native Court made a 'law' that no 'chief' should smoke a pipe in court, and how one Chief Nwachukwu Nwadike when sitting as a vice-president smoked a pipe in court and was fined two pounds at the instance of the court clerk for contravening government 'law'. No record of the fine was made, however.[60]

[57] Memo. No. 461/1915 dated 10.6.18 by DO, Awka, and Minutes of Meeting with Chiefs dated 24.10.18 in OP 307/1917 Chief Igwegbe, etc.
[58] Based on information collected from Jacob Aweze of Ezzagu, an ex-court messenger.
[59] Information collected from Chief Nwancho Atuma of Ikwo, and Chief Ukpai Ereshi of Agba, all in the Abakaliki Division.
[60] Information collected from Chief James Onwunali of Obowo, Okigwi, a former Warrant Chief.

This position which the clerks illegally carved out for themselves was so firmly established that Warrant Chiefs and aspirants to that office had to seek the court clerk's favour with presents; at times of their beautiful daughters. A chief who played his cards well, especially by directing litigants who came to him for help to the clerk as the power who could make or mar a case, could easily win, with the support of the clerk, a prominent position in court. Igboji Ola of Igboagu, one of the first Warrant Chiefs of Izzi (Abakaliki), was in the habit of asking his people to send gifts of yams, fowls, firewood and the like to the court clerk, the district interpreter, and some policemen. In this way his people were constantly reminded that he had these highly placed men as friends and that it would be dangerous to fall foul of him. At Ezzagu (Abakaliki) the first Warrant Chief was Akuma, but it was Ukoro Edene of the same place who used to entertain court clerks, messengers, interpreters and other officials whenever they visited Ezzagu, while Akuma remained splendidly aloof. These officials in time formed the habit of looking up to Ukoro Edene as the real man at Ezzagu. Ukoro and Akuma were at loggerheads over many things but Akuma was never able to secure a conviction in the court against Ukoro. When Akuma died Ukoro directly stepped into his shoes as Warrant Chief as if he were his legal heir, thanks to his good relationship with the right men at headquarters.[61]

An Ikot Ekpene man who was a court clerk in Abak District between 1921 and 1923 has told the story of how he settled a difficult land case there. The struggle for this particular piece of land had split a ward of the village from top to bottom and the case had been in the court for so long that everybody had tired of it. This man, as the local court clerk, went into the matter, investigated and adjusted the claims and warned all concerned that he would not want to hear anything more of the case. According to him this ended the matter.[62] Thus the influence of court clerks was not confined to the court premises: it was also a factor of great importance in intra-village politics.

[61] Information collected from Mr Abraham Ejidike, of Abakaliki Town, who served as a court messenger at Abakaliki during the second decade of this century, and from Chief Idika Igboji of Izzi (Abakaliki), son and successor of Igboji Ola, a Warrant Chief.
[62] Based on information from Mr Kenrick Udo of Ikot Ekpene Town, ex-court clerk.

There is evidence that more often than not the so-called decisions of the Warrant Chiefs were in many courts, especially in those far away from district headquarters, the decisions of the court clerks. Chief Elei Adagba of Mgbo (Abakaliki), himself formerly a Warrant Chief, said 'the chiefs took decisions with the aid of the Court Clerk who told them when a decision would please the white man and when it was likely to infuriate him'. Chief Ukpai Ereshi of Akwurakwu Agba (Abakaliki) a very intelligent man and a former Warrant Chief, said that 'many a time what the clerk said was law was accepted as law since he was the only man in the court who knew what was in "the white man's book"'. Stories are also common of court clerks refusing to record certain decisions until the chiefs had reconsidered – that is, reversed – them. There is sufficient proof that certain sitting chiefs regarded the clerk as the judge and they themselves as his advisers. Chief Mbabuike Ogujiofor of Ihube, Okigwi, who became a court messenger in 1909, said there were occasions in certain courts where he served when the court clerk would refuse to appear in court and the chiefs would go and kneel before him to beg him to 'come and try cases for us'. The whole position was an unbelievable one to anybody who knew that by the theory of the system the clerk was or should be the servant of the chiefs who should employ and pay him. Said Okereke Aka of Alayi, a former Warrant Chief: 'How could the Clerk be our servant when he could tell us to shut up and we would shut up; otherwise if he reported us to the District Officer the latter would say "all right"?'[63]

The court messengers themselves benefited from this absurd situation. A former court messenger told of an instance when as a head messenger he was approached by a chief who wanted to be taken to the court clerk. Because the chief did not come with a bottle of 'English wine', he said, 'I ordered him out of my house. It was only after he had knelt down and addressed me as "master" that I consented to go on condition that the wine would be produced later.'[64]

[63] According to the informant the DO's 'all right' was understood to mean that the chiefs would be punished.
[64] Based on information collected from Chief Elei Adagba of Mgbo in Abakaliki, Chief Ukpai Ereshi of Agba in Abakaliki, Chief Mbabuike Ogujiofo of Ihube in Okigwi, Chief Okereke Aka of Alayi in Bende and from Chief Madumere of Olokoro, Bende.

Five factors facilitated and sustained the ascendancy of the clerks for a long time. First and foremost was the way the office of the court clerk evolved among the people, especially in the hinterland. Owing to the difficulty of obtaining educated men for the post of court clerks in the early days of British rule, the district commissioners were often the clerks as well as the presidents of Native Councils. The district commissioner H. S. Burrough was for at least eight months his own court clerk at Okigwi. Even a missionary, Mr Kirk, was for a time the clerk of the Etinan Native Court.[65] In District Courts where divisional and district officers sat with selected chiefs who acted as assessors when trying certain classes of cases, for instance cases of murder, political officers were also their own clerks. When therefore this duty devolved on educated Africans it was only natural that the chiefs should attribute to them the same position and power which the more highly placed European 'clerks' of the Native Courts had enjoyed.

Secondly, there was the fact that for many years and in many courts only the clerks had any education. The whole idea of education was new, and people who could speak or write English were regarded as having extraordinary powers and were both respected and feared. The use of printed writs in the Native Courts and the fact that the courts were required to administer some of the laws made by the Protectorate government, gave the clerk much advantage over the chiefs. The sitting members, who sometimes thought that they were required to administer an entirely new body of law, looked up to the clerk for guidance. Furthermore the illiteracy of the chiefs, or the fact that the clerk lived where he could easily be got at by the political officer or both, dictated that all communications between the political officer and the chiefs should pass through the clerk. Thus orders issued under the Roads and Rivers Ordinance, or for the supply of carriers, as well as the list of chiefs selected to sit for the month went to him. When transmitting these messages to the chiefs the clerk did not scruple to pretend that the orders emanated from him. There are stories that certain clerks would send for the chiefs selected to sit for the month to see them some four or five days before time. These chiefs, it is widely admitted,

[65] E 3828/08 Report on Okigwi for Nov. 1908. Report on the Qua Ibo sub-district for quarter ending 30.9.02 by A. C. Douglass in Calprof 10/3 Reports 1900–2

would take goats or fowls and yams to the clerk 'for selecting them to sit'.[66] This method of transmitting messages to the chiefs thus helped to foster and propagate the idea that the clerk was superior to the chief.

Thirdly, even within the limits recognised by law the clerk's powers were very extensive. He issued all the processes of the court and so determined whether a case was criminal or civil, and whether the accused was to be arrested and confined to the guardroom. He was directly in charge of the court messenger establishment and, it is said, some of the more presumptuous clerks used to flog messengers. One former court messenger admitted that he was flogged by court clerks even when he was head messenger, and named one Mr Iyala and one Mr Pepple as having been particularly prone to flog messengers.[67] The fact that the clerks could deal with messengers, who were the terror of the countryside, in this way made a great impression on people. The fact is that for a long time the clerks, as the 'direct representatives' of the central government, were allowed to exercise great powers. The fact that they stood between the political officer and the people and could understand both was greatly in their favour. In this position they did not infrequently help political officers to make up their minds on local matters. The truth of this statement can be fully appreciated from an examination of the powers which a man like Magnus A. Duke, clerk of the Calabar Native Council, was allowed to arrogate to himself with regard to the decisions of the court.

In April 1897 the Native High Court of Calabar heard a land case in which one Okon Ekpo Iso was seeking to recover from another Ekpo Iso a piece of land which the family of the former had given to the family of the latter. The court dismissed the claim on the ground that 'a gift is a gift' and cannot be taken back at will. The plaintiff, however, appealed to the District Officer, A. A. Woodhouse. In a memorandum which Duke attached to the appellant's letter he commented: 'I do not from the writer's point of view consider that he has any just ground for appeal.' It can hardly be doubted that this opinion helped to account for

[66] Information collected from the men listed in footnote 64, above, as well as from Chief Udo Udo Ibanga of Ikot Ekpene Town, and from Mr A. O. Okori of Ikot Ekpene Town, the latter being a petition writer.
[67] Based on information collected from the field. The informant requested for his identity to be kept secret.

Mr Woodhouse's confirmation of the court's ruling without further investigation.[68] In November of the same year the court dismissed the case of one woman, Atim Udo Messembe, against her husband 'for not treating her as a wife should be treated'. In transmitting the proceedings of the case to the political officer this same clerk urged that the decision was in accordance with native law and custom and that he trusted the government would confirm it. The government did.[69] It was clerks who had acquired positions as powerful as that just described who in the post-1914 period had to conduct the affairs of the courts with minimum supervision from the political staff.

The fourth factor which redounded to the benefit of the clerks was the fact that in many court areas they played various and prominent parts in the people's day-to-day life, a state of affairs which made them highly respected. They were often advisers in agriculture and first-aid administration, preachers in churches on Sundays and local magicians. One Mr Pepple, who served in the Ngbo Native Court, which was established in the early 1920s, had a great reputation as a magician and fortune-teller. He used, it is said, to 'foretell' big commotions in Ngbo at certain times of the year and these invariably occurred. Political Officer G. B. Chapman was said to have later found that Mr Pepple's reputation depended on his working hard underground to embitter relations between any two opposing groups in order to precipitate a breach of the peace. Then he would round up those involved and subject them to ruthless blackmail.[70] When the district officer at Calabar visited Akpabuyo court district in 1917 and found that the hundreds of para-rubber trees at the station were flourishing, it was the clerk that he instructed to collect the seeds and issue them to local farmers.[71] Doubtless he was also expected to instruct them on how to care for the seedlings.

The clerk of the Afunatam Native Court in Ikom District was, in addition to his other duties, the transport clerk at the Marine. In that capacity, he received all loads going from the above place

[68] Minutes of Native Court held on 11.4.97 and Memo. from Magnus A. Duke dated 17.8.97 in Calprof 8/5 Minutes
[69] Minutes of Native Court held on 11.11.97 and Memo. from Magnus A. Duke dated 12.11.97 in Calprof 8/5 Minutes
[70] Based on information collected from Mr B. N. Aniekwe, a former court clerk, living in Abakaliki Town, and from Chief Elei Adagba of Mgbo in Abakaliki.
[71] Report on Akpabuyo in Calprof 14, C 517/17, Report on Akpabuyo

to Ikom and other stations down the Cross River. Though he did not issue tickets to passengers, they had to report to him on arrival and he would direct them to the appropriate quarters. All Europeans and other important government officials arriving at Afunatam had to inform him well in advance so that he could arrange for carriers, or they might be stranded for upwards of three days. The clerk was also responsible for the despatch of all mails arriving at Afunatam by road or river.[72] The clerk of the Afunatam Court must have appeared to the rustic villagers as the *primum mobile* of their little world. No other single person in their political experience had ever had in his hands so many strings of authority. Addressing this 'colossus' as 'master' was indeed an inadequate expression of the awe in which he was held.

Fifthly the dominance of court clerks also derived from the great wealth they commanded. Lugard had believed that the tendency of clerks to be corrupt in the period before 1914 was the result of their low salaries. He therefore increased their pay. The significance of this lies in the fact that at the same time the sitting fees of the chiefs were declining.[73] The following table produced in 1924 illustrates the disparity in official material remuneration between the chiefs, the court messengers and court clerks and which helped to tip the scale in favour of the clerks.[74] In comparing the figures it should be borne in mind that none of these

[72] Handing Over Notes on Ikom found in the Onitsha Province file No. 427/1/22

[73] The decline in the sitting fees paid to chiefs started about 1911, when it was found out that the chiefs deliberately refused to speed up the trials with the result that simple cases were allowed to drag for days. By this trick, since they were paid on a daily basis, they got more pay. As a counter-measure the government ruled that a *sitting* would no longer necessarily mean each day the court sat except such a meeting led to the trial of between 17 and 20 cases; failing that, a *sitting* was to be taken as three days' meetings. From that time to the collapse of the Warrant Chief System court members vainly asked for increased pay to enable them to meet the steadily rising cost of living. See Calprof 14, C 940/16 Calabar Chiefs, Petition for increased power in Native Courts, etc. OW 435 Bonny Native Court – Sitting fees; see all the Enclosures. Memo. No. C 14/1915 dated 21.5.15 from Commissioner, Calabar Province, to SSP in 540/15 lieutenant governor's meeting with chiefs of Ikot Ekpene District. Memo. No. OW 659/1923 dated 16.6.28 from the Resident to all DOs in OW 30/1928A Circular Instruction to DOs

[74] Report on the Working of the Native Courts in the Eastern Provinces, *Sessional Paper*, No. 31 of 1924, pp. 3–7

courts had fewer than twenty-five chiefs who had to share the total sitting fees for the year:

Court	Salary of clerk £ s. d. (p.a.)	Fees for chiefs £ s. d. (p.a.)	No. of CMs	Total pay for CMs £ s. d.
Calabar	240 0 0	132 0 0	8	150 0 0
Creek Town	108 18 0	102 10 0	4	84 0 0
Akpabuyo	134 8 0	136 0 0	5	96 0 0
Oban	112 0 0	64 0 0	4	78 0 0
Adiabo	144 0 0	113 15 0	5	96 0 0
Uwet	144 0 0	55 2 6	18	78 0 0
Owerri	309 0 0	323 0 0	12	318 0 0
Nguru	359 0 0	187 0 0	10	210 0 0
Awka	188 0 0	165 5 0	—	147 15 0

In 1928 about four clerks in Onitsha Province earned above £190 per annum, Mr L. N. Nzekwu topping the list with £240 per annum. Six had their own motor-cars, often with private chauffeurs. 'It is almost impossible,' contended Captain W. Buchanan-Smith, Resident of Onitsha Province, 'that the chiefs can regard such a man, whose car is infinitely more decorative than the Resident's dilapidated Ford, as their social inferior.'[75] In addition to earning such high salaries at a time when the cost of living was relatively low, the clerks were often wealthy farmers. Chiefs seeking for favour supplied clerks with unpaid labour, and it is said that the latter often asked for more carriers than the government wanted and then turned over the surplus into their farms. They were also in the habit of causing accused persons detained in the local guardroom to work for them without pay. They were notorious for lending money at exorbitant rates of interest. It was because of all these that the court clerks were, comparatively speaking, generally very rich.

In the years before 1914 the court clerks were to some extent overshadowed by the district officers who sat as presidents. However infrequently the political officers sat, their presence reminded the chiefs that the clerk was not the head of the Native Court. By inflating the salaries of the clerk and excluding the district officer from court membership Lugard removed the last remaining obstacles to the final emergence of the 'golden age' of court clerks.

[75] CSO 26 No. 11672, vol. i, Government Native Court Clerks – Proposed abolition of Office, pp. 64–5

Under the morally blind leadership of the clerks the Warrant Chiefs and their courts lapsed into the most appalling state of corruption and oppression. Mr Purchas, assistant district officer, after nine months' service in Opobo Division, described these tribunals as 'courts of injustice'. Mr F. P. Lynch estimated that about 50 per cent of cases tried by the courts came to the political officer for review, and that if an officer were delegated to devote all his time to hearing complaints of corruption against the chiefs, the result of his labour would be that about 90 per cent of the Warrant Chiefs would be in prison. Every political officer in the service believed that the courts were corrupt though they differed as to how far deep the courts were steeped in corruption. [76]

Cases of corruption were uncovered from time to time. At Aba in 1919 Lynch charged one of the most influential chiefs in the Aba Native Court with taking bribes in a debt case between one Ogbonna (defendant) and one Anyatanwa (plaintiff) and was astounded by the attitude of the chief. The latter argued: 'I think it is quite all right to take money [bribe] as I did not ask for it. This is always done throughout the Native Courts. When people have cases in court they come and dash [give presents to] the sitting chiefs beforehand.' The other members of the court did not deny this statement. [77] On 18 April 1920 the Orlu Native Court convicted four boys who were related to one influential Warrant Chief of Awomama on a charge of larceny of livestock and sentenced each to three months' imprisonment with hard labour. That day the Awomama chief was in court as a spectator rather than as a sitting member. An hour after the court rose this chief and the court's president for the day came to the court clerk and persuaded him to grant bail to the convicts. The following morning the case was retried and the boys sentenced to a fine of one pound each. The fines were paid by the Awomama chief. For this gross perversion of justice the two chiefs were made to lose their warrants. [78]

Such perversions of justice were rampant under the Warrant Chief System. Mr C. Howard, District Officer Obubra, said that

[76] See all the Memos. enclosed in C 176/19, Remarks by F. P. Lynch
[77] Memo. No. 594/45/19 from F. P. Lynch to Resident, Owerri Province, in Abadist 1/1/39 Native Court Chiefs, etc.
[78] See Memo. by H. B. Bedwell dated 25.4.20 in C 46/1920 Chiefs Orisakwe and Amanfor, Members of Orlu Native Court. In the same file see Memo. from SSP C 46/1920 dated 4.5.20 in which the cancellation of the Chiefs' Warrants was granted.

bribery existed wholesale and that the average civil case was a five-shilling lottery.[79] Frank Hives, who served as Resident at Onitsha, Owerri, Calabar and Warri, said the decision returned by the chiefs in any case was determined in most instances by how much money they had received from the parties. 'Bribes of this kind,' he continued, 'are not confined to money alone, but to cows, goats, and I have known cases of a girl for a wife.'[80] Everywhere in this area visited by the present author, it was admitted that a poor man could never hope to get justice in the Native Court and that litigation was another version of competitive bidding. Chief Obiukwu Nze of Umulolo an ex-Warrant Chief, said, in explanation of the material prosperity of most Warrant Chiefs, that no insect would grow fat if it did not first feed on weaker ones. At Izzi the son and successor of Igboji Ola, who was a Warrant Chief, said that in this period it was a waste of time for anybody to seek redress in the courts if he lacked the material bribes to give to the chiefs and the court staff. These bribes, he said, could 'make falsehood true and truth truer'.[81]

In order to reduce the pressure on the Native Courts the Warrant Chiefs had been granted the power to try minor disputes at home. But they abused this power. It was admitted by all the ex-Warrant Chiefs interviewed by the author that the private courts they held competed with the smaller Native Courts in the number of cases tried in them. The chiefs believed that they were allowed to try all grades of civil cases privately. An ex-Warrant Chief, Ngadi Onuma of Oloko, looked on his own private court as the court of first instance for his people and the Native Court as the Court of Appeal. He argued that just as a man could go first to the Native Court and then to the district officer if he was not satisfied, so he could go from his own private court to the Native Court. Chief Okugo's own private court at Oloko, Bende, was said to be larger and more dignified and better disciplined than any Native Court. In it men were frequently given twelve strokes of the cane for the slightest noise or disturbance which was treated as contempt of court. Obiukwu Nze

[79] Memo. by Mr C. Howard, Acting DO Obubra, marked 'C' in the file C 176/19, Remarks by F. P. Lynch
[80] Memo. by F. H. Ingles and Conf Memo. No. W 9/1919 dated 2.2.20 by F. Hives in C 176/19, Remarks by F. P. Lynch
[81] Based on information from Chief Obiukwu Nze (Umololo, Okigwi) and Chief Idika Igboji (Izzi, Abakaliki).

(Umulolo, Okigwi) admitted having a lock-up in his private compound where accused persons were detained until their cases came before his private court. Chief Ogayi of Inyimagu, Abaka-liki, was also said to have had his own private lock-up. In the private courts it cost the same thing as in the Native Courts to take out a summons and fines were freely levied. The proceeds went to the Warrant Chief and not to the government.[82] On this issue of private courts, C. Howard, who was at Obubra, said: 'Indeed it is the conception of the Warrant fostered by the average chief that it does empower him to judge cases in the town.'[83] In these private courts enforcement of decisions given was often ensured by making the litigants swear on a dreaded deity before the trial that they would abide by the verdict or that if they decided to take the matter to the official Native Court they would not tell the political officer that an effort had been made to deal with the matter privately in the chief's court.[84]

Warrant Chiefs, clerks and road overseers exploited orders given them under the Roads and Rivers Ordinance as well as orders to recruit carriers. In either case the chiefs, whether they called out an age-grade *en masse* or recruited people indiscriminately, generally produced more men than any specific work in hand demanded. The surplus hands they either made to work in their farms or distributed between the clerk, the road overseer and the district interpreter. Mr Grier, during his tour of the Eastern Provinces in 1922, saw Ibibio men so recruited cultivating a farm in front of a road overseer's house. Uniformed

[82] Information from Chief Ngadi Onuma (Oloko, Bende), Chief Obiukwu Nze (Umulolo, Okigwi) and Mr Jacob Aweze (Ezzagu, Abakaliki).

[83] Memo. on the Native Courts by Mr C. Howard, Acting DO, Obubra, marked 'C' in the file C 176/19, Remarks by F. P. Lynch. This development was not strictly in keeping with the traditional practice by which people took their disputes to a local lineage head for settlement. Firstly the Warrant Chief was not generally a lineage head, but often an upstart, the type of man to whom people would not normally refer their cases. Secondly, under the traditional system it was the parties to a quarrel who chose the lineage head to whom to refer their case, but Warrant Chiefs were reputed for compelling people to refer cases to them. Thirdly, unlike the traditional lineage head under the indigenous system, it was the Warrant Chief who dictated how much he would charge for each case he investigated for his people.

[84] Memo. on the Native Courts W 9/1919 dated 12.11.19 by F. Hives in C 176/19, Remarks by F. P. Lynch

road overseers, said another political officer, were an unmitigated curse with 'endless opportunities for blackmail'.[85]

The greatest proof of the corrupt use to which these chiefs put their powers was the fact that every one of them was very wealthy when compared with his non-warranted neighbours, in spite of the fact that the sitting fees were very paltry. Even today one can single out the compound of a former Warrant Chief. These men competed with each other in the erection of two-storeyed buildings of fantastic shapes and sizes for those days and often of the crudest architectural description which were at times put to very little use. In many places the present author was told such and such a Warrant Chief was the first indigenous son of the clan or village to own a bicycle or a motor-cycle, a double-barrelled shotgun, or even a car. Obiukwu Nze (Umulolo, Okigwi) claimed to have been the first in the Otanzu clan to possess any of the above-mentioned novelties.[86] Frank Hives reported the case of a Warrant Chief who before his appointment had practically nothing, but as soon as he was made a court member became very wealthy. When convicted on a charge of slave-dealing and child-stealing his visible property consisted of a two-storeyed wooden house with corrugated-iron roof, 130 wives (the bride-price in each case being nothing less than fifteen pounds), sixty head of cattle, seven bicycles, a double-barrelled shotgun and numberless sheep, goats and extensive farms. He was able to pay easily a fine of one hundred and fifty pounds and heavy costs. This fact of the wealth which possessing a warrant could bring helps to account for the number of people who sought for warrants in this period and for the lengths to which they were ready to go to attain their ends. One candidate offered a sum of fifty pounds in ready cash and promised thrice that sum more if given a warrant and made to sit as president for three consecutive months.[87]

Though after reading the reports sent in by his officers, Sir Hugh Clifford had no doubt that the Warrant Chief System was

---

[85] S. M. Grier, *Report on a Tour in the Eastern Provinces*, etc., pp. 6, 13, Comments by Mr Purchas on Grier's *Report* dated 12.8.22 in C 176/19, Remarks by F. P. Lynch, etc.
[86] Based on information collected from Chief Obiukwu Nze (Umulolo, Okigwi), Chief J. N. Nwansi (Ikeduru, Owerri), Chief J. O. Njemanze (Owerri Town) and Chief J. N. Wachukwu (Ngwa, Aba).
[87] Memos. on Native Courts W 9/19 dated 12.11.19 and 2.2.20 in C 176/19, Remarks by F. P. Lynch

in great need of reform,[88] it was only in 1922 that he took the first hesitant step in the direction of reform by sending Mr S. M. Grier, the Secretary for Native Affairs, to tour the Eastern Provinces and report on the working of the existing local government system. The report which Grier submitted on his return to Lagos was a thoroughgoing indictment of the system and it went far to confirm the pessimism which characterised the reports and memoranda sent in by various officers between 1919 and 1920. Grier came to the conclusion, in no way radically new, that as a result of the reforms of 1914 the Native Courts were 'doing a great deal of harm' and had become 'one of the principal disintegrating forces in the country'. He attributed the whole unsatisfactory situation to four factors, some of which had been harped upon by many officers before him. These were:[89] the corruption of the courts; the fact that the Warrant Chiefs were for the most part men who had no standing in the indigenous political system; the ascendancy of the court clerk over the chiefs; and the fact that the Native Court areas had been demarcated without attention to ancient clan boundaries.

Convinced of the need for a desperate remedy, Mr Grier recommended some far-reaching reforms. He called for a clean sweep of all Warrant Chiefs who had no 'traditional' claims to their positions, the recognition of all the 'hereditary chiefs' of all villages and towns and the recruitment of Native Court members from among them. He counselled the revival of 'traditional' village and clan councils which had continued to function in secret in spite of the concerted attempt made under Section 26 of the Native Courts Ordinance to suppress them. This last measure, Grier believed, would check 'the flood of litigation which flows into the Native Courts and is in itself a proof of the disintegration of native society'. These councils were to enjoy limited jurisdiction and deal with cases touching bride-price, farm disputes, minor debts and cases of petty assault. Lastly he recommended that the political officer should re-enter the court as president in order to curb the pretensions of the court staff and keep the chiefs 'something like straight'.[90] Indeed, some

---

[88] Comment by Governor Clifford B 713/1920 dated 26.11.20 in EP 1308/6, Annual Report, Owerri Province for 1919. See also Minute by Governor Clifford dated 9.1.21 in C 176/19, Remarks by F. P. Lynch.

[89] S. M. Grier, *Report on a Tour in the Eastern Provinces*, pp. 5–7, 26

[90] *Ibid.*, pp. 11–12. See also Memo. on the Aba Riots by Major C. T.

of the recommendations meant the reversal of Lugard's policy.

The Grier report had a mixed and stormy reception. On the one hand it was an eloquent statement of the case of the majority of the officers who had sent in the reports of 1919–20 on the Native Court System. An officer like Mr Purchas wrote: 'If I may be permitted to say so, I consider that Mr Grier has written a well-deserved condemnation of the Native Court System since 1914.'[91] On the other hand there were officers who were disturbed by the radicalism of Grier. Colonel Moorhouse contended that it must be remembered that the Native Court System, with occasional modifications, had been in existence for nearly twenty years; that the older people, even if they did not like it, had got accustomed to it; and that the rising generation had known no other form of 'Native jurisdiction'. 'I would strongly deprecate,' he warned, 'any drastic changes in their constitution by a stroke of the pen and suggest more gradual measures of reform.'[92] F. N. Ashley, District Officer at Ikot Ekpene, and other officers of his turn of mind also detested any root and branch reform and pointed out that there was no alternative to the Native Court System. Neither Mr Ashley nor James Watt, Resident of Owerri, accepted that the Native Courts were as corrupt and vicious as Grier had represented them.[93]

The causes of this seeming change of front by officers in the Eastern Provinces make an interesting study. In the first place the reactions of the governor and lieutenant governor to the report, enshrined in their comments, were published as an appendix to the main report and circulated to all the residents and the officers under them. It was therefore widely known that the trenchant tone of the report was unpopular at headquarters.[94] The second reason is to be found in the composition of the officers in the field at the time. Grier's report leaned heavily on the opinions on the Native Courts voiced between 1919 and

Lawrence, Secretary, Southern Provinces, in the *Aba Commission of Inquiry Reports* (hereinafter *ACIR*), pp. 144–6
[91] Comment by Mr Purchas on Grier's *Report* dated 12.8.22 in C 176/19, Remarks by F. P. Lynch
[92] S. M. Grier, *Report on a Tour in the Eastern Provinces, etc.*, p. 28
[93] Memo. on the Aba Riots by Major C. T. Lawrence, SSP in *ACIR*, pp. 149–52. See also Memo. dated 15.10.22 by F. N. Ashley in Calprof 14, C 582/22D, Pedigrees of Chiefs, etc.
[94] S. M. Grier, *Report on a Tour in the Eastern Provinces*, etc., pp. 25–33

1920, by such officers as F. P. Lynch, R. B. Brooks, Frank Hives and others. The memoranda from Calabar Province in 1919 were sent in by E. Falk at Ikot Ekpene, D. Castor at Calabar, M. D. W. Jeffreys at Eket and H. O. Swanston at Opobo. But in 1922 it was men like F. N. Ashley at Ikot Ekpene, Captain Hanitch at Eket and E. J. Price at Aro who commented on the report from the Calabar Province. The same reshuffling of officers, perhaps brought about by the arrangement for leave, had taken place in many of the other provinces. At Owerri, instead of R. B. Brooks there was James Watt as resident and it was his comment on the report that was recorded. In Owerri Division there was F. L. Tabor instead of Mr Ferguson and it was he who commented on the report.[95]

This fact was of great importance and perhaps more than anything else accounts for the apparent *volte-face* noted above. A man like Ashley had been continuously at Ikot Ekpene since 1915. In 1919 Falk was merely acting for him while he was on leave. It was then easy for Falk to write: 'If I may say so, the whole system of administration is unsatisfactory.'[96] Ashley could not be expected to admit that all his labour in the division for about seven years had only led to a dismal failure. In any case the general feeling was that 'it would be a grave reflection on the vigilance and sagacity of Political Officers in the Eastern Provinces' if corruption were accepted to exist on the scale portrayed by Mr Grier.[97] The seeming change of sides was a game of 'politics' played, unfortunately, at the expense of the local people and, it would seem, of outspoken critics like Lynch. On the report Watt had observed 'I should feel disposed to tell any officer who said that 90% of the judgments given were corrupt I should look to him patiently to improve it.' Sir Hugh Clifford minuted: 'I agree with Mr Watt's contention.' These two damaging statements were incorporated in a later report and circulated to all officers in the Eastern Provinces.[98] Lynch felt this aspersion cast on his 'sagacity' so much that as late as 1925 he was still complaining of it. He said:

[95] Compare the list of officers mentioned in Tomlinson's *Report* of 1923 with those who sent in the Memos. on the Native Courts in 1919.
[96] Memo. on the Native Courts Conf No. 17/1919 dated 30.12.19 by Mr Falk in C 176/19, Remarks by F. P. Lynch. Mr. Falk's comments were supposed to be based on his experience in the Ikot Ekpene Division.
[97] G. J. F. Tomlinson, *Report on a Tour in the Eastern Provinces*, p. 4
[98] *Ibid.*, pp. 4, 27

I submit that there is not a single Political Officer in the service, there is not a clerk, nor an interpreter, who does not know and openly admit that in nearly every case the chiefs receive their bribe beforehand. But my bringing this matter up in 1919 resulted merely in censures on myself, printed moreover in an official pamphlet with a wide circulation and endorsed apparently by His Excellency.

When the lieutenant governor dismissed the complaint as 'impertinent in tone and . . . uncalled for' Lynch replied: 'I would assure His Honour that I felt and still feel very keenly the slur cast on me, in my opinion most unfairly, by Mr Tomlinson and Mr Watt. . . .'[99] Those officers who felt as Lynch did, also learned a lesson from his fate. Between 1923 and the final collapse of the Warrant Chief System there was no other trenchant report on the system. It was an era of 'make-believe'.

It is therefore likely that when Mr G. J. F. Tomlinson, the assistant secretary for native affairs, was sent on another tour of the Eastern Provinces in 1923, the aim of which was to report on the system a second time, he knew he was required to produce a report different in tone from that of his chief. It is not surprising therefore that he came out with one which was moderate in tone and which, by maintaining that the Native Courts were corrupt but not so corrupt, earned the sobriquet 'thoughtful' from both Clifford and Moorhouse because at least, so they thought, it saved them from the apparently unwelcome necessity of introducing speedy and far-reaching changes.[100] Tomlinson's report contained nothing that was radically new, independent or original. Aware that speedy reform was unpopular at headquarters, he insisted on 'gradualism' as the keynote of his recommendations. Whatever the drawback of the courts, he counselled, 'we are not in a position to deal urgently with a crying scandal nor with a worn-out machine which is on the verge of breaking down . . .

---

[99] Memo. No. Conf 3/25 dated 7.3.25 and Conf 3/25 dated 29.6.25 from F. P. Lynch, DO Awka and No. A 679/1925 dated 4.6.25 from SSP to resident, Onitsha, in OP 176/25, Misconduct of Chiefs of Awka Native Court. In reply to the rebuke Mr Lynch further contended 'I would assure His Honour that I have throughout acted from one motive only, namely the interests of the ignorant natives, who are easily victimised by many of those fortunate enough to have acquired the position of Member of a Native Court, and for whose welfare I consider I have a moral responsibility.'

[100] G. J. F. Tomlinson, *Report on a Tour in the Eastern Provinces*, pp. 26, 29

it is, I submit, important to proceed with great caution in considering schemes of reform.'[101]

The Warrant Chiefs 'without hereditary status', he advised, should not be dismissed *en masse* because such a step would be too violent and too sudden, because it would be unfair to these men who, in the difficult early days, had been useful to the government in bringing their people under control and because such a step would split towns and villages into ex-Warrant Chief and new-Warrant Chief factions. In any case, he said, gradual replacement was working wonders in a place like Ezza in Abakaliki. Since he knew that at headquarters there was some doubt about the advisability of reinstating political officers as presidents of the courts in view of the general shortage of European staff he advised against it. On the positive side, however, Tomlinson made four main recommendations, one of which reiterated an earlier suggestion made by Resident R. B. Brooks, while the others merely reproduced ideas already expressed by Grier in his own report.[102] Mr Tomlinson had no illusions about his contribution to the whole debate. He even went so far as to describe his recommendations as 'no more than an elaboration of the proposals in Grier's report'.[103] The second tour was a great waste of time and the essence of the report could have been produced by a judicious use of the papers already available at headquarters by 1922.

After the noise and fury of the controversy created by the two reports, what left the headquarters was the most modest of reforming plans hedged in by counsels of 'caution' and 'patience'. Governor Clifford was clear on a few things, equivocated on one

[101] *Ibid.*, p. 5

[102] These recommendations were as follows: (i) The reorganisation of the Native Courts on clan basis. As already seen, this was the idea of S. M. Grier. (ii) The examination of the credentials of all existing Warrant holders with a view to gradually displacing upstarts and replacing them with 'hereditary chiefs'. Here he merely replaced Grier's 'speedily' with Moorhouse's 'gradually'. (iii) The recognition of all the traditional heads of villages and quarters with a view to achieving a more equitable representation of the various units and to giving excluded heads some measure of authority in their units. R. B. Brooks had suggested this as far back as 1919. (iv) The discovery of the parent town of each clan with a view to seeing whether the chief of that town could be made a Paramount Chief. S. M. Grier had also advocated this in his report.

[103] G. J. F. Tomlinson, *Report on a Tour in the Eastern Provinces*, etc., pp. 5–18. Compare these with Grier's *Report*, pp. 7–15

or two and remained silent on many other issues of reform. He came out clearly on the side of those who deprecated any attempt to turn out all Warrant Chiefs who were 'without hereditary status'. Gradual replacement after careful inquiries was enjoined. He supported those officers who thought it retrograde to reinstate political officers as members of the courts after eight years of their exclusion. On the positive side he recommended the prosecution of research into clan boundaries with a view to seeing that no clan was severed into two or more parts by administrative divisions. On the 'revival' of village and clan councils he was vague. He said where these existed they should be 'revived' but warned that there was a tendency to assume that 'the tribal system of government was more complete, more elaborate and of a higher type than it . . . ever was'. He was afraid the whole process would end up in imposing on the people 'a tribal organisation of an alien character'. In any case, no definite injunction was issued requesting research directed towards finding if these councils existed. Clifford was silent on the question of the more equitable representation of clans, villages and wards in the Native Courts and on the programme for according some form of official recognition to the heads of all units from the ward up and for giving unit heads excluded from the bench for the time being some minor executive powers.[104]

In the final analysis the only positive action enjoined was that all member units of a clan should attend the same Native Court. Even in this officers were given neither a free hand nor a clear lead. Each political officer in a division was to mark out on any available map the existing Native Court areas as well as the clan or other ethnic group boundaries, and attach to the latter reports showing on what information the recommended demarcation of clans was based. These data were to go up to the residents, who would comment on them and make recommendations on the redistribution of court areas. After this a special officer was to be appointed to go into the details of ethnic group organisation and make further recommendations. 'I should then,' said Moorhouse, 'be in a position to put forward definite recommendations in accordance with generally accepted principles.'[105]

For the rest only negative action was wanted from officers. They were to exclude themselves from membership of Native

[104] G. J. F. Tomlinson, *Report on a Tour in the Eastern Provinces*, pp. 26–8
[105] *Ibid.*, pp. 26–8

Courts. They were not to dismiss any Warrant Chiefs except on charges of misconduct; instead they should wait patiently for death to do this dirty job. But to beguile the time, as it were, they were to conduct investigations into the reasons for the appointment of existing Warrant Chiefs and group the chiefs into those who had 'hereditary right', or were appointees of 'hereditary chiefs', who, owing to age, infirmity or 'callousness', refused warrants; or who were 'elected' by the communities; or were merely government nominees. Where the Warrant Chief had no hereditary position political officers were to find out, before his death, who was the 'hereditary chief' so as to appoint him when a vacancy occurred. Since, as already pointed out by Reginald Hargrove, succession to village headship was not governed at all times and in all places by the principle of primogeniture, one would question the wisdom of such inquiries. Read differently the governor's directives meant that even when a vacancy occurred political officers should be chary of appointing anybody a Warrant Chief until there was indisputable evidence that a would-be successor was a 'hereditary chief'.[106]

Officers addressed themselves to the work of regrouping clans with varying degrees of enthusiasm. In Owerri Province, for instance, officers who derived inspiration from the Grier report of 1922 had already plunged into the work before the visit of Tomlinson in 1923. To Mr Purchas, District Officer at Onitsha, the work was neither interesting nor worthwhile, and he did nothing about it until 1927.[107] A large number of the required reports had however reached headquarters by August 1924; in fact those from Owerri Province probably got there either late in 1923 or early in 1924. Colonel Moorhouse ordered that the recommendations be analysed into four categories: cases in which no change was needed; cases in which rearrangements could be made without altering divisional boundaries; those needing rearrangements which would affect divisional but not provincial boundaries; and those requiring the alteration of provincial boundaries. But G. H. Findlay argued that this would entail 'many days assiduous' labour and should be held over until the secretarial staff was at full strength again. Under this minute,

---

[106] *Ibid.*, p. 29
[107] OW 722/23, Events of Importance in 1923. See also Memo. Conf No. 1/1924 dated 24.6.27 by Mr Purchas, DO, Onitsha, in C 38/1923 Native Courts, Tribal Areas

Captain W. Buchanan-Smith, another officer in the Secretariat, suggested that the work should await the return of Mr H. O. S. Wright. The work was in fact never done.[108] Here the grandiose scheme envisaged by Moorhouse in 1923 fizzled out. What was left was a slipshod policy which approved the setting up of one clan court here and another there. The result was, as will soon be shown, near-chaos.

The fact is that the proposed reorganisation turned out to entail more work than the administration had anticipated. Some reports from the Calabar Province did not reach the headquarters in time. Mr Murray's report on Calabar Division left the resident's office only in the first week of July 1925. M. D. W. Jeffreys's report on the Eket, which was much famed in those days, was not finished until June 1925.[109] In some places officers did not find it easy 'discovering' clans. Mr Purchas wrote from Onitsha Division to say that no clans existed and that 'the unity and coherence' already created by the existing Native Court System should not be destroyed in a vain bid to return to what existed in the days of Methuselah. Mr J. G. Lawton, who was at Awka, reported that the clan system had vanished and insisted on a return to the old practice by which the district officer sat as president of the Native Court.[110] Mr H. T. B. Dew, then at Enugu, deprecated any rearrangement in his division, since the existing groupings were convenient from the point of view of the distance each village had to cover to reach the court it attended. One clan, for instance, consisted of Nsude, Eke, Abia and Udi. Under the existing arrangement only Nsude and Eke were included in the Udi court area. If it were insisted upon that the four villages must attend the same court, he argued, it would mean one of the existing courts being closed down. This, he said, would upset the position of many other villages in the Agbaja group and the four towns in question might not welcome such a drastic change, which, instead of engendering harmony,

---

[108] Minute No. 96 dated 1.8.24 by H. C. Moorhouse; Minute No. 102 dated 13.8.24 by G. H. Findlay and Minute No. 103 dated 13.8.24 by W. B. Smith in C 38/23 Native Courts, Tribal Areas

[109] Memo. No. C 582/1922 'C' dated 28.9.25 by Resident, Calabar Province, Memo. No. B 1193/24 dated 27.5.25 by M. D. W. Jeffreys in C 38/23, Native Courts, Tribal Areas

[110] Memo. Conf 1/1924 dated 9.6.27 by Purchas and Conf No. 94/MP 54/22 dated 8.3.24 by Mr Lawton in C 38/23 Native Courts, Tribal Areas

would precipitate jealousy and enmity. These facts, he said, applied *mutatis mutandis* to the Nkanu group.[111]

Partly because of these conflicting opinions and attitudes and partly because of the immensity of the problems which varied from province to province and from division to division the rearrangements effected by 1927 were on non-uniform lines and at different stages of completion. In the Calabar Province the most remarkable progress was made in Ikot Ekpene Division, thanks to the efforts of F. N. Ashley and M. D. W. Jeffreys. By 1924 the lieutenant governor had sanctioned the opening of clan courts for Ibiono, Ikpe, Ikono, Ika and Itam. The Ihe, Ututu, Isu and Ukwa groups were separated from the Aro Court, where, they alleged, the Aro had hitherto oppressed them.[112] In Owerri Province officers gave their attention more to ensuring that no clan was dismembered by divisional boundaries than to the creation of purely clan courts. Thus up to 1927 and after in Okigwi Division, for instance, each court served more than one clan. The Okigwi Native Court served the Otanchara, Otanzzu, Isuochi, Nneato and Umuchieze clans; the Umuduru Court served Osu, Ugiri, Agbaja, Isu and Mbama clans; the Obowo Court served Ihitte and Agbaja clans. The two courts in Orlu District served three clans each.[113] In Ogoja Province the clans and groups were somewhat more clearly demarcated. In Abakaliki Division the Ikwo, Ezza, Ngbo, Ishielu and Eshupum clans each had their courts. But the small non-Ibo-speaking Orri had to attend the Ngbo court, since the establishment of a separate clan court for them was precluded by the fact that they were few and did not occupy a continuous block of territory. In Ogoja Division the 'tribes' were quite small and were given courts on that rather than clan basis. The Boki villages, however, which were separated by hills and marshes, could not, on grounds of distance, be brought under one court.[114]

In spite of the isolated achievements recorded above the fact

[111] Memo. MP No. E 118/23 dated 25.8.23 from Mr Dew, DO, Enugu Division, in C 38/23, Native Courts, Tribal Areas

[112] EP 1138, vol. x, Annual Report, Calabar Province 1924, pp. 4–5. Minute by LGSP attached to Memo. No. C 106/24 dated Dec. 1924 in Calprof 14, C 582/22, Pedigrees of Chiefs, etc.

[113] CSO 26/3, No. 20645 Assessment Report Okigwi District of Okigwi Division, Aug. 1927, pp. 20–3

[114] Memo. No. 699/6/1923 dated 24.9.23 by G. G. Shute, DO, Ogoja, in C 38/23, Native Courts, Tribal Areas

remains that the administration failed to prosecute this reorganisation scheme to a successful conclusion by 1927 when questions of direct taxation drove every other administrative scheme to the background. A lack of clear guidance from the centre nearly led to administrative chaos. The provincial boundaries should have been adjusted first, then the divisional and district boundaries, before any attempt to regroup clans within each district. But as it happened, each district officer was allowed to alter court boundaries without regard for his neighbours' efforts in the same direction. The adoption of this opposite procedure and the failure to work out the whole scheme on paper led to a breakdown of central control. In certain districts reorganisation was impeded by the fact that at times sections of a clan were either in different districts or divisions or provinces.[115] Even after the period covered by this study Owerri Province was still handing over the administration of some Ijo villages to Warri Province and receiving some Umuchieze and Isuochi towns from Onitsha Province. By 1932, even within Owerri Province, the adjustment of district boundaries had not been finally settled: the controversy was still raging about which division to place all the Isu group.[116]

Also it was not clear to anybody which overrode the other: the principle of maintaining the integrity of clans or the stubborn needs of administrative convenience. The views of officers were therefore widely divergent on this point. Thus Mr A. E. F. Murray at Calabar produced an ambitious scheme which involved making the Cross River, up to the point where it enters the present-day Cameroun Republic, the northeastern boundary of Calabar Division. By so doing, he hoped to include all the Ekoi and related clans in Calabar Province to which he said they 'naturally' belonged, and also he hoped to give the province a good natural boundary to the northeast. This meant that Obubra Division, once in Calabar but at the time in Ogoja Province, would return to Calabar Province. The scheme would however not have achieved the economy in staffing which was dear to the heart of the Acting Lieutenant Governor, Captain Davidson. It was therefore thrown overboard because, argued

---

[115] EP 1138, vol. xi, Annual Report for Calabar Province 1925, p. 8
[116] CSO 26/3, No. 29003 Intelligence Report on Mbama Clan, Okigwi, 1932, pp. 1, 11, 15. CSO 26/3, No. 28583, Intelligence Report on Isuochu, Nneato, Umuchieze Clans, Okigwi, 1932, pp. 17–18. EP 1308, vol. viA, Annual Report Owerri Province for 1929, p. 8

Resident Falk, 'we cannot entirely set aside administrative imponderabilia in order to establish pure unified clan councils'.[117] Nor was clan integrity itself a principle to which all groups were ready to adhere. Neither the fragment of the Mbama clan in the Okigwi nor that in the Owerri Division was ready to leave the division to which it had become accustomed and in which it had contracted new associations for the other divisions in order to act in harmony with the principle of clan solidarity.[118] At Ikot Ekpene many Warrant Chiefs representing various clans argued against proposed regroupings with the lieutenant governor. One group went so far as to say they were not ready to attend the same court with a section of their clan, whose inhabitants they accused of being cannibals. In many places villages preferred a court in the immediate neighbourhood, no matter its clan composition, to another in a distant village of the same clan.[119]

What was more, clans were not always neatly arranged. The migrations and dispersions of the pre-colonial era had produced in places a mingling of clans and groups which the British found baffling. This was particularly so in the Cross River basin. Mr Murray, in his grandiose scheme for Calabar, had done all he thought possible to keep clans together, but in the plan he eventually submitted it was found he had severed the Aro clan into two.[120] The Otanchara and Otanzu in Okigwi so melted into each other that no decision could be taken until the 1930s as to whether or not Otanzu should leave the court built on Otanchara grounds.[121] In 1927 Mr Falk, Resident, Calabar, was found complaining that the boundaries of the clans were frequently indeterminate, that enclaves were frequent and that practical

[117] Memo. No. 176/23 dated 5.10.24 by A. E. F. Murray, Memo. C 38/23 of 12.10.25 from SSP to Resident, Calabar Province, in C 38/23 Native Courts, Tribal Areas. Memo. No. Conf R 12/24 dated 20.10.24 by Resident, Calabar Province, in file 106/24 Creation of Tribal Councils and Reorganisation of Native Courts

[118] CSO 26/3, No. 29003 Intelligence Report Mbama Clan, pp. 1, 11. See also Enclosure No. 72/1932/6 from DO, Okigwi, to Resident, Owerri Province

[119] EP 1138, vol. xi, Annual Report, Calabar Province, 1925, p. 8. C 428 Calabar Province Annual Reports 1925–6, para. 70

[120] Memo. dated 12.10.25 from SSP to Resident, Calabar Province, in C 38/23 Native Courts, Tribal Areas

[121] Memo. No. 800/72/1929 dated 26.8.29 by A. Leeminz in the file EP 6036, Report by K. A. B. Cochrane, DO. See also para. 1 of the Report

problems of administration rendered certain suggested changes inadvisable.[122]

In addition to all these there was the perennial staffing problem. A short peep into the situation in Calabar Province in 1925 would reveal the reality of this handicap. The district officer at Opobo said he could not carry out the inquiries into the distribution of clans for some time to come because the frequent changing of the assistant administrative officers working with him had thrown the whole work of the division on him. The situation elsewhere in the province was worse. The Abak district was vacated for lack of officers. The assistant district officer at Itu was also the local treasurer at Ikot Ekpene. The officer at Eket had the second-class township of Oron and a Supreme Court area twenty-eight miles away from his station to supervise. The district officer at Calabar, owing to his assistant being ill, had to work single-handed. When in 1927 Falk continued to complain of shortage of staff the lieutenant governor made the revealing comment that Calabar Province with a staff of fourteen at their posts and nine on leave 'has been as liberally treated as possible'.[123]

The situation in 1927 has been lucidly portrayed by Resident Falk. 'The introduction of taxation,' he complained, 'finds the province in a state of transition and confusion. A lack of staff to terminate this state of affairs quickly, just at the moment when it is vital to have no subsidiary problems on our hands, is embarrassing.'[124] This administrative chaos was not limited to the Calabar Province. Where inquiries about clan boundaries were not going on, disturbing questions were being asked about the genealogical trees of Warrant Chiefs and their would-be successors. At Owerri in 1925 Mr Ferguson had disturbed the hornets' nest by making some people Warrant Chiefs merely because they were *Ofo*-holders. All candidates for Warrant Chiefs soon got themselves possessed of *Ofo*; in some families three of these symbols were found. Streams of petitions poured into the district office

[122] Memo. MP No. C 582/1922 'C' dated 18.6.27 from E. Falk, Resident, Calabar Province, to SSP in C 38/23 Native Courts, Tribal Areas

[123] Memo. No. C 582/1922 'C' dated 28.9.25 from F. N. Ashley, Resident Calabar Province, to SSP in C 38/23 Native Courts, Tribal Areas. Memo. Conf No. C 17/1927 dated 1.8.27 from E. Falk, Resident, to SSP in same file C 38/23 Native Courts, Tribal Areas. Memo. C 38/23 dated 1.6.27 from SSP to Resident, Calabar Province, in same file

[124] Memo. MP No. C 582/1922 'C' dated 18.6.27 from Falk, Resident, Calabar Province, to SSP in C 38/23 Native Courts, Tribal Areas

against the new appointments. By 1927 the feverish search for *Ofo*-holders had penetrated into the Onitsha Province at the suggestion of the anthropological officer, H. F. Matthews.[125]

The point is that the whole situation throughout the Eastern Provinces at this time was very unsatisfactory. There was much truth in the contention of Major T. Lawrence, the Secretary for Southern Provinces in 1930, that 'direct taxation was in reality introduced into the Eastern Provinces before the ground had been fully prepared for it. Reorganisation was incomplete and the native machinery was not in order. In a sense the cart had been put before the horse.'[126] On the whole the point was that the period from 1919 to 1927 was, in the field of local government in the Eastern Provinces, one of little actual achievement. The feverish desire and attempt to make the Warrant Chief System more efficient and more acceptable to the people reached its climax with the tours and reports of Grier and Tomlinson. The rest of the story was a wretched anti-climax. The introduction of direct taxation, which, it was hoped, would strengthen the system, not only made it as unpopular as it could ever be, but proved to be a fatal remedy.

[125] EP 7000, Status of ofọ-holders in the appointment of Members of Native Courts. See all the enclosed memos. The lineage ofọ is a staff of office symbolising moral authority and was generally in the custody of the oldest member of the group. Apart from the lineage ofọ there were others – for personal gods, divination, titles and so on, each symbolising something different and held by many people irrespective of their traditional status within the kinship group. It is thus understandable why Mr Ferguson ran into trouble when he attempted to act on the basis of the information that ofọ-holders were the traditional authorities in Iboland.

[126] Memorandum on the Aba Riots by Major C. T. Lawrence, SSP in *ACIR*

6 The coping stone of Lugardism or the fatal remedy, 1927–9

On 4 April 1927 a bill entitled 'Ordinance to Amend the Native Revenue Ordinance 1927' was passed into law by the Legislative Council in Lagos.[1] This enactment extended the provisions of the Native Revenue Ordinance to the Warri Province and to the four Eastern Provinces of Calabar, Ogoja, Onitsha and Owerri. It marked the decisive step in the protracted attempt to confer on these provinces what were considered to be the benefits of the institution known as the Native Treasury. Since within less than two years of coming into force this measure proved fateful for the Warrant Chief System, it is necessary to study in detail the reason behind its introduction as well as the methods by which its provisions were implemented.

Thanks to Lugard's influence, the Native Treasury had come to be regarded by the advocates of Indirect Rule as a main cornerstone of their system, and the introduction of taxation as the logically necessary first step towards its institution. Lugard, after he had left Nigeria finally, had enshrined this credo in a sentence which his successors and admirers quoted as an article of faith. 'Without a tax,' he had pontificated in 1922, 'there can be no treasury and without a treasury no real eventual measure of self-rule.'[2] Since the men who in 1928 imposed direct taxation on the Eastern Provinces regarded themselves as following in Lugard's footsteps, it is not surprising that their foremost argument in support of the measure was not radically different from that already spelled out by Lugard. In fact as far as these men were concerned Lugard's *Political Memoranda* and his *The Dual Mandate* provided the necessary philosophical basis for the project. It was maintained in Lugardian circles that direct

---

[1] *Legislative Council Debates*, 4 April 1927, pp. 4, 36–8
[2] Lord Lugard, *The Dual Mandate In British Tropical Africa*, Edinburgh 1922, p. 219

taxation was being introduced out of consideration for the interest of the people themselves and that the benefits which direct taxation could confer on the taxed should be appreciated by observing the results of its introduction into other parts of Nigeria. 'The outstanding and most beneficent consequence,' it was argued, 'has been the strengthening, consolidation and development of the Native Administrations.' In the Northern and Western Provinces the imposition of direct taxation had been accompanied by the establishment of Native Treasuries which provided funds for the payment of salaries of chiefs and other local government officials, for building and maintaining roads, bridges and hospitals and for carrying out numerous other public works. In short, only the creation of Native Treasuries could enable any system of local government in Africa to perform its proper functions. It was confidently asserted that Native Administrations and Treasuries constituted the most potent instrument for the stimulation of local patriotism and local development and for inculcating in chiefs and other local authorities a sense of responsibility to the communities entrusted to their charge.[3]

This belief that the introduction of direct taxation into an African community meant injecting into it the germs of life and future development had won uncritical acceptance even in the Colonial Office. After his tour of West Africa in 1926 the Honourable W. A. G. Ormsby-Gore, the Parliamentary Under-Secretary of State for the Colonies, recommended the introduction of direct taxation into the remaining provinces of Southern Nigeria, for, he said, 'the absence of Native administrations with local revenues in South-Eastern Nigeria [was] one of the factors accounting for the less developed state of these provinces compared with the rest of the country'.[4] When in 1927

---

[3] CSO 26/2, No. 17720, vol. ii, Taxation of the Colony, Warri, Onitsha, Owerri, Ogoja and Calabar Provinces (hereinafter Taxation), pp. 239C–239D. *Legislative Council Debates*, 4 April 1927, pp. 26, 30. By and large Lugard and the Lugardians used similar arguments to justify the introduction of direct taxation into various parts of Nigeria, on each occasion modifying these arguments slightly to suit their particular purpose. For a brief statement of their arguments for taxation in the Northern and Western Provinces, see M. Perham, *Lugard: The Years of Authority, 1898–1945*, London 1960, pp. 164–6, 442–4

[4] W. A. G. Ormsby-Gore, *Report of a Visit to West Africa*, Cmd. 2744 (1926), p. 116

the Colonial Secretary was told of the decision to carry out this recommendation he wrote elatedly to the governor:

> Your proposal marks a definite step in the advancement of the peoples of the Southern Provinces. . . . There can be no doubt that the introduction and establishment of direct taxation and Native Administration deriving their principal revenue from such taxation has promoted the progress of the Southern Provinces where it has been introduced.[5]

It is therefore easy to understand the jibe of the Hon. W. F. Becker that the government would have the Legislative Council believe that the payment of taxes was one of the joys of civilisation and a jealously guarded privilege which it was about to extend to a number of undeserving people in the former Eastern and Central Provinces.[6]

The government also saw the imposition of direct taxation as the only way to end the subjection of Warri and the other four Eastern Provinces to the régime of forced labour, which was not only wasteful but burdensome. The Roads and Rivers Ordinance under which this type of labour was recruited had, it was argued, become grossly anachronistic. Enacted at the beginning of the century to promote the construction of rough-and-ready roads from one government centre to another, the ordinance had come later to be used in maintaining the network of roads in these provinces in such a state of repair that many of them were good enough for wheeled traffic. By 1920, however, it had become clear that the ordinance was being used in situations which meant straining its provisions.[7]

By October that year the need for a change of system had become so urgent that the governor was ready, on recommendation from Moorhouse, to place funds at the disposal of the residents of the affected provinces for the payment of labour employed on the roads. Eventually no grant was made, as the financial condition of the Protectorate was far from sound. In 1921 Moorhouse renewed the request and secured a grant of

[5] CSO 26/2, No. 17720, vol. ii, Taxation, p. 279
[6] *Legislative Council Debates*, 4 April 1927, p. 29. Becker represented the banking interests in the Legislative Council. He was not opposed to the introduction of taxation but he was merely commenting on an impression he had gained regarding official attitude in the matter which bordered on levity.
[7] Minute by H. C. Moorhouse dated 21.6.21 in B 593/1921 Labour for Road Work in the Provinces

three thousand pounds for this purpose for the year 1922–3. In the following year the sum was increased by nine hundred pounds.[8] It was clear from the beginning that this special grant could be only a temporary relief and that a permanent alternative to forced labour had to be found. This alternative, it was agreed, had to be a system by which people would buy relief from forced labour by paying direct taxation.

There were many in the high reaches of government – men like G. J. F. Tomlinson, the Acting Secretary for Native Affairs; the governor and Major U. F. H. Ruxton, who succeeded Moorhouse as lieutenant governor – to whom the introduction of direct taxation into these five provinces was, to an extent, a matter of obeying the logic of historical and moral necessity. In the first place a glance through the history of the introduction of direct taxation into other parts of Nigeria revealed to them a simple but fascinating logic of procedure. In the Northern Provinces the government started by imposing taxes on the Muslim emirates, which apart from being used to such impositions 'from time immemorial' also possessed the necessary machinery for their collection. After this, direct taxation had been imposed on 'the relatively unorganised pagan communities' of the North. The extension of taxation to the Southern Provinces had followed much the same pattern in being piecemeal and gradual. There, taxation had started at Oyo, from where it had spread to Egba and Benin. These were areas where 'the people were familiar with the idea of payment of tolls and tributes and the machinery of Native Administration was readily available for systematic collection'. 'In the South then, as in the North', said Governor Graeme Thomson, 'the procedure has been to inaugurate taxation in highly organised provinces and then to extend it to less advanced communities.'[9] Seen in this light, therefore, the imposition of direct taxation on the Eastern Provinces in 1928 was an effort to obey the logic of this procedure.

Also the administration regarded the introduction of direct taxation as morally inescapable. Adherence to the procedure just analysed had by 1927 led to a situation in which the whole of the Northern Provinces, and the whole of Southern Nigeria west of

[8] *Ibid.*
[9] Draft of Speech by the Governor to the Legislative Council in CSO 26/2, No. 17720, vol. ii, Taxation, etc., pp. 239A–239B. The draft was made by Mr Tomlinson.

the Niger excepting the Warri Province, were taxed while the latter place and the Eastern Provinces were not. To the adminstration this seemed unjust. 'Indeed,' argued the governor, 'I find it easier to justify the extension of taxation than to defend a system which compels the people of Kano and Ibadan to pay taxes while the people of Owerri and Calabar escape scot-free.'[10] In urging this side of the issue these officials achieved great heights of oratory. Before the Legislative Council of 4 April 1927 the lieutenant governor, Major Ruxton, beautifully argued thus:

> Reviewing the speeches in general [that is, those against] there seems to be an absence of the higher point of view. It is not taxation taken in a limited sense and its effects on one little community; it is not a question of revenue to the Government that has been the motive behind us. The main motive of introducing this [taxation] Bill has been that of equity, of fairness. The whole of the British Empire is taxed, and the whole of Nigeria is taxed with the exception of five provinces; really you cannot argue that those five provinces should not be taxed.[11]

Considerations for the maintenance of abstract principles of uniformity and equity, which the natives could hardly understand, played no small part in the decision to bring Warri and the Eastern Provinces under the operation of the Native Revenue Ordinance in 1928.

But it must not be thought that the government was not interested in the financial argument for the introduction of direct taxation. Though nobody was ready to concede the fact that this was the premier consideration, there was nobody who thought that it was not an important one. Mr Tomlinson argued before the Legislative Council in 1927 that though the measure was 'not primarily' a revenue-raising trick, yet that it could 'not be denied that Government has a duty to raise revenue'.[12] In the same forum, the following year, the clerk of the Executive Council, Mr H. E. Priestman, asserted: 'We have never admitted that taxation was only for the purpose of equity. We also admitted that we wanted revenue. . . .'[13] This was considered justified in view of the increasing demands which the people were coming to make on the government for modern amenities. Many requests for these had been received by the lieutenant governor during his

---

[10] *Ibid.*, p. 239B
[11] *Legislative Council Debates*, 4 April 1927, p. 34
[12] *Ibid.*, p. 26
[13] *Ibid.*, p. 11

tour of the Eastern Provinces in 1924. At Uyo, the chiefs asked for a medical officer and a government school. Both the Uyo and Etinam chiefs asked for bridges across the Qua Ibo River. At Owerri the chiefs wanted a railway line through their town.[14] However, it is necessary to emphasise that important as the consideration for raising money was, it took an inferior place to the desire for uniformity and equity.

Some argued that taxation would prove a beneficial stimulus to economic growth and would be a good tonic to the people of the provinces concerned. At this time there was a general complaint that those who had come under the influence of the missions and their schools, in fact a large section of the younger generation, were growing 'idle, useless and immoral'. The fresh burden of taxation would force them to work. In this way the wage-earning class would increase, people would travel out to seek employment and, said Major Ruxton, 'this is good for the country'.[15] Becker complained that in spite of the 'huge' sums of money which had been sunk in port, road and railway development in the Eastern Provinces, Port Harcourt, the chief outlet for the produce of this region, had shown very little progress for a period of about six years. He hoped the introduction of taxation would do something to remedy the situation, and optimistically said,

> It may be that we may here stumble across the secret that is agitating the minds of many of us, and that is, of conserving the palm oil industry of the country. There is no doubt that the payment of taxes will bring the people into closer touch with Government and is bound to affect educational work in connection with our premier products.[16]

Mr F. P. Lynch, Resident for Calabar in 1926, hoped that taxation would force the people to do a little more work and to spend less time on litigation, which, according to him, they regarded as a pastime.[17]

All other reasons notwithstanding, it cannot be over-emphasised that direct taxation was introduced for the same reason as had been advanced by Lugard earlier, namely the needs of Native Administration. Apart from the growing necessity to provide the funds sorely needed for local development, there was the fact that

[14] CSO 26/1, No. 09098, vol. ii, Inspection Notes by the Lieutenant Governor, Southern Provinces (hereinafter Inspection Notes), p. 11
[15] *Legislative Council Debates*, 4 April, 1927, p. 33
[16] *Ibid.*, p. 29
[17] C 248/25 Annual Report Calabar Province for 1926, para. 63

the need to build up and strengthen further the power, authority and standing of the Warrant Chiefs had grown and was daily growing. As has already been shown, with the exit of Lugard it was discovered that his reforms and projects had done nothing to solve the fundamental problem of lack of influential chiefs in the Eastern Provinces. But the belief still persisted in official circles that such chiefs were necessary for the establishment of an effective Native Administration in the region. While some officials, as has also been shown, believed that it was Lugard's so-called reform which had upset their apple cart in local government in Southern Nigeria, there were others who held the view that the trouble derived from the fact that the Warrant Chief System was not Indirect Rule of the orthodox hue, since it did not enjoy the benefits of an independent revenue derived basically from direct taxation. To this latter group the surest remedy for the lack of centralised leadership in the communities of the Eastern Provinces lay in the introduction of direct taxation and the institution of Native Treasuries. In 1921 Mr W. F. Gowers, the Acting Lieutenant Governor, Southern Provinces, maintained in a minute to the Chief Secretary that everywhere direct taxation was in force and the courts were not the sole means of earning local revenue there was a chance of the courts becoming really useful. 'The receipt of tribute,' he continued, 'is . . . indissolubly bound up, in the native mind, with the idea of authority, and it is my idea that the latter will perish without the former.'[18]

In 1922 Captain Hanitch, Assistant District Officer, Eket, supported Mr Grier's recommendation for the introduction of direct taxation with the argument that such a step would give a measure of power to the chief, whose position, he said, was sinking lower and lower each year.[19] Mr Ormsby-Gore contended in 1926 that only through direct taxation could Native Authorities on the scale of those of the Northern Provinces and Southwestern Nigeria be developed in the Eastern Provinces.[20] The heads of houses in the coastal communities were argued into accepting taxation with the promise that it would help them to

---

[18] Minute dated 30.3.21 from W. F. Gowers to the Chief Secretary in C 176/19, Remarks by F. P. Lynch, etc.
[19] Memo. No. 757/36/22 dated 5.10.22 by Captain Hanitch in Calprof 14, C 582/22D, Pedigrees of Chiefs in the Calabar Province
[20] W. A. G. Ormsby-Gore, *Report of a Visit to West Africa*, p. 116

recover the powers over their members which they had lost through the abolition of the House Rule Ordinance in 1915.[21] Direct taxation in the Eastern Provinces was thus, in its origin, mainly a remedial measure designed to cure the Warrant Chief System of its besetting weakness of lack of 'big chiefs', and by so doing to help it to evolve into something resembling the 'classical' pattern of local government in the Fulani emirates.

The first of the last series of steps which ultimately led to the imposition of direct taxation on Warri and Eastern Provinces was taken in August 1924. On that date the Lieutenant Governor, Colonel Moorhouse, addressed a minute on the subject to the Governor, Sir Hugh Clifford.[22] But because the days of his governorship were already numbered, Clifford decided to leave all action on the matter to his successor. On 17 November 1925, a few days after his arrival in Nigeria as governor, Sir Graeme Thomson held a meeting with the Chief Secretary to the Government, the Acting Lieutenant Governor, Captain Davidson, and the Acting Secretary for Native Affairs, Mr Tomlinson, and found that these high officials were unanimous on the fact that the time had come when the Colony of Lagos, Warri and the Eastern Provinces should be taxed directly. The following day he instructed that the residents of the provinces concerned should be asked to submit reports on the machinery which they would recommend for carrying out the intentions of the government on the matter, on the extra staff which they would require for the purpose and on the rates at which they felt each adult male could be taxed without undue hardship.[23] The circular letter which left the Secretariat in consequence of this instruction, apart from requiring the residents to supply information along the lines requested by the governor, enjoined on them a study of Lugard's *Political Memoranda* Nos 5 and 6, which were said to enshrine the accepted principles on which taxation should be introduced and Native Administration founded.[24]

The memoranda which the residents sent in reply to this circular letter were, to the chagrin of the men at headquarters, 'unimaginative', 'unenthusiastic' and characterised by anxiety at

[21] Memo. dated 15.9.27 on Interview granted by HE to the Chamber of Commerce Calabar and to the Chiefs in CSO 26/2, No. 18417
[22] CSO 26/2, No. 17720, vol. i, Taxation, p. 2
[23] *Ibid.*, p. 2
[24] *Ibid.*, pp. 2–3

the serious mention of the intention to impose direct taxation. Major Ruxton described the replies as devoid of 'any great value', and attributed what he considered the shortcomings of the reports to the fact that these memoranda were written by officers with no previous experience of taxation and to the fact that being overworked and steeped in what he called 'that soul-destroying non-constructive labour known as court work' they could not be expected to show great enthusiasm for direct taxation and Native Administration, which would enormously increase their burden.[25] Whatever their limitations, however, these memoranda contained the considered opinions of men who had appreciable intimate knowledge of the different political situation of the Eastern Provinces. It was unfortunate that their cautious, matter-of-fact attitude exercised little influence on the method ultimately decided upon for the introduction of direct taxation.[26]

On 7 November 1926 a meeting, which was later to prove fateful for the Warrant Chief System, was held by the Deputy Governor, T. S. W. Thomas; the Attorney-General, Donald Kingdon; the Secretary for Native Affairs, Tomlinson; and the Lieutenant Governor, Major Ruxton. At that meeting it was decided by a majority vote to recommend the extension of the Native Revenue Ordinance to the Provinces of Calabar, Ogoja, Onitsha, Owerri and Warri.[27] Since this decision ran counter to the advice of the political officers in charge of these provinces and later led to disaster it is necessary to examine in full why it was made.

[25] *Ibid.* See the enclosed memos. Conf OP 43/1925 by the Resident, Onitsha Province, dated 26.4.26; Conf No. C 38/1925 by the Resident, Owerri Province dated 17.2.26; strictly Conf Memo. No. OG 12/25 by the Resident at Ogoja dated 14.5.26. It may be pointed out that on 1.9.26 the political staff numbered seventeen short of the approved establishment.

[26] Unfortunately we do not have the memoranda which individual local political officers seem to have submitted on direct taxation; only the summaries of their views by the residents. The general trend of opinion was against income tax with its implications of enumeration and assessment – the measures which eventually brought the Riot. Some officers warned against associating the already discredited Native Courts and their members with taxation, others against introducing taxation until the ground had been thoroughly prepared through, at least, one and a half years of propaganda by officers who had stayed long enough in their districts and divisions to win the confidence of the people. None of these views received serious consideration.

[27] CSO 26/2, No. 17720, vol. i, Taxation, etc., pp. 152–3

At the same time as the residents of the provinces concerned were called upon for their views on the machinery necessary for the introduction of direct taxation, the newly appointed lieutenant governor, Major Ruxton, was requested by the governor to submit a comprehensive scheme on the same issue. It is a tribute to his clear-headedness and pragmatism that in spite of his Northern political experience Major Ruxton was prepared to take into account the fact that the political situation of the Eastern Provinces differed from that of the Hausa-Fulani, Yoruba and Benin Provinces. Thus he saw that although it was tempting to make the Native Revenue Ordinance, the legal basis of taxation in the North and West, applicable to these provinces, it would be indeed unwise and impracticable to do so. That ordinance, he pointed out, was framed in 1904 to meet conditions in a predominantly Muslim country organised on autocratic lines and uncontaminated by ideas of English law, but in a quest for uniformity it had been amended later and applied by Lugard to the Yoruba and Benin Provinces of the South. Now Ruxton saw that there was nothing in the political conditions of the hitherto untaxed provinces to justify the application of the same ordinance. 'The whole basis on which the Native Renue Ordinance rests in the Northern and Yoruba Provinces,' he said, 'is completely absent so much that its wording is unmeaning to officers in the eastern provinces.'[28]

Bearing in mind the strikingly different political and mental climate of these five provinces, Ruxton proposed that initially only the simplest form of capitation tax should be aimed at but that elaboration could follow after ten years, when the administrative officers might have acquired experience in collecting, and the people become accustomed to the idea of paying, tax.[29] In a memorandum accompanying the draft bill which he submitted in October 1926 Ruxton argued that

> whereas in the Northern Provinces chapter 74 (The Native Revenue Ordinance) is but the statutory background on which taxation rests, an ordinance scarcely consulted in practice and totally unknown to the taxpayer, in the Eastern Provinces the new ordinance will have to lie open on every office table and copies will be in the hands of every lawyer's tout. The interpretation of almost every clause will be argued before the Supreme Court. It will certainly not lie on the top shelf in Provincial and District Offices.[30]

[28] *Ibid.*, pp. 5–6   [29] CSO 26/2, vol. No. 17720, i, Taxation, etc., p. 6
[30] *Ibid.*, p. 8. This was prophetic. By Nov. 1928, the Amended Native

In order not to offend the educated elements Ruxton carefully avoided the word 'Native' and the draft bill was entitled 'General Tax Ordinance', while the treasuries to be set up were to be called 'local' rather than 'native' treasuries. For similar reasons the bill was to apply to members of all races in these provinces to avoid any charge of racial discrimination. In the absence of chiefs through whom assessment along the lines of Sections 4-6 of the Native Revenue Ordinance could be made, the bill imposed a poll tax with a ceiling rate of ten shillings per head.[31]

The form of this draft bill enjoyed the approval of the residents of the provinces concerned and was in agreement with the ideas of Ruxton's immediate predecessor, Colonel Moorhouse. Like Ruxton, Moorhouse had suggested the levying of a poll tax 'not on logical grounds' but in order to avoid the unforeseen difficulties that were bound to arise from an attempt to make assessments in these areas for purposes of an income tax.[32] But in the discussions that followed Ruxton's practical proposals, it was the utopian idealism of men like Sir Richmond Palmer, the Lieutenant Governor of the Northern Provinces, and Cyril Alexander, the Resident of Kano, that triumphed.

On 15 September 1926 Ruxton had forwarded a copy of his draft bill to Palmer for his comments. This step proved a turning-point in the history of the introduction of direct taxation into the Warri and Eastern Provinces. Palmer argued that though in practice direct taxation could not be levied in these provinces without government sanction, yet there was much to be gained from making the theory on which taxation in the five provinces (including Warri) would be based more in keeping with the theory of the Native Revenue Ordinance as interpreted and understood in the emirates. This theory was that the local chief levied the direct taxation and collected it by his own authority. The application of this theory throughout Nigeria, Palmer contended, would promote the closer amalgamation of the Southern and Northern Provinces and would also discourage Northern Nigerians living close to the border with the Eastern Provinces from crossing the Northern boundary to evade their customary

Revenue Ordinance was before the Supreme Court in Calabar. Certain of its provisions were already being disputed. See CSO 26/2, No. 18417, vol. ii, the enclosed Memo. No. C 4681/1928 dated 4.11.28
[31] CSO 26/2, No. 17720, vol. i, pp. 8-9, 12-13
[32] *ACIR*, p. 3

obligations. Ruxton's projected system, he feared, would force the Northern Authorities too to levy tax as a direct government imposition with dangerous consequences for the authority of the Emirs. Palmer argued that, except perhaps in the Colony of Lagos and its immediate environs, the resident should not be regarded as levying the tax '*ex proprio motu*' or as a government agent but on behalf of the community.[33] Supporting this line of thought, Cyril Alexander, the Resident of Kano, said that it was only by doing as Palmer advised that the ambition to uphold the authority of the chiefs through taxation could be attained. He argued that however 'primitive' the members of an African community might be, they would understand that they owed duties to their community. They would also understand the embodiment of these duties in a money payment. Therefore, he went on, if the tax was presented to the public as levied at the instance of the heads of local communities it would be more readily accepted by the people than if they were encouraged to regard it as enforced by a 'nebulous authority of which they know little or nothing'.[34]

In the draft bill it had been provided that the resident would receive from the government half of the tax collected for the purpose of meeting local needs. This was anathema to the Northern pundits, for it conjured up before them the danger of giving more powers to the Legislative Council, a body which they detested because, they said, it was alien and unrepresentative of real African opinion. If the local share of tax were regarded as a dole or grant from the central government, the Legislative Council would be entitled to pry into the mode of its expenditure. This, it was said, was bound to breed constant collision between enthusiastic residents immensely aware of local needs and eager to fulfil them, and an unappreciative, wrong-headed legislature devoid of any intimate knowledge of distant provinces and districts. Palmer and Alexander recommended that the reverse should be the theory; that is, that the share paid into the government treasury should be regarded as a direct contribution to government from the public funds of the local community. This argument appealed very strongly to the men at headquarters, who said they were not prepared to allow the Legislative Council to intrude into Native Administration affairs.[35]

[33] CSO 26/2, No. 17720, vol. i, pp. 108–9
[34] *Ibid.*, p. 115   [35] *Ibid.*, p. 273

The proposal for a poll tax was equally unacceptable to men like Palmer and Arnett, the latter being at the time the Resident of the Cameroons Province. He had also seen the draft bill. Arnett, who had had his political education in the North, argued that a poll tax on all male persons of sixteen years and over would constitute a charter of liberty to every youth who wanted to 'kick over the traces of paternal and tribal discipline' and therefore was undesirable. A youth of sixteen, he said, had no independent income, but on the contrary was still a charge on his father. In this belief Arnett advocated an income tax imposed on the family as the taxable unit. This, he said, would prevent the evil of youths who had earned the few shillings needed to pay the tax claiming immunity from family control.[36]

To Palmer a poll tax was obnoxious because it could hardly be equitable. He cited Adam Smith, who had pointed out long ago that the incidence of any tax which was not unjust must be based on ability to pay. To achieve this equity, Palmer maintained, it followed that somebody must study, even if very crudely and sketchily, the relative wealth of the various sections of the community in order to determine what would be a fair rate for each area. This, he said, was in effect an assessment, albeit a very unsatisfactory one. If the poll tax was not going to be clearly unjust by infringing Adam Smith's maxim, Palmer concluded, to choose it in the hope of avoiding having to undertake an assessment was glaringly untenable.[37]

The provision in the bill for taxing 'non-natives', including Europeans, in these five provinces was also seen as a weak point. Cyril Alexander argued that if Europeans must pay tax, then they should be taxed by the central government rather than by the local government. If Europeans paid taxes levied by local communities they would soon ask for representation on the local government bodies which controlled the expenditure of such taxes. Such a development, he said, would destroy the 'nativeness' of Native Administrations while on the other hand it was unlikely that Europeans would meekly submit to taxation without representation.[38] Tomlinson pointed out that the proposal to tax 'non-natives' in the five provinces would impede rather than promote the passage of the bill in the Legislative Council. It

[36] *Ibid.*, p. 150
[37] *Ibid.*, pp. 366–7
[38] *Ibid.*, pp. 199–200

would raise a storm of opposition from those provinces hitherto subject to taxation but where 'non-natives' had never paid. If 'non-natives' were to pay anywhere they would have to pay everywhere, and that meant that in places where income tax was the rule they would be taxed on their income. This involved the question whether His Majesty's subjects should be taxed twice on the same income within the British empire. [39]

These were the arguments and attitudes of mind which led to the adoption of the Native Revenue Ordinance as the legal basis for the introduction of taxation into Warri and the Eastern Provinces. It must be stated unequivocally that to the government the strongest case against Ruxton's draft bill was what was called its 'lack of idealism' in failing to take into account the 'higher' principle of uniformity of practice throughout Nigeria. If the problem of taxing Europeans were the overriding concern the result would not necessarily have been the decision to adopt a legal enactment framed for places of dissimilar conditions. It would have been sufficient to drop the section bringing Europeans under the bill. This decision taken on theoretical grounds to extend the Native Revenue Ordinance to the Eastern Provinces committed the government to the assessment of the wealth of the people as a step to fixing the amount to be paid by each individual and by each local community, and to special methods of tax collection. The rest of what follows in this chapter will show that in fact it was *more* the attempt to carry out these specific demands of the Native Revenue Ordinance than taxation *per se* that precipitated the riot of 1929 which brought the Warrant Chief System to disaster.

As soon as this decision was taken in spite of the protests of Major Ruxton and his residents the implementation of the scheme moved apace. On 18 November 1926 the Colonial Secretary was sent a despatch informing him of the decision to tax these five provinces and of the reasons for the line and method of action adopted. [40] The latter sent his 'full approval for the general policy' proposed in a telegram of 1 January 1927 and followed it up twenty days later with a despatch in confirmation of this approval. [41] In February the amendment bill, which was to make the Native Revenue Ordinance applicable to the five provinces, was published.

[39] *Ibid.*, pp. 136–9, 197–9
[40] CSO 26/2, No. 17720, vol. ii, pp. 191–200   [41] *Ibid.*, pp. 242, 27–96

When the bill came before the Legislative Council the debate on it showed that nobody from the floor had thought seriously of it. Though K. Ata-Amonu (member for Calabar), I. O. Mba (member for Ibo Division), S. H. Pearse (member for Egba Division), Mark Pepple Jaja (member for Rivers Division) and S. C. Obianwu (member for Niger African Traders) spoke against it, none of their arguments was particularly telling. They all conceded the fundamental point, that taxation was one of the inescapable duties one incurred from membership of an organised community. Their main, if not only, appeal was for a postponement of the date for introducing the scheme so that there would be time to tell the people about it. But neither in literary style nor in factual content did the case of these opposers sound brilliant, especially if placed by the side of the well-reasoned and brilliantly argued case of the government bench. The fact that there was a period of twelve months between the passage of this bill in April 1927 and its coming into force on 1 April 1928, destroyed the case of men like Obianwu, who asked for a postponement by six months during which the people would learn about taxation.[42]

That the opposition was a sham was revealed by the fact that when the member for Calabar moved that the consideration of the bill be postponed for six months his motion was lost by twenty votes to six and that among those who voted against him were Mark Pepple Jaja and S. H. Pearse, both of whom had earlier made a show of opposition. None of the European un-official members voted against the bill, which was finally carried with the same vote.[43] The uneventful way the bill passed through the Legislative Council showed that the members did not quite realise the implications of the action they were sanctioning.

The same day and without any argument the Roads and River Ordinance was repealed, the repeal being scheduled to take effect from the date the new tax ordinance would become law. The reason for the repeal was the classic one that with the extension of direct taxation to all the provinces of the Protectorate this ordinance had lost its *raison d'être*. The repeal was also a propaganda measure. Forced labour had become so unpopular with the people and so resented by the educated elements that it was hoped its abolition would make taxation more acceptable. The tax

[42] *Legislative Council Debates*, 4 April 1927, pp. 25–36
[43] *Ibid.*, 36–8. CSO 26/2, No. 17720, vol. ii, p. 428. Four of the ten African members voted in favour of taxation.

ordinance was not to come into effect for twelve months so that before the actual payment active opposition would die down and the administration would have 'ample' time to prepare for the enforcement of its provisions.[44]

With the passage of these bills the scene of the drama shifted from the sheltered floor of the Legislative Council in Lagos to village squares and Native Court halls in Warri and the Eastern Provinces, where rough and turbulent rallies were held to advertise the new measure. The period of confidential despatches and hushed discussions was succeeded by one of open propaganda and public disputations. Immediately after the Legislative Council Session of April 1927 rose, the Lieutenant Governor, Ruxton, despatched Mr W. E. Hunt, Resident, an officer who was said to have had some experience of the working of the Native Revenue Ordinance, to the five provinces concerned to explain to the chiefs the provisions and objectives of the new Ordinance.[45] In the course of the tour, Mr Hunt held meetings with Warrant Chiefs at Ikot Ekpene, Itu, Aba, Okigwi, Ahoada, Umuahia, Afikpo, Awgu, Enugu, Nsukka, Awka, Onitsha, Warri and Sapele; and discussed problems of taxation with such prominent chiefs as Mark Pepple Jaja of Opobo, Chief Dogho of Warri and Chief Onyeama of Eke.[46] Meanwhile instructions had left the Southern Secretariat for the provinces asking the residents and their staff to commence telling people of the imminence of taxation and at the same time to start gathering information as part of assessment.

The official propaganda designed to make taxation acceptable to the people followed much the same pattern throughout the Eastern Provinces, and in fact constituted most of the arguments presented to the Legislative Council which were now amplified into a form suitable for popular and rustic consumption. Many towns and villages were visited. Warrant Chiefs, village and ward heads were told taxation would help to enhance their importance in their people's eyes; along the coast they were told the new measure was virtually a compensation for the repeal of the Native House Rule Ordinance. It was also spread about by political officers that all chiefs who helped with assessment

[44] *Legislative Council Debates*, 4 April 1927, p. 38. CSO 26/2, No. 17720, vol. ii, pp. 16, 430

[45] *ACIR*, p. 4

[46] Memo. No. C 194/1925/80 on Direct Taxation in the Eastern Provinces by W. E. Hunt, in CSO 26/2, No. 18417

and collection would get ten per cent of what they collected as reward, and that before the expenditure of any part of the local share of tax they would be consulted.[47]

Before the populace it was emphasised that everybody in the world, even in England, which had produced 'the highest civilisation', paid tax, that their immediate neighbours in Western and Northern Nigeria already paid tax and that in any case 'the big Governor' in Lagos had already enacted a law that they too must pay. The amount, it was emphasised, would not exceed ten shillings per head and that this 'small' payment was to relieve them of the burdens of the forced labour and the carrier system. What was more delightful, the sugar-coated argument ran, the money was not going into any private pocket, European or African, but was to be used for public purposes. The administration, however, did not trust in reasoned persuasion alone; its determination to force the issue, if need be with the help of the army, was not left in doubt. All intelligent and enlightened men would support direct taxation, it was added, while only deluded obscurantists would oppose it and by so doing bring untold calamities on themselves and their people.[48]

In Calabar Province, Resident Falk made use of the pulpit and the press to spread the propaganda. The Calabar weekly, *The Dawn*, of 2 July 1927 not only carried the resident's case for taxation but followed it up with a comment urging the people to respond enthusiastically to this new evangel and reminding them that 'the mother-country [Lagos]' had at first strenuously opposed the Water Bill but now was enjoying clean and good water and would not for any reason part with such a valuable asset. To support the scheme, the newspaper argued, meant to support 'the future good of this country'. Falk went further and printed one thousand five hundred leaflets carrying his message in English and Efik, for distribution among the people.[49] On 1 October 1927

[47] Conf Memo. SP 2676/64 dated 3.8.27 with Extracts from *The Dawn* of 2.7.27 attached in CSO 26/2, No. 18417. Memo. on propaganda attached to MP No. NA 4/1/1927 dated 4.5.27 from DO, Aba, to Resident, Owerri, in OW 363/1926: Introduction of Local Administration

[48] *Ibid.* The same documents cited, see also CSO 26/3, No. 20610. Assessment Report Aba Division 1927, pp 7–8. OP 522/1927 Annual Report Onitsha Province 1927, p. 6

[49] CSO 26/2, No. 18417, p. 2. *The Dawn* was published by Mr W. Coulson Labour, a Wesleyan Methodist. I owe this information to Dr F. I. A. Omu of Lagos University.

Native Treasuries were established in all the Districts of the Eastern Provinces and Warri with revenue from Native Court fees and fines. This was a return to the financial *status quo ante* 1914, a reversion to Moor's policy six months before taxation. It was done for purposes of propaganda, to enable the people to have concrete proof of the government's good intentions even before being called upon to bear any new burdens.[50]

The Resident of Onitsha Province, to reinforce the general propaganda, arranged a tour of the already taxed provinces of the West for a number of Warrant Chiefs and influential men in the province. The tourists were Mba, Obianwu and Ebosie of Onitsha, Kodilinye of Obosi, Amobi of Ogidi, Ezeokoli of Nnobi, Obodeze of Umulokpa, Obodojie of Ihiala, Orizu of Nnewi, Idigo of Aguleri, Onyeama of Eke and Chukwuani of Ngwo. The tour lasted from 2 to 12 February 1928 and was led by Mr Purchas, the District Officer at Onitsha. The men visited Agbor, Benin City, Akure, Ilesha, Ife, Ibadan and Oyo. At Ilesha, the Assistant District Officer, Mr Chadwick, helped them to study the Native Treasury system as well as the court books and took them to the local public buildings. At Oyo the Alafin offered them 'good advice' and they inspected buildings such as the dispensary, school and waterworks, all of which were Native Administration projects. At Ibadan the Bale showed them the Native Administration prison, treasury and 'the tribute collection building' and, it was reported, 'the cheerfulness of the payers and the fact that no Government officials, either European or African, were present made a deep impression on the touring chiefs'. At Ife, the Oni 'described the benefits of taxation, pointing to the prosperity of his town which was indeed obvious'. Both Mr Purchas and the Resident, Captain Buchanan-Smith, thought the trip was a great success and would 'considerably facilitate the institution of Native Administration' in Onitsha Province.[51]

Side by side with the spread of propaganda went the collection of materials for compiling the assessment reports which were to guide the government in fixing an equitable and uniform tax rate for each area. By law the residents were to cooperate with the chiefs or elders or other persons of influence in each district

[50] CSO 26/2, No. 17720, vol. i, Taxation, etc., pp. 12, 13, 16–17
[51] Memo. No. 111/1927 dated 15.2.28 by Mr Purchas and Memo. No. OP 523/1927 dated 21.2.28 by the resident in OP 523/1927, Visit of Certain Chiefs from Onitsha Province to Oyo Province

and 'in accordance with native custom and tradition' estimate or compute

   (i) 'the annual value of the lands and produce thereof used, occupied or enjoyed by members of each community';

   (ii) 'the annual value of the profits or gain from any trade, manufacture, office or employment in which the members of each community may be engaged';

   (iii) 'the value of all livestock owned by each individual or by each community'.[52]

In the attempt to carry out the injunctions of this law the residents and their officers directed their energies in the year preceding taxation towards computing what the farmer, who was taken as the average taxable male, could pay as annual tax. To get at this figure each assessing officer visited a number of individual farms, estimated their annual yield, and added this to what he reckoned to be the annual income from palm produce and livestock. The tax rate per head was two and a half per cent of this total average income.[53]

The first test of the effectiveness of the official propaganda came during this work of assessment. The experiences of assessment officers, who took the first practical step that suggested to

[52] *ACIR*, p. 4. Laws of Nigeria (1933 ed.), i, p. 808

[53] It was from the beginning agreed upon that one of the pre-conditions for a successful introduction of taxation was that, as much as possible, there should be a uniform flat rate for each area, though not necessarily for each district, since it was admitted that the district or division was not a natural economic, but an artificial administrative, unit. Consequently the rates for the first and second years of taxation in Owerri Province, for instance, worked out as follows:

Division or district	Recommended rate (s.)	Division or district		Recommended rate (s.)
Degema	7	Okigwi {	Isuochi	4
Ahoada	7		Remainder	6
Owerri	7	Orlu {	Ebem	4
Aba	7	Bende {	Remainder	6

These rates, as well as those for other provinces, were approved by the governor on 2 April 1928; that is, a day after the Ordinance had come into force.

See *ACIR*, pp. 4–5. CSO 26/3, No. 20621, Assessment Report Degema Division, Owerri Province 1927, pp. 110–11. CSO 26/2, No. 18417, pp. 80–1. Memo. No. 18417/99 dated 2.4.28 from the Chief Secretary to LGSP in CSO 26/2, No. 18417

the people that the talk of taxation could be seriously meant, consistently showed that the people and the majority of their chiefs had refused to be convinced by the concerted propaganda. Even the reception given to William Edgar Hunt, whose propaganda was meant to win the support of the chiefs, was sufficiently indicative of the fact that the path which the government had decided to tread was a steep and rugged one whose end was invisible. In one of the meetings he held with court chiefs in Ikot Ekpene Division Mr Hunt was told to his face that the manner in which the tax was being imposed savoured more of German than of British methods. Here one can see the effect on the people of British wartime propaganda against the Germans. At Itu, Aba, Okigwi, Bende, Nsukka and Onitsha the chiefs were hostile to the whole idea of direct taxation. The Aba chiefs solemnly told Hunt that 'they had always obeyed the orders of the Government but this order [the one asking people to pay tax] they could not obey'. At Bende, after a heated discussion, the chiefs stood up and dramatically offered to surrender their Warrant Chief caps to Mr Hunt rather than have anything to do with the taxation of their own people. Even at Enugu, where Onyeama of Eke, who was ever-ready to appear to be pro-government, overshadowed the other chiefs, there were some who declined to be identified with the novel imposition, or even with the announcement of it to their people. In Owerri Division Hunt was advised not to hold a meeting with the chiefs, since just before his arrival there the resident had attempted to hold such a meeting but had been forced to disband it halfway through as the recalcitrance of the chiefs had nearly led to incidents.[54]

Whether in the Owerri, Calabar, Ogoja or Onitsha Province assessment officers who conducted the propaganda at the level of the ordinary people had unpleasant experiences. In Aba Division, where the propaganda was said to have been very thorough and mass meetings were held in most towns to explain the scheme, the beginning of assessment was 'received with sullen and obstinate signs of defiance and refusal to entertain the demands'.[55] At Owerri, when people heard that the assessment was connected with the proposed taxation, they refused to offer the required

[54] Memo. No. C 194/1925/80 on Direct Taxation in the EPs by W. E. Hunt in CSO 26/2, No. 18417. Most of the chiefs were genuinely afraid of their people's reaction on this issue.
[55] *ACIR*, p. 5

information, deserted their compounds and assaulted chiefs who were inclined to cooperate with the government. Here the storm-centres were Olakwo and Okpala, where even policemen were assaulted and molested.[56] In the Bende Division the assessment officer, Mr A. L. Weir, had an easy time in Oloko and Ayaba Court areas, where he told the people the white lie that the assessment and census had nothing to do with taxation. Before he got to Alayi Court areas, however, the cat had got out of the bag and therefore things became more difficult for him. Chiefs refused to give any useful or reliable information and the public meetings he summoned were widely boycotted.[57] From Calabar Province Resident Falk reported that as soon as assessment began 'a storm of angry protests broke out from many parts'.[58]

The opposition in Onitsha and Ogoja Provinces was not as vociferous as that in Calabar and Owerri Provinces. The most serious anti-tax attitude reported in Onitsha Province came from Awka. Towards the end of November 1927 Awka blacksmiths had returned home from their annual occupational tours and started preaching the doctrine 'no taxation and no Native Courts'.[59] Only in Obubra Division of Ogoja Province was an attempt made to obstruct assessment. At Ugep, Onyenn and Nkum Okpambe the people had to be overawed with immediate prosecutions in the courts.[60] However, the experience of the first year of collection in the Onitsha and Ogoja Provinces later showed that this rather mild opposition to assessment did not mean that direct taxation was more acceptable to their people than it was to those of Owerri and Calabar.

Not surprisingly the peoples of the Eastern Provinces did not show any enthusiasm for taxation. It is true that taxation, when seen as the duty which every man owes to contribute to the upkeep of his community, was really no new idea. It existed in pre-colonial times in various forms of labour and contributions given in the public interest. As Hunt put it: 'No people in the era before money was invented paid a tax but every society of persons

---

[56] *Ibid.*
[57] CSO 26/3, No. 20646, Assessment Report on Bende Division, Owerri Province 1927, p. 13. *ACIR*, p. 9. EP 4126, Assessment Report Bende, para. 56
[58] EP 1138, vol. xi, Annual Report Calabar Province, 1927, p. 4. EP 3976, Assessment Report Opobo Division, Calabar Province, 1927, p. 2
[59] OP 522/1927, Annual Report, Onitsha Province, 1927, p. 3
[60] EP 755, vol. vi, Annual Report, Ogoja Province, 1928, p. 18

must have had a system of contribution in services or kind to a common fund for common good and in essence this was tantamount to a tax.'[61] Forced labour, which obtained up to 1 April 1928, was taxation commuted to labour. Many communities were already used to payments at locally assessed rates either for the building of a church or for a school or for hiring a lawyer when there was communal litigation. So prevalent was this latter practice that Ingles, Resident of Owerri, asserted that payment at assessed rates was already 'staple food', a development to which he attributed the fact that the initial work of preparing for taxation met with less obstruction than might otherwise have been the case.[62]

Nevertheless, taxation in the form and manner it was imposed on the Eastern Provinces in 1928 was a novel experience. Contribution towards the building of a church or the prosecution of any other project the need for which sprang spontaneously from the community was one thing, and the British tax was another. The tax was to be annual, it was directed towards no specific project but was for something vaguely labelled 'development', something which most of the communities themselves did not propose. What was more, taxation was understood to imply tribute to a conquering power. This was what the people protested against when at Okigwi, Awka, Onitsha and elsewhere they told Hunt that his proposals were against their custom.[63] The peoples of the Eastern Provinces never regarded themselves as having been conquered by the British. At Onitsha and Okigwi the chiefs pointed out that while it was understandable that the British should tax the 'Hausas', whom they had conquered and enslaved, it was utterly bewildering to hear that they also planned to tax the free peoples of Eastern Provinces, whom they had never conquered but who, out of their own munificence, had leased to the British the land on which they settled.[64] Among the fundamental objections to taxation was this feeling that it implied political subjugation and enslavement.

Another aspect of the question which shocked all, except

[61] Memo. SP 4002/vol. ii/90 dated 29.2.27 in EP 4002
[62] EP 1308, vol. v, Annual Report, Owerri Province, 1927 and 1928, p. 22
[63] CSO 26/2, No. 18417, pp. 5, 7, 9
[64] *Ibid.* See C 194/1925/80, Memorandum on Direct Taxation in the Eastern Provinces by W. E. Hunt, 1927. Erroneous though this point of view was, it is historically important in that it helped to determine the reaction of some people to direct taxation.

perhaps the few educated youths who were used to being counted at school, was the census of the population which accompanied the assessment of taxation. Throughout these provinces the counting of human beings, especially of free men, was contrary to custom. In traditional Ibo belief a man could count what was his own; for instance, his slaves, livestock, yams and the like. But free men belong ultimately to the earth goddess and it was not for anybody to attempt to count the free. Again counting of men was believed to cause death. It was held that counting reminded Death that human beings had multiplied and were multiplying and ought to be pruned down.[65] But census was part of assessment, for it was necessary to obtain the number of taxable males in each tax unit in order to know the net revenue to expect from it. Though ever since the establishment of the colonial régime annual returns had generally contained population figures there had been no actual census of any village or of its units. Even the haphazard count which now accompanied the assessment revealed the hopeless inaccuracy of the so-called census of 1921.[66] It was the attempt to obtain an accurate census and all the obscure ruses to which political officers resorted to attain that end which helped to make taxation all the more suspect and obnoxious. The general question was: 'In taking a census of the peoples of the Eastern Provinces was the Administration implying that the people had become its slaves or property or was it out to decimate them?'[67]

These moral and psychological objections were further strengthened by the economic burdens of taxation. This aspect of the problem was one of the important factors which determined most peoples' response to the whole question. The Resident of Calabar reported in June 1927 that 'relief from corvee labour did not seem to appeal to the peasantry if they were to pay money in lieu of this old form of taxation'. Even the promise of giving a ten per cent rebate to village heads did not prove a very enticing

[65] Based on information collected from Okereke Aka (Alayi, Bende), Ọfọ Onuoha and Oji Eberebe (Isuikwuato, Okigwi), Chief G. O. Iheanacho (Ugwa, Owerri), Chief Udo Udo Ibanga (Ikot Ekpene) and from many other old men.

[66] *ACIR*, p. 4. EP 1138, vol. xi, Annual Report Calabar Province, 1927, p. 3. CSO 26/3, No. 20621, Assessment Report Degema Division, Owerri Province, 1927, pp. 116, 119

[67] This question was put by Chief Okereke Aka of Alayi, Bende.

bait.[68] The argument that the money was to be used for local development had no magic appeal. One chief shrewdly pointed out that to whomsoever the money went the important thing was that it had left the people's pockets. During his propaganda tour Hunt was confronted in many places with the complaint that there was no money in the country. In one Native Court area in the Ikot Ekpene Division the chiefs argued that people had been impoverished since the abolition of the slave trade and slavery and that insistence on taxation would lead to people selling or mortgaging their children. Already, they argued, people had to borrow money to pay court fees. At Itu Hunt was asked to pledge his word that the government would not prosecute people who pawned their children to raise the money with which to pay tax.[69]

Another objection to taxation on economic grounds was the result of a general misunderstanding on the part of the people of government policy regarding forest reserves and oil palm plantations. At the same time as tax assessment inquiries were being prosecuted, the government was unwisely taking steps to institute forest reserves without explaining fully to the people the purpose of the whole scheme. In Calabar Province, for instance, extensive areas were gazetted as forest reserves before any effort was made to explain to those affected that the move was for their ultimate benefit. When people refused to give information regarding their income and property, assessment officers counted their palm trees, measured their farms and assigned arbitrary values to these. Wherever assessment officers adopted this strategy it led to the conclusion that assessment would lead directly to the government seizing the peoples' lands and palm trees. In the Eastern Provinces, where the economy rested heavily on these two items, this conclusion meant trouble for the government.[70]

It was in an atmosphere that was highly charged with widespread suspicion of government and unpreparedness to entertain

[68] Memo. on taxation in the Calabar Province by the Resident dated 8.6.27 in CSO 26/2, No. 18417
[69] Memo. No. C 194/1925/80 on Direct Taxation in the Eastern Provinces by W. E. Hunt in CSO 26/2, No. 18417
[70] EP 1138, vol. xi, Annual Report, Calabar Province, 1927, p. 4. Annual Report, Southern Provinces, 1927, pp. 20, 62. ACIR, pp. 5–7. For indigenous reaction to direct taxation in the neighbouring Warri Province (West of the Niger), see Obaro Ikimẹ, *Niger Delta Rivalry*, Longman 1969, ch. 6.

novel burdens that the administration tried to impose direct taxation through the hated Warrant Chiefs. The result was disaster. Since orthodox Lugardism placed great emphasis on the collection of direct taxation through the chiefs, regarding it as one of the most effective ways of increasing the authority and influence of chiefs, the story of the first tax collection in the Eastern Provinces is very illuminating and must be told in some detail.

The method of collection most acceptable to the administration was 'lump sum collection', because, the government believed, it threw a great deal of responsibility on the chiefs and thus gave them a chance to show their mettle. Under this system the village was taken as the tax unit and over it the village head or a Warrant Chief was made the tax agent. The sum expected from the village was made public, and the agent was given as many tax-receipts as there were taxable males in his village. He was also given a piece of paper advising him on the sum required from each compound. The compound head collected the assessed rates from his people and handed the proceeds over to the village head, who paid it in at the district headquarters. This was the system which was employed in Okigwi Division of Owerri Province, in parts of Nsukka in Onitsha Province and in practically the whole of Ogoja Province. In Onitsha Division the ward head was the official agent, but throughout the Nnobi Court area it was Warrant Chief Eze Okoli who did the collection.[71]

In the rest of the region the methods adopted were a travesty of that regarded as orthodox by the administration. In Owerri Division, for instance, the rate per head and the net demand from a village as well as the day for collection were made public. On the appointed day the taxable males met the district officer and his contingent of record clerks in the village square. There the village head collected the assessed rates from his people and presented them to the district officer. The names of the payers were there and then written on the tax receipts, which were presented to them.[72] In a number of villages in Nsukka Division the village heads confessed that it would be impossible for them

---

[72] EP 1308, vol. v, Annual Report, Owerri Province, 1927 and 1928, p. 6
[71] EP 755, vol. vi, Annual Report, Ogoja Province, 1928, p. 15. EP 1308, vol. v, Annual Report, Owerri Province, 1927 and 1928, pp. 6–7. Nsukka Division Annual Report, 1928, p. 3 in OP 348/1928. Onitsha Division Annual Report, 1928, p. 3 in OP 348/1928

to do the first collection since the young men would suspect them of pocketing the proceeds. So they asked the government to play a more direct part in the first year's collection. As a result the same method was adopted in these places as was in Owerri Division.[73]

In some other places, for instance in Bende and Degema Divisions, the whole pretence of collection through chiefs broke down from the outset.[74] In Ohuhu, Bende, tradition has it that there were no official tax agents; instead, the district officer came with record clerks and court messengers, called the people out to the village square and presented before them a bag into which each adult male dropped the assessed rate in return for the receipt which he collected from the record clerks. For the purpose of collecting from those who dodged these meetings Warrant Chiefs were subsequently given court messenger escorts with whom to hunt down defaulters. One informant, Agomo Adiele Ogbuishi of Ama-Ogwugwu, told the story of how he was chased by court messengers until he collapsed in a palm grove. He was then seized, given six strokes of the cane, and forced to pay.[75]

The mode of collection in the Alayi Court area is even more revealing. On 6 June 1928, so goes the story, the assistant district officer (ADO) of Bende went to Warrant Chief Oji Eberebe of Ovim in Isuikwuato and asked him for what he had collected. To escape punishment, Oji, a very wily man, who had until then made no effort to collect from anybody, gave the ADO twenty pounds out of his own private savings. Immediately, the political officer handed back to Oji ten per cent of the sum as official rebate. With Oji as guide, the ADO went to the houses of the other Isuikwuato Warrant Chiefs, who also had refused to take any step to advance the cause of taxation. At Umuasua, Warrant Chief Okeite 'foolishly' said he would neither pay his own tax nor collect from his people. The ADO immediately seized Okeite's cap and dropped it into the collection box. When the party came to Warrant Chief Ofo Onuoha of Isu Amawo they were told that he was 'not at home': he had been warned of the approach of the ADO and had taken to the bush. At Amaeke and Ohurohu the

[73] Nsukka Division Annual Report, 1928, p. 3 in OP 348/1928
[74] EP 1308, vol. v, Annual Report, Owerri Province, p. 7
[75] Based on information collected from Chief Samson Onyeama, ex-Warrant Chief; Agomo A. Ogbuishi and Anosike Ugbo, all of Amaogwugwu, Ohuhu Bende

Warrant Chiefs were similarly 'not at home'. When the party got to Alayi, court messengers were sent to call the three Warrant Chiefs of the place. Of these only one, Okereke Aka, showed some money 'as what he had collected', while the other two at first pleaded that they were unable to face their people on the issue. When however they learned of what happened to Okeite's cap they 'remembered' they had collected something. Court messenger escorts then took them to fetch 'what they had collected'. They later confessed to having got the money from their private savings. A Warrant Chief cap was worth some sacrifice. It was soon discovered that the above method could not satisfactorily and speedily effect the collection, and as a result a more direct method was adopted. Some people paid to record clerks, others still to the political officer.[76]

Serious as the resistance to taxation was or threatened to become, the fact remains that the first year of collection gave a false impression of safety. The absence of violence of grave proportions was mainly owing to two factors. It needed the shock of the first payment for people to realise what taxation meant in practical terms. At the end of 1928 O. W. Firth, the Resident of Owerri, prophetically observed: 'The full effects [of taxation] cannot yet be known, but it will undoubtedly have far-reaching results.'[77] Also the widespread use made of the police and of prosecutions in the law courts was apparently effective. Before men, or rather women, became utterly desperate this was a strong steadying factor.

Thus the first year of tax collection, 1928–9, did not give any clear indication as to the future. The experience of that year also failed to indicate from what part of the Eastern Provinces any subsequent trouble would come. Throughout Owerri Province, which was later to become the trouble-spot, tax was collected without much difficulty.[78] On the other hand in Onitsha Province, later to remain absolutely immune from disturbances, the collection was accompanied by anxiety in one or two places. In

[76] Based on information collected from Ọfọ Onuoha, ex-Warrant Chief, Okereke Aka, ex-Warrant Chief, Oji Eberebe, ex-Warrant Chief, Iheke Oghaji, Onwuka Aka and Aka Ekeoma, all of the former Alayi Court area. It is necessary to point out that those who paid out of their private savings said they went back and recouped themselves by undertaking the actual collection.
[77] EP 1308, vol. v, Annual Report, Owerri Province, 1927 and 1928, p. 4
[78] EP 1308, vol. v, Annual Report, Owerri Province, 1927 and 1928, p. 4

the Ihiala Court area the people at first refused to pay, making much fuss over the approved rate per head, but later paid when the government threatened to move in its forces.[79] In the Agbaja area of Enugu Division, the discs, which were given as a token of payment, ran short halfway through the collection. The people around Oji River who had not paid by the time this happened concluded that it was no longer necessary to pay as the year was already running out. A dangerous situation nearly developed when they so ridiculed those who had already paid that the latter threw away their discs and swore vengeance on the tax collectors, who, they felt, had tricked them. It was the timely arrival of the required stock of discs that saved the situation.[80] The Calabar Province came next in turbulence, for there it was actually necessary to move in the police on one occasion to overawe the people before they agreed to pay.[81]

The government experienced the most anxious moments in Ogoja Province. Here, as the appointed day approached, whispers of discontent were heard and as collection stood two weeks off the whispers developed into a roar. The people of Afikpo clan did not agree to pay before they had received reliable information that Lagos and Calabar had paid, and since payment in Calabar was delayed this made matters difficult. Attempts by the government to hold propaganda meetings there ended in turbulent demonstrations by angry women. Only stern measures eventually brought the clan under control.[82] In Abakaliki Division the Ezza clan first refused to pay anything, then offered to pay ten pounds per village (about ten per cent of the total assessment); but after protracted negotiations paid. Their neighbours, the Izzi, proved more recalcitrant. When in July 1928 the Assistant District Officer, Captain E. F. G. Haig, attempted to issue discs to some villages of the clan mobs of irate women seized the discs and threw them away. Meetings held to 'educate' the people broke up in disorder. In October the same year in the Igboagu section of the clan, elders and followers of Warrant Chiefs who acquiesced in government orders were assaulted and forced to flee to the district headquarters for safety. When Resident G. S. Hughes called a public enlightenment rally the seven or eight hundred

[79] Onitsha Division Annual Report, 1928, p. 6 in OP 348/1928
[80] Enugu Division Annual Report, 1928, pp. 4–5 in OP 348/1928
[81] *ACIR*, p. 8
[82] EP 755, vol. vi, Annual Report, Ogoja Province, 1928, p. 18

men who attended came armed with matchets. The situation was brought to normal by the arrest and prosecution of the supposed ringleaders.[83]

In Obubra Division payment was made but not before the Nkomoru and Assiga had offered a lot of resistance. In May 1928 'riotous mobs' at Nko and Ugep declared their unpreparedness to pay and forced the divisional officer to withdraw from their area. At the end of the month two police constables who went into Nkomoru to execute Provincial Court warrants were assaulted. The situation threatened to get out of hand and the divisional officer had to visit the area with a police escort of twenty-five men. The ringleaders were arrested, tried and punished on the spot.[84]

Nevertheless, the first collection was indeed a resounding success for the government and the lieutenant governor heaped praises on his officers, especially on Hunt, who was described as the 'chief propagandist and instructor in Native Administration methods'.[85] The total yield of tax was £357,267, as against an estimated sum of £288,630. Of the thirty-one Native Treasuries (including those in Warri) fifteen collected within six months of the coming into effect of the law sums which exceeded the estimate for the whole year. In Ogoja Province, where the greatest difficulties were met with, collection was finished by the end of the year and the estimated revenue was exceeded in five out of the six Native Treasury areas. In Owerri Province the estimate was exceeded in all divisions except Bende, which had a deficit of £5000 owing to an over assessment of the Ayaba and Oloko areas.[86]

From April to October in the second year of collection everything seemed to point to the likelihood of the success of the first year being repeated. As Major C. T. Lawrence, the Secretary, Southern Provinces, put it, 'nothing in [the middle of] 1929 pointed to the possibility of an explosion'. The markets were well attended by both men and women, who looked cheerful and

[83] *Ibid.*, pp. 19–20, 47
[84] *Ibid.*, pp. 21, 48
[85] Memo. MP No. OW 302/1928 dated 14.11.28 in OW 36/1928A Circular Instructions to DOs
[86] *Ibid.*, ACIR, p. EP 755, vol. vi, Annual Report, Ogoja Province, 1928, pp. 14–15. EP 1308, vol. v, Annual Report, Owerri Province, 1927 and 1928, pp. 9–10

friendly. The Native Courts were continuously flooded as usual. The collection of taxation itself went on fairly smoothly.[87] However, this apparent calm was entirely misleading. As the rest of this chapter will show, the peoples of the Eastern Provinces were not yet reconciled to direct taxation. Nor were they happy with many other aspects of the colonial system.

In September 1929 Captain John Cook, Assistant District Officer, was sent to Bende as Acting District Officer. He took over from Weir and was to hold the division until Captain Hill returned from leave in November. When he assumed duties Cook found the nominal rolls of adult males 'very unsatisfactory', since the record did not indicate to what ward or compound each payer belonged. He therefore decided on a more detailed and scientific roll that would give this information and also carry against each payer's name such details as how many wives, children, goats, sheep, fowls and the like he had. Cook called his Warrant Chiefs together in October, told them they were to conduct this new and more detailed count and rather irrelevantly added that the exercise had nothing to do with a tax on women.[88]

The mere mention of women in this context gave rise to the rumour that the government in fact had a plan to tax women. What made this story convincing was that in 1926 the government had unwisely deceived the people of Oloko and Ayaba in Bende and this fact had become widely known. The assessing officer, Mr Weir, had told them that the counting of heads was a mere 'count' and not a 'census' and had nothing to do with taxation; 1927 had revealed that the reverse was the case. To make matters worse, the Warrant Chiefs now amplified Captain Cook's injunction as they understood or rather as they were ready to understand it. Chief Ananaba of Umuala in Oloko solemnly declared before a meeting of the elders of his village that the government had ordered him to count women and domestic animals 'so that they would be taxed'. Instead of stopping there, he proceeded to remind the elders of the devious methods by which they had been counted at the inception of taxation. As soon as the meeting dispersed this news became common talk.[89]

[87] Memorandum on the Aba Riots by C. T. Lawrence, SSP in *ACIR*, para. 238
[88] *ACIR*, p. 11
[89] *Ibid.*, pp. 11–12

The women reacted swiftly to what seemed to them a new and dangerous threat. Those of Umuala and Ugbebule held meetings at which they resolved 'to wait patiently until anybody made a move to count them and they would make trouble'. At Ezima chiefs Oleka, Ezima and Oboro, when approached by women unsettled by the rumour, plainly told them that the government 'had ordered them to count women for purposes of tax'. *Maka tax*, the phrase used, is a vague Ibo expression which could be easily understood to mean 'so that they would be taxed'. Ezima also went on to tell the women that he was not satisfied that women should pay tax at the same time as men paid.[90]

Before the end of October the women of Oloko were convinced that there was a secret and wicked plan to tax them and had made up their minds to resist. Chief Okugo of Oloko, one of the Warrant Chiefs whose unpleasant duty it was to conduct the count, finding the whole business unpopular and explosive, refused to do anything about it until 18 November, when Captain Cook stampeded him into action with the order that he had to be ready with the census figures within eight days or face disciplinary action. Still Okugo refused to take a direct part in the count. On the contrary, he delegated it to a mission school teacher, Mark Emeruwa, who went to Bende and received instructions from Cook. There, runs the story, Emeruwa was told to count only men but to obtain from them details relating to their wives and livestock. The count went on without incident until Emeruwa came to the compound of one Ojim, where he saw Nwanyeruwa, one of Ojim's wives, preparing palm oil. The details of what happened are extremely obscure, but probably Emeruwa requested the woman to count 'her people' and livestock. Nwanyeruwa replied aggressively, asking Emeruwa pointedly whether his mother was ever counted. By the time the altercation got to this point both parties had completely lost their tempers and had gone for each other's throats in earnest; Nwanyeruwa clutching at the mission teacher with her oily hands.[91]

Unfortunately for Emeruwa, Okugo, Cook and the government, there was a mass rally of women in a neighbouring compound, a rally which, the women said, had met to discuss issues unconnected with tax, but which the Donald Kingdon Commission of Inquiry into the subsequent Riots said had met on the tax question. In any case whatever was its purpose, Nwanyeruwa ran

[90] *Ibid.*   [91] *Ibid.*, pp. 12–13

to this meeting in a state of frenzy to announce that the awaited enumerator of women had arrived. The women did not hesitate to act. They went at once to Emeruwa's house in the mission compound and, since they had come to regard 'counting' as synonymous with taxation, asked him why he had said 'women should pay tax'. They also sent messengers 'armed' with fresh folded palm leaves to women of neighbouring villages inviting them to come to Oloko. Thus began the Women's Riot of 1929, which, starting in Owerri Province, spread to Calabar Province.[92] A full-scale study of the Women's Riot will not be gone into here. The episode is important in the present context as a historical divide between the era of the Warrant Chiefs and a period in the local government history of the Eastern Provinces in which official policy and action were directed towards evolving a system in keeping with the democratic traditions of the people. All that will be attempted in the present study is a brief analysis of certain aspects of this large movement which will throw helpful light on the Warrant Chief System and its problems.[93]

There were causes other than the rumour of a plan to tax women which helped to precipitate the Riot. First among these and closely allied to the premier cause was the fact that the people already felt very keenly, especially in the areas affected by the Riot, the burden of the taxation on men. The incidence of the first year's tax in places like Owerri Division was too high and by 1929 had become unbearable. When the government fixed the rates in 1927 it bore in mind not only what a man made from farming but also what he made from the trade in palm oil and kernel. But after 1927 the price of palm produce had fallen sharply, reaching its lowest point in 1929. In 1928 Ferguson and in 1929 Royce, both administrative officers at Owerri, had reported that the rate of tax per head for the Nguru area, for

---

[92] *Ibid.*, pp. 13–14
[93] Professor Gailey has recently published a book on the Riot entitled *The Road To Aba*. My review of this book is appearing elsewhere. Here however one can only point out that Professor Gailey followed the British administration and other later writers on the subject in referring to the movement as *Aba* Riots. This is misleading and at times has created the impression that the episode was centred on Aba. The Riot did not start at Aba and did not reach its peak there. The women did not and do not refer to it as the Aba Riot. They call it *Ogu Umunwanye*, meaning *Women's War*. There is probably still a place for a full-scale study of the episode based on an intensive use of local sources and traditions.

instance, was too high, but nothing had been done to remedy this obvious source of grievance by the time the Riot occurred. Added to the effects of the decline in the palm produce trade was the fact that in places where the Riot began, especially in Oloko Court area, the number of taxable males had been over-estimated. Since people here and in some other villages and lineages had deliberately inflated the number of men 'under their control' in order to emphasise their importance, hoping to be made Warrant Chiefs as a result, when taxation was imposed and assessment based on the census returns the result was consternation, disillusionment, hardship and anger at what they regarded as a dirty trick which the government had played on them. Furthermore the so-called taxation on men had in fact in places meant taxation on men and women. Some women helped their husbands with their earnings and some widows paid for their sons of sixteen years or thereabouts. The threat of a tax on women was to some women not just a threat to lay on them a completely new burden but a threat to add to an already existing and excessive one.[94]

Next in importance to grievances arising from rumours of taxation and actual taxation was the grievance against the Warrant Chiefs. For many reasons people had lost confidence in the chiefs, and to some extent in the administration that kept them in being.[95] Then came general economic grievances which helped to intensify the hatred for taxation. The produce trade, which had become a mainstay of the cash economy of the region, was experiencing a slump in this period. The slump of 1929 was probably one of the worst the people had faced since the establishment of British rule. The following statistics collected from a few of the places worst hit will help to illustrate some aspect of the trade conditions of the period.[96]

(*a*) OPOBO (Calabar Province)

	Average price of palm oil							*Average price of palm kernel*					
Year	*Per cask*			*Per ton*			*Year*	*Per measure*			*Per ton*		
	£	s.	d.	£	s.	d.		£	s.	d.	£	s.	d.
1926	15	1	2	23	8	6	1926	8	12	10	13	17	6
1927	13	13	0	21	4	3	1927	8	8	0	13	10	0
1928	15	10	0	24	2	3	1928	9	7	0	15	0	0
1929	13	19	0	21	15	3	1929	7	7	0	11	16	3

[94] *ACIR*, pp. 95–7 [95] See ch. 7
[96] Memorandum on the Aba Riot by C. T. Lawrence, SSP, in *ACIR*

(b) OWERRI PROVINCE

	Palm oil per four-gallon tin		Palm kernel per 50 lb.	
	1928	1929	1928	1929
	s. d.	s. d.	s. d.	s. d.
Aba (Dec.)	7 0	5 10	5 9	4 6
Umuahia (Dec.)	6 10	5 8	—	—

Going hand in hand with the fall in price of the chief exports of the people was the rise in price of imported goods like tobacco, cigarettes, spirits and grey baft, largely owing to increases in import duties. Another grievance had arisen from the fact that in places like Itu, Opobo and Imo River the firms had dropped the method of buying produce by measure, which the people understood, in favour of buying by weight, which they did not understand.[97]

This economic grievance was important only in so far as it helped to make the burden of direct taxation more keenly felt. Some scholars, for instance C. K. Meek, impressed by the fact that articles such as palm kernel and tobacco, which were usually sold by women, featured prominently in their complaints, and also by the fact that the riot was mainly limited to the palm belt, have tended to regard grievances connected with the slump in produce trade as the chief cause of the disturbances.[98] Here it is enough to point out that there was a slump in 1927 but no riot and that the 1929 slump, like all slumps, affected men and women alike. It would be inaccurate to regard the Riot as a palm-belt phenomenon. It is indeed a limited view which portrays the Riot as a response to a passing economic crisis. British administration, especially through the Warrant Chief System, had struck and undermined indigenous society at many vital points. This was highly disquieting to a people who saw their past in terms of quiet balance and even serenity.[99] But that a Riot would have occurred in 1929 and that it would have taken the form it did without the introduction of direct taxation and the effort made to ensure that it conformed in many details with what obtained in Northern Nigeria and Yorubaland is most unlikely.

[97] *ACIR*, pp. 102–3
[98] C. K. Meek, W. M. Macmillan and E. R. J. Hussey, *Europe and West Africa*, Oxford 1940, p. 25
[99] For the people's vision of their pre-colonial history see A. E. Afigbo, 'Revolution and Reaction in Eastern Nigeria', in *JHSN*, iii, 3, Dec. 1966

The Riot was a complex episode but its complexity can be explained mainly in terms of thirty years of blind British rule and the reaction which it evoked. The Riot did not spread beyond the palm belt where it began largely because of the government's intervention and the severity with which the rioters were dealt with. According to the official figures the casualty list in Calabar Province alone was as follows:[100]

Place	Killed	Wounded
Opobo	32	31
Abak	3	—
Utu Etim Ekpo	18	19

News of these slaughters usually spread very fast and the number of victims also grew as the story passed from mouth to mouth. By the time the news of the shootings at Abak got to Opobo the number of the dead given by the government as three had grown to sixty. The bloody encounters between the troops and the women easily dispelled the illusion which the women had at first, that the troops would not shoot at them. The slaughter taught them the sobering and tragic lesson that a colonial power would stop at nothing to maintain its position of authority in time of crisis. Also the limited territorial coverage of the Riot owed something to the limitations in the means at the disposal of the women for spreading their propaganda. Being unable to avail themselves of modern means of spreading information the women used the following method: each village which joined the movement sent a fresh palm leaf, through one or two of its women who travelled on foot, to the next village with the call to join in the riot against the government; then the woman who first got this message would take steps to rally round her fellow women. At the general meeting the women would decide whether to join in the rioting and what form their action would take.[101] For short distances this system was probably very efficient, but it failed to draw women in places as remote as Ogoja and Nsukka into the movement before the government, which had at its disposal modern means of transport and communication, mastered the situation.

The Women's Riot was characterised by attacks on three institutions – Warrant Chiefs, Native Courts and European

[100] *ACIR*, Appendix III (15)
[101] *Ibid.*, pp. 12–14

factories. The women of Oloko had not only succeeded in securing the arrest of Chief Okugo but had also seen him uncapped and imprisoned by the government.[102] This set the pattern for the attack on the Warrant Chief régime for many of the Native Court areas affected by the Riot. At Owerrinta the women started by stopping the proceedings of the Native Court, then proceeded to chase the chiefs away and ended by looting the house of the court clerk and damaging those of the court messengers.[103] On the whole nine Native Courts were burnt, three ordinarily destroyed and four damaged throughout the area touched by the Riot.[104]

The attack on the chiefs and their courts derived partly from the old grudge which many people bore them for past oppressions,[105] and partly from the fact that the chiefs were regarded as having secretly agreed with the government on the introduction of taxation. Here the evidence of Nwatu, a Warrant Chief of Owerrinta, is illuminating. On 11 December 1929, when thousands of women from the Owerrinta Court area had assembled, Nwatu tried to ride through their midst on a bicycle, wearing his judicial cap and carrying a shotgun. The women immediately set upon him, seized his bicycle and gun, tore his clothes and chased him into the bush. Nwatu afterwards confessed before the Donald Kingdon Commission in 1930 that he was attacked because of the part he had played in taxation. Just before the introduction of taxation he and a number of other chiefs had visited Lagos on the invitation of the government. Many people later saw the object of the visit as conspiracy with the white man on the introduction of taxation.[106] The Native Courts were not only places where chiefs and clerks had given many an unfair verdict, they had also been used in many places as centres for the collection of tax. When a group of demonstrating women attacked the clerk of the Nguru Native Court, Mr Williams, they cried 'kill him' and said 'his was the house where all the Government money was stored and where all the tax money was kept'.[107] The women must have thought that after the tax had been collected in the court house it would be transferred to the house of the court clerk.

[102] *Ibid.*, pp. 14–17   [103] *Ibid.*, pp. 36–7
[104] *Ibid.* See the enclosed map   [105] See the next chapter
[106] *ACIR*, pp. 55–6, *Aba Commission of Inquiry Notes of Evidence* (hereinafter *ACINE*), para. 3434   [107] *ACINE*, para. 5030

The looting of factories was a side-development which some in the administration magnified at the time to justify their act in shooting down women with machine-gun and rifle fire at Utu Etim Ekpo, Abak and Opobo. On 11 December 1929 bands of Ngwa women were passing through Aba to Eke Akpara on the Aba–Owerrinta road when the car of the Medical Officer at Aba, Dr Hunter, knocked two of them down. To escape from the mob which got infuriated at the fate of their two comrades, Dr Hunter took shelter in the factory of the Niger Company. The women looted the property of the company because its factory gave shelter to their quarry.[108]

Before the accident, the women had confined their menaces to harassing the persons of white people, all of whom were identified with the government, the Native Courts and all those connected with them. It was only after the Aba incident that other women at Imo River, Utu Etim Ekpo, Umoba, Mbawsi, Okopedi and Ntan, who, as long as nobody had been shot, did not want to be surpassed in their demonstration of anger at the supposed plot to oppress them, proceeded to loot or to attempt to loot European factories and shops. Here it is enough to point out that at Opobo and Umuahia, where there were many factories and where looting would have been more rewarding than in some of the places where looting actually took place, no attempt was made to loot. Also the Oloko women, when they heard the turn events had taken at Aba, sent a telegram to the District Officer Aba to tell their fellow women that the destruction of houses and the raiding of stores were not part of their programme for securing redress on the tax question. The Donald Kingdon Commission which subsequently inquired into the Riot was of the opinion that the looting at Aba was a direct consequence of the motor accident and the lootings elsewhere a direct result of the desire of other mobs to rise to the peak of the example already set at Aba.[109]

The outbreak of the Women's Riot is of great interest in many ways. It showed that the Warrant Chief System, as a system of local government, had become thoroughly discredited for a

[108] *ACIR*, pp. 44–50
[109] *Ibid.*, pp. 50 5. A minority report by Mr Osborne argued that the looting at Aba had nothing to do with the accident, but was part of a previously worked-out plan of violence by the women. See pp. 132–4 of the Report.

number of reasons which will be analysed in the next chapter and some of which have already been mentioned. Inquiries conducted in the area in which this system operated have shown that but for the intervention of the government and its stiffness the demonstration against the colonial régime would have become more widespread and perhaps more violent than it actually was.[110]

The Riot marked the end of an era in the local government history of the Eastern Provinces in more ways than one. Ever since 1922-3 it had become clear that the Warrant Chief System had failed to meet the requirements of the government which instituted it or to evoke the enthusiastic acceptance of the people whom it was designed to serve. Consequently a reforming movement had set in which, it was hoped, would make the system more effective and efficient for achieving the purposes of the government as well as make it more popular with the people. But because it was not realised that the system was rotten to the core the pervading spirit of this reform was gradualism.

The result was that seven years after Mr Grier's report on the Eastern Provinces inquiries into clan boundaries the first step towards the creation of clan courts were still going on and the rearrangements already effected were not far-reaching enough to make the people aware of the fact that the Warrant Chief System was undergoing substantial changes.[111] Up to the outbreak of the Riot it was still thought in official circles that one little reform here and another there could make the system

[110] In the areas of Onitsha and Ogoja Provinces which I covered during my field work I got the information that one main factor prevented the women in these two provinces from taking part in the Riot. This was the official version of the Riot that first reached these provinces. When people asked for the cause of the trouble, I was told, officers told them that a certain chief had asked the women in his area of authority to pay tax, not that there was a rumour that government wanted to tax women. This, of course, made the Riot appear like a local issue. By the time the real immediate cause of the trouble, i.e. the rumour that Warrant Chiefs and the government were plotting to tax *all* women, became common knowledge, the government had had time to demonstrate that, contrary to popular belief, it had no objection to shooting women. Based on information collected in the Onitsha and Abakaliki Divisions of the Onitsha and Ogoja Provinces respectively, especially on information collected from Luke Obiasogu (Nnewi, Onitsha), Onyejuluwa Njoku (Nnewi, Onitsha), Chief Nwancho Atuma (Ikwo, Abakaliki) and Chief Ukpai Ereshi (Agba, Abakaliki).

[111] *Annual Report Southern Provinces for 1929*, pp. 3, 12–13, 23–4, 33

traditional, efficient and popular. In a conference of residents held in Lagos in 1928 the decision was taken that Native Court clerks and messengers should be natives of the court areas they served, they were to be recommended by the chiefs and were not to be sent on transfer. It was hoped these minor changes would help to end the domination of each court by the court staff.[112] In the same year it was decided, at the instance of the lieutenant governor, that every effort was to be made to do away with the titles 'Native Court Chief', 'Native Court Warrant Chief' and 'Warrant Chief'. The government thought it was the widespread use of these terms which engendered the idea 'that Government created chiefs by giving them a warrant' whilst 'all Government did was to appoint certain persons to be members of a Native tribunal'.[113] The point is that nobody in the upper reaches of the administrative pyramid, where official policy was made, realised the need to go fast with reform. To learn this lesson they needed the shock of mobs of irate women tearing down Native Court houses, snatching Warrant Chiefs' caps and hurling themselves in desperation at trained troops armed with rifles and machine-guns.

Nor did the government realise before 1929 how radical the reforms should be to become effective and satisfactory. Up to the riot the government clung to the idea that the true redemption of the Warrant Chief System lay in the appointment of 'hereditary chiefs' to the position held by Warrant Chiefs. In 1929, just before the riot, the Southern Secretariat had sanctioned the appointment of Warrant Chief Obiukwu Nze of Umulolo, Okigwi, as the District Head of the Otanzu clan on a salary of five pounds per month.[114] In the Ogoja Province a similar scheme was receiving energetic execution. In Ogoja District the 'clan chiefs' of Mbube, Yako, Akaju and Ikerri 'were found' and recommended for appointment as District Heads. In Afikpo Division the heads of Edda, Afikpo and Okposi clans were similarly 'discovered' and appointed to similar positions. It was the same in Obubra district, where the *Kudedin* of Adun and the *Ntul Asiene* of Atam

---

[112] Memo. No. OP 135/1927 dated 18.4.28 from the Resident of Onitsha Province to his Divisional Officers in OP 156/1928 Provincial Circulars
[113] Memo. No. OW 120/1927 dated 9.8.28 from the Resident, Owerri Province to his DOs in OW 30/1928A: Circular Instructions to DOs
[114] EP 6036, Appointment of District Head, Okigwi Division – the whole file

were said to have 'come forward' on their own.[115] This reversion to the Paramount Chief policy of Lugard passed through the Southern Secretariat without adverse comment. It was in line with the accepted policy of the time.

By the time the annual reports for 1929 were sent in the Women's Riot had taken place. The residents, located as they were in their remote provincial headquarters, failed to appreciate how far this event had caused a rethinking of the government's attitude to the whole question of local government in the Eastern Provinces. When therefore they wrote their reports along the lines of 1928 and announced with joy some more 'discoveries' of 'clan chiefs' they found their reports severely criticised. The comment of the Lieutenant-Governor, C. W. Alexander, on the Calabar report for 1929 is illustrative of the wind of change which was blowing at headquarters. 'All officers,' he warned, 'must get out of their heads the idea that the pursuance of a policy of native administration is possible only where there are ruling potentates, that is, paramount chiefs.'[116] The significance of this warning stands out very clearly when it is pointed out that it was this man, Cyril Alexander, who in 1926 had urged the closest conformity to Northern Nigeria local government practices, even in the matter of the law on which taxation was to rest.[117]

When in 1930 the Ogoja Resident rather anachronistically and unrepentantly persisted in talking of chiefs, instead of village and clan assemblies, the disapproval from the Southern Headquarters became actually denunciatory. Mr F. B. Carr, one of the officers in the secretariat, castigated the way the Resident used 'the word chieftainship . . . in an unqualified form, the tendency to ignore councils and to endeavour to find or make a district head. It is most unfortunate,' he concluded, 'that the head of Ngbo is being recognised. The report acknowledges that there is not a head and that there never was a head but it is perfectly clear that there are and always were village group councils and it seems a pity not to utilise these and to introduce an alien form of government as convenience.'[118] The habit of discovering chiefs in spite of all the

[115] EP 755, vol. vi, Annual Report, Ogoja Province, 1928, pp. 8–13
[116] EP 1139, vol. viii, Annual Report, Calabar Province. See minute by C. W. Alexander enclosed in the Memo. SP 1139/vol. viii/26 dated 3.5.30
[117] See above pp. 217–9
[118] EP 755, vol. viii, Ogoja Province, Annual Report. See comment by F. B. Carr dated 2.3.31.

evidence to the contrary was in the tradition of the era which the Riot had effectively ended in 1929. 'The search for such officials [District Heads] and the Paramount Chief,' noted Walter Buchanan-Smith, the lieutenant governor, 'is a relic of the first days of Amalgamated Nigeria and in certain parts of the South has been shown to be a most futile proceeding.'[119] Much as here and there one finds officers who after 1929 continued to linger on mentally in the past, the Riot of that year effectively caused a change of policy as regards the basis of local administration in the Eastern Provinces.

It also inaugurated a change in methods. Mr Palmer's inquiries of 1914, on which Lugard greatly relied in introducing aspects of his 'new policy', were made among the administrative staff. As far as Palmer was concerned the people on whom the new system was to be applied might as well not have existed. It was much the same thing with the tours and inquiries of Mr Grier and Mr Tomlinson in 1922 and 1923 respectively. Though a few natives were questioned and their opinions recorded, the deciding factor was the opinion of the European political staff. Even the natives whom Grier and Tomlinson interviewed were all Warrant Chiefs, a group who to some extent had lost touch with their people.[120] After 1929 the procedure changed. Before then investigations into issues of local government policy had been very haphazard. But from 1930 the peoples of the Eastern Provinces witnessed investigations into their political system 'of a range and depth to which there has been nothing comparable in Africa since the researches directed by Sir Donald Cameron as a prelude to his reorganisation of Tanganyika'.[121]

The Donald Kingdon Commission into the Riot, with its patient collection of opinions from all natives who volunteered to give evidence and with its attempt to find out from them what system of local government they would rather have, was the herald of this supersession of the earlier slipshod and cavalier treatment of local government questions by scientific investigation. In fact, in the methodology and the approach it adopted the commission was not only an epilogue to the Warrant Chief period but also a prologue to the era which began immediately

[119] *Ibid.* See comment by W. Buchanan-Smith dated 23.3.31
[120] S. M. Grier, *Report on a Tour in the Eastern Provinces*, Lagos 1922, pp. 7, 9
[121] M. Perham, *Native Administration in Nigeria*, Oxford 1937, p. 221

after the Women's Riot. Truly, some of the old Native Courts continued to linger on for many years after 1929 because the problems of staff shortage and the need to make thorough investigations the basis of the reorganisation caused delay. But in point of fact the policy and system of local rule through chiefs came to an end with the Women's Riot.

7 The Warrant Chief System anatomised

Too many harsh criticisms have been made of, and hasty conclusions drawn on, the Warrant Chief System without an attempt to ask the right questions let alone investigate them. Thus Professor Anene on the basis of a general study which ended in 1906, when the system in question was just being established and extended, declared it the *'greatest blunder'* of the British administration and asserted that it *'effectively undermined the tribal system and produced chaos'*.[1] In order either to dispel or confirm these conventional assumptions and assessments it becomes necessary to ask and answer in some detail three related questions. The first is whether the system was, in all respects, an unmitigated failure or whether it had any redeeming features.

[1] J. C. Anene, *Southern Nigeria in Transition 1885–1906*, Cambridge 1966, pp. 250, 257. Most books on Nigeria which have touched on this topic are strewn with such conclusions. I have chosen to illustrate the case from *Southern Nigeria in Transition 1885–1906* because this book, with all the usual airs of detailed scholarly investigation and objective assessment, is bound to carry so much weight that, if unchallenged, it will erect the conclusions into established dogma. Professor Anene took his departure from a general assumption of questionable validity. 'It is a generally accepted thesis', he writes, 'that when backward peoples are suddenly confronted by a powerful modern state and were not given time to adjust themselves to the new situation, the peoples invariably lost their stability and became disorganised' (p. 1). One may ask who has 'accepted' this thesis? When a 'primitive' people have already come into contact with 'a powerful modern state' how do you give them 'time to adjust themselves to the new situation'? Are we being told that all situations of culture contact between Europe and Africa since 1800, for instance, produced instability and chaos and that this applied to the Ibo and their neighbours? This view would be hardly pardonable in a European writer who knows nothing of the continuing vitality and richness of village life in Ibo, Ibibio, Ijo and Ogoja communities. It is astounding in an Ibo from Nando, a community whose rich indigenous culture even to this day strikes a visitor as having been only marginally touched by European impact.

The second is about what its basic demerits were. The third is whether having dominated and to some extent determined the local political life of the people of this area for about three decades the Warrant Chief System effected far-reaching changes in their indigenous political system. It is with these vital questions, which are indispensable for a full understanding of the history of the system, that this chapter deals.

An assessment of the Warrant Chief System based only on the opinions of the vast majority of the peoples of the Eastern Provinces must irresistibly lead to the conclusion that it is impossible to speak of the system in terms of merits; that is, in terms of benefits conferred on, or gained by, the people. The general view would appear to be summarised in the assertion of Chief R. J. Onyeneho of Umuariam Obowo in Okigwi that while 'the people gained nothing from the Warrant Chief System, the British did since it helped them to rule the peoples of the Eastern Provinces'.[2] While the first half of this statement may be disputable the second is not. In the early years of British rule the Native Court, which was the most visible expression of Warrant Chief rule, played an indispensable part as 'an outpost of the British Empire'. It was the cheapest and most effective means of 'planting the British flag' wherever it became possible to do so after a military conquest. Each administrative division was usually too large for the small European staff posted there to cover effectively, and means of communication was very poor. Consequently a political officer could not visit every part of his district frequently. The function of reminding people living in places remote from district headquarters that, in spite of the departure of the military forces which had subdued them, the British had come to stay was performed by the Native Court. It was for this reason, argued F. N. Ashley, the Resident of Calabar Province in 1924, that 'it was invariably the rule to open a Native Court in an area after a patrol'.[3] Without the Native Court, Mr F. P. Lynch said in 1926, 'it would have been difficult for the native to realise that there was such a thing as permanent Government Officer'. But when he (the native) saw these buildings which were well

---

[2] Collected from Chief R. J. Onyeneho (Obowo, Okigwi). It is necessary to point out that this majority view may well be wrong, but it is historically important in that it helped to determine the attitude of the majority to the Warrant Chief System.

[3] EP 1138, vol. x, Annual Report, Calabar Province, 1924, p. 5

maintained and situated in large and cleared compounds and also saw the court messengers in action, continued Lynch, he began to realise that the government meant more than a visit, probably every eighteen months, by a white man.[4] Mr E. G. Hawkesworth, another administrative officer, did not overstate the issue when in the early 1930s he said in Churchillian phrase that without the aid of the Native Court 'it would have been impossible for the meagre European staff to have brought so difficult an area under control so rapidly'.[5]

The Native Courts also performed judicial functions which the British were equipped neither by their numbers nor experience to satisfy. For instance in the third quarter of 1907 the Native Courts of the Eastern Provinces alone dealt with 4493 civil and 3246 criminal cases.[6] In 1924, two years after Grier had ventilated the shortcomings of the existing Native Court System in his report, the courts in Okigwi Division dealt with the following number of cases:

Native Court	Year	No. of civil cases	No. of criminal cases
Okigwi	1924	553	1011
Orlu	1924	496	1379
Umuduru	1924	245	1037
Obowo	1924	319	790
Uruala	1924	307	759
Afikpo Road	1924	?	?
Total		1920	4976

There were about one hundred and thirty-four other Native Courts in the Eastern Provinces then and each dealt with about the same number of cases.[7] The annual returns of cases settled by Native Courts give validity to the contention that though these courts fell short of some people's idea of courts of justice they were indispensable from the point of view of the administration.[8]

Though the administration of justice was one of their most important assignments, the Native Courts also served very

[4] C 428/25, Calabar Province Annual Reports, 1925–6, para. 79
[5] CSO 26/3, No. 26506, Intelligence Report on Okun and Afaha, Ikot Ekpene Division, Calabar Province, 1931, p. 22
[6] *Government Gazette Supplement*, 13 Nov. 1907, p. vii
[7] *Report on the Working of the Native Courts in the Southern Provinces Sessional Paper*, No. 31 of 1924, pp. 3–7
[8] EP 1138, vol. vii, Annual Report, Calabar Province, 1922, p. 4

important executive needs. They bolstered up the authority of Warrant Chiefs and thus made it possible for the latter to enforce the provisions of the Roads and Rivers Ordinance, and thus bring about the building of the motor roads and bridges which spanned the Eastern Provinces by the end of the period of Warrant Chief rule. 'The very roads they [the courts] stand on today,' wrote Ashley in 1924, 'were made through their presence.'[9] It was also through the Warrant Chiefs that much of the labour for the construction of the railway running from Port Harcourt to the Benue was recruited. Between January 1913, when the work on the railway started from Port Harcourt, and June the same year, five thousand labourers were recruited for the purpose through the chiefs. By the end of the year the number rose to thirteen thousand. In the same period the number of men who voluntarily presented themselves for employment was between four and seven thousand. Even this voluntary labour depended largely on propaganda which was spread with the aid of chiefs.[10] For many years the Colliery Department at Enugu depended on Warrant Chief Onyeama of Eke for miners and other menial workers.[11] Carriers recruited through the chiefs eased the transport problems of the administration in the years before the general availability of wheeled carriages. The general improvement in communication and travel brought about by the Warrant Chiefs was a great service to the economy of the region.

Exercising their powers for making by-laws, the chiefs enacted and enforced regulations which promoted economic progress. In 1902 a proclamation and in 1906 an order were made fixing the exchange rates of brass rods at four for one shilling, and of *okpoho* manillas at twelve for one shilling but no penalties were provided for cases of non-adherence to these rates. The result was that rates varied according to the whims of coastal middlemen, a state of affairs that caused consternation and confusion among the interior producers and hindered trade. To stabilise rates of exchange, and therefore trade, Native Courts in the Eastern Provinces, in 1907, passed rules enforcing the rates of exchange established by law. Refusal to accept payment in English or indigenous currency became punishable by a fine

[9] EP 1138, vol. x, Annual Report, Calabar Province, 1924, p. 4
[10] EP 1308/2, Annual Report, Owerri Province, 1914, p. 36
[11] G. J. F. Tomlinson, *Report on a Tour in the Eastern Provinces*, Lagos 1923, p. 9

of not more than five shillings or imprisonment for not longer than
seven days in default. Attempts to cheat anybody with regard to
the value of English currency became punishable with a fine of
not more than ten shillings or imprisonment for not longer than
two weeks.[12] This rule helped to put a check to the practice by
which the middlemen exploited interior producers through fixing
fictitious values for English and indigenous currencies. In 1910
the Native Courts made rules prohibiting the felling or tapping of
palm trees without the consent of the district commissioner. This
was designed to protect and foster the produce trade.[13] The same
year Native Courts situated in areas where there were rubber
plantations made rules regulating the time and method for tapping
the vines.[14]

One of the first tasks which the administration set out to
accomplish in Southern Nigeria was to stamp out 'the so-called
barbarous practices which still formed a part of the social and
religious life of the communities' and this objective was to some
extent achieved through the Native Courts.[15] The very existence
of these courts and the fact that they only had the right under the
law to deal with certain classes of cases arising among the people
were in themselves campaigns and measures against the use of
poison ordeals or oracles in the settlement of cases. The Warrant
Chiefs gained materially the more cases that came to their courts
and so developed intense interest in tracking down those who
indulged in those practices which the administration regarded
'with horror'. Another 'obnoxious' practice against which the
Native Courts also fought was the destruction of twins and the
expulsion of twin-mothers from the community of their fellow
human beings. In 1907 the Native Court of Ikot Obong in Ikot
Ekpene instituted proceedings 'for desertion and non-support'
against men who drove away their wives for giving birth to twins.
In consequence the men agreed to take back their wives while
many other men learnt their lessons from the fate of their
neighbours.[16]

[12] *Native Council Rules East and Central Provinces 1907–13*. See Ikot
Ekpene Native Council Rule No. 1 of 1907. *Government Gazette Supplement*, 13 Nov. 1907, p. vii
[13] *Native Council Rules East and Central Provinces 1907–13*. See Awka
Native Council Rule No. 2 of 1910.
[14] *Ibid*. See Onitsha Native Council Rule No. 1 of 1910.
[15] CSO 26/3, No. 26506, Intelligence Report on Okun and Afaha, Ikot
Ekpene, p. 23   [16] *Government Gazette Supplement*, 13 Nov. 1907

The Native Courts, which were thronged by litigants and news-mongers, though not by the staid elements, to an extent enabled people to hear what went on locally,[17] and were used by the government to spread propaganda and information. It was in them that government officers, especially senior officers like residents, the lieutenant governor and the governor met the Warrant Chiefs and their retinue to discuss aspects of official policy. On 14 October 1910 W. Fosbery, the Commissioner for Eastern Province, held at the Abak Native Court a meeting which was attended also by chiefs from Ikot Obiama and some other neighbouring villages. There various matters like the state of the produce trade and the currency question were treated, and the people were told the commercial advantages of soft oil. The natives on their side complained that Opobo men still refused to accept English coinage. They also seized the opportunity to express their strong objection to the hole in the penny and its tenth. At Azumini and Aba Native Courts similar questions were discussed with local representatives and the opportunity was taken to 'educate' the people on the economic benefits of the penetration of the interior by European firms.[18] Hunt's pro-tax campaigns of 1927 were conducted in the Native Courts.[19]

The courts were useful even in fields not specifically assigned to them by law. All cases of murder and other serious crimes were generally reported first to the clerk of the nearest Native Court, who then committed the verbal reports received into writing and despatched the court messengers to arrest the accused. As a result, by the time the case reached district headquarters it had assumed an intelligible form.[20]

The court compound itself influenced the life of the village in which it was located. To the local people the way of life of the court staff was generally a model and a reminder of the new ways which the British brought with them. On the court compound stood the court house, which carried the prestige of a centre of authority. Around it, but a little removed from it, stood the rest house where the political officer lodged when he came on tour, the houses of the clerk and his assistants as well as the quarters

---

[17] EP 1138, vol. vii, Annual Report Calabar Province, 1921, p. 5
[18] EP 489/10, Inspection Notes by the Honourable Provincial Commissioner Eastern Province, 1910
[19] See ch. 6
[20] EP 1138, vol. x, Annual Report Calabar Province, 1924, p. 3

of the court messengers, the roadmen and the telegraph linemen. Then there was the dreaded lock-up where criminals awaiting trial, or those already sentenced but awaiting removal to the district prisons, were lodged. Some of the men who lived in this new settlement had official uniforms in which they often strutted about even when not on duty. That the whole arrangement made an appreciable impression on the people is clearly shown by the fact that in many areas the court compound came to be known as 'barracky', a vernacular rendering of the word 'barracks'.[21] The ostentatious court clerk was at times an object of admiration by local youths who had a smattering of education and often uncritically imitated his manners and mode of dress. One Mr Allen, a court clerk, was said to have introduced fashion-conscious youths around Obohia and Akwete to check trousers.[22] A court compound, as Lynch put it in 1926, was 'a little oasis of quasi-civilisation'.[23] Also court compounds were used as hostels by benighted travellers. They served as relief centres for people involved in accidents or vehicle breakdown. A traveller no matter his complexion, asserted Lynch in 1926, always looked upon the court compound as 'a refuge'.[24]

While these services which the Warrant Chiefs and their courts rendered were obvious to the British administration, they were less so to the people. If it was true that the courts accomplished much in the way of settling disputes, it was also true that before these courts came into being the people had their own means of settling cases, that the courts and the chiefs often fomented litigation,[25] and that the fairness of many of their decisions was often in doubt. If the new communication routes encouraged trade and commerce, it is also true that the hardship which people went through under forced labour to bring the roads into existence overshadowed in native eyes this advantage which was not, and could not have been, immediately obvious. In short, even in those fields where the British considered the Warrant Chief System most useful, it failed to appeal strongly to the people. Apart from these more or less negative objections, there were

[21] *Ibid.*, p. 3. CSO 26/3, No. 26506, Intelligence Report on Okun and Afaha, Ikot Ekpene, p. 44. CSO 26/3, No. 27615, Intelligence Report on Edienne and Itak Clans Ikot Ekpene, 1932, p. 47
[22] Based on information from Claudius E. Abonta (Akwete, Aba), Nwankwo A. Akato (Akwete, Aba)
[23] C 428/25, Calabar Province Annual Reports, 1925–6, para. 79
[24] *Ibid.*, para. 79   [25] See below, pp. 286–7

positive reasons why the Warrant Chief System failed to win, and never could have won, the acceptance of the peoples of the Eastern Provinces.

The supreme handicap or demerit of the Warrant Chief System was its lack of any real root in the political traditions of the people. The very idea of a man, no matter what he was called, who had powers to 'issue' orders to his village and/or its neighbours or to a whole clan was a political novelty. Unfortunately for the administration the very conferment of a judicial warrant on anybody in this area no matter how the appointee was selected or his traditional position among his people, meant the creation of this hitherto unheard-of political prodigy. A warrant or even a headman's cap invested on the recipient more powers and prestige than any single individual enjoyed within the indigenous political order. The conferment of the warrant was a public proclamation that the recipient, from the time of his appointment, had behind him the authority of the hardly understood Native Court and ultimately the support of the protectorate police and army, forces which were beyond the control of those over whom he was placed.[26] From the point of view of the people this government appointee more or less had his own standing army and police.

Neither public opinion nor any other force the people could muster, not even actual violence, was as effective against this 'new man' as it could have been in pre-colonial times against a lineage head, a self-made leader or the head of a title or secret society. No group of people could remove or simply ignore a Warrant Chief or set aside the orders of a Native Court without incurring the displeasure of the government. The Warrant Chiefs saw the situation in this light. Asked whether the people ever thought they had any control over the Native Court and its members and staff, Chief Ngadi Onuma of Oloko, a former Warrant Chief, replied:

> The Native Court belonged to the Government. It was not established by the people nor could it be closed down by them, if they attempted to close it down they brought upon themselves a military patrol. Warrant Chiefs feared the Government more than the people. The latter could not unseat a chief but the Government could.[27]

[26] See below, pp. 281–2, for the use of these forces to support chiefs whom the people disapproved of and rebelled against.
[27] Based on information collected from Chief Ngadi Onuma, ex-Warrant Chief (Oloko, Bende).

There were many practical demonstrations of this new help-lessness of the people against their supposed rulers. In 1917 the members of the Enyamba ward of Calabar 'for many good reasons and in accordance with Native law and custom and . . . with the consent and concurrence of all interested members of the said house', 'removed' one Etubom Obo Obo Offiong from the headship of Enyamba ward and placed in his stead one Edem Efiom John Enyamba XI. In pre-British days if this move had the support of the majority of the ward members it would have been the end of the matter. But this was not so in the period under discussion. The protectorate government refused to recognise Offiong's removal because the grounds for it did not 'appear sufficient' and because 'the attack on the old man was rather a mean one'.[28]

The fact that Warrant Chiefs were not accountable to their kith and kin was a proof to the people that the chiefs, like the court messengers, the police, soldiers, court clerks, and the like, were civil servants. Revelling in their new position, the Warrant Chiefs exercised powers which were unprecedented in scope in the political experience of the people. Everywhere the question was put it was admitted to the author that anybody who got a cap or a warrant or both became more powerful than he could ever have been under the indigenous system, and for as long as he enjoyed the confidence of the government was more powerful than all the people under him. He could conscript anybody ostensibly to work on government roads or stations but in practice to do his own private bidding,[29] and though when hold-ing a private court he could call to his aid elders who were in his good books, he was not bound to accept even their unanimous opinion. On this question Obiukwu Nze of Umulolo said: 'When settling a case out of court I used to call on some elders to help me. First I listened to their opinion, but if this contradicted mine I ignored it and gave mine which always stood.' Asked whether his

[28] See Letter dated 2.8.17 from E. E. Bassey Enyamba and others to the DO; Petition dated 17.6.19 to the governor and the DO's comment dated 13.12.17, all in Calprof 14, C 1207/17, Obo Obo Offiong (Etubom Eyamba Family), Deposing of, etc.

[29] Under the old régime any influential man could obtain the labour of an age-grade but this depended entirely on his being popular with all. He was also bound to feed the members of the age-grade when they worked for him. But a Warrant Chief did not need to fulfil these conditions to 'get' people to work for him free of charge.

father, who in his time had been the village head of Umulolo, treated the opinion of his elders in this way he retorted: 'Had my father a warrant? What do you think a warrant was?' To Obiukwu as to many others the warrant 'made many things possible' in the politics of the villages.[30]

For the first time in the people's history a scrap of paper had the power to change the course of events. The warrant led to a serious, though transient, constitutional revolution. Take the case of Ama-Ogwugwu in Ohuhu (Bende), where the warrant was given to Ezechulam Akaeme, the head of the senior ward, while the other five ward heads were made ordinary headmen. In the indigenous constitution Ezechulam Akaeme was no more than *primus inter pares,* but the result of the supersession of this constitution by the Warrant Chief System was the creation of political inequality where it had never existed. The other five ward heads who were not subject to the command of Ezechulam before the establishment of British rule, after that event became his political subalterns and had to take orders from him on issues (and these were many) in which the colonial government had an interest. They found themselves in a position where they were often treated with as little consideration as Obiukwu Nze at Umulolo treated his own elders. Udo Udo Ibanga of Ikot Ekpene confessed that his father became an autocratic *Obong Isong* after getting a judicial warrant.[31] In places where the traditional ward heads were not made headmen the result was equally the creation of an unusual political situation.

Among the Izzi of Abakaliki, where headmen were generally 'the most intelligent and sophisticated young men' in the wards, they gained precedence and ascendancy over the elders in non-ritual aspects of the public life of the wards and treated these elders with scant ceremony. In 1932 the Izzi told Godfrey Allen, who wrote the report which formed the basis for the reorganisation of their local administration, that this was one of their greatest objections to Warrant Chief rule.[32]

[30] Based on information collected from Chief Obiukwu Nze (Umulolo, Okigwi).

[31] Information collected from Chief Samson Onyeama (Ohuhu, Bende), Agonmọ A. Ogbuishi and Anosike Ugbo (Ohuhu, Bende) and from Chief Udo Udo Ibanga (Ikot Ekpene Town).

[32] CSO 26/4, No. 30192, Intelligence Report on Izzi Clan Abakaliki Division, Ogoja Province, 1932, p. 192

The untraditionalism and therefore the tragedy of the Warrant Chief System lay not only (though greatly) in the fact that it side-tracked the indigenous institutions of the communities of this region in favour of a handful of arbitrarily selected men, but it lay also in the fact that the Native Court, its most prominent manifestation, contravened traditional practices and usage in all the vital aspects of its constitution and function. Prominent in this category of demerits was the territorial extent of a Native Court's jurisdiction. As already shown, the largest unit of political authority among the Ibo, Ibibio, Ijo and Ogoja peoples in pre-British days was the village or the village-group.[33] But in determining the size of a Native Court area the colonial government was concerned to ensure that each court made enough money from fees and fines to be self-supporting and that no district officer had too many courts to supervise.[34] The result was a situation in which the vast majority of Native Courts served not just a number of villages but also clans and at times 'tribes'. Up to 1924, when a futile attempt was made to ensure that no court served more than one clan, the following courts in Owerri and Bende Divisions of the Owerri Province served the ethnic groups shown:[35]

Division	Native Court	Clans or sub-tribes into which village served by each court fell
Owerri	Owerri	Oratta, Isu.
	Nguru	Agbaja, Ohuhu.
	Okpala	Ohuhu, Etche, Oratta.
Bende	Umuahia	Ohuhu, Ubakala, Ibeku.
	Alayi	Isuikwuato, Item, Igbere.
	Bende	Akoli, Item, Ibeku, Bende, Nkalu, Abam, Abiriba.

The shortcomings of this arrangement were legion. Since there was nothing in traditional political arrangements as territorially extensive and as ethnically diverse in scope as the Native Courts, there could be no question of the people looking upon these courts as indigenous. The arrangement entailed the grouping together of either former enemies or areas with small, but nonetheless important, differences in custom or both, a situation that

[33] See ch. 1
[34] CSO 26/3, No. 20645, Assessment Report on Okigwi District, 1927, p. 25
[35] C 38/23, Native Courts, Tribal Areas, see the enclosed map prepared by John Jackson, ADO in the Resident's Office, dated 16.4.24

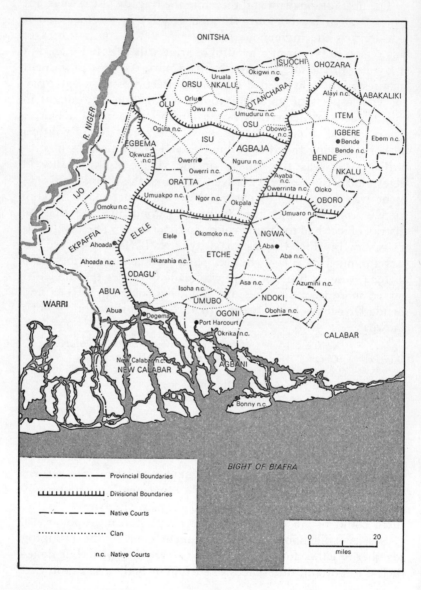

Owerri Province, 1924

turned out to be very unsatisfactory. To bring all the villages of either the Oratta or the Isu sub-tribe, both formerly politically independent, under one court was bad enough; it was still worse to bring some Oratta and Isu villages under the same court. The Oratta, who claimed to have been great warriors in the past, were openly contemptuous of the Isu, whom they described as mere traders. While an Oratta man could marry an Isu woman, an Isu man could not marry an Oratta woman. On the cultural plane bride price was higher among the Isu than among the Oratta, and while the former had *Ozo* title lodges the latter had nothing of the sort.[36] The existence of cultural differences of this degree within one court did not ensure that things went on smoothly within it, nor did it qualify chiefs from one group to deal with cases which arose from the other group. A similar situation obtained in the Okigwi Native Court in which Ihube village, the head of the Otanchara clan, and Uturu of the Otanzu clan, both of which had a long history of mutual hostility, were included.

From the size of these courts many other practical problems arose and the failure of the administration to deal with these issues to the satisfaction of all concerned helped to make the Warrant Chief System more unpopular than it would otherwise have been. The town in which a court was located generally tried to treat her neighbours who attended the court as inferior or subordinate to her. A case in point was the treatment which the Andoni received in the Opobo Native Court. The Andoni were the owners of the island on which Opobo stands and had leased it to King Jaja after his flight from Bonny. From then on the people of Opobo, thanks to their great wealth and sophistication as traders, proceeded to assume mastery over the Andoni who, like many other neighbouring groups, had an ancient tradition of independence. The establishment of the Opobo Native Court and the inclusion of the Andoni in it strengthened Opobo's unjustifiable pretensions. Through the Native Court, heads of Opobo houses made the Andoni supply them with timber, mud, mats and other building materials without any payment. The Andoni, who spoke a different language from the Opobo and had no representatives in the court, never won any case in which Opobo men were on the opposing side. Up to 1921, when the Andoni got their own court, the Opobo Native Court,

[36] C. K. Meek, *Law and Authority in a Nigerian Tribe*, Oxford 1937, pp. 91–2.

which was supported by the might of the colonial government, was, for the Andoni, the most hated manifestation of Opobo 'imperialism'.[37]

Another illuminating case was the treatment which the people of Ekulu and Ulubi villages received in the Nnewi Court. These two villages found attendance at Nnewi Court very irksome. They complained of their men being forced to work for Nnewi chiefs for long periods without pay, and of receiving no justice in that court, since some of their cases were tried and punishment imposed in the absence of the litigants. In 1918, during a serious influenza epidemic, Nnewi chiefs asked Ekulu and Ulubi to supply two hundred men ostensibly to work on the court compound but in fact to do their private bidding. As most people were ill because of the epidemic these villages could supply only half the required number of workers, most of whom were small boys. Nnewi Warrant Chiefs drove the boys back and threatened Ekulu and Ulubi with a government military patrol in the event of failure to send the right number and grade of men. This was the height of provocation to Ulubi and her neighbours who reacted violently. The villages swore to prevent processes issued by the Nnewi Court being served in their areas, and to assault any messenger in the service of that court who intruded into their territory. 'We will never be satisfied,' they told the district officer, W. H. Cooke, in 1919, 'unless you give us another court, we have suffered too much from this court and we will not attend it. We have been ruined.'[38] Whatever the position which Nnewi enjoyed *vis-à-vis* her neighbours in the pre-colonial days she was not an administrative centre which had a right to dictate to them on any issue. But one of the results of the Warrant Chief System with its court which exercised jurisdiction traversing all hitherto known political divisions was the investment of this very position on Nnewi.

Another aspect of the Warrant Chief System which gave offence and which was connected with the size of Native Court areas was the great distance which some litigants had to travel in quest of justice. One of the complaints of Ulubi, Ekulu and their neighbours against the Nnewi Court was the fact that it was very

---

[37] Calprof 14, C 429/21, Opobo District Annual Report, 1920, pp. 7–9
[38] Memo. No. 792/1918 dated 30.10.18 from DO, Onitsha, to the Resident, and Conf No. 1/19 dated 13.3.19 from DO to the Resident in OP 354/1918, Request by Ulubi and other towns, etc., for a Native Court

far from them.[39] In 1919 the people of Ibaka on the Mbo River (Calabar Province) asked for a court of their own in order to reduce the number of canoe accidents which their people had in going to Idua Native Court and because many of their people did not have the money to pay fares to Idua and back. What was worse, the people of Ibaka argued, after one had 'used up all his savings' to travel to Idua he generally found that his case was adjourned.[40] This last inconvenience – that is, frequent adjournments, which caused much hardship and bred discontent – was also a direct result of the very large area which each court served. The courts were usually congested with cases and Warrant Chiefs found it difficult to cope successfully with the mass of litigation which came before them. Consequently cases were kept pending for months. The fact that the courts lacked an effective means of ensuring that litigants attended when wanted caused further confusion.[41] Because of this latter factor, said the Warrant Chiefs of some towns on the Opobo–Aba road in 1920, a murder was committed among them by an irate litigant who had found it impossible to get his victim with whom he had a land case to attend court. Other litigants who were less ready to take such a drastic step as this 'besieged' their chiefs to settle their cases for them privately.[42]

The fact that every Native Court had jurisdiction over a wide area and the fact that each court usually had more cases coming to it than it could deal with expeditiously were in part responsible for the unjust decisions which the Warrant Chiefs were notorious for. When a case eventually came up for hearing after a series of adjournments the time that could be spent on it was generally too limited to allow for a very careful investigation of the claims advanced by the parties. And to make matters worse the chiefs coming, as they at times did, from villages far removed from that in which a dispute arose, generally lacked that deep knowledge of

[39] Memo. No. 792/1918 dated 30.10.18 from the DO, Onitsha, to the Resident in OP 354/1918, Request by Ulubi and other towns, etc., for a Native Court

[40] Petition dated 8.10.19 from the people of Ibaka to His Excellency in Calprof 14, C 622/19, Calabar Province, Petitions to the Governor

[41] Memo. attached to No. 757/37/22 dated 5 10 22 from Captain Hanitch, Eket, to Resident, Calabar Province, in Calprof 14, C 582/22D, Pedigrees of Chiefs in Calabar Province

[42] Petition dated 13.7.20 in Calprof 14K 533/20, Petitien for the Establishment of a Native Couri on Gpobo–Aba government road

the local conditions, and details of the custom and history of the village concerned, to be able to come to a just decision quickly, especially as many of the cases were very complicated.[43]

Structural shortcomings apart, the law administered by Native Courts was another factor which helped to make the Warrant Chief System untraditional and unpopular. The operation of the principle that Native Courts were to be guided by 'native law and custom not repugnant to British ideas of justice' led to the growth of a body of laws which, from the point of view of the people, was far from indigenous. The story of the handling of cases of adultery and debt, two of the three types of cases which tended to dominate the sittings of the courts,[44] will help to illustrate the nature of this novel and bastard legal system.

Among the Ibo, for instance, adultery fell into two broad groups. In the first category was adultery committed within the kinship group, which was regarded as an offence against *Ala* (the earth deity) and against the ancestors. The settlement of this varied from place to place but invariably included a ceremonial removal of the pollution of the community by the priest of *Ala*. At Mgbidi the male adulterer could be sold into slavery, while at Mmako the guilty couple were banished for this class of offence. In the second group was adultery committed outside the kinship group which involved no offence to *Ala* nor to the ancestors, and which was regarded as a private injury and was settled as that, generally with compensations to the injured man.[45]

But in Native Courts no distinction was made between the two types of adultery. It would seem that in some courts the Warrant Chiefs up to 1921 gave compensation to the husband of the adulterous woman but made no effort to ensure that the supernatural elements which a particular case of adultery outraged were propitiated. In 1921 even the practice of awarding compensation was stopped because it seemed to the British to be open to abuse. The resident of Onitsha Province argued rather academically that if the practice were continued with, an unscrupulous man in embarrassed financial circumstances could

[43] Memo. attached to No. 757/37/22 dated 5.10.22 from Captain Hanitch, DO, Eket, to Resident in Calprof 14, C 582/22D, Pedigrees of Chiefs in Calabar Province

[44] In 1921 Mr F. N. Ashley, DO Ikot Ekpene, wrote as follows: 'The vast majority of the civil cases are debt and dowry.' See EP 1138, vol. vii, Annual Report Calabar Province, 1921, p. 5

[45] C. K. Meek, *Law and Authority in a Nigerian Tribe*, etc., pp. 218–24

arrange for his wife to pass a night with another man and then make money from subsequent prosecution.[46] On this point of Native Court attitude to adultery ọfọ Onuoha of Isuikwuato, a former Warrant Chief, said:

> The Native Courts were guided by English law. Take the case of adultery. Under traditional law and custom a man found guilty of this offence not only gave seventy shillings to the injured husband, but also produced a dog for sacrifice in propitiation of *Ala*. But in the Courts introduced by white men the outraged man got nothing, nor was the pollution of *Ala* removed.[47]

Allied to this matter was the ruling by which a man could through the Native Court claim his natural child which under traditional law belonged to the husband of the woman if she was married, or to her people if she was unmarried.[48] On this point Nnubia of Ọzubulu, a former Warrant Chief, said that on one occasion some Warrant Chiefs were forced to ask the district officer whether it was the colonial government that paid the bride price on their wives.[49]

It was in debt cases that one of the most far-reaching and most unsatisfactory innovations was made by the British through the Native Courts. There were three fundamental principles in the traditional law of debt. The first was that the community had a duty to enforce the payment of a debt however contracted. The second was that a debt once contracted became the responsibility of all in the debtor's kinship or local group. A debtor's successors and heirs inherited along with his property, or rather lack of property, his debts and other obligations, and actions could legally be taken against any of them for the recovery of the debt. The third was that a creditor had legal rights to the body or property or both of his debtor or of those of the debtor's people.[50] The justification for these rather strict provisions in traditional law lay in the fact that they arose in a society where there were no

[46] A 375/22, Annual Report, Onitsha Province, 1921, para. 59
[47] Collected from Ọfọ Dnuoha (Isuikwuato, Okigwi), an ex-Warrant Chief.
[48] L. T. Chubb, 'Out in the Sun All Day', *Ibadan* (journal published at University College, Ibadan), No. 3, June 1958, p. 13
[49] Information collected from Chief Nnubia (Ọzubulu, Onitsha).
[50] EP 1138, vol. vii, Annual Report Calabar Province, 1921, p. 5. EP 4045, Native Court Questions, etc. See Memo. EP 4045/5 dated 1.3.28 and Memo. No. OG 97/1927 dated 10.9.27 from the Resident, Ogoja, to SSP. C. K. Meek, *Law and Authority in a Nigerian Tribe*, etc., pp. 205, 231–4

banks, stock exchanges or other institutions where money could be deposited with safety and at the same time accumulate interest. The need for security of wealth was therefore keenly felt and fully provided for.

The law of debt which evolved in the Native Courts undermined traditional law and creditors' security. The abolition of slavery and the slave trade destroyed a creditor's rights to the person of his debtor or to the persons of the debtor's relations.[51] On 31 May 1918 the government ruled that no punishment for debt should take a form which would make it a lever for forcing the family of the debtor to pay on his behalf.[52] This order, by undermining the principle of collective responsibility by the kinship or local group for a debtor's liabilities, struck at the root of traditional society.

The Native Court, which was supposed to be the indigenous system of government and should therefore have performed the functions of 'the community' in enforcing the payment of a debt, adopted a very unsatisfactory attitude in this matter, since the British looked at the problem of debt in a way that differed from the native approach. The government argued that most debtors were not criminals any more than the directors of a company who through no fault of theirs were no longer able to pay interest, and that the responsibility for a bad debt lay heavily with the creditor. In any country, argued one officer, those who place themselves in the position of creditors must be prepared to incur a portion of the bad debt and to go to some trouble to recover sums due to them.[53] As a result it was laid down that a certain percentage of all debts collected through the Native Courts must be paid into the courts' funds.[54] An institution which should have been for the protection of the creditor was thus used to exploit him. The heavy expenses a creditor ran into under the new régime in order to recover what was his own caused a great deal of discontent.

[51] EP 4045, Native Court Questions, etc. See Memo. No. OG 97/1927 dated 10.9.27 from Resident, Ogoja, to SSP
[52] EP 4045, Native Court Questions, etc. See Memo. EP 4045/4 dated 1.3.28
[53] EP 4045, Native Court Questions, etc. See Memo. No. OG 97/1927 dated 10.9.27 from the Resident, Ogoja, to SSP. See also OW 942, Recovery of Debts in Native Courts, Enclosure No. 38/1931/53 of 1.10.31 from DO Owerri to the Resident
[54] See ch. 3, above

Although it was accepted that Native Courts could sentence debtors to imprisonment there was disagreement on the question of how the judgment debtor should be maintained in prison. Up to 1916 the government unwillingly bore the cost of this. But in August that year Mr Bedwell, Resident of Calabar, suggested that creditors should be responsible for the maintenance of all the debtors they sent to prison. The legal adviser, Mr T. D. Maxwell, advised that 'imprisonment for debt should only be resorted to when a debtor can pay but will not pay, that is, when he commits contempt of court'.[55] This decision meant, firstly, that a creditor had little redress against a bankrupt debtor; secondly, that even with debtors able but unwilling to pay the punishment inflicted was not for debt as such but for disobeying the orders of a Native Court. It is necessary to point out here that indigenous law made no distinction between bankrupt and non-bankrupt debtors. A creditor had adequate protection against both.

On 28 October the same year (1916) the resident of Calabar was authorised to apply the opinion of the legal adviser to his province. Eight months later he wrote back that the attempt met with total failure owing to the difficulty of proving what property actually belonged to a debtor, since houses and lands were generally held as family property and other personal property was often of insignificant value. On a number of occasions when a debtor's supposed livestock was seized, the resident complained, it was generally found that the debtor owned only a part of it.[56] This method was abandoned precisely because its application involved the enforcement of a principle acceptable in traditional law – the principle of collective responsibility.

In 1918 the whole debate on how to deal with debtors was reopened. Some residents were in favour of arrangements under which the government maintained the judgment debtor in prison because they believed it was more in keeping with indigenous ideas on the matter, but others insisted on the burden being borne by creditors. In 1919 the resident of Calabar was advised to try the latter method. Its introduction naturally caused great dissatisfaction, most of the chiefs warning that creditors would

[55] Memo. No. EP 4045/4 dated 1.3.28 in EP 4045, Native Court Questions, etc.
[56] Memo. No. OG 97/1927 dated 10.9.27 in EP 4045, Native Court Questions, etc.

take the law into their hands. The motive for the government's ruling on this matter of debt, said F. N. Ashley, was to discourage people from lending money to, or going into other financial arrangements with, 'economic men of straw'.[57] Though the decision of 1919 had not become of general application throughout the Eastern Provinces even by 1930,[58] it was, for Calabar Province at least, a startling innovation. Some experienced officers considered it absurd. F. P. Lynch described it as 'unreasonable', while Mr R. A. Roberts, the senior resident of Onitsha, said it denied the creditor any legal remedy against his debtor.[59]

In 1930 Mr G. I. Jones, administrative officer, pointed out that one reason why the Warrant Chief System was unpopular 'was the complete divergence in theory and practice between native law and custom and the law actually administered in the Native Court'. He continued,

> Theoretically, [the] . . . Native Court is supposed to administer native law and custom . . . not in opposition to the principles of English law, [but] . . . this almost amounts to a contradiction in terms. One might as well tell a court of the hundred or shire in Medieval England that it could continue to administer its native law and custom as far as these did not differ with modern Anglo-Saxon ideas of jurisprudence. The two differ so radically that all that would happen would be either that Anglo-Saxon law and custom would continue to be administered or that modern English law took its place.[60]

Though one may not accept Jones's comparison of an Ibo or Ibibio community of 1930 with a medieval English community, or his contention that either the one or the other body of law must triumph, his criticism sufficiently illustrates the absurdity of the attempt to 'reform' indigenous law to suit English conscience. This reform was one of those factors which made the Native Courts neither 'native' nor 'English', but all the same alien to the people.

Another unsatisfactory feature of the Warrant Chief System was the ineffectiveness of the punishments meted out by the

[57] EP 4045, Native Court Questions, etc. See Memo. No. OG 97/1927 dated 10.9.27 from Resident Ogoja, and Memo. EP 4045/4 dated 1.3.28
[58] By 1931 in the Owerri Province, for instance, the issue was still undecided. See OW 942, Recovery of Debt in Native Courts
[59] Memo. No. EP 4045/4 dated 1.3.28 in EP 4045, Native Court Questions, etc.
[60] CSO 26/3, No. 27002, Intelligence Report on Ngbo and Ezzangbo (1930), pp. 51–2

Native Courts to convicted criminals, for instance to thieves. To the peoples of this area theft, especially of livestock and farm produce, was a very grave offence, and on certain occasions was punishable by death, especially where the offender was caught *in flagrante delicto*. In some other cases the thief was adorned with broken utensils and empty snail shells, paraded in the locality or market and subjected to devastating ridicule. In the days of the slave trade unrepentant thieves of particular articles were sold to the Aro, who in turn sold them through coastal middlemen to European slavers, who carried them off to the New World.

But under the Warrant Chief System the highest punishment permitted for theft was imprisonment. In the pre-1914 period there were courts which could sentence a thief to as much as two years' imprisonment. With the reforms of Lugard the powers of Native Courts were drastically curtailed and courts of 'C' grade, the highest grade allowed by Lugard at first in the Eastern Provinces, could sentence criminals to only six months' imprisonment. By 1918, however, it was found that the courts needed wider powers. In Okigwi, for instance, various Native Courts sent delegations to the district officer for increased powers in cases of larceny because, they contended, mild punishments encouraged theft. In consequence residents were called upon to, and did, send names of courts which they considered fit to wield the power to sentence people convicted of larceny of livestock and farm produce to a term of imprisonment of up to one year. By 1922 chiefs were again convinced of the futility of this limited power as a means of checking the spread of this particular brand of crime. Once again the courts were granted powers to sentence this category of thieves to two years' imprisonment.[61]

The point was not just that Native Courts had not the power to sentence thieves of farm produce to long terms of imprisonment, but that when compared with traditionally accepted forms of punishments for this brand of crime imprisonment for theft appeared to the people like child's play. An Abakaliki Warrant Chief, disgusted with the futility of imprisonment as a deterrent for crime, told the lieutenant governor in 1924 that a prison was 'a feeding house to which people repair to get fat and fit'.[62] The

[61] OW 112/18, Native Courts Increased Powers to, in cases of Larceny. See Enclosures Nos 1, 2, 3, 4, 5, 6, 7, 8, 14, 15, 16
[62] CSO 26/1, No. 09098, Lieutenant-Governor, Southern Provinces, Inspection Notes, p. 255

fact was that six or more months in the prison which was an alien institution carried less moral stigma than being paraded for less than one day in a crowded village market. Nor did imprisonment provide a means of permanently getting rid of a hardened criminal. The Native Court was expected to provide a deterrent for crimes in order to protect society against the evil-minded but it failed.[63] 'The inadequacy of the punishment for thieving,' noted G. I. Jones in 1930, 'has become one of the standing grievances of the people.'[64]

The procedure adopted by the Native Courts was another feature which made people regard the Warrant Chief System as an alien institution. In the first place the arbitrary selection, every month or so, of four men to try all the cases which might arise within a Native Court area made up of villages and clans of non-uniform customs and traditions was novel. Secondly, if any case arose it was to the clerk, who was generally a stranger and therefore ignorant of variations in local custom, not to the local Warrant Chiefs, who at least were mainly sons of the soil,[65] that the complainant went. Since the clerk issued the summons it was he who determined whether a case was civil or criminal, a decision which could be correctly made only by the elders of the village in which the matter arose. Added to these anomalies was the fact that the Native Courts adopted certain practices which were characteristic of the Supreme Court. There was the taking of evidence in writing, which was an entirely new idea. There was the use of printed forms or writs. By 1924 the forms used by a Native Court included the warrant instituting the court, the warrant appointing the members, summons to the accused, summons to witness, civil summons, warrants of arrest, warrant of imprisonment and three other forms for returns. A move to reduce the number of these forms in 1925 paradoxically led to the addition of another – the search warrant.[66] These forms the clerks generally ostentatiously displayed to the view of people in court. Then there were judgment and cash books and the other

[63] For the reaction of the indigenous system to this situation, see below
[64] CSO 26/3, No. 27002, Intelligence Report Ngbo and Ezzangbo (1930), p. 54
[65] There were cases of ex-slaves who were Warrant Chiefs. See ch. 2, above, and S. M. Grier, *Report on a Tour in the Eastern Provinces*, Lagos 1922, pp. 22–3
[66] CSO 26/1, No. 03547, vol. i, Native Court Books and Forms. See the entire file

paraphernalia of ink-pots, pencils, pens, blotting-paper and the like which the clerk needed for his work. If none of these articles was directly contrary to tradition, they were all new and their purposes generally misunderstood.

The courts swore litigants and their witnesses before taking statements from them but did so in a manner that made the ritual unconvincing and a parody of the practice in traditional judicial procedure. Meek has left an interesting account of how this ritual was performed in a Native Court. The materials used rightly varied from court to court. In one court these were a diviner's *ofo* and its paraphernalia, the skull of a goat taken from a shrine of *Ala* and the cloth of a madman. In another court the materials were the skull of a horse sacrificed to a local deity, the figurines of the god of divination and a diviner's *ofo*.[67] When a man was to be sworn a court messenger took one of these symbols, placed it on the man's head or chest and told him: 'If you tell lies may *this* kill you.' Then the man swore on all the objects put together.

This mode of swearing had no value. In the first place it was not traditional to swear on more than one god; it was believed some gods neutralised each other. Also by indigenous usage the god on which a man swore had to be called by name. 'This', as underlined in the above quotation, was the name of no god and would kill nobody. Also before a god was sworn upon it had to be invoked by the man who tended it, for, it was believed, the god immanent in the visible symbol sworn upon could be 'on tour' at the moment in question. In the indigenous legal system the oath ordeal was resorted to only when a dispute could not be settled otherwise. People were not made to swear as a prelude to giving evidence. The infringement of these requisites for a 'proper oath' made litigants contemptuous of Native Court swearing. Hardened criminals saw nothing in it to compel them to tell the truth, while the honest and conservative saw nothing in it to make them have faith in the procedure. Traditionalists did not take Christians seriously when they swore on the Bible, nor did the Christians regard swearing on ancestral symbols as worth anything. In fact Mr Nwosu of Umuakwu in Oloko Native Court area was voicing a generally held belief when he told the Donald Kingdon Commission: 'Because people who give evidence in the

[67] C. K. Meek, *Law and Authority in a Nigerian Tribe*, etc., p. 237, including footnote 1

court are not given proper juju to swear on, they do not tell the truth.'[68]

In the final analysis there was a fundamental difference between the Native Court and the indigenous system in their attitudes to the whole question of law administration. There was a difference between the Native Court and the traditional conception of 'community'. The settlement of a crime against the community under the indigenous system began with the punishment of the offender and reached its climax with a ritual propitiation of the deity who was believed to have been specifically offended by the crime in question. But in the Native Courts the satisfaction of an outraged community in proved criminal cases was supposed to be achieved with the imprisonment of the criminal or some such punishment. This involved a civil conception of the community and of law administration which was psychologically and emotionally alien to the people. The point was that, as G. I. Jones pointed out in 1930, justice was administered for and by the community, not by an arbitrarily selected group for the white man.[69] It therefore did less harm to society if a man who was innocent was punished because the community believed him to be guilty than, as often happened in the Native Courts, if a man whom the community believed to be guilty was declared innocent because the case against him was not proved. As Jones also pointed out, law administration was 'primarily a religious and not a civil matter'. 'It is,' he continued, 'God who punishes the wrong doer, those who judge cases are merely his agents. They are not "triers of cases" but "speakers of truth" and in every case where the truth appears doubtful the case is at once referred to a divine power for trial either by oath or ordeal.' This was so even in the settlement of private wrongs. The civil attitude to law and its administration was, as the same authority put it, 'presumptuous impiety' to conservative indigenous opinion.[70]

The unpopularity of the Warrant Chief System derived not only from its utter divergence from the indigenous political system but also from the fact that it was to many people a reign

[68] *ACINE*, para. 1805
[69] Justice in the Native Court was for the white man, since, as many Warrant Chiefs admitted, they always sought to give a decision that would please the white man. See ch. 4, above.
[70] CSO 26/3, No. 27002, Intelligence Report on Ngbo and Ezzangbo (1930), pp. 52–3

of terror. The enforcement of the Roads and Rivers Ordinance, the use of conscripted carriers as the main means of transportation, the depredations of the court messengers, the use of the court itself as an instrument for oppressing the weak and the fact that owing to a number of factors the people had little effective redress against these ills engendered in many a sense of oppression which alienated them from the Warrant Chief régime. The surprise is not that the system collapsed at all and in the manner it did, but that it did not meet with that fate earlier.

The labour given under the Roads and Rivers Ordinance was unpopular not only because it was both forced and unpaid, but also because it brought heavy burdens on the people. Grier and Tomlinson after their tours of the Eastern Provinces in 1922 and 1923 respectively confessed that the burden of this work had exceeded what was originally intended.[71]

Closely allied to forced labour was what might be called the 'carrier system'. This was an arrangement by which each Warrant Chief, on order from the government, recruited young men for the purpose of transporting the luggage of a government official, of an army or police detachment as required from one station to another. Though people were paid for this work, it was one of the most dreaded aspects of the Warrant Chief régime and details of hardships and privations endured by carriers still loom large in the traditions surviving in many communities about the system under study. Each band of carriers was escorted by a contingent of court messengers, policemen or soldiers depending on whether the loads in question belonged to a member of the African staff or a European or whether the carriers were likely to pass through 'hostile' towns and on which kind of escort was available at the time and place in question. These escorts were said to have treated carriers with great brutality.[72]

The relevance of all these is that it was the chiefs who were blamed for every mishap that befell a fellow villager who was conscripted either as a carrier or for work on the roads and government station. 'Relatives of men who have not come back

[71] B 593/1921, Labour for Road Work in the Provinces. See the entire file
[72] Based on information from Chief Mbabuike Ogujiofor (Ihube, Okigwi), Chief Ukpai Ereshi (Agba, Abakaliki), Chief Nwancho Atuma (Ikwo, Abakaliki), Mr Luke Obiasogu (Nnewi, Onitsha), Mr Kenrick Udo (Ikot Ekpene Town), Chief Oji Eberebe (Isuikwuato, Okigwi).

from military expeditions or railway work,' reported District Officer E. Falk from Owerri in 1919, 'invariably consider the chiefs who recruited the men to be guilty of a species of homicide or slave dealing.'[73]

There is also evidence that Native Courts were deliberately used by Warrant Chiefs and clerks as instruments of oppression. The chiefs in particular abused the privilege they had to prosecute people for 'disobeying lawful orders'. In the Native Court what orders the chief had issued were not generally probed. Usually the trial centred on whether the defendant had disobeyed an order from his chief. The chiefs and clerks were also accused of being in league with disreputable men whom they used to bring rivals to court for liquidation. On this point Chief R. J. Onyeneho said:

> It was under the Warrant Chief System that the terrible thing called *Akwukwo Nwannunu*[74] came into being. It was a system by which a chief could contrive to bring to court a man whose only offence was that he was forceful and progressive. Chiefs regarded such men as a threat to their positions and used the Court to liquidate them. Once such men were dragged to Court the cases against them which were often groundless ended only after they had spent in defending themselves all the wealth which made them 'proud'.

The Aro, who were displaced from their former position as monopolist middlemen and who for much of this period were still looking for a way of retaining their 'dominance', were generally the agents of the Warrant Chiefs and clerks in the execution of this tyrannous plot.[75]

The feeling of oppression which was widespread under the Warrant Chief System was not lessened by the fact that there was little real opening for redress. On paper there were many avenues through which the aggrieved could make his complaint reach the ears of the government. A dissatisfied litigant could ask for the review of his case by a political officer, while for other complainants he could petition the government. There was also the chance that during his monthly tour the political officer could

[73] Memo. No. 327/1919 dated 20.5.19 from E. Falk, DO, Owerri, to the Resident, in OW 215/19

[74] This literally meant *Bird's Summons*. It was so described because it was *summons from the air*; that is, from a fictitious enemy. It is said that if the practice did not originate after 1914 it at least became more rampant then.

[75] R. O. Igwegbe, *The Original History of Arondizuogu 1635–1960*, Aba 1962, pp. 99–100. Supplemented with information collected from Chief R. J. Onyeneho (Obowo, Okigwi)

get wind of local happenings and squabbles and perhaps probe them. But there is evidence that none of these channels was foolproof or rather that all the channels were ineffective to an astounding degree.

The review of Native Court cases by the political officer was supposed to help control the quality of justice administered by Warrant Chiefs. But the fact was, especially from 1914, when the problem of understaffing worsened and departmental and routine duties took an upward leap, that review as a system of check was nugatory from the point of view of the people. The district officer, who sometimes worked without an assistant, had little time to give the Native Courts the attention they deserved. As a result each court received what F. P. Lynch in 1919 called 'one flying visit in a month'.[76] During such a visit the officer was often faced with as many as fifty cases which he had to go into in one day and rush back to headquarters for other work.[77] In the circumstance he depended greatly on the recordings of court clerks, which officers generally complained were unintelligible and in which few people had little confidence. As a political officer serving in Calabar Province put it in 1916: 'A copy of the proceedings in any case is almost useless to go upon and very often suggests carelessness or injustice on the part of the chiefs. . . . The one thing which holds back the Courts is the Clerk's notes of the cases.'[78] Also Mr P. O. Onwughalu, who worked as an interpreter during part of this period, said: 'The main weakness of review lay in the fact that what the District Officer saw in the judgment book as the proceedings was often what the Clerk, after the bewildering manœuvres which generally preceded a case, decided to put down rather than what actually was said in Court.'[79]

To circumvent the dishonesty of clerks, district officers – when they had the time – asked the chiefs their reasons for each verdict they gave. This procedure appeared to losing litigants like making a mockery of the government's intervention. Alfred of Egbelu, himself a Warrant Chief of Ngor Native Court, told the Donald

[76] Memo. by F. P. Lynch on the Native Courts dated 14.10.19 in C 176/19, Remarks by F. P. Lynch, etc. See also the other memoranda in this file for the ineffectiveness of review

[77] *ACINE*, paras 4799–805

[78] EP 1138, vol. ii, Annual Report, Calabar Province, 1966, p. 9

[79] Information collected from Chief P. O. Onwughalu (of Onitsha Town), a former district interpreter.

Kingdon Commission that the only way to remedy the discontent of the people with the Native Courts was to allow dissatisfied litigants to appeal to a higher court. The appeal to the district officer did not satisfy them, he said,

> because when that officer came to review cases he asked the very people who tried the cases for their views and when they expressed them he would agree with them. The result was that the dissatisfaction of the people continued since they believed that the District Officer had leagued together with the chiefs to undo them.[80]

When the reviewing officer had the time to ask litigants to restate their cases, the parties which lost went away with the belief that it was the interpreter who ruined their case.[81]

Also there is no doubt that it was not infrequently that district officers confirmed and the courts enforced unjust verdicts. Apart from this situation arising inevitably from the very fact that the political officer could not know all the manœuvres that had taken place to make a case assume the shape it did before it reached him, there was also the fact that it was official policy not to reverse the decisions of the chiefs too often in order not to undermine the power and prestige of the chiefs and their courts. H. E. Jones, district officer at Onitsha noted in 1920,

> Judging from the number of complaints brought by losing parties, there appears to exist a very grave lack of confidence on the part of the people in their Native Courts, though in the great majority of cases the judgment, of the chiefs are upheld in review. In most cases this is done . . . on the point of policy. Were this not so the whole work of the Courts in this division would speedily become a farce.[82]

In March 1921 Mr F. H. Ingles watched the trial of a case in the Umuduru Native Court, Okigwi. Though he was convinced that the course of justice was perverted when the court discharged and acquitted the defendant in spite of the strong and well-corroborated case of the prosecution, he let the verdict stand because, he said, the case was 'rather a minor one' and ordering

---

[80] *ACINE*, paras 3617–19

[81] In spite of all inducements, there was hardly any political officer in this period who was able to acquire a working knowledge of the indigenous languages. This was partly because Europeans found the indigenous languages difficult and partly because they did not stay long enough in any one area to get down to actually studying the language. See CSO 26/1, No. 09098, LGSP's Inspection Notes, p. 143

[82] Conf Memo. No. 2/1920 dated 2.1.20 by DO, Onitsha, in C 176/19, Remarks by F. P. Lynch, etc.

its retrial in the Provincial Court 'would have considerably undermined the chief's judgment'.[83] It is disputable how far the litigants themselves considered the case 'minor'. In any case it was such incidents that tended to teach the people that in the Native Court truth unsupported by material means could be singularly unconvincing.

Touring was urged as a means by which the political officer could learn of people's complaints and, if possible, effect redress. But it soon became clear that officers rarely toured their divisions. There were two other factors apart from overwork which accounted for this. In the pre-1914 days, when there were very few motor-cars in the Eastern Provinces and when political officers travelled either on foot or by means of hammocks, they toured more often and more thoroughly than in the succeeding era. This was because with the availability of cars officers would dash from headquarters to any part of their districts to deal with a matter that called for immediate attention and rush back in a matter of hours.[84] But in the earlier days the situation was different. If a serious matter arose in a remote section of a district the political officer travelled either on foot or by a hammock. For him this involved sleeping in some of the villages which situate between the headquarters and the village in which the crisis arose, a situation which gave the officer immense opportunities for useful contacts with the people. The pre-1914 period was also the era of travelling commissioners who did much to forge close links between the people and the government.[85]

Another factor which hindered touring was the fact that as the Protectorate settled down and comfortable accommodation became available even young officers were, contrary to earlier practice, allowed to come to West Africa with their wives. The European women refused to travel except in considerable comfort and there was no question of leaving them alone in certain headquarters where there were no other Europeans for many miles around. On this matter, the Lieutenant-Governor, Captain W. Buchanan-Smith, wrote:

[83] Memo. No. 384/35/21 dated 7.3.21 from the DO, Okigwi, to the Resident, Owerri Province, in OW 347/21 – Omodoru Native Court General Paper

[84] *ACINE*, paras 6685-8. This type of trip, made in order to deal with an urgent matter, was not regarded as touring and was useless as a means of knowing the people and getting to understand their problems.

[85] See ch. 3

There is an aspect of the question which has not been mentioned ...
though to my mind it has a very definite bearing on the matter, and this
is the ever-increasing number of ladies who are allowed to come out to
Nigeria to join their husbands. No one would like to deny the improvement in Nigerian conditions resulting from the increased number of
ladies who have come to the country of recent years. But it would be
equally futile to pretend that from a political point of view the in-
discriminate permission now given to the most junior administrative
officers to bring out their wives is for the benefit of the service or of the
natives generally. Quite a number of ladies dislike travelling otherwise
than in comfort and by motor car and are in other respects unsuited to
the rough life of the bush. Similarly I have known officers deliberately
to neglect to visit outlying villages owing to the fact that they did not
possess rest houses suitable for their wives.

He decided for the future to tighten up the interpretation of the
regulations.[86] The effect of this feminine factor on the efficiency
of political officers is adequately illustrated from the following
telegram sent by the resident of Owerri Province to the lieutenant
governor in the heat of the Women's Riot of 1929 about one of
his officers. It reads: 'Have evacuated Mrs Blank Port Harcourt
enable Blank be more mobile at night.'[87]

There is no greater proof of the administration's loss of touch
with the people than the startling fact that most of the complaints
against the Native Court and its officials absolutely failed to
filter into the official records. There is no record on what forced
labour or head porterage meant to the people or on how court
messengers carried out their duties in practice. To an unbelievable
extent political officers, as time went on, relied on Warrant Chiefs,
court messengers and clerks for information about the people,
that is, the government relied on the same iniquitous combine
against whom the people complained. Throughout the divisions
covered by the present author during his field work there was
not a single village where the elders or the former court staff
admitted that before 1929 the administration held general meetings of the people or of their elders to know how they took the
new régime. The administration held general meetings with the
people only for the purpose of selecting 'hereditary chiefs', but
then the clash of claims and counter-claims of individuals and

[86] CSO 26/3, No. 25512, vol. ii, Comments on the Report of the Aba Commission, Memo. Conf No. SP 7213/vol. ii/215 dated 20.3.31 from SSP to
Honourable Chief Secretary
[87] L. T. Chubb, 'Out in the Sun All Day', in *Ibadan*, No. 3, June 1958,
p. 14

of groups made such rallies useless as a means of recording the political pulse of the people. In 1928 the lieutenant governor, Major Ruxton, minuted in a memorandum sent to him by one of his residents: 'I agree with the contention that we are losing touch with the mass of the people.'[88] This was self-delusion, for by 1928 the administration was not 'losing' but had already lost touch with the masses.

The effect of this loss of touch was not only that even imagined wrongs were left undispelled and to continue to wear the visage of real wrongs, but that at a period of time when a veritable revolution was taking place in many aspects of indigenous life, people were not adequately educated as to the meanings of many new measures which affected them. The impression which the tour of many of the divisions left on the present author is that few people, if any, actually appreciated the necessity for forced labour and head porterage. Consequently the hardships which these imposed were greatly resented. The extent to which people failed to understand where the government was leading them to is revealed by what Okereke Aka of Alayi, a former Warrant Chief, said he and his people thought about taxation by 1939. He said: 'We never understood what the white men did with our money until the Second German War broke out and then we knew they used it to prepare for the war.'[89] If this former Warrant Chief, who was reputed for being fearless in his youth and who even in old age had a powerful intelligence and memory, could hold such an opinion on an issue like taxation, in which a definite attempt at propaganda through the Native Courts was made, it can then be understood how far the non-court-going majority of the people failed to appreciate the series of innovations which came with the new régime and most of which were resentfully blamed on the Warrant Chiefs.

Also petitions were not very effective in securing redress for complainants. In the first place a petition was costly and that meant only people of more than average means could afford it after a costly litigation. James Watt, when he was the resident of Owerri Province in 1920, estimated that the average petition cost about twenty-five shillings. In the second place petition writers

[88] Memo. No. SP 2485/vol. viii/13 dated 3.9.28 from SSP to Honourable Chief Secretary in CSO 26, No. 50225, Circulars issued by the Secretary, Southern Provinces
[89] Information from Chief Okereke Aka (Alayi, Bende)

were found mainly at headquarters, which meant only the court-going population usually got at them. The rustic villager who hardly visited headquarters except when conscripted for one type of work or the other hardly ever went to headquarters to consult petition writers on oppressions, real or imagined, which he suffered in the village at the hands of Warrant Chiefs. In the third place most petition writers were very ill-educated and could not state clearly the cases of their clients. In 1920 James Watt complained:

> No one would object to a letter-writer who made careful enquiries into matters on which he was asked to write and stated his client's case clearly and briefly. But very few petitions are of any assistance to political officers in stating even one side of the case. As a rule they are grossly inaccurate and do not benefit petitioners.[90]

Petitions merely drew the attention of the political officer to a complaint and whether the grievance was remedied depended on whether the European officer had the time to go into the case and whether the interpreter was honest with his interpretations. Fourthly, the manner in which the administration dealt with petitions was not understood by the people. According to official regulations on the matter all petitions going to government officers above the rank of district officer had to go through the latter.[91] Then the authority petitioned asked the district officer to investigate the complaints and report to him. In cases which the district officer had already dealt with and on which he was believed to have made up his mind, complainants regarded this way of attending to petitions as farcical.[92]

In any case Warrant Chiefs, court clerks, messengers and district interpreters usually formed a coalition in each district designed to frighten people away from the district officer and make it difficult for the latter to get at the truth even on those matters which managed to get to him. Many such combines were exposed from time to time. In 1913 in the Awka Division it was discovered that there was 'a widespread conspiracy on the part of an interpreter, of certain court officials and policemen all of whom in some degree or the other were connected with Onitsha town, to establish a system of intimidation and blackmail through-

---

[90] EP 1308/7, Annual Report, Owerri Province, 1920, pp. 4–5
[91] CSO 26/3, No. 23610/35, Rules Regarding Petitions
[92] Information collected from Chief J. N. Wachuku (Ngwa, Aba)

out the district'.[93] The brain behind this league was one J. M. Mba, the head interpreter, who having been at Awka since 1905 had become more or less an institution there. As soon as this league was broken up by the cancellation of the warrants of two of the chiefs involved and by the arrest of Mba, the people felt safe enough to tell the government that some of their chiefs owed their position to Mba, and compelled them to farm for Mba and to supply him gratis with yams, maize and vegetables when he was in charge of purchasing prisoners' food. The people also said that they were unable to approach the district officer hitherto because the interpreter and some policemen cooperated to prevent complaints from reaching the government.[94] Also investigations at Awa Native Court (Eket) in 1916 revealed that the clerk, one Ijeoma, allied with two of the most influential chiefs, Ifon and Akpabio, to convert the court into an instrument for feathering their own nests. Among their exploits was regular embezzlement of fines imposed by the court.[95] Because of this collusion, which was a feature of many courts, a great number of people who had genuine grievances got no redress.[96]

There was also a general belief that the government used the army and the police to support chiefs and court officials in all they did, and there is evidence to show that this belief was in fact based on practical experience. About 1910 the Warrant Chiefs of Okija in the Onitsha Division locked up some *Ozo* men for not responding to a call for forced labour. The people of Okija, who were infuriated by this unprecedented disgrace to their aristocracy, marched on the court, broke into the lock-up, released the men

[93] A 543/13, Annual Report, Onitsha Province, 1913, para. 10
[94] *Ibid.* See Enclosure dated 21.6.14 and entitled 'Mr Mba, Interpreter at Awka'
[95] Letters dated 27.1.16 and 8.6.16 from the DO, Eket, to the Resident, Calabar, in Calprof 14, C Conf 7/16, Miscellaneous Information about Chief Joseph Ifon of Awa Native Court, 1916–30
[96] This fact needs qualification. The league was not always intact especially when, as was admitted, the parties suspected each other of keeping back part of the bribe received, or when, as at Nnewi, the court was split into two camps which competed for dominance and each camp raked up charges against each other. In spite of this, however, the contention about the power of such a combination to frustrate a poor complainant remains valid. There is reason to believe that harmony between the court staff and the chiefs was the rule rather than the exception. But the understanding was not always based on equality of status, for the clerk was generally the sun around which the other planets of the court revolved.

and then burnt the court. What the government did was to send a military patrol to Okija without investigating the origins of the outbreak. The people of Okija drew their conclusions from the incident.[97] There were many other such cases. In the first quarter of 1915, when the Ifite ward of Nteje (Onitsha) rose against their 'head chief' Okuefuna, the district officer immediately visited the place with a police escort and imposed on the people a fine of fifty pounds and one hundred guns. In the last quarter of 1915 a section of the Isu in Udi murdered a road overseer and a 'minor chief' and drove out the police, presumably for exactions connected with work on the roads. The reaction of the government was to despatch a military expedition against the 'rebels'. Thus it was official policy that wherever the people were found refractory a 'punitive expedition' should be sent against them either instead of or before an officer to investigate the cause of their grievances. The policy was to support the chiefs as much as possible. As Resident Roberts of Onitsha put it in 1915: 'The chiefs frequently abuse their power and if they are not supported the boys get out of hand and refuse to do anything they are asked to do.'[98] The evils of this policy were that it strengthened the popular conviction that a common man had no chance against a Warrant Chief or the court staff, and that it prevented the administration from understanding to what extent there was deep-seated hostility to the Warrant Chief System.

It must be pointed out that the tragedy of the Warrant Chief System also lay in the fact that the people judged it not on its own merits but in relation to what they considered a past millennium during which the indigenous system functioned without alien disturbance and when 'justice rolled like a mighty stream'. This, therefore, raises the question of which of the two systems administered justice more equitably and gave greater satisfaction than the other.[99] To the peoples of the Eastern Provinces there was no doubt that the establishment of the Warrant Chief System marked the end of an era in their judicial history. As Chief Ogueri of Uboma in Okigwi put it: 'Immediately white

[97] Based on information collected from Chief Ejedeghobi (Okija, Onitsha). His father, who was a Warrant Chief, was accidentally shot during this patrol. The informant later became a Warrant Chief himself.
[98] A 1364/16, Annual Report, Onitsha Province, 1915, paras 6, 7, 8, 10, 20, 27, 28, 32, 36 and 41
[99] Justice here should be construed as the decision of cases through the impartial assessment of the facts made available to the judges.

men came justice vanished.'[100] To see what made people hold
this kind of view it is necessary to show those factors which the
people regarded as responsible for the perversion of justice under
the Warrant Chief System and which did not exist under the
indigenous system.

The first factor derived from the territorial extent of a Native
Court's jurisdiction. Since Native Courts were sited with an eye
on whether they were central to all the people they served or for
some other such reason, they were psychologically and ritually
out of focus, and were therefore free from those occult controls
which in pre-British days helped to ensure the maintenance of
equity. Traditional bodies which dealt with important matters
met in those places where the shrines of the group were located.
Those centres were also believed to be haunts of the spirits of the
departed members of the group, all of which were believed to be
keenly interested in the maintenance of justice and right relations
within the group. Even the house of the lineage head in which
elders generally met to take decisions was also regarded as
hallowed ground since it contained the highly venerated ancestral
symbols. Furthermore the meetings were generally held either
early in the mornings or late in the evenings and on certain
market days when these spiritual members of the community
were believed to be 'at home'. There was also the belief that the
administration of justice was a religious duty. Indigenous
councils were manifestly aware of the existence of these forces
and this awareness ensured that blatant or deliberate injustice was
not done since unjust decisions were believed to entail grave
consequences for 'judges'. It was to escape giving unjust verdicts
that difficult cases were generally settled on oath or by any other
ordeal acceptable to the litigants.

The Native Court community, being untraditional, appeared
to many people as non-moral.[101] Traditionally the community

---

[100] Based on information collected from Chief Ogueri of Lowa in Uboma,
Okigwi.

[101] I owe the information on the working of the traditional system of
government to seven old men who want to remain anonymous – two from
Okigwi, one from Owerri, two from Abakaliki, one from Ikot Ekpene and
one from Onitsha. Their views are important not because they are
necessarily unbiased and correct accounts of the indigenous system, but
because they give a vivid picture of the ideal, real or imagined, against
which the Warrant Chief System was measured by the conservatives.
Their account helps us to understand the state of mind of Etak Eto, the

outside the clan, or in fact sometimes outside the village-group was not conceived of as having the same convocation of gods and spirits of dead ancestors, and since it was those elements which upheld morality within the 'traditional community', the Native Court community had no moral code enjoining on the chiefs' honesty and fair dealing in human affairs. In fact traditions of conflict and duplicity mutually engaged in among villages and clans in the past dictated that one should strain to get the better of the man from a village outside one's traditional 'moral unit'. If therefore Opobo Warrant Chiefs took bribes to pervert justice in cases involving the Andoni or the Ibibio or both, they did not see themselves as committing any moral offence which could incur severe consequences from the spirit world. Nor did their fellow Opobo men think the worse of them. 'The power of the ancestor to support morality,' said Monica Hunter about the Nyakusa of South Tanganyika, 'is believed to be effective only within the immediate group of kinsmen and affines. . . . In pagan belief morality is rarely sanctioned outside the group of near relatives or that of the chiefdom.'[102] This was practically true of the Eastern Provinces in this period.

The second factor working to promote injustice in the Native Court was the 'alien' extraction of the court staff, and the fact that the latter lived apart from the communities they served. For the greater part of this period court clerks and interpreters were mostly men from the coastal communities, Onitsha, Sierra Leone and the then Gold Coast.[103] The object uppermost in the

village head of Ukam (Opobo), who, though a Warrant Chief, told a political officer in 1921: 'In plain words we are dissatisfied with British rule and want the Government to leave us so that the country may be governed by Ekpo and like societies. . . . I repeat my statement that the British are not fit to govern this country.' For saying this Etak Eto was charged with sedition and deprived of his warrant. C 35/1921, Petition from certain Chiefs of Opobo re the actions of mission boys – the whole file

[102] M. Hunter, 'An African Christian Morality', *Africa*, x, 3, July 1937, p. 291. There were cases of bribes offered and received within the maximal or even major lineage. This was said to derive from the fact that the chiefs and their headmen did not see themselves as performing the traditional functions.

[103] In 1910, the DO at Owerri wrote of the Ngor Native Court: 'The Ngor Native Court suffers from an inefficient clerk from the Gold Coast who requires an interpreter in his dealings with the Natives.' E 2224/10, Owerri District Half-Yearly Report dated 4.7.10, p. 3

minds of these strangers was not the service of humanity but the accumulation of wealth. Even later, when education penetrated the hinterland of the coastal states, and produced there some men who joined the local government service, the practice by which a court clerk or interpreter was treated as government servant and frequently transferred from station to station continued to ensure that these officials were generally strangers in the communities they served. The same thing applied to court messengers. In 1931, when the Native Court of Okun and Afaha in Ikot Ekpene Division was being reorganised, it was found that the court clerk and four out of the six court messengers were 'aliens', the remaining two being from the Okun clan.[104] In 1932 it was also found that the staff of the Ediene and Itak Court were drawn indiscriminately from all over Ikot Ekpene Division.[105] Away from their kith and kin these men were not passionately interested in seeing that justice was done, but were more concerned to feather their own nest. Closely allied to the foregoing was the fact that these men did not live among any of the people they served, but lived in the Native Court compound, where they were thus far removed from public opinion, one of the very effective agencies within the village for keeping men truthful. It was therefore easy for them to accept bribes and disregard justice.

It must be stated that the Warrant Chiefs and the court staff were not men innately morally depraved, but who, having found themselves in a new situation, decided to make the best use of it. The very existence of the court, its size, procedure and jurisprudence and the whole superstructure of the colonial régime were all indicative of changed times. Neither the people nor the Warrant Chiefs looked upon the court as performing traditional functions. Said E. G. Hawkesworth:

> The Warrant Chiefs regard their appointment as bestowing upon them executive authority of a new type which did not exist before the advent of the British. . . . Even where the Obong Isong is appointed he does not regard such appointment as a recognition of his natural position but considers that he has received a Government office. . . .[106]

[104] CSO 26/3, No. 26506, Intelligence Report on Okun and Afaha, Ikot Ekpene Division, Calabar Province, p. 43
[105] CSO 26/3, No. 27615, Intelligence Report on Ediene and Itak Clans, Ikot Ekpene Division (1932), p. 49
[106] CSO 26/3, No. 26506, Intelligence Report on Okun and Afaha Clans, etc., pp. 31–2

It was in this new mental environment and as agents of a remote central government that the Warrant Chiefs and the court staff performed their functions. In this new situation traditional sanctions and modes of procedure were regarded as inapplicable. It was this fact that shocked and alienated conservative opinion and that was responsible for the bribery and corruption which now came to obtain even within traditional moral units.

But under the traditional system these novel factors making for injustice did not exist. Men operated a system whose purposes they understood, treated cases whose origin they had intimate knowledge of, dealt with litigants whose history and character they knew very well and gave each case the attention it deserved since there were not too many cases to deal with at a time. Everybody who had anything to contribute was heard and not interrupted or hushed to save time or out of some ulterior motive as was the case in Native Courts.[107] Furthermore the traditional system did not take delight in the multiplication of litigation and therefore always sought to give a final solution to each case, if need be by sending it to an oracle that would settle the issue for all time by 'eating' one of the parties. But the Native Court had an interest in the multiplication of cases for it meant more openings for bribes. The very existence of such an institution designed almost only to settle cases was an invitation to litigate.[108] It brought into being professional money-lenders, petition writers and lawyers' touts, all of whom were interested in multiplying litigation. In this period the Nkwerre people from Orlu as well as the Aro earned a notoriety for hanging around Native Courts to foment litigation which gave them the opportunity to pursue their trade of lending at exorbitant rates.[109] Igwegbe Odum first made his name as a money-lender at the Ajalli Native Court before he embarked on his political career.[110] None of these men or groups

---

[107] One of the common complaints of litigants against the Native Courts was that their witnesses were not called or listened to with patience. In 1920 Mr Lyon, DO, Udi, wrote: 'There is the frequent complaint by appellants that their witnesses were not invited. The truth of this is substantiated by the frequent appearance on the record book [of the statement] ... "the chiefs require no further evidence".' See Memo. Conf L/4/1919 dated 11.1.20 by DO, Udi, in C 176/19, Remarks by F. P. Lynch, etc.

[108] CSO 26/3, No. 20645, Assessment Report, Okigwi District

[109] C. K. Meek, *Law and Authority in a Nigerian Tribe*, p. 234. See also footnote 1 on same page.   [110] R. O. Igwegbe, *The Original History*, p. 122

was interested in the dispensation of justice for its own sake. They were all out for what they could get and the more injustice there was the more litigation there was and the more they got. There is every reason to believe that in this type of environment there was less justice and satisfaction for the people than existed under the traditional system.

An interesting but difficult question deals with the impact of the new on the old. Its difficulty derives from the fact that the functioning of the old in the new environment, like its functioning in pre-British days, is not documented, and many institutional or procedural changes which took place were too subtle to survive in popular tradition. Also, since change is immanent in every social system,[111] it is not easy to say which particular development or decline was due to the impingement of a new factor or was itself logical in the system. Furthermore when the factors which are new and which impinge on a social system are many and various it becomes all the more difficult for a student of one of these forces to say what changes, even if these were brought about by the new forces, were owing to the force which is the object of his study. And the period under study was one during which very many new forces – economic, educational, political, religious – were in action. This section of the work therefore deals only with the broad question of whether the indigenous system atrophied and died as a result of the attempt to get it superseded by the Warrant Chief System or whether it continued to operate.

In spite of the drive to make the Warrant Chief System the sole agency of local government[112] and in spite of the zeal with which Warrant Chiefs were said to have prosecuted non-warrant holders who attempted to try cases outside Native Courts, the indigenous system continued to function. This is not at all unexpected, since the political system of the old order was inextricably embedded in the lineage system and the latter has continued to function to the present day as a basis of social life and relationship within the village. Furthermore the indigenous system was not designed solely for the settlement of cases. It was a full-fledged political organ and the attempt to deprive it of its

[111] This is one of those principles of sociology to which needed emphasis has been given by Professor Pitirim Sorokin. See A. K. Davis, 'Lessons from Sorokin', in *Sociological Theory, Values and Socio-Cultural Change*, ed. E. A. Tiryakian, Ontario 1963, pp. 3–4
[112] See ch. 3, above.

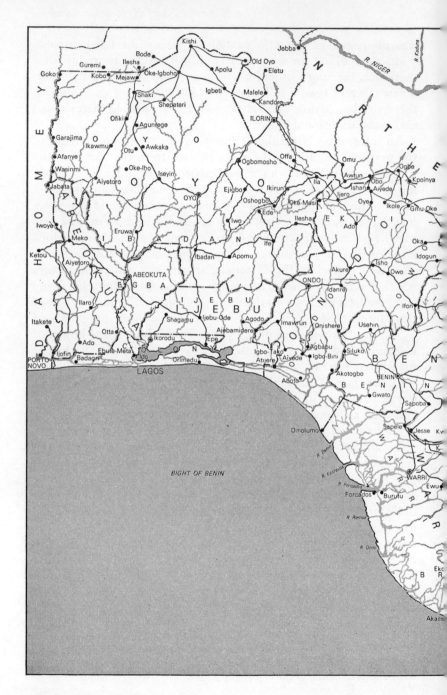

The Southern Provinces, 1926

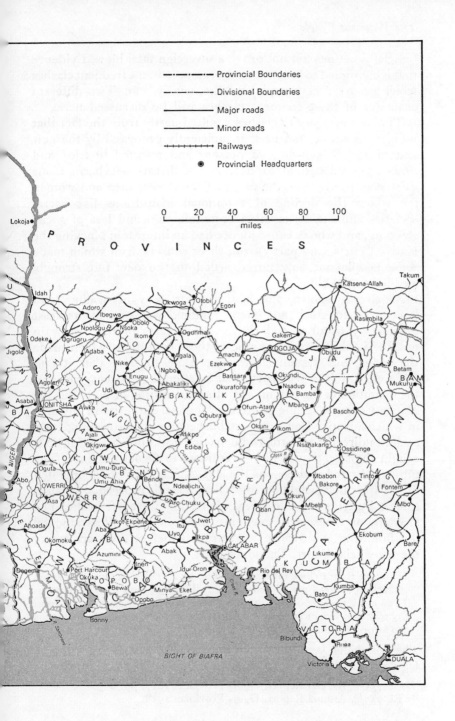

judicial functions did not prove a sovereign fatal blow. Evidence that it continued to function actively is seen in the frequent clashes which occurred between it and the new system. Two different examples of these frequent clashes will be discussed here.

The first category of clashes resulted partly from the fact that indigenous society felt itself insufficiently protected by the new system against evil-minded persons and resorted to tried and time-honoured methods for dealing with threats to its harmonious existence; partly from the fact that there were men and women for whom the decline of traditional institutions like secret societies and oracles entailed economic ruin and loss of social standing, and who in consequence had an interest in blocking the Native Courts; and partly from sheer conservatism which made some people not only unreconciled to the new but strongly wedded to the old.

As already shown, the Native Court way of dealing with larceny of livestock and farm produce was one of its least satisfactory features, and the fact that cases of theft grew in number in this period was one of those conditions which made the indigenous system show from time to time that it still functioned. In the year 1917, that is, after about twenty years of the operation of the ban on any other institution or body but the Native Court exercising political or judicial authority in any area in which a Native Court was established, a number of indigenous societies directed towards the detection and punishment of theft caught the attention of the government in Ogoja Province. The most celebrated of these was the *Akpokisi* society, which operated in Afikpo and neighbouring villages and proceeded against thieves by tying them to trees, where they were left to die. The strength of the society even in 1917 is clearly illustrated by the following evidence of a Warrant Chief of Amaseri before the Provincial Court. The chief said:

> If anyone went to look for a man tied up by *Akpokisi* he would be killed . . . as head chief I would be killed. . . . Through the action of *Akpokisi* I ran away to Afikpo [headquarters] and remained there an exile from my town for five months under Government protection. The society is too strong for the chiefs to do anything.[113]

The following year similar societies were found operating at Ugulangu and Oshiri in the same province.[114] In 1929, that is

---

[113] EP 755/2, Annual Report, Ogoja Province, 1917, pp. 6–7
[114] EP 755/3, Annual Report, Ogoja Province, 1918

nearly thirty years after the supposed supersession of the old institutions by the new, the *Ezeputa* society, an organisation of the Izzi of Abakaliki, was revived to deal with thieves and to eradicate the influence of the Izzi Native Court. Chita Eledo, a Warrant Chief of Izzi, was attacked and his son wounded, court messengers and all other agents of the government were chased out. Chief Idika Igboji of this clan said to the present author: 'The society was revived by the elders of each village who were dissatisfied with the lenient way the Native Court dealt with "criminals".'[115]

The feature just described was not peculiar to the Ogoja Province. In 1924 in Abak District of Calabar Province the indigenous Anang Society, called *Ekpo Akai* – 'ghosts from the bush' – was revived to deal with the increasing crime of larceny. In each village all the freeborn adult males held a meeting in which they enrolled into the society on special oath, and modified the traditional methods of dealing with thieves. Any person suspected or accused of theft was brought before the *Ekpo Akai* for trial. Accused men who insisted on their innocence were put on oath ordeal. All delinquents caught in the act were handed over to the society, who fined them, stripped and paraded them round the neighbouring market. When this modified punishment was found ineffective as a deterrent to crime, the old law of death for convicted thieves was revived. Criminals who were caught were first tortured and then executed publicly.[116]

The continued operation of these institutions, which were either the executive agents of the indigenous system or some of the agencies at the disposal of that system for dealing with difficult cases, was clear evidence that the Native Courts did not effectively supersede let alone destroy the former. That an institution like the Aro Long Juju, whose influence was very extensive and against which the British never relaxed their vigilance, should continue to operate up to 1921[117] is a pointer as

[115] CSO 26/4, No. 30192, Intelligence Report, Izzi Clan (1932), Abakaliki Division, para. 106. Supplemented with information collected from Idika Igboji (Izzi, Abakaliki)

[116] EP 1138, vol. x, Annual Report, Calabar Province, 1924, pp. 9–10. Some Warrant Chiefs were involved in this matter – a situation suggesting that they were not satisfied with the Native Court handling of this class of crime.

[117] EP 755/6, Annual Report, Ogoja Province, 1921, pp. 4, 14–16. EP 755/7, Annual Report, Ogoja Province, 1922, pp. 7, 10, 23

to the extent the indigenous system continued to function under the Warrant Chief System. Under normal conditions the indigenous system functioned mainly with regard to those aspects of the community's life which were not much touched by the Native Court System and where it was not likely to incur the anger of the Warrant Chiefs. Those occasions on which its votaries clashed with the colonial government were occasions when they considered the times as being out of joint and decided to restore things to normal by using the swift old methods.

The second category of evidence for the continued existence of the indigenous system comes from the fact that the indigenous principle of decentralisation of authority triumphed over the opposite ideal represented by the Warrant Chief System. The reorganisation which set in in 1930 was an attempt to give official recognition to the indigenous principle. In fact the very attempt made under the Warrant Chief System to channel authority within the village and sometimes within the clan through one man or a handful of men paradoxically helped to encourage segmentation and decentralisation. Since there was no segment or group with a traditional right to produce a man entitled to the type of position the British wanted to build up for a Warrant Chief, each segment, after the initial fear of the white man had died down, pushed forward a candidate for the position.

This craze for caps and warrants, already dealt with,[118] was not entirely a craze for a new status symbol but was also the result of the attempt of the indigenous constitution to reassert itself and the ancient principles of equal participation by all segments in all matters of general concern.

In another way 'caps' and 'warrants' intensified the tendency of the old political system to segment. As already shown it was the habit of 'warrant' and 'cap' seekers to erect the segment from which they came into autonomous villages. In 1927 Mr J. C. Mackenzie, Cadet, asserted that the Warrant Chief System had a revolutionary effect on the ancient clan structure and that in some places it had split up the indigenous organisation. An example was the case of Umu-Igbo of Obia clan in Ahoada, where the Warrant Chief came from Umu-Omenyi, which was the strangers' quarter of the section called Umu-Arada. Having become the most important man in Umu-Igbo and perhaps scheming to establish a 'dynasty' and consolidate his position, this Warrant

118 See ch. 5, above.

Chief proceeded to declare his ward independent of the other five wards of the village.[119] Some time in the early 1920s Uzuakoli, one of the five wards of Uruala in Orlu, claimed to be a separate village owing to the schemings of one Adebonu, who wanted a warrant for himself.[120] The village of Umuowa in the Orlu district, like many other Ibo villages, divided into two main sections, Umubu and Owerre, each of which under the Warrant Chief System had a 'capped' headman. Rivalry between the two headmen, no doubt caused by the quest for a warrant, threatened the village with complete disruption. By the time the political officer at Orlu went into the matter in May 1920, the conflict had reached a stage where the two sections would not assemble in the same place. Umubu made a new Nkwo market and met the officer there, while Owerre assembled in the original Nkwo, where the village assembly had traditionally met. In a bid to bring the two sections together again the political officer appointed their other market, Eke, as the new centre for village meetings.[121] An identical thing took place at Olakwo in the Owerri Division, where a Warrant Chief was appointed from each of the two sections of the village. This fact came to light in 1929, when the town was visited by a military patrol during the Women's Riot. To meet the officer in charge of the patrol each section met in a place of its own. 'It was found out,' said the officer, 'that this was due to a Court member having been appointed in each section, an instance of the disruption caused by the Native Court System.'[122]

However, it must not be thought that the thirty years or so of Warrant Chief rule left no scars on the indigenous system. Continued survival was achieved at a price. Indisputably what was revived in the 1930s as the indigenous system would have appeared as only pseudo-indigenous to any native of this area who died about 1850 had he been able to return ninety years later. For one thing the oracular and other spiritual agencies which in pre-British days occupied a very prominent place in village government had by 1930 lost much of their importance. The so-called destruction of the Long Juju at Arochukwu, *Igweka-Ala* at Umunneoha, *Agbala* at Awka and hundreds of other lesser

[119] CSO 26/3, No. 20634, Intelligence Report, Ohia Clan, pp. 11–12
[120] Orlu Intelligence Book, 1921–30, p. 165
[121] *Ibid.*, p. 42
[122] EP 6659, vol. v, Disturbances on Aba Owerri Road. See report dated 29.12.29

oracles and shrines reduced the use to which they were put in political matters. Mostly only the old irreconcilable die-hards continued to retain great faith in them. The generation which was born between 1900 and 1930 grew up with a Native Court mentality. Political officers were impressed by the comparative youth of the crowds they saw in the Native Courts.[123]

Also age-grades and secret societies underwent progressive decline as political forces not only because they could no longer act as the fearless executive agents of village councils without being prosecuted in Native Courts but also because of the corroding effects of western education, the economic attractions of the new urban centres and the growth of general sophistication which resulted from increased travel. 'Capped' headmen and court messengers virtually usurped the executive functions of indigenous institutions. If an age-grade was called out for work on the road, it was the Native Court, not it, that punished defaulters. Also, since more and more cases left the village council for either the private court of the Warrant Chief or for the Native Court, less and less use was made of age-grades as instruments for enforcing the decisions of the village elders. In the same way the title societies lost political influence because the possession of a warrant or cap gave more perceptible power than the highest indigenous title. It therefore became more fashionable to use one's money to lobby chiefs, court clerks, court messengers and interpreters to support one's quest for a cap and warrant or to invest it in new economic ventures than to spend it on title-taking. The upshot was that age-grades, title and secret societies more and more took the form of social clubs and institutions whose political significance became progressively a matter of anti-quarian interest. The most obvious proof that these institutions had lost much of their political importance by 1930 lay in the fact that nobody agitated for a place for them in the new scheme of things ushered in by the reorganisations of the 1930s. As these traditional institutions lost their political influence an increasing number of people resorted to the Native Courts for the redress of grievances.[124]

Thus though the Warrant Chief System failed to cause the

[123] S. M. Grier, *Report on a Tour in the Eastern Provinces*, Lagos 1922, p. 6
[124] CSO 26/3, No. 26506, Intelligence Report Okun and Afaha Clans, Ikot Ekpene, p. 43

complete dissolution of the traditional system it nonetheless made appreciable inroads into it. But in so far as it failed to destroy or modify the principle of lineage equivalence or to institutionalise chieftaincy exercising meaningful political power and authority, it failed to modify that constitution in the way and to the extent the colonial administration had hoped for.

8 Conclusion

The history of the Warrant Chief System is a tale of wrong
assumptions leading to wrong decisions and wrong remedies and
finally of failure. In so far as the system was untraditional it
carried a fatal flaw from its inception. It is understandable that
since they were not prophets, were not guided by practical
anthropologists and worked at a time when the problem of
conquering the people had to be tackled together with the
problem of administering them, Moor and Egerton made a
serious mistake while implementing their policy of ruling through
what they considered 'the tribal system'. But it is not out of place
to ask whether if they had an intimate knowledge of the indigenous
system of government of the Ibo, Ibibio, Ijo and Ogoja peoples
Moor and Egerton would have wanted to work through it. In the
early years of the Protectorate, when the imposition of British
rule was a matter of great urgency, it was very unlikely that any
administrator of a practical turn of mind would have considered
it advisable to rule each village or clan through its own informally
organised assembly or council. Even if there were an administrator romantic enough to adopt such a system, he would still have
singled out a member of that assembly or council through whom
the government was to transmit instructions and advice to the
village council. This would have needed giving such an inter-
mediary some insignia which would distinguish him from a
common impostor. Such a system would probably have equally
led to the evolution of a system more or less like the Warrant
Chief System.[1] Yet it is unlikely that such an agent, if closely

[1] Compare with the following opinion expressed by P. A. Talbot, Resident
of Onitsha Province, in 1920. 'The abolition of the Native Courts,' he
said, 'is, it seems to me, out of the question. They form the main spring of
administration. Even if it were possible to multiply by ten the number of
Europeans, the latter will still be compelled to have native accessors to

controlled by the government, could have become as independent of, and therefore as alienated from, the village elders as the classic Warrant Chief was, especially if the office was rotated from lineage head to lineage head in consultation with the village council. On the other hand it may well be sheer romanticism to think that the staid and proud elders, titled men, priests and leaders of secret societies who in the early years of British rule thought that only the worthless should take appointment under the white man would have agreed to convert their ancient institutions into the obedient instruments of the colonial government. In the circumstances Moor's version of the Warrant Chief System was perhaps a realistic attempt to solve a very difficult problem. This in no way means that it had any chance of ultimately succeeding in winning the acceptance and appreciation of the people. How and when it would have met its end is a matter for conjecture, since before it had made its full impact on the people and their socio-political system it was remodelled and infused with new ideas by Sir Frederick Lugard.

By 1912 effective British occupation was about twenty years old in certain parts of the Eastern Provinces. By that year also it had been discovered that, contrary to earlier official belief, the house system was a coastal socio-political phenomenon rather than an institution common to all the peoples of these provinces; that is, one of the misconceptions on which the Warrant Chief System was founded had been exploded. What was more, even along the coast the so-called chiefs (house and ward heads) were speedily losing whatever measure of power they had enjoyed in the past. These facts called for a reconstitution of the local government system of the Eastern Provinces along lines dictated by the results of a sincere and sustained effort to understand the nature of the indigenous political system. But this was not done. Lugard was not completely unaware of the differences in political organisation which existed between the former Fulani empire and the Eastern Provinces. In fact it was his awareness of these differences that spurred him on to try in the latter place a number of policies which he hoped would help chieftainships

advise them on local customs and the system would soon adumbrate to the present one.' See the Memo. OP 35/1919 dated 3.2.20 by Talbot in C 176/19, Remarks by F. P. Lynch, etc. The 'reforms' ushered in by the Reports of Grier and Tomlinson (ch. 5 above) also presumed the same thing.

to evolve there. To Lugard chiefs were greatly to be desired because they made his particular brand of Indirect Rule possible.

It would be misleading to over-emphasise the difficult conditions created by the First World War in order to explain the failure of Lugard's schemes in the Eastern Provinces, as has been done by Dame Margery Perham in her *Native Administration in Nigeria*. An objective opinion on Lugard's local government policy in this area must be based on an assessment of how far that policy took into account objective local conditions and on how successful it was. It would be unfair to criticise Lugard for believing that the system of local government in the provinces east of the Niger needed some reform. This much was recognised by even the Southern officers who considered it basically sound. Lugard became blameworthy when he saw change in the Southern system as synonymous with the imposition of the Northern system, when he made no real effort to understand the local government problems of the Eastern Provinces, when he failed to trust those officers who after years of service in the South could be described as having acquired a tolerably sound general knowledge of the South.

Thus Lugard's reforms were designed not to meet the functional defects already detected in the Warrant Chief System in the years before 1914, nor to achieve the necessary reconciliation between that system and the indigenous political organisation, but to realise his ideal form of Indirect Rule through revolutionising some of the most deep-seated political instincts and traditions of the people. The frenzied attempt to modify a society radically in order to fit it for a particular interpretation of a certain policy shows Lugard as lacking in that flexibility of thought and outlook which should characterise people who would grapple successfully with the problem of bringing peoples with different institutions and ways of life under the umbrella of one state. Said that sage historian W. E. H. Lecky:

> It is a great error both in history and practical politics, to attach too much importance to a political machine. The essential consideration is by what men and in what spirit that machine is likely to be worked.[2]

This does not seem to have been one of Lugard's political maxims. In fact Lugard's second period of office in Nigeria or, to be more specific, his association with the Eastern Provinces

[2] W. E. H. Lecky, *The Political Values of History*, London 1892, p. 52

was disastrous for his reputation as an administrator to an extent that has scarcely been realised hitherto. One of Lugard's legacies, and a dangerous one at that, was the tradition that uniformity in local government policy throughout Nigeria was a consummation devoutly to be wished. This tradition haunted his successors, or rather put them in chains from which they were released only by the shattering experience of an anti-government Riot organised and carried out entirely by women.

Though as soon as Lugard left the country finally in 1919 it became clear to the majority of the political officers working in the Eastern Provinces that the reforms he introduced were a mistake, neither Sir Hugh Clifford, who succeeded him, nor Sir Graeme Thomson after Sir Hugh was able to save the Warrant Chief System from ultimate disaster. If Clifford was convinced that the Warrant Chief System was in great need of change, he was far from clear as to what to do.[3] He was further fettered by the assumption, propagated by men like Colonel Moorhouse, that the intractable local government problems of the post-Lugardian years derived from Lugard's abrogation of the arrangement by which the political officer sat as the president of the Native Court.[4] This misleading diagnosis, which assumed the answer to the fundamental question of whether local government in the Eastern Provinces must necessarily mean rule by chiefs, helped to create the belief that what the Warrant Chief System needed was tinkering with rather than radical reconstruction. To confuse the issues further, when in the early 1920s Clifford created a Department of Native Affairs he put it into the hands of S. M. Grier and G. J. F. Tomlinson, men who had their political education in Northern Nigeria and had acquired the bias for a particular brand of Indirect Rule. It is therefore not surprising that the remedies which were applied on the advice of the

---

[3] Minute No. 5 dated 8.11.19 by H. Clifford in C 176/19, Remarks by F. P. Lynch, etc. It may be necessary to point out that, although Clifford became aware of the need for reform in 1919, it was only in 1923 that what might be called a programme of reform was formulated, and even then he was positive only on the issue of clan courts and the quest for hereditary chiefs. By the time any positive steps had been taken in these directions, he had recommended the introduction of direct taxation and left the country. See ch. 5

[4] Minute No. 38 dated 7.5.20 by the LGSP in C 176/19, Remarks by F. P. Lynch, etc. S. M. Grier, *Report on a Tour in the Eastern Provinces*, Lagos 1922. See comment on by Moorhouse dated 22.3.22

Secretary for Native Affairs and his assistant were either marginally relevant, like the scheme for clan courts, or absolutely irrelevant, ill-conceived and in fact dangerous, like the vain search for hereditary chiefs.[5] On his exit Clifford handed over to his successor, Sir Graeme Thomson, a crumbly and rickety system as well as the legacy of introducing direct taxation through it.

Sir Graeme Thomson thus came to head a government which had already been ensnared by an unrealistic tradition. His imposition of direct taxation on the Eastern Provinces along the lines dictated by the Native Revenue Ordinance was the last attempt to force the Warrant Chief System into the Lugardian mould. The system crumbled in the process. It can thus be concluded that the uneasiness which in the post-Lugardian years afflicted the administration with regard to the Warrant Chief System failed to produce in the upper reaches of the administrative hierarchy a man with sufficient vision and resolve to hack his way through what was considered to be a forest of confusion to the high-road of a clear-cut policy.

With the probable exception of Major U. F. H. Ruxton,[6]

[5] The reports on the Native Courts sent in by officers east of the Niger between 1919 and 1920 were in general so critical and pessimistic that anybody unhampered by Lugardian blinkers would have re-examined more critically the whole question of rule through chiefs in the Eastern Provinces. An officer like Jeffreys at Eket wrote: 'The average chief in this district is not a chief, but usually a trader or at most staggers under the dignity of being the elder of a hamlet. There are no native rulers [chiefs] in this district.' Mr Howard at Obubra, writing in the same vein, said: 'They [the Warrant Chiefs] really are not chiefs, but simply town headmen hall-marked by a warrant in which alone lies their superiority over the common herd.' Some officers went so far as to call, or hint at the need, for the abolition of Native Courts and the introduction of Resident Magistrates. But when Grier and Tomlinson toured these areas they sent in reports which diverted official energies into the vain search for the very institution which local officers said did not exist. In this way the administration failed to realise that the basic evil of the Warrant Chief System lay in its utter divergence from the indigenous system. See Memo. No. DC 20/20 by ADO Mr M. D. W. Jeffreys, as well as Memo. marked 'C' by Howard in C 176/19, Remarks by F. P. Lynch

[6] Apart from serving in the non-Emirate provinces like Lower Benue, Yola and the Cameroons, Ruxton also served in Gwandu and Bornu and had at one time acted as Lieutenant Governor of the Northern Provinces. See Robert Heussler, *The British in Nigeria*, London 1968, pp. xix–xx. Mr Dorward, in his recent article on 'The Development of the British Colonial Administration among the Tiv 1900–1949', in *African Affairs*

service in the Northern Provinces unfitted political officers for service in the Eastern Provinces. Many Europeans who had long contact with and intimate knowledge of the Eastern Provinces in this period came to the same conclusion after seeing some of these 'transplanted' officers in action. Around 1922, P. A. Talbot, who had risen to the rank of a resident after many years' service east of the Niger, wrote 'a strongly worded minute . . . in which he expressed the opinion that officers trained in the North were unsuitable for work in the South'. Mr Grier, who had first served in the North and then in the Western Provinces, agreed with him in part and said that while unsuitable for work in the Eastern Provinces such officers could be useful in the Western areas.[7] Talbot's point was again made with greater poignancy before the Donald Kingdon Commission of Inquiry by the Methodist Reverend Minister, W. T. Groves, who knew the Eastern Provinces well. He said,

> It is no good sending a man from the North to this country. That is my experience and I know a few of them. They do not understand the people. Neither is it any good bringing a man from another colony to change everything in about three months, without knowing the conditions of the people.[8]

In essence this was an indictment of the men with Northern Nigerian experience from Lugard down. To round off this point it is illuminating to note the opinion of Captain Buchanan-Smith, who came to Southern Nigeria in 1909, served for many years in the Eastern Provinces and became the Lieutenant-Governor of the Southern Provinces in 1930. Discussing the whole question of the failure of the Warrant Chief System, he argued:

> Since 1914 when Mr Palmer was sent by Sir Frederick Lugard to report on the position in the Southern Provinces there has been a definite tendency for Government to be guided by the views of officers whose knowledge of Native Administration has been derived from experience gained mainly in the Northern Provinces or in the Cameroons. These officers though extremely able had but little personal experience of the conditions prevailing in the smaller but much more densely populated Ibo provinces, and their views on affairs in these provinces did not always merit the considerable weight apparently attached to them. In some respects the results have been unfortunate.

(1969), has shown that Ruxton was never captivated by the orthodox emirate pattern.
[7] S. M. Grier, *Report on a Tour in the Eastern Provinces*, etc., p. 20
[8] *ACINE*, para. 18742

Firstly, he said, this gave rise to the opinion that officers east of the Niger were not as hard-working as their counterparts elsewhere, since apparently they did not produce the same results. This opinion, he said, was demoralising. Secondly, he continued, 'officers in the Eastern Provinces have often been led astray in their endeavour to discover conditions which might satisfy their critics but which did not, in fact, exist or they have been disheartened by the incredulity with which their views have been received and have hesitated to repeat them'.[9] The fact is that from 1914 there were three traditions in conflict. The first was the indigenous traditions of the people, the second the tradition of Sir Ralph Moor and the third the tradition of Sir Frederick Lugard. It cannot be said that the administration clearly recognised this tripartite character of their dilemma. In any case, because they failed to resolve the minor conflict between Moor and Lugard they could not tackle successfully the larger issue of harmonising alien rule with the indigenous political traditions of the people.

The question whether Indirect Rule could have succeeded in the Eastern Provinces would normally be dismissed as speculative and unhistorical by purists to whom history is concerned with what actually happened rather than with what might have been. But framed differently as 'under what conditions could Indirect Rule have succeeded in the Eastern Provinces?' it has attracted the attention of at least two scholars. Writing on the Umor of Obubra Division in 1939, Professor Daryll Forde said that the policy of Indirect Rule

> depends for success on more than a general grasp of the outlines of native social organisation. Native standards of value as expressed in individual and collective behaviour, the operation of balances and checks in the social system, current trends which are tending to cause some institutions and customs to lose strength at the expense of others, and the economic forces that have been or are in future likely to be operative in the society, must all be analysed and assessed in their mutual relations as interrelated elements in a complex process.[10]

One must dismiss this prescription as utopian, impossible of realisation in any place and at any time no matter who rules whom.

[9] CSO 26/3, No. 25512, vol. i, Comments on the Report of the Aba Commission of Inquiry, p. 49

[10] D. Forde, 'Government in Umor, Obubra Division: A Study of Social Change and the Problems of Indirect Rule in a Nigerian Village Community', *Africa*, xii, 1939, p. 129

Is it recommended that a colonial power should carry out such an all-embracing study before setting up an administration or can the two go on hand in hand? How many social anthropologists would be engaged to carry out the study in a place like the Eastern Provinces, where, though the broad principles of social organisations might be similar, significant local differences exist? Since it is impossible to insulate a community from the impact of alien forces in order to carry out such a study, the prescribed course would not only engage all the staff a colonial government could possibly employ bearing in mind its limited resources. It would also go on *ad infinitum*, as even the advent of the anthropologist and the political officer in each community would constitute a factor for change which the anthropologist would also have to analyse and assess. This would reduce colonial government to an area research scheme in anthropology.

What is more, no people ever recognise at any one time all the forces making for change in their society, in what directions changes are likely to take place, all the checks and balances built into their system, all the codes guiding individual and collective conduct and so on. It is the experience of history that social changes are not always recognised before they have taken place, after which any study of them can only take the form of a post-mortem, the conclusions from which would not necessarily constitute a sure guide for the future. Probably Professor Forde is saying that Indirect Rule can never be sufficiently *indirect* in the sense of utilising not only the structure of indigenous political institutions but also making them function in their proper social or cultural context infused with the traditional ethos and philosophy of right government and right conduct.

Nearly thirty years after Professor Forde, Professor Anene argued that the colonial government in carrying out its policy of Indirect Rule would have been better advised if it had 'sought out the elders in each village-group'[11] as agencies of rule. Fortunately, however, on the same page Professor Anene wrote his own refutation when he observed that among the Ibo and their neighbours the elders were not primarily political leaders but 'merely . . . intermediaries between the dead ancestors and the living'.[12]

Professors Anene and Forde would thus seem to attribute to

[11] J. C. Anene, *Southern Nigeria in Transition 1885–1906*, Cambridge 1966, p. 258   [12] *Ibid.*, p. 258

the British alone responsibility for the failure of the Warrant Chief System, and probably rightly too, for those who arrogate to themselves the right to rule other races or nationalities should be prepared to do everything possible to make their rule effective and successful. But then nothing that happens in a situation of culture contact between two races or nationalities can be explained entirely in terms of the wisdom or stupidity of only one of the parties unless the other is completely inert. And even then there are moments in history when inertness could have far-reaching consequences. But the Ibo and their neighbours were far from inert during the period covered by this study. Thus to some extent the failure of the Warrant Chief System derived from the fact that each of the two groups involved, the British and the natives, for a long time failed to see that they had much to learn from each other in the field of government. 'The natives here,' asserted Sir Ralph Moor in 1901 of the people of the then Southern Nigeria, 'are wanting in that instinct for government bred in the white races by centuries of systematic rule, wanting in all experiences and judgment. . . .'[13] Later Governor Clifford also felt that the difficulty of fashioning a satisfactory local government system for the Eastern Provinces derived to a large extent from the backwardness of the natives. 'During the whole course of my service in the Tropics,' he wrote in 1919, 'I have never yet encountered any natives whose standards of culture approximate to that of the Ibos, Ibibios and Efiks whose chiefs could be safely entrusted with a fraction of the power with which the so-called chiefs in these Districts . . . are invested.'[14] The British were in fact convinced in this period that they had everything to teach the peoples of these provinces in the art of government. It was this unshakeable confidence which was in part responsible for the British refusal in this period to carry out detailed researches into the structure and mechanism of the indigenous political organisation. If through such research they had recognised that authority amongst the Ibo and their neighbours was at root *delegatory* in character and that politics and government had a broad democratic base they might have come close to evolving a system which the people would understand.

[13] CSO 1/15, Southern Nigeria Confidential Despatches to CO 1900–7. See Despatch No. 15 dated 14.12.01, Moor to CO
[14] Minute No. 5 dated 8.11.19 by Clifford in C 176/19, Remarks by F. P. Lynch, etc.

On their part the elders of the Eastern Provinces were convinced that they were the heirs of a civilisation which made it possible for men to live in harmony with the universe, as they understood it, through adherence to traditions and customs which they believed embodied the wisdom and experience of their forebears. The vast majority of the people thus found it difficult, if not impossible, to appreciate the wisdom of the new ways being peddled by the British. 'In plain words,' the village head of Ukam, who surprisingly was also a Warrant Chief, said to the political officer at Opobo in 1921, 'we are dissatisfied with British rule and want the Government to leave us so that the country may be governed by *Ekpo* and like societies. . . . I repeat my statement that the British are not fit to govern this country.'[15] Eight years later, Ohuhu women told Chief Nwatu, who tried to argue with them during the Riot, that 'they were going to Owerrinta to demolish the Native Court; that they did not want the Native Court to try cases any longer; and that all white men should return to their own country so that the land in this area may remain as it was many years ago before the advent of the white man'.[16] The tragedy of the Ukam chief and of the militant women was a failure to face facts. They had no alternative to Warrant Chief rule but their pre-colonial system. Here they failed to recognise that alien rule had come to stay or had made a significant break with the past and that their world could not remain as it was in the days of yore, not even if the British accepted the invitation to pack bag and baggage.

Probably Indirect Rule might have succeeded in the Eastern Provinces if the people and their imperial masters had understood each other better; that is, if the British had learned that chiefly rule was not possible in every society and the local people that their traditional system of democratic village republics needed substantial modification if it would successfully meet the needs of the twentieth century. But with both sides arguing on two different planes as shown there could scarcely have been an easy solution to the problem. It is not surprising, therefore, that the Warrant Chief experiment was brought to an abrupt end by open conflict and bloodshed.

[15] Calprof 14, C 35/1921, Petition from certain chiefs of Opobo re the actions of mission boys. See the entire file
[16] *ACINE*, paras 9769–70

Appendix

The following are extracts from my field notes. The two witnesses whose accounts are given here are the traditional heads of the two neighbouring clans of Otanzu and Otanchara, which were in the Okigwi Native Court area in the period covered by this study. A comparison of these two accounts shows the general consistency which marks the oral evidence used in this work.

(a) Obiukwu Nze of Umulolo (the Clan Head of Otanzu and a former Warrant Chief)

The subjugation of Umulolo. 'Umulolo was subdued by a military patrol which entered the village from the direction of Ogbunka (in Awka Division). No member of the village had previous warning of this disaster. Immediately the patrol entered the village it attacked my father's compound, and in the process my father and I were wounded while my paternal grandmother was killed. Everybody in the village took to the bush and stayed there for about six days. Parts of my father's compound were burnt. A few days after the attack, my father died of heartbreak "for seeing what his father never saw"; that is, the insult of having war carried into his compound and for having his ancestral "gods" destroyed in the process.

'Four days after my father's death, the soldiers came back, and everybody again took to the bush. We ran away because we were frightened.[1] When the white men found nobody to parley with, they burnt the remaining portions of my father's compound, but in spite of or even because of this, nobody came out of his hiding in the bush to parley with them. Later the white men sent word

[1] Asked why the people ran away, Obiukwu replied: '*O mere onve ma ihe ha wu.*' (Who knew what they – the white men who were in charge of the patrol – were?)

306

through an Aro guide that they would burn down the whole of Umulolo village if my father and I were not surrendered to them. Our old men had a hurried meeting there in the bush at which they decided to hand me over to them in order to save the rest of Umulolo from being razed to the ground.

'When I was taken to the white men I told them that my father had died as a result of the previous shootings. I was terribly frightened because I thought I was going to be killed. When given what later I understood to be English wine to drink I refused it because I thought it was poison. But it was forced down my throat. In the parley which followed between the elders of my village and the white men the former learned that futile attempts had earlier been made to arrange a peaceful meeting between the leaders of the patrol and my father. Since no message to this effect was received by my father or by any other elder of the village we concluded that the Aro and Awka men who accompanied the expeditions as guides must have lied maliciously against my father. I am not saying, however, that our elders would have agreed to hold such a meeting, but an early warning would have given our people time to prevent a surprise attack. In the parley with our elders the white men said they came specially to know who were Nze Osuoji of Umulolo and Ogujiofor Umeojiaku of Ihube of whom they had heard through Aro agents.

'Ogujiofor Umeojiaku of Ihube suffered worse things than I did at the hands of the same military patrol, for it was alleged that he refused to respond promptly to an order to meet the white men. When eventually he appeared he was seized and tied to a tree, and later forced to guide the patrol to a number of neighbouring villages. He was subsequently released at a place about ten miles away from his village. I think it was at Ngodo in Isuochi clan that he was released.'

The Native Court. 'Whether a Native Court was good or bad depended on the court clerk. There were good and bad court clerks, the good clerks were usually friendly with the chiefs and both sides used to exchange visits. But the bad ones used to ruin the courts altogether, especially when they formed the bad habit of taking money from litigants and keeping it to themselves. *Nwoke n'ibe ya n'azo gini ma obugh nkem g'aka?*' [What else but greed causes trouble between man and man?]

'The court was often converted into an instrument of oppression not only by the chiefs and clerks, but also by ordinary people who had the money for litigation. A case in point was Osu Okpara of Ihube, who specialised in taking people to court only to expose them to the greed of certain chiefs. Though some of the actions he instigated in the court were never tried, nonetheless his victims had to give "presents" to the chiefs and the court clerk. I was always opposed to this practice because I was convinced that it was evil.

'A court clerk was feared and respected more than a Warrant Chief. If a litigant incurred the ill-will of a court clerk he was sure to lose his case. This was why clerks were usually very wealthy, for each litigant bought their favour to prevent their inserting "No" where he had said "Yes". But most chiefs were also to blame for the fact that it was generally the man with the longest purse who won a case. A case came up once when I was a sitting member. One of the parties lavishly distributed presents of money, goats and cocks to the chiefs and the clerk. In a private session in the court clerk's house I pointed out that the readiness with which this party distributed presents brought the justice of his cause into question. This argument did not make much impression on my fellow-chiefs, nor did it prevent me from taking my share of the presents. There was nothing else I could do. Usually chiefs and clerks maintained friendly co-operation, trouble arose only when one side kept back what litigants offered as bribes.

'Still, the Native Courts were juster in the days of the Warrant Chiefs than they are now. In our day it was possible for a litigant to secure an audience with a chief or a court clerk by giving him the paltry sum of ten shillings. Today nobody can get an audience with a Customary Court Judge for a sum less than twenty-five shillings.

'It would be wrong to compare the Native Courts with village assemblies of the people. The chiefs were employed by the white man to try cases according to the white man's laws. We were government workers, or at least that was what we thought. When I tried cases in my house I followed traditional law and custom, but in the Native Court it was a different matter: this was why we used to rely on what the clerk told us was the white man's law.'

The Warrant Chief. 'The rule of the Warrant Chiefs varied from place to place. There were good and bad chiefs. Chiefs like myself who ruled according to traditional law and custom are still alive, but people like Ike Nwaji of Aku, who ruled with an iron hand, are no more. There is nobody left in this man's family because he did not realise that he should not treat people from his village the way he treated litigants in the Native Courts. As a result *"elu na ala we puta zachara Ike Nwaj"* [Heaven and earth combined to sweep him away]. There is nobody left in this man's extended family, and our tradition attributes this disaster to the fact that he was a dreadful chief. It is true that I, like Ike, had a private lock-up but I did not use it the way Ike did. Ike was never reported to the government for exceeding his powers because he did not keep all his ill-gotten gains to himself. He had court clerks, interpreters, and court messengers as his friends. If a man gave an indication of the intention to make trouble for Ike, he would find himself in prison before he had in fact made a complaint to the political officer.

'The Warrant was a very powerful weapon, it was the only thing that could make a man a chief. Chiefs of these days are chiefs in name only. A man like Ike Nwaji had a hammock in which he was carried about in the same way as district officers were in those days when there was no wheeled traffic. At first I could not buy a hammock, but later I was able to buy a bicycle, then a motor-cycle and later still a car.[2] Then I was the only man in Umulolo who owned these new gadgets or had a house roofed with corrugated-iron sheets. Then when a man came to Umulolo he could easily say which was my compound. Those who became court members after the Women's Riot were chiefs in name only. Some of them could not earn enough from the court to maintain their families. By then everything had been spoilt, people had got "wise".'

Asked how the Warrant Chiefs made the money that made them so rich Obiukwu answered, *'Ma ukpara erigh ibe ya o nagh ebu'* ('to grow fat an insect must feed on fellow insects').[3]

The court messenger. 'Another group of people associated with the Native Court who inspired fear and respect as well as hatred were the court messengers. To many people they were the government. There was nobody they could not arrest. What was worse, they were often mistaken for policemen. If they reported anybody, the white man would say "all right", and this was

[2] The body work of this car could still be seen as one entered the informant's very extensive compound.

[3] Further attempts to continue the discussion along this line failed.

generally taken to mean that punishment would be meted out to the person complained against, even if he was a chief.

'In those days, when handcuffs were rare or when a court might be short of them, court messengers generally used ropes to ensure the safe custody of those they arrested for crime or recruited to carry loads for the white man. In Ishiagu there were many cases of people who committed suicide rather than allow themselves to be arrested and treated like this. Some of the men would climb very tall palm trees and would fall down and die if court messengers insisted on having them arrested or recruited as carriers.

'If a court messenger came to serve Native Court summonses on people under me, or came to get men for work on the road or to recruit carriers, he would call on my boys [headmen] to help him. In the process they could take anything given to them for their "wine". At first, when a court messenger told me that the political officer wanted me to recruit able-bodied men to meet government needs, I used to rally my people by beating my gong. But within a short time this method became ineffective, as young men would run into the bush whenever the gong sounded. It even became very difficult to get the village together for anything by this traditional method. This was what forced me to appoint one man in each ward of the village as my headman. It was these headmen who, in cooperation with the court messengers, went from ward to ward recruiting men as wanted. Even then it was still necessary to chase the people about, especially if the purpose of the recruitment was known to be the procurement of carriers. Some Warrant Chiefs allowed each ward of the village to elect their own headmen, but I appointed and dismissed those who worked with me.

Forced labour. 'Though carriers were paid, the carrying aspect of forced labour was very unpopular. This was partly because some people died from being made to carry what was clearly too heavy for them, and partly because it was generally difficult to find food on the way. Each carrier had to take along his own food, but since carriers often spent upwards of six days on one journey the food easily got bad and people were forced to starve. The distance covered was sometimes great, there were occasions when people from Umulolo were compelled to carry loads from Okigwi to Port Harcourt – a distance of about 110 miles. After travelling these great distances young men usually became more difficult to control partly because they would blame the chief for their bad luck and so bear him a grudge, and partly because having seen so many new places they would come back more sophisticated than they were before the trip.

General. 'On the whole before the First World War [known in the Eastern Provinces as the First German War] ended, things became difficult for many Warrant Chiefs. In places where the Warrant Chiefs were of slave descent the free-born who had pushed them forward, when it was thought that the demand for chiefs was a demand for slaves, started to angle for Warrants; in fact in places Warrant Chiefs were sued in the Native Court for refusing to surrender their Warrants as requested by the free-born.' [Chief Obiukwu declined to give an example. According to him an old man does not say all he knows.] 'Since I was a free-born and ruled my people well nobody challenged my position.' Asked what he meant by ruling his people well, Chief Obiukwu gave an example. He said: 'When trying cases in my house I usually called some elders to help me. First I would listen to their opinion. If this was contrary to mine I would dismiss it and give my own verdict, which always stood. But a man like Ike Nwaji would never accord an elder of his village this respect.' Asked whether his father could have dismissed the opinions of his elders in this way before the coming of the British, Obiukwu said: 'Had my father a Warrant? What do you think the Warrant was?'

The introduction of direct taxation. 'It was the introduction of direct taxation that spoilt everything. When the government first told us [the chiefs] of its intention to introduce direct taxation we resisted, partly because we did not know what it was. It was called *Utu ala* by interpreters. We were therefore worried that we should be called upon to pay rent on our own land. We asked the local political officer why the government needed money and why it would not mint enough to cover its needs. The chiefs of the Okigwi Court area were particularly obstinate on this taxation issue, and the government had to win us over by foul means. We were invited to a party at the Native Court. There I found that the oil which was used in the preparation of the stew was not the ordinary palm oil. I warned many of my colleagues that the food contained "medicine" and that if we ate it we would find ourselves consenting to the introduction of direct taxation. The chiefs could not resist the appeal of the food. The day after the party all the chiefs who had spiritedly opposed the new measure started raising arguments in its favour. The "medicine" had done its work. I knew that this would lead to the ruin of Warrant Chiefs, for I could think of no argument which would persuade our people that white men who minted money were so poor that they wanted the people to give them part of their meagre earnings.

'The accuracy of the first count leading to taxation varied from place to place. In most of the areas under the Okigwi Native Court the general tendency was to count only a fraction of those who had reached taxable age. This was because the counting gave rise to a rumour that the government wanted to find out the number of soldiers to send to slaughter the young men. Also people were not used to being counted. But there were a number of Warrant Chiefs who thought they would be made "big" chiefs if it was found they had many people under them. In places like Ihube and Uturu, where the people were wise, though only a fraction of the taxable males were enumerated, every person who had reached the appropriate age shared in the burden of taxation. But in this village, where the people are usually shortsighted, those who were not enumerated refused to share in the burden of the first payment. Consequently in the second year of taxation those who felt betrayed the previous year undertook to do the counting themselves in order to ensure that nobody was omitted. That is why the tax still weighs heavily on this village.

'The only advantage people gained from paying direct taxation was the abolition of forced labour, but this was quickly forgotten. The government promised us development; but tell me [addressing the present writer] what development there is in Umulolo today after more than thirty years of taxation?

'Before the second year of taxation was over the Women's Riot occurred and Warrant Chiefs were treacherously sacrificed by white men. The Riot was caused by the rumour that there was a secret plan to tax women. Though this was denied when the Riot took place, it must be pointed out that the white men had it in mind to tax women. When this wicked plot was discovered, the white men shifted the blame to Warrant Chiefs and dismissed them. Later the government spread the false story that the Riot was caused by the fact that the chiefs oppressed the people. If this were the cause I would not have been attacked by the women, for I was a very good chief. I was attacked because since I was the Paramount Chief of Otanzu clan it was believed that I accepted taxation on behalf of the people. The Riot had nothing to do with the oppressive rule of chiefs.

'The government seized the opportunity offered by the Riot to get rid of the chiefs who had already got a firm grasp on government and put in their position new men who knew nothing about the tricks of white men. By the time the Riot came the white men were already getting afraid of the chiefs. If the women had not risen we would have started ruling ourselves earlier than we did. It was this that frightened the white men.' Asked what plans the Warrant Chiefs had for expelling the British, Obiukwu answered: 'There was no definite plan, you are a native of this area and you [addressing the present writer] know our local saying that *enyi mara ihe enyi ya mara ha anagh adi na nma* [people who are equally cunning are never good friends].

(b) Chief Mbabuike Ogujiofo of Ihube (the Clan Head of Otanchara and a former court messenger)

The advent of white men. 'The first white men who entered Ihube did so from the direction of Awka. When they insisted on seeing the head of the town, my father, Ogujiofo Umeojiaku, was sent to them. Through him, they got from our people many heaps of yams with which they fed the soldiers who came with them. They were shown the way to Ihube by two Awka men, Nwosu Agbaka and Nwozugha, who had been living in the village as blacksmiths. It was these two men who told the white men that my father was the head of Ihube, and Nze Osuoji the head of Umulolo. When the white men and their soldiers left for Isuikwu-ato we gave them four men to show them the way.

'On the second occasion the white men came from the direction of Umulolo, where they had burnt Nze's compound and killed his mother. On this occasion the white men sent word in advance to Ogujiofo saying that they would be passing through his town and wanted shelter built for them in the town's central market. Unfortunately Ogujiofo was not at home when the messenger came, for he had gone to Bende where he had to give evidence in the case of an Aro man who was charged with murder. When he came back from Bende and went to the white men to explain why no shelter was built as ordered, he was arrested and tied to a tree. Though already a man of advanced years, he was forced to carry bareheaded a very heavy box which our people said contained bullets. In Isuochi and Lokpa he helped to introduce the white men to the leaders of the people. After fourteen days he came back when our people had already given him up for dead. Later he was invited to Umuduru, which was then the District Head-quarters, and given a Warrant. The representatives of the other wards of the village became headmen under him.

The Warrant Chief. 'The work of the chiefs was to sit in the Native Court to hear such cases as they did not settle at home and to recruit carriers and road-makers. In the Native Court the district commissioner first sat as president, but later that position rotated among the chiefs.

Forced labour. 'Forced labour helped to make chiefs and court messengers very unpopular because it was very tedious. Carrier work was singularly dreaded because it was not infrequently that people were forced to carry loads which were too heavy for them and for long distances too. No carrier dared complain vociferously for fear of being mercilessly beaten by the escorting court messengers or soldiers or policemen. On one occasion an Uturu man died while carrying a very heavy load from Okigwi to Orlu. The man died because when he complained that the load was too heavy for him the soldiers who formed the escort beat him with the butts of their rifles. The political officer whose load was being transported asked me to provide the cloth with which the man's corpse was covered while it was being carried back to Uturu by the same men who had brought the officer's load. I was called upon to do this because the other carriers who came with the dead man had no money on them and because being an Ihube man I was regarded as their brother.[4]

'There was another case in which some Ihube men were conscripted to carry an unsplit coconut trunk to Okigwi. On the way the men stumbled and fell as court messengers tried to hurry them along. One of the carriers was knocked to death by the trunk. It is difficult to determine the number of people who died as a result of forced labour, especially as a result of the carrier system. Some died while engaged in the assignment, many more finished the assignment only to come home and die.

The court clerk. 'In the Native Court the clerk was master and his word was law. The chiefs did not understand that the clerk was their servant. The result was that the clerk did not only

[4] Ihube and Uturu are neighbouring village-groups but belong to Otanchara and Otanzu clans respectively.

record the proceedings of the court, but actually took part in the trial of cases. I remember a number of occasions on which different clerks refused to put in an appearance in the court and the chiefs went to beg them on bended knees to come and try cases for them. The fact is that in those early days of British rule, when the chiefs used to sit with the political officer in the District Court to try murder cases, it was the political officer who recorded the proceedings. Even in the Native Courts some political officers used to record the proceedings themselves. After hearing the case the political officer used to ask the chiefs to go and confer and bring him their opinion. This opinion he could accept or reject. When the political officer ceased to be a member of the Native Court and the clerk became virtually the only literate man in the court and had to record the proceedings he was taken to occupy the same position as the political officer. It was because of this that the chiefs came to call the clerk "master".

'Then also the clerk alone sat on the dais of the court room, whereas the chiefs sat lower down. It was on the dais too that the political officer sat when he came to review cases. This fact redounded to the benefit of the court clerk, especially as nobody could talk in the court without first obtaining his permission. Another factor which helped to bolster up the prestige of court clerks was the fact that they could control with an iron hand the court messengers, who were greatly feared and respected by the chiefs and their people. It was the general practice at the time for clerks to flog court messengers. One Mr Iyala and one Mr Pepple, who served in this division as court clerks, were singularly prone to flog court messengers. It was because of the arrogance with which court clerks treated both chiefs and court messengers that my father before he died vowed that whoever he reincarnated would be literate in order to become a court clerk and be addressed as "master".

'The literacy of the court clerks thus won them an unchallenged position in the Native Court. The roster for the monthly sittings generally went to the clerk from the political officer. The clerk then sent court messengers to inform the chiefs whose names appeared for the month, and the chiefs would take goats and cocks to the clerk because *Nna anyi ukwu nyere anyi ikpe.* [Our master has appointed us to sit.] The chiefs did not know that the order came from the political officer. As none of the chiefs could read or understand English, it is not unlikely that at times the clerk altered the lists in order to make it possible for chiefs friendly with him to sit more frequently.

'The clerk used to take part in the proceedings and used to force the chiefs to reconsider a decision which went against his interests by telling them that the political officer would cancel their Warrant for so flagrantly going contrary to government law in their decision.'

The court messenger. 'In remote villages court messengers were regarded as the incarnation of the government, hence they were often the first victims of any village that decided to throw off the yoke of British rule. Onyechere Agbuonu, a court messenger, was killed by Umukabia. He simply disappeared and no trace of him has been found till today because the people of Umukabia said they did not want to have anything to do with the British. In the same way and for the same reason Anu Dike, another court messenger, disappeared in Umukabia. Nkpa killed Okoronkwo Anyada of Amaigbo for the same reason. When two court messengers were sent to Awgu to prepare the way for the visit of the district officer at Okigwi, they disappeared because they were the agents of "Nwamba". The people of Awgu called the British "nwamba" [cat] because of the close resemblance which they saw between the eyes of a Briton and the eyes of a cat. It was because of this type of undeclared war which often existed between the people and the court messengers that the latter were very brutal with the people and vice versa. It was a vicious circle. Court messengers were known in many places as "okpunudo" because they often tied and dragged arrested culprits or even unruly carriers with rope.' ('Okpunudo': 'those who drag with rope'.)

'Sometimes it was through court messengers that chiefs approached court clerks. I remember an occasion when a chief called on me to take him to the court clerk. Because he did not offer me a bottle of English wine, I ordered him out of my house. It was only after he had knelt down and addressed me as "master" that I consented to go on condition that the wine would be forthcoming.

'At first there were no court messengers attached to the Okigwi Native Court. The practice then was for the man who took out a summons against an opponent to deliver it to his adversary. This continued until Ahiara people killed two Isu men who had gone to deliver a court summons taken out by the Isu against the

Ahiara. After this incident the government was forced to recruit court messengers who were generally understood to be the agent of the administration.

'As court messengers it was also our work to escort from village to headquarters men recruited for work on the road or as carriers. Half-way between the village and the headquarters some of these people used to escape. If there were deserters we used to conscript anybody we met on the way to make good the loss. After some time we adopted the practice of asking for more men than we were required to bring so that in spite of desertions we would still have men up to the stipulated number by the time we got to the scene of work. Where it was impossible to start off from the village with more than the officially required number, we used to tie and drag the recruited men like a slave gang to guard against losses.

'For many years the work of a court messenger was thus a very tedious and unpopular one and nobody was prepared to be recruited into the service. I was myself conscripted into the service. I went to Okigwi to see the court clerk on behalf of my father, who was a Warrant Chief. There I was caught and given a uniform. On more than two occasions I deserted, but each time I was caught, thrashed and confined to the lock-up for days in a bid to persuade me to continue in the service. It was only after my family had begged me to stay "if I did not want the white man to kill them" that I reconciled myself to the situation.'

The introduction of direct taxation. 'It was in 1926 that some chiefs were selected and sent on a tour of Lagos. My father was one of them and he came back to say that they had been forced to thumb-print a document which purported to show that they accepted the introduction of a thing called "takisi" or "utu ala". A year after this, Mr Cochrane undertook the enumeration of the people without telling anybody the purpose of it.

'Long before this time Captain Ambrose, DO, had surveyed a piece of land which incorporated bits of land belonging to Ihube and some other neighbouring villages and labelled it crown land. Villagers who planted on it were astounded to see themselves prosecuted or at least arrested for "spoiling the white man's land".[5] Thus when Cochrane not only counted people, contrary to

[5] Crown land was rendered into Igbo as 'ala beke'. But 'ala beke' is a vague term which also means 'the home-country of white men'. Thus there was an amusing case of a man who was arrested for trespass on

tradition, but also measured people's farms, the rumour that the government wanted to appropriate more of the people's land gained currency.

'Because the government succeeded in collecting the first year's tax without any serious trouble, in 1929 it gave the order that women should be counted as the first step to taxing them. Captain Cook, a very stupid man who was DO at Bende, at once tried to conduct this count and so precipitated the Women's Riot. Other wiser DOs refused to conduct the count, but then Captain Cook wanted promotion.

'The women attacked the chiefs because they believed that if the chiefs had not agreed to the suggestion the government would not have introduced taxation. The women also seized the opportunity of the Riot to revenge themselves on the chiefs for past oppressions.

'When the plot to tax women was discovered, the white men sacrificed the chiefs in order to save their faces. Later the government said that the Warrant Chiefs were dismissed because they were corrupt, oppressive and untraditional. This is not true. If the government wanted to stamp out corruption it should have allowed the people to govern themselves in their villages as was the case before the British came. Instead of doing this the government merely increased the personnel of Native Courts. The clerks and court messengers, who were no less corrupt than the chiefs, were not dismissed. Only a foolish man will take what the white man tells him at its face value. Unfortunately our people have also learned the white man's ways. In consequence one can never rely on what a fellow-man tells him.'

crown land and who asked to be told when he had been to 'ala beke' by which he meant 'England, to spoil it'.

Sources and Bibliography

A. PRIMARY SOURCES

1. Records kept at the National Archives Headquarters, Ibadan

Records collected from the Office of the Chief Secretary, to the Government, Lagos.

(i) CSO 1/13   Oil Rivers, Niger Coast and Southern Nigeria Despatches to FO and CO 1891–1906

  ,,   1/14   Oil Rivers, Niger Coast and Southern Nigeria Despatches from FO and CO 1891–1906

  ,,   1/15   Southern Nigeria Confidential Desptaches to CO 1900–7

  ,,   1/16   Southern Nigeria Confidential Despatches from CO 1900–7

  ,,   1/18   Southern Nigeria Circular Desptaches from CO 1890–1904

  ,,   1/19   Colony and Protectorate of Southern Nigeria Despatches to CO 1907–13

  ,,   1/20   Colony and Protectorate of Southern Nigeria Despatches from CO 1907–13

  ,,   1/21   Colony and Protectorate of Southern Nigeria Confidential Desptaches to CO 1908–13

  ,,   1/22   Colony and Protectorate of Southern Nigeria Confidential Despatches from CO 1908–13

CSO 26   This is a very large group of records. Its chief distinguishing characteristics among the CSO group of records are (*a*) unlike the other groups it does not consist of bound volumes but of filed papers, (*b*) the file jacket of each record in

319

this group bears a five-digit number. The records in this group which were found useful for this work include half-yearly and annual reports, special reports on events of particular significance in the provinces, policy papers, circulars, intelligence and assessment reports, etc. These fall under the following subgroups:

CSO 26/1 the 'o' series or files bearing numbers starting with 'o'
„ 26/2 the '1' series or files bearing numbers starting with '1'
„ 26/3 the '2' series or files bearing numbers starting with '2'
„ 26/4 the '3' series or files bearing numbers starting with '3'

(ii) Calabar was the Headquarters of the Oil Rivers (later Niger Coast) Protectorate, and also from 1900 to 1905 of the Protectorate of Southern Nigeria. The records which accumulated here in this period have been grouped as Calprof papers 1–10. These papers are now housed in the Ibadan branch of the National Archives. Those of them which have been found useful for the purpose of this work are:

Calprof 6/1 In-Letters to the Commissioner and Consul-General 1891–9
„ 6/2 Out-Letters from the Commissioner and Consul-General 1891–9
„ 6/3 In-Letters from the Vice-Consuls, District and Assistant Commissioners 1891–9
„ 6/5 Miscellaneous Correspondence 1891–9
„ 8/1 Minutes 1896–9
„ 8/2 Reports 1893–9
„ 8/5 Court Records 1891–9
„ 9/1 In-Letters to the High Commissioner 1900–2
„ 9/2 Out-Letters from the High Commissioner 1900–6
„ 9/3 In-Letters from District and Divisional Commissioners 1900–6
„ 9/4 Out-Letters to District and Divisional Commissioners 1900–6
„ 10/1 Minutes 1900–6
„ 10/2 Proclamations 1900–2
„ 10/3 Reports 1900–2
„ 10/4 Court Records 1900–5

2. Records kept at the Enugu Branch of the National Archives

Records from the Office of the Secretary Southern Provinces.

In 1914 the provinces of Nigeria were grouped, for administrative purposes, into the Northern and Southern Provinces, each group with its own lieutenant governor and secretariat. Under this arrangement the provincial administration in each group reported directly to its lieutenant governor. This led to the accumulation of a large amount of records in each of the secretariats. The Secretariat of the Southern Provinces was first at Lagos but later moved to Enugu. Its records have now been collected by the National Archives Department, classified and deposited at Enugu under the code 'CSE' (Chief Secretary, Enugu). Since however there has been cause to alter again and again the classification under the CSE code, and since there is no reason to believe that the process has come to an end, I have decided to use the original reference numbers of the files when referring to them in this work. The records from this group which I found useful for this study fall under the following main sub-groups:

Conf Series	Covering the years 1904–6
Conf CSO Series	Covering the years 1906–12
Conf C Series	Covering the years 1912–25
Conf 'A' Series	Covering the years 1912–25
Conf 'B' Series	Covering the years 1909–25
The 'C' Series	Covering 1917
The 'SP' Series	Covering the years 1916–24
The 'EP' Series	Covering the years 1924–33

Records from the Office of the Resident of Calabar Province.

Calprof 11	EP	Series covering the years 1906–7
,, 12	E.	,, ,, ,, ,, 1908–13
,, 13	T	,, ,, ,, ,, 1908–11
,, 14/1	C	,, ,, ,, ,, 1914–39
,, 15		Covering the years 1925–33
,, 21		,, ,, ,, 1919–23

Records from the Office of the Resident of Owerri Province.

E Series covering the years 1907–13
EP „ „ „ „ 1906–7
OW „ „ „ „ 1913–33

Records from the Office of the Resident of Onitsha Province.

OP Series covering the dates after 1914

(Between 1906 and 1914 much of the area which in 1914 became Onitsha Province was included in the Central Province, which had its headquarters at Warri, but the records of the Warri Provincial headquarters for these years are missing – it is said the office of the Resident of Warri was burnt in the 1940s. However, information on Onitsha Province for these years can be got from the CSO group of records.)

Records from the Office of the Resident of Ogoja Province.

OG Series covering mostly the years of the 1920s and after

(Information on the earlier years of the Ogoja Province can be got from the CSO and SSP groups of records. It has not been possible to trace the records which accumulated in the office of the Resident of Ogoja for the earlier years. It is possible they no longer exist.)

Official Publications (lodged in the Ibadan Branch of the National Archives)

Correspondence respecting the affairs of West Africa: *Africa* 11 of 1893

Report on the Niger Coast Protectorate: August 1891–August 1894 Africa 1895

Laws of Southern Nigeria 1900 and 1901

Protectorate of Southern Nigeria Blue Books 1904–5

Colony and Protectorate of Southern Nigeria Blue Books 1906–13

Government Gazettes 1906–33

Nigeria Blue Books 1914–33

Political Memoranda 1918 by F. D. Lugard

Report on the Amalgamation of Northern and Southern Nigeria by F. D. Lugard, London 1920

Report on a tour in the Eastern Provinces by the Secretary for Native Affairs, Lagos 1923

Report on a tour in the Eastern Provinces by the Assistant Secretary for Native Affairs, Lagos 1923

Sessional Paper No. 31 of 1924

Report of the Aba Commission of Inquiry, Lagos 1930

Aba Commission of Inquiry Notes of Evidence, Lagos 1930

Ethnographic Report on the Peoples of Nsukka Division by C. K. Meek, Lagos 1930

Report on Social and Political Organisation in Owerri Division by C. K. Meek, Lagos 1934

Report of the Native Courts (Eastern Region) Commission of Inquiry, Enugu 1953

Report of Commission into the position, status and influence of chiefs and natural rulers in Eastern Region by G. I. Jones, Enugu 1957

Report of Commission into the Onitsha Chieftaincy dispute by R. W. Harding, Enugu 1963

4. Oral Evidence

The material from written sources was supplemented with oral evidence collected by the present writer in the course of tours of the Eastern Provinces undertaken for the purpose in 1962 and 1963. For samples of this kind of evidence, the reader is referred to the Appendix.

B. SECONDARY SOURCES

1. Published Works

Achebe, C. *Things Fall Apart*, London,1958
Akpan, N. U. *Epitaph to Indirect Rule*, London, 1956
Anene, J. C. *Southern Nigeria in Transition*, Cambridge, 1966
Apthorpe, R. (ed.) *From Tribal Rule to Modern Government*, Lusaka, 1959
Basden, G. T. *Niger Ibos*, London, 1938
— *Among the Ibos of Nigeria*, London, 1921
Buchanan, K. M. and Pugh, J. C. *Land and People in Nigeria*, London, 1955
Buel, R. L. *The Native Problems in Africa*, 2 vols, New York, 1928
Burns, A. C. *History of Nigeria*, London, 1942
Cameron, D. C. *My Tanganyika Service and Some Nigeria*, London, 1938
Cary, J. *The Case for African Freedom*, London, 1944
Coleman, J. S. *Nigeria: Background to Nationalism*, California, 1958
Crocker, W. R. *On Governing the Colonies*, London, 1947
Crow, H. *Memoirs*, Liverpool, 1830
Crowder, M. *The Story of Nigeria*, London, 1962
— *West Africa Under Colonial Rule*, London, Second Impression, 1970
Davidson, B. *Black Mother*, London, 1961
Dike, K. O. *Trade and Politics in the Niger Delta*, Oxford, 1956
Flint, J. E. *Sir George Goldie and the Making of Nigeria*, London, 1960
Forde, D. (ed.) *Efik Traders of Old Calabar*, Oxford, 1956
Forde, D. and Jones, G. I. *The Ibo- and Ibibio-speaking Peoples of South Eastern Nigeria*, Oxford, 1950
Fortes, M. and Evans-Pritchard, E. E. *African Political Systems*, Oxford, 1940
Gann, L. H. and Duignan, P. (eds) *Colonialism In Africa*, vol. I, *The History and Politics of Colonialism 1870–1914*, Cambridge, 1969
Geary, W. N. M. *Nigeria Under British Rule*, London, 1929
Goldie, H. *Calabar and its Missions*, London, 1901
Green, M. M. *Ibo Village Affairs*, London, 1947

Hailey (Lord) *An African Survey*, Oxford, 1938
— *Native Administration in British African Territories*, HMSO, 1951
Heussler, R. *The British in Northern Nigeria*, London, 1968
Igwegbe, R. O. *The Original History of Arondizuogu*, Aba, 1962
Ikime, O. *Niger Delta Rivalry*, London, 1969
Jones, G. I. *The Trading States of the Oil Rivers*, Oxford, 1963
Kingsley, M. *West African Studies*, London, 1901
— *Travels in West Africa*, London, 1900
Kirk-Green, A. H. M. *The Principles of Native Administration in Nigeria*, Oxford, 1965
— *Lugard and the Amalgamation of Nigeria: A Documentary Record*, Cass, 1968
Lecky, W. E. H. *The Political Value of History*, London, 1892
Leith-Ross, S. *African Women*, London, 1939
— *Beyond the Niger*, London, 1951
Leonard, A. G. *The Lower Niger and Its Tribes*, London, 1906
Livingstone, W. P. *Mary Slessor of Calabar*, London, 1914
Lugard, F. D. *The Dual Mandate in British Tropical Africa*, Edinburgh, 1922
Mair, L. P. *Native Policies in Africa*, London, 1936
Meek, C. K. *Law and Authority in a Nigerian Tribe*, Oxford, 1937
Morel, E. D. *Nigeria: Its Peoples and Problems*, London, 1912
Nemo (Douglas, A. C.) *Niger Memories*, Exeter, n.d.
Nicolson, I. F. *The Administration of Nigeria 1900–1960*, Oxford, 1969
Partridge, C. *Cross River Natives*, London, 1905
Perham, M. (ed.) *Ten Africans*, London, 1936
Perham, M. *Native Administration in Nigeria*, Oxford, 1937
— *Lugard: The Years of Authority*, London, 1960
Pratt, J. A. *Brief Historical Sketch of Opobo*, London, 1910
Ranger, T. (ed.) *Emerging Themes of African History*, Nairobi, 1968
Robinson, R. and Gallagher, J. with Denny, Alice, *Africa and the Victorians*, London, 1961
Talbot, P. A. *Peoples of Southern Nigeria*, 4 vols, Oxford, 1926
— *Tribes of the Niger Delta*, London, 1932
— *In the Shadow of the Bush*, London, 1912
— *Life in Southern Nigeria*, London, 1923
Talbot, P. A. and Mulhall, H. *The Physical Anthropology of Southern Nigeria*, Oxford, 1962

Thomas, N. W. *The Ibo-Speaking Peoples*, part I, London, 1914
Tiryakian E. (ed.) *Sociological Theory, Values and Socio-cultural change*, Free Press of Glenco, 1963
Uchendu, V. C. *The Igbo of Southeast Nigeria*, New York, 1946
Waddell, H. M. *Twenty-nine Years in the West Indies and Central Africa 1829–1858*, London, 1863

2. Theses

Anene, J. C. O. *Establishment and consolidation of imperial government in Southern Nigeria 1891–1904*, M.A. thesis, London, 1952
— *Boundary Arrangements for Nigeria 1891–1906*, Ph.D. thesis, London, 1960
Ifemesia, C. C. *British Enterprise on the Niger 1830–1869*, Ph.D. thesis, London, 1959
Jeffreys, M. D. W. *Diploma thesis on the Ibibio.* (There is little information about this thesis, which was for a Diploma in Anthropology. The copy which I saw was in loose filed sheets, gave no information as to date of production or the university to which it was submitted, and was at the time lodged in the Ikot Ekpene District Office. Later I found identical copies lodged at the Enugu Archives.)
Nzimiro, I. *Chieftaincy and Politics In Four Niger States*, Ph.D. thesis, Cambridge, 1966
Ottenberg, S. *The System of Authority of the Afikpo Ibo*, Ph.D. thesis, Northwestern University, 1957
Tamuno, S. M. *The Development of British Administrative control in Southern Nigeria, 1900–1912*, Ph.D. thesis, London, 1962

3. Articles

Afigbo, A. E. 'Herbert Richmond Palmer and Indirect Rule in Eastern Nigeria 1915–1928', *JHSN*, iii, 2, Dec. 1965
— 'Oral Tradition and History in Eastern Nigeria', Parts I and II, *African Notes*, Bulletin of the Institute of African Studies University of Ibadan, iii, 3, 1966, and iv, 1, 1966
— 'The Native Treasury Question Under the Warrant Chief

System in Eastern Nigeria 1899–1929', *ODU, Journal of African Studies*, University of Ife, iv, 1, 1967

— 'Revolution and Reaction in Eastern Nigeria: The Background to the Women's Riot of 1929', *JHSN*, iii, 3, Dec. 1966

— 'Chief Igwegbe Odum: The Omenuko of History', *Nigeria Magazine*, 90, 1966

— 'The Warrant Chief System: Direct or Indirect Rule', *JHSN*, iii, 4, June 1966

Chubb, L. T. 'Out in the Sun All day', *Ibadan*, a Journal Published at the University College, Ibadan, 3, June 1958

Dorward, D. C. 'The Development of British Colonial Administration Among the Tiv, 1900–1949', *African Affairs*, 1969

Forde, D. 'Government in Umor (Obubra Division). A study in social change in a Nigerian village community', *Africa*, xii, 1939

Ikime, O. 'Reconsidering Indirect Rule: The Nigerian Example', *JHSN*, iv, 3, 1968

— 'Sir Claude Macdonald in the Niger Coast Protectorate – A Reassessment', *Odu*, a Journal of West African Studies, New Series, 3, April 1970

— 'Nigerian History in the Making', being a review of *Southern Nigeria in Transition*, by J. C. Anene, *JHSN*, iv, 2, June 1968

Lloyd, P. C. 'Lugard and Indirect Rule, *Ibadan*, a Journal Published at the University College, Ibadan, October 1960

Ottenberg, S. 'Ibo Oracles and Inter-group relations', *Southwestern Journal of Anthropology*, xiv, 3, 1958

Perham, M. 'A Re-statement of Indirect Rule', *Africa*, vii, 3, 1934

— 'Some Problems of Indirect Rule in Africa', *Journal of the Royal Society of Arts*, 18 May 1934

Robinson, K. 'The Making of British Nigeria', *The Journal of African History*, ii, 2, 1961

Index

80, 108, 111, 172, 186–7, 189;
Province, 74, 100, 130–1, 140,
141, 142, 144, 150, 154, 162, 166,
171, 172, 179, 191, 196, 201, 202,
203, 204, 205, 206, 207, 211, 212,
215, 223, 226–7, 229, 230, 238,
241, 246, 250, 263, 267–8, 289
Calabar, New, 31, 55, 94
Cameron, Sir Donald, 247
Cameroons, 46, 55, 148, 152, 203,
219, 301
cannibalism, 204
cap and staff system, 105, 257, 290,
292
Carr, F. B., 246
carrier system, 273
Caster, D., 196
census, 228–9, 239
Central Provinces, 100, 106, 156,
209
centralisation, 138, 175
Chadwick, 224
Chapman, G. B., 187
charismatic leaders, 26
Christianity, 94
Chukwuani, Chief, 142, 172, 224
clan structure, 18ff, 139–40, 199,
201, 204, 244, 246, 290, 300
Clifford, Sir Hugh, 166, 168–9,
193 4, 196 9, 214, 299, 304
climate of West Africa, 47–8
coastal communities, 27, 31–2, 38,
48–9, 59, 60, 99, 103, 148, 154–5,
269, 295
Coleman, James, 9
Colonial Office, 86, 147, 149–50,
160–1, 208–9, 226
Commissioner's Court, 101
constitutional village monarchy
system, 16ff, 27ff
Consular Courts, 81, 91–2
continuity, 47–8
Cook, Captain John, 236–7
Cooke, W. H., 262
Copland Crawford, W. E. B., 151,
165
court clerks, 109–11, 124–5, 135,
154, 166, 167–8, 180ff, 245, 255,
275–6, 280–1, 284–5

court messengers, 136–7, 162, 167–
168, 175–6, 245, 273, 280–1, 284–
285
Court of Equity, 37ff, 78
Creek Town, 16, 30, 61, 108, 171,
172, 189
Cross River, 7–8, 10, 54, 55, 64, 72,
100, 188, 203, 204
Crown Colonies, 4–5, 44, 118
Crowder, Professor Michael, 59,
82
customs revenue, 120, 147

Daaku, K. Y., 12
Dahomey, 11–12
Davidson, Captain, 203, 214
Dawn, The, 223
Dayrell, E., 152
decentralisation, 7–10, 13, 18, 138,
175, 290
deities, local, 34, 271, 286
Degema, 38, 42, 55, 60, 75, 79, 94,
108, 111, 113, 178, 179, 232
democratic village republic system,
16ff
Dew, H. T. B., 201
Dimneze, 62
Direct Rule, 2–5, 44
Dogho, Chief, 222
Douglas, A. C., 68
Duke Ephraim, 31–2
Duke, Magnus A., 184–5
Duke Town, 16, 27, 30, 38, 171

Eastern Provinces, British rule in,
1ff, 34–6, 40, 48–9, 58ff, 83–4,
93, 100, 120ff, 143ff, 206, 207ff,
287, 294–305; indigenous political system in, 7ff, 38–9, 47, 140,
285–7; Native Courts in, 37ff,
84ff, 102, 106, 111, 123ff, 138ff,
174ff, 256, 272; reforms in, 162ff,
194–202, 298–300; reports on,
51, 74, 194–5, 197–8, 206, 216,
247, 277–8; structure of society
in, 19ff, 32, 228–9, 264ff, 289–92
Ebrohimi, 54
economic developments, 38, 44, 82,
86, 139–40, 146

333